Equity in the Classroom:
Towards Effective Pedagogy for Girls and Boys

Edited by

Patricia F. Murphy and Caroline V. Gipps

RoutledgeFalmer
Taylor & Francis Group

LONDON AND NEW YORK

D0227721

First published in 1996 by Falmer Press

Reprinted 2003
by RoutledgeFalmer
11 New Fetter Lane, London EC4P 4EE

Transferred to Digital Printing 2003

RoutledgeFalmer is an imprint of the Taylor & Francis Group

A catalogue record for this book is available from the British Library

Library of Congress Cataloging-in-Publication Data are available on request

ISBN 0 7507 0540 X (cased, Falmer Press)
ISBN 0 7507 0541 8 (paper, Falmer Press)

ISBN 92–3–103302–6 (UNESCO)

Jacket design by Caroline Archer

Typeset in 10/12pt Times by
Graphicraft Typesetters Ltd., Hong Kong.

Printed & bound by Antony Rowe Ltd, Eastbourne

Contents

Preface   vii

Introduction   1
Caroline Gipps

I Pedagogy and Gender   7

1 Defining Pedagogy   9
   Patricia Murphy

2 A Girls' Pedagogy 'In Relationship'   23
   Jane Roland Martin

3 Citizenship, Difference and Marginality in Schools: Spatial and
   Embodied Aspects of Gender Construction   34
   Tuula Gordon

4 The Pedagogy of Difference: An African Perspective   46
   Sheila Parvyn Wamahiu

5 Gender Identity and Cognitive Style   59
   John Head

II Differential Learning and Performance   71

6 Scholarship, Gender and Mathematics   73
   Elizabeth Fennema

7 Girls and Information Technology   81
   Karen Littleton

8 Research on English and the Teaching of Girls   97
   Janet White

9 Girls' Achievement in Science and Technology — Implications
   for Pedagogy   111
   Jan Harding

10 Is There a Space for the Achieving Girl   124
    Michèle Cohen

11 A Socially Just Pedagogy for the Teaching of Mathematics   136
    Leone Burton

Contents

III Interventions   147

12 Redefining Achievement   149
    Gaell M. Hildebrand

13 Single-sex Settings: Pedagogies for Girls and Boys in Danish
    Schools   173
    Anne-Mette Kruse

14 Intervention Programs in Science and Engineering Education:
    From Secondary Schools to Universities   192
    Sue Lewis

15 How Do We Get Educators to Teach Gender Equity?   214
    Jo Sanders

16 Gender, Teachers and Changing Practices: Voices from Schools   228
    Liz Wyatt, Jo Whitehead and Christina Hart

17 The Emotional Dimensions of Feminist Pedagogy in Schools   242
    Jane Kenway, Jill Blackmore, Sue Willis and Léonie Rennie

18 Review and Conclusions: A Pedagogy or a Range of
    Pedagogic Strategies?   260
    Caroline Gipps

UNESCO/Institute of Education Colloquium 10–12 January 1995
'Is There a Pedagogy for Girls?'   272

Notes on Contributors   274

Index   279

Preface

In virtually all countries, educational opportunities for girls have traditionally been more limited than those for boys. Correction of this imbalance has been one of UNESCO's major concerns since the organization was founded fifty years ago. Much progress has been made in reducing male–female gaps in access to formal education as such, yet, as the number of countries which are able to ensure a broad measure of equality of access for boys and girls to the different levels of formal education gradually increases, questions of equal treatment and of equal opportunities for access to the different fields of study within education have become more salient at both national and international levels. Of particular concern to educators in many countries, both industrial and developing, is the widespread tendency for girls to participate less than boys in technical and science-related studies. The persistence of this phenomenon has given rise to an increasingly critical scrutiny of existing pedagogical practices, which in many cases are now known to provide more rewarding educational experience for boys than for girls.

These considerations prompted UNESCO to approach the Institute of Education, London University, with a view to organizing an international colloquium in 1995 on the theme 'Is there a pedagogy for girls?', chosen so as to stimulate a wide-ranging discussion of gender aspects of current pedagogical practices, especially in western industrial countries. This book represents one of the outcomes of the colloquium. The colloquium was organized in the context of the preparation of UNESCO's *World Education Report 1995*, for which 'the education of women and girls' was chosen as the main theme. The colloquium was chaired jointly by the two editors of this book, Caroline Gipps and Patricia Murphy. A full list of the colloquium's participants, as well as the papers delivered, is given in the Appendix.

UNESCO is grateful to the Institute of Education, to Caroline Gipps and Patricia Murphy, and to all the participants in the colloquium for their cooperation.[1] However, the views expressed in this book are the authors' and do not necessarily represent those of UNESCO. The designations employed and the presentation of material throughout this publication do not imply the expression of any opinion whatsoever on the part of UNESCO concerning the legal status of any country, territory, city, or area or its authorities, or concerning the delimitation of its frontiers or boundaries.

Note

1 The editors would like to thank Fulden Underwood, Sue Crook and Kate Myronides for their meticulous preparation of the manuscript.

Introduction

Caroline Gipps

In January 1995, we organized, on behalf of UNESCO, a colloquium at the Institute of Education on the theme 'Is there a pedagogy for girls?'. The outcome of the colloquium was to contribute to the *World Education Report* on the education of women and girls. The driving force for UNESCO was, within a global frame, a shift from access issues in education for girls, towards a focus on what happens to girls *within* the classroom. Their concern was girls' performance, and whether traditional approaches to learning and pedagogy favoured boys in some way.

We set up a small, invited, colloquium rather than a large conference so that we could generate discussion of the issues and move the debate forward. Eighteen educationists from England, Africa, Finland, Denmark, America and Australia wrote papers and attended the three-day session in which we discussed issues around pedagogy, girls, boys and teaching. The papers focused on: framing the debate about the education of girls; developments in learning theory; research reviews of girls' performance in various subject areas; and intervention projects focusing on girls' performance. Contributors came from a range of backgrounds: philosophers, feminist educators, assessment specialists, cognitive scientists, specialists in language, mathematics and science education. This ensured a wide-ranging and lively debate across traditional boundaries. One of the first tasks was to agree on a definition of pedagogy which, as Chapter 1 shows, is a complex and contested term.

This book represents the outcome of the colloquium: the colloquium papers form the bulk of the chapters, but we have written introductory and concluding chapters to complete the book. Our aim is that by drawing on learning theory, research and interventions from a range of countries, we can move forward the debate on how best to approach the teaching of girls. But we came to see that to try to separate out pedagogy for girls from that for boys would be to misconstrue the issue: unless we understand and deconstruct the dynamics of gender in schooling we cannot develop effective pedagogy for either gender. Including boys in the frame is particularly appropriate since in the UK, at least, there is considerable concern about the overall poorer performance of boys through the period of compulsory schooling.

But first we have to recognize the limitations of this book in terms of the countries and backgrounds from which our contributors come: we are virtually all from advantaged, developed, first-world nations: America, Australia, the UK, Northern Europe, with one voice from Africa. This limitation is, undoubtedly, unfortunate; the outcome is that what we write will be from our particular background and experiences. We do not intend to imply that our experiences, our suggestions and findings should be viewed as being appropriate for all pupils. Indeed it is clear that the situation for girls in many developing countries is such that the niceties of pedagogic strategy are much less significant than issues of access to schooling and relief from domestic responsibilities to allow for study. Having addressed the background and limitations we now start to frame the debate.

Setting the Scene

Issues concerning the education of boys and girls have been discussed for hundreds of years: for example, in 1693, in his essay 'Some Thoughts Concerning Education', John Locke addressed the issue of the teaching of boys and girls in order to promote the conversational method in the teaching of Latin to boys. As Michele Cohen points out, the conversational method had previously been used very effectively for the teaching of French, but was not generally considered appropriate for training the male mind in the classics. During the latter half of this century the focus of discussion has generally been in terms of appropriate subject content, physical provision, classroom interaction amongst teachers, boys and girls, the gendered construction of knowledge, and more recently in terms of appropriate assessments for the two genders. In this book, however, we now turn attention specifically to questions of pedagogy within the education of girls, and of boys.

The underlying question posed by UNESCO was: why is it that boys and girls experience schooling differently? Is it possible that styles and approaches that we consider to be appropriate for teaching *pupils* are in reality more appropriate for boys? Much of the subject matter of science is embedded in activities with which males are more familiar; role models in science and key figures in the history curriculum are also predominantly male. If this is the case with curriculum materials can it also be the case with teaching and the way pupils are expected to learn? Beliefs about the different abilities and appropriate roles for the sexes have led to differentiated curricula, and to differential access to particular aspects of the curriculum. This is a world-wide phenomenon. However, changes have occurred which have been associated with strategies to enhance girls' access to, and engagement in, subjects where their representation and performance with regard to boys' was poor, e.g., science and mathematics. Change has been effected in many countries (England, USA, Australia, Scandinavia, Finland) leading to increased participation and improved performance for girls. The question, then, is what do these shifts imply? Is this enhanced performance due to changing content, changing teaching approaches or assessment techniques, or changes in attitude towards the role and status of women and girls?

Before making progress on these questions we had to come to an agreed definition of pedagogy. To summarize, and preview the next chapter, we used a working definition of pedagogy as *the interactions between the teacher, pupils, the learning environment and tasks*. This definition incorporates the taught curriculum, the hidden curriculum and teaching method used by the teacher as well as her planning. The focus on interaction is a conscious one and the broad scope of the definition is one that allows for the inclusion of the relationship between teacher and pupil, the inter-actions among pupils, the teaching style of the teacher (which may vary with sub-ject and setting) the cognitive style of the pupil and the selection and presentation of the material. Another element which also bears on the interaction is the assess-ment process, since the assessment process itself affects what is taught and the way in which it is taught. The complexity of this definition forewarns us that there will be no simple answer to the original question: is there a pedagogy for girls?

A Theoretical and Philosophical Frame

First, we take a brief look at feminist approaches. The historical battle of women educators to have girls treated as the equal of boys, and to move away from a separated, two-track approach to schooling has resulted, through treating girls as a homogenous group, in a denial of difference among girls. This denial of difference among girls and women has led to a simplification of the issues and a belief among some feminists that one approach should suit all girls.

It has been only relatively recently that the differences which exist among women and girls have entered into discussions about their education; this has challenged many of the assumptions of feminism, in particular, that there is one overarching approach. In line with postmodern approaches to the interpretation of knowledge and 'truth', feminism has acknowledged the importance of difference, the context-bound nature of individual views and beliefs and the limitations of grand theory (including feminist theory). Meanings are socially constructed; texts are 'read' or interpreted by individuals and groups according to their cultural and social backgrounds, their experience of power relations and their individual bio-graphies. Thus Jane Kenway and colleagues in their chapter argue that feminist educators and teachers need to ask not only how and what to offer to girls but also how different girls respond to that which is offered. They argue (as has Walkerdine) that some feminist teachers' approach can be construed as equally authoritarian as previous patriarchal approaches: 'this (curriculum) is good for you'. Girls who resist the message are then seen as problematic, while for some girls the voice of feminist authority is actually oppressive rather than liberating. What needs to be considered is the meaning that the particular message has for those girls and its relevance to their lives: the slogan 'girls can do anything' is a liberal fantasy which has little purchase in the reality of many girls' lives. Furthermore, Kenway argues that the 'normal' girl on which much gender reform is based is middle class and white (or Anglo); as the norm, these girls receive an education which is couched in their own terms while girls who do not meet this norm are problematized as dis-advantaged or deficient. The 'disadvantage' model has also been widely critiqued in relation to boys' and girls' educational performance: in schooling it is the (middle class) boy who is the normal pupil and other pupils, including girls, are disadvant-aged and must become like the normal boy in order to succeed (Gipps and Murphy, 1994) since success is defined and measured in middle-class male terms.

In the western world, the discourse of achievement is male and educational practices have traditionally had the achievement of boys as their main concern. As Michele Cohen points out, in Europe, girls' good performance in a particular subject has served to lower its status (whilst arguing that boys would succeed in the subject if they really wished to); girls' academic competence has been construed as indicating mediocrity of mind (and compliant hard work) while boys are seen to have potential and 'a habit of healthy idleness'. Boys' failure tends to be attributed to something external to them (poor teaching, inappropriate method) while girls' failure is attributed to something *in* them (their intellect or nature). Thus, improving performance has meant for boys changing the methods or the practice, while for girls it has meant changing them (the disadvantage model again) including the way they work.

Jane Martin urges in her chapter that we use a gender-sensitive approach: take gender into account where and when it makes a difference. 'A gender-sensitive approach allows us to explore the topic of a pedagogy for girls without being committed to a traditional two-track education system such as the one that Rousseau designed for Sophie and Emile. It allows us to maintain — without being inconsistent — that gender is irrelevant to the question of, for instance, who should receive an education in critical thinking, who should study math and science, who should be computer literate, who should develop self-confidence and self-esteem, while insisting that gender does make a difference to the pedagogy one harnesses to those goals, and also to the ways in which the goals are defined.' However, pedagogy, Jane Martin reminds us, is only one aspect of education. Pedagogy is embedded in a larger educational system consisting of curricular goals and subject matter, institutional forms and structures, definitions of the function of school, conceptions of an educated person etc. Dealing with issues to do with the education of girls abstracted from its systemic context, as has been done consistently in the past, makes the task easier and more publicly acceptable. But to treat issues such as girls' low self-esteem, boys' harassment of girls, and curricular misrepresentations of girls and women as unrelated phenomena is to ignore the deep connections between knowledge and power, between gender and education thus perpetuating the status quo, including the masculine structuring and shaping of knowledge.

In the USA, Australia, England and Africa there is evidence that girls are experiencing increasing harassment and hostility in their interactions with boys in school. How can this *not* make a difference to girls' self-esteem and academic achievement? Is it possible to, and should we, design a pedagogy for girls that overcomes, or compensates for, the deleterious effects of boys' attitudes and behaviour? To do this would be to miss the point: that it is in everyone's interests to address the source of boys' misogyny directly, (and do not forget the taunting and exclusion of boys who do not fit the 'normal' masculine mould in school) if the goal of education is the development of human beings who respect and have a concern for others. As Anne-Mette Kruse points out, boys are not personally responsible for sexist behaviour, but they will remain unwitting propagators of a sexist culture if they are not challenged and helped to see how they can change their approach to girls.

Learning Theory and Cognitive Style

No discussion of pedagogy can be framed without a consideration of learning. Developments in views of learning have had a significant impact on teachers' practice which is examined in the chapter on Pedagogy. The struggle to understand gender differences and ameliorate them has had an impact on how learning is now understood to occur.

Traditional learning theory, with its origin in the work of famous male psychologists, does not have particular assumptions about the differences between boys and girls, because it *ignores* differences; it simply takes the normal pupil to be a boy (Walkerdine, 1988) and, it turns out, a white, middle-class boy. However, the view of student learning built up during the 1970s and 1980s under the 'constructivist' label, which sees students as active constructors of their own world view and which insists that to be useful new information must be linked to the knowledge structures, or schemata, already held in long-term memory, suggests that learning will be different across individuals. The roots of the constructivist view of learning can in fact be traced back to Dewey and Piaget who saw that the teacher has to understand the individual's ways of making sense of learning situations. Howard Gardner (Gardner, 1991) too argues that students possess different 'kinds of minds' and therefore learn, remember and understand in different ways. Some take a primarily linguistic approach, others a quantitative approach; some perform best when asked to manipulate symbols, others when they have to perform at a practical level. Gardner argues that these differences challenge educational systems that assume that everyone can, and should, learn the same materials in the same way. The work on girls' and boys' learning adds weight to Gardner's argument.

Another important strand is childhood socialization. Early socialization processes are central to children's learning of their social and gender roles; the formation of social and gender identity leads to emotional, cognitive and psychological differences. John Head argues that similarities in early socialization processes occur across cultures. These affect pupils' cognitive and learning style, there being clear gender differences in a number of areas. He presents research to show that:

- males tend to extract information from context while females tend to pay attention to context in a study or problem;
- in considering moral reasoning, or other problem solving, males tend to take analytical rule-based approaches while females tend to take a holistic approach and emphasize empathy;
- males tend to be more hasty, impulsive and willing to take risks while females exercise more care and deliberation;
- males tend to attribute success to their own efforts and failure to external factors while females show the reverse; the perception of personal failure may inhibit subsequent performance;
- interactions among males, including their discourse, are marked by competition while females appear to prefer to work in cooperation; their discourse is relational with reference made to the previous speaker.

The implication of this is that boys and girls are likely to prefer different learning approaches and procedures; teachers must, then, be flexible in their choice of teaching methods. The consequences of these 'learnt' preferences for learning in a range of curriculum subjects are exemplified throughout the chapters in this book.

We also know that teachers' expectations, their teaching style (including the level of public interaction required with the teacher) the content, context and presentation of the material, and assessment mode, all interact with learning and performance (for all pupils). As we wrote elsewhere: 'Differences in achievement, the APU, NAEP and international surveys show, are related to differences in opportunity to learn to a large extent . . . Attitudes, APU studies have shown, also have an important effect on achievement . . . the psychosocial variables affect how boys and girls come to view themselves, how they become viewed by others, how the subject is "constructed" and how achievement within it is defined' (Gipps and Murphy, 1994, p. 264). Thus the picture around teaching and learning is a complex one, suggesting that pedagogy should be seen as an array of practices — what we come to call pedagogic strategies. First we turn to a more detailed discussion of pedagogy based on different theories of learning and cognition, and look at feminist and liberatory pedagogies and how these fit within the educational debate. Then follow the chapters contributed by the colloquium members. Some of these we have previewed in this chapter in order to set the scene. The others — focused on research into girls' and boys' performance and effective interventions — we will review in the final chapter, as we move towards our concluding comments.

References

GARDNER, H. (1991) *The Unschooled Mind*, USA, Basic Books.
GIPPS, C. and MURPHY, P. (1994) *A Fair Test? Assessment, Achievement and Equity*, Milton Keynes, Open University Press.

I

Pedagogy and Gender

1 Defining Pedagogy

Patricia Murphy

Introduction

Pedagogy is a term widely used in educational writing but all too often its meaning is assumed to be self evident. An examination of how the term is used and the implicit assumptions about teaching and education that underlie its use is a valuable way of understanding how the education process is perceived. Many of the strategies that have been developed to redress inequity in schooling have targeted classroom practice and teaching as an important site for change. For this reason, attention has been paid to pedagogy, its meaning and relationship to curriculum. Feminist research has revealed how particular relations are reflected and reproduced in schooling at a number of levels. At the ideological level, ideologies of 'race', 'ethnicism' and 'gender' act to socialize students for their future roles. At the structural and organizational level of institutions, both in their overt and covert practices, messages are relayed to students about the relative power positions of different groups and individuals; and about the subjects and aspects of those subjects which are deemed appropriate for them to study. These subject divisions typically reflect the occupational structures in societies and the sources and selection of knowledge represented in curriculum subjects.

In different cultures at different points of time in history, the meaning and status of pedagogy has shifted. Simon (1981) describes the situation in Britain where the 'dominant educational institutions . . . have had no concern with theory, its relation to practice, with pedagogy' (p. 11). The absence of critical accounts of pedagogy in Britain contrasts with other western and eastern European countries where pedagogy has a tradition of study. However, in spite of this tradition or because of it, the study of pedagogy is one of confusion, ambiguity and change (Best, 1988). In Best's view, the status and meaning of pedagogy has changed in recent times and has been 'devalued, deflected from its original meaning or even discredited'.

The failure to examine pedagogy limits the potential for effecting change through education. Simon quotes Fletcher's (1889) view that 'without something like scientific discussion on educational subjects, without pedagogy, we shall never obtain a body of organised opinion on education.' This viewpoint is echoed by Shulman (1987). He argues that to advance teacher reform it is essential to develop 'codified representations of the practical pedagogical wisdom of able teachers'. For Shulman, one of the major problems for understanding teaching is that 'the best

creations of its practitioners are lost to both contemporary and future peers . . .
teaching is conducted without an audience of peers. It is devoid of a history of practice' (1987, p. 12). For Shulman, accounts of practice must include the management
of students in classrooms and the management of *ideas* within classroom discourse.

There has been recognition in recent years of the unique, interactive nature of
pedagogy. This interactiveness makes it difficult to capture and represent professional expertise as practised in classrooms. Interventions that have been developed
to enhance female participation in aspects of the education process or to challenge
sexist ideology in schools and society provide detailed accounts of practice. They
are, therefore, invaluable sources of illumination of a pedagogy that is seen more
as an art than a science.

In this chapter we consider some of the historical accounts of pedagogy and
identify some of the key elements in its conception. We then turn to more current
debates that extend this conception and draw upon developments in understanding
about the nature of human learning and knowledge. Finally, we consider feminist
research and review the characteristic of feminist pedagogy and how these relate
to the general debates about pedagogy. The intention here is not to provide an
exhaustive account about developments in relation to pedagogy. Rather, it is to set
a framework for the issues raised in the chapters that follow.

Changing Perceptions of Pedagogy

Simon, in his critique of pedagogy in the British context, highlights the important
link between views of ability and learning and education. He describes how early
attempts to integrate theoretical knowledge with the practice of education during
the late nineteenth century in Britain were based on associationist psychological
theories of learning. In these theories, learners are viewed as passive responders to
external stimuli. The pedagogy emerging from elementary schools in the 1890s and
secondary schools in the early 1900s reflected this. Walkerdine (1984) described
the purpose behind the introduction of compulsory schooling in Britain as social
and disciplinary, to inculcate in the populace good habits to redress the perceived
consequences of bad habits, i.e., crime and poverty.

The next significant change in the form of pedagogy, Walkerdine associates
with the emergence of the term 'class' in the discourse that developed when population statistics became available. This led to a shift in the organization of educational apparatuses from school rooms to classrooms, from mixed age groupings to
same age 'class' groupings. Education for regulation and citizenship was now to be
achieved not through coercion as previously believed, but through the development
of rational powers of the mind, hence the content of what children were to study
also changed. As Walkerdine points out these changes in pedagogy emerged as a
result of conflicts and struggle and were 'simultaneously a discursive transformation and a transformation of apparatuses and practices'. The next development in
approaches to pedagogy was influenced by the new emphasis on psychometrics in
education.

Psychometric constructs such as mental age are premised on the concept of the norm, i.e., normal behaviour, normal achievement, the normal child. These constructs were appropriated by psychologists who believed that humans were possessed of a general innate ability that was distributed in the population normally (Spearman, 1927). Individuals' innate ability sets the ceiling on their achievements: it follows from this that teaching cannot alter children's *potential* to learn. Such a perspective fits well with those educators who hold a hereditarian view of intelligence (see Gould, 1981). As Walkerdine (1984) put it, 'the development of the "child" as an object both of science in its own right and of the apparatuses of normalisation . . . provided the possibility for a science and a pedagogy based on a model of naturally occurring development which could be observed, normalised and regulated.'

The emergence of new theories of learning which challenged the notion of innate ability independent of environmental, social and educational influences reasserted in the education community the belief in the human capacity to learn. Child-centred theories of learning led to what is commonly and often misleadingly referred to as discovery approaches to pedagogy or non-directive pedagogy. In these theories of learning the child is believed to possess certain qualities and potentials which can be realized, given the appropriate environment. The focus on individual potential in these theories introduced the notion and possibility of an individualized rather than a class-based pedagogy. The teacher's role was also recast. She was no longer the inculcator of rational powers of the mind, but the 'guide' who enabled individual growth. This theory of pedagogy drew heavily on interpretations of aspects of Piagetian theories including notions of stages of development and 'readiness' for learning. Central to the pedagogy was the belief that a child's development towards scientific rationality emerges spontaneously as she explores and 'plays' with the environment. However, a child can only learn from certain experiences if 'ready', i.e., at the appropriate stage of development.

Walkerdine (1984) has described the circumstances that led to Piagetian theories being taken up in the particular ways they have been in classrooms. She details inherent conflicts between Piaget's theories that aim to normalize children's behaviours and a pedagogy that is premised on the aim of liberating the individuality of the child. Of particular value is Walkerdine's analysis of the web of related practices and apparatuses (such as record cards, classroom layout, work-cards, teacher training) which together 'produce the possibility and effectivity of the child-centred pedagogy'. The continuing and important message from Walkerdine is that the apparatuses of the pedagogy are not merely applications, but a site of production in their own right. Feminist research has paid particular attention to the apparatuses of pedagogy and how they are implicated in producing and maintaining differentiation in schools. For example, assessment practices or forms of questioning may only enable certain students to reveal what they know and may act as barriers to others (Murphy, 1995). Less obvious are those practices and customs to which Gordon refers (Chapter 3 of this volume) which make assumptions about gender differences. Gordon refers, in particular, to the way the physical school constructs a different 'place' for girls and boys by unduly restricting the use of space for girls.

She describes how this, in turn, becomes one of the influences that affects teachers' judgments and expectations of girls.

Developments in Views about Learning and Teaching

Whilst Piagetian theories continue to be reinterpreted and applied to aspects of education other influential theories have emerged in recent years, in particular other forms of constructivism and socio-cultural theories of learning. Common to all of these theories, however, including Piaget's, is the notion of the student as agent, the active constructor of meaning and knowledge. Although views vary about the nature of this agency, it is generally agreed that in order to teach one must first establish what students know, how they know it and how they feel about that aspect of their experience. The concept of agency has other implications for teaching and learning. If it is the student who constructs meaning out of the opportunities school offers, then, to progress, students need to gain an explicit understanding of what they know and how they come to know it, i.e., to develop *operative* knowledge that allows them to select from their knowledge appropriately in order to solve the problems and dilemmas they face in making sense. This operative knowledge (von Glasersfeld, 1989) has to be *taught* and requires teachers to develop strategies to make students' thinking explicit to them. The development of such metacognitive awareness relies crucially on language.

This focus on the role of language in learning coupled with a quite different perception of human ability distinguished social constructivist and socio-cultural theories of learning from certain Piagetian based and behaviourist perspectives. For example, on the conception of students' ability Bruner (1986) considers that children develop an understanding of others' minds from a very early age. He considers the shared use of language to be the key which unlocks others' minds to us. Learning how to use language involves 'both learning the culture and learning how to express intention in congruence with the culture.' For Bruner, culture is the 'implicit semi-connected knowledge of the world, from which, through negotiation, people arrive at satisfactory ways of acting in a given context.' If we consider differential power relations in schools and the differing cultural experiences and values of teachers and students, we can begin to anticipate how such negotiation could, in certain contexts, break down or operate to the disadvantage of individuals and groups.

Bruner's thinking was influenced by the Russian psychologist Vygotsky (1978). Vygotskian perspectives have been increasingly applied to the process of education in recent years. Vygotsky similarly saw language as intimately involved in the process of learning and development. Through the use of language, children mediate their actions. As such, egocentric speech represents the transition between external and internal speech. Faced with difficulties a child communicates with another adult or peer, and this socialized speech is subsequently internalized by the child. Seen in this way, language comes to form higher mental processes. It structures and directs thinking and concept formation, and is the product of social experience.

Vygotsky's view of development, and his concern with language and communication as central to learning, has major implications for teaching. In his view, students' potential for learning depends both on their existing knowledge and their capacity to learn. The potential for achievement can be realized through the help of a more informed adult or peer — a quite different conception to that of age-related staged development. Learning triggers developmental processes that only operate when the learner interacts and cooperates with people and the environment. In Bruner's words, the teacher 'serves the learner as a vicarious form of conscious-ness until such time as the learner is able to master his own actions' (Bruner, 1985, p. 24). The teacher's role is now much more demanding than that of a 'guide'. From this notion of the teacher's role, the term 'scaffolding' was coined (Wood, 1988). Scaffolding describes how teachers act to focus students' attention on 'relev-ant and timely aspects of the task and highlight things they need to take account of' (Wood, 1988, pp. 80–1). The teacher actively structures the support students need until they attain 'stand alone' competence. The ability to scaffold tasks suggests that teachers are aware of individual students' different needs. Indeed it is one of the reasons for the current focus on formative assessment practice. However, it is documented in research, as John Head's chapter shows, that many boys and girls approach learning activities in different ways. The 'scaffolds' that teachers provide for students would need to take into account the influence of students' different cognitive styles if they are to serve as supports for them.

Bruner talks of students establishing joint reference between each other on the basis of shared contexts and assumptions. However, meaning produced through this process of reference is always 'undetermined and ambiguous'. Von Glasersfeld applies this to teaching and argues that teachers construct models of students' notions and operations. The teacher's goal is to gain understanding of the students' understanding. The 'best' that can be achieved in this process is a model that re-mains 'viable within the range of available experience'. These notions of modelling and referencing place both teachers and students in a *dialectical relationship*. The theory of learning once again redefines the teacher's role and relationship to the student. Paulo Freire similarly viewed the process of learning as a dialectical move-ment (Freire, 1971). 'The act of knowing involves a dialectical movement that goes from action to reflection and from reflection upon action to a new action' (Freire, 1985). For Freire, the learning process implies the existence of two interrelated con-texts. These he labels as 'authentic dialogue' between students and teachers, and the second the 'social reality' in which people exist. The teacher's role in Freire's perspective is to pose problems about 'codified existential situations in order to help learners arrive at a more critical view of their reality'. Whilst it is not possible to go into theories of learning and knowledge in any great depth here, it is import-ant to raise a few other central ideas that have come to the fore in thinking about the learning process. These ideas have particular relevance to the equity debate and, to an extent, extend the notions already discussed.

One significant issue is the context dependency of learners' knowledge. Con-text in this debate is seen as the common knowledge of the speakers invoked by the discourse (Edwards and Mercer, 1987). Context is therefore an integral aspect of making sense along with learners' prior knowledge and understanding. Many of the differences in girls' and boys' responses to teaching and assessment activities indicate that the common knowledge invoked by the activities is not shared (Murphy, 1996). Jan Harding (Chapter 9) describes how in similar circumstances girls and boys perceive different problems because their view of what is relevant differs. These differences mean that the opportunities that students have to develop particular understandings will vary in spite of the apparent commonality in teaching provision. The teachers' selections and those reflected in textbooks can therefore support the learning of some students to the disadvantage of others. Traditionally, it has been the meanings that girls more than boys value that are marginalized in curriculum activities — English being an exception. For many teachers and students these context effects are invisible and their impact on learning unanticipated. A similar phenomenon is described by Karen Littleton concerning the choice of contexts in computer software (Chapter 7 of this volume).

Traditionally, knowledge has been viewed as an 'integral, self-sufficient substance, theoretically independent of the *situations* [my emphasis] in which it is learned and used' (Brown, Collins and Duguid, 1989). Situated cognition theorists challenge fundamentally the separation of what is learned from how it is learned and used. Knowledge in their view is not separable from the activity and situation in which it is produced. Rather, knowledge is like language, 'its constituent parts index the world and so are inextricably a product of the activity and situations in which they are produced' (Brown, Collins and Duguid, 1989). Conceptual tools are seen to reflect the cumulative wisdom of the culture and are a product of *negotiation*. According to Brown *et al.* 'activity, concept and culture are interdependent'.

For those educators concerned with equity in the classroom, the force of situated cognition is in the implications it raises for school knowledge systems. The social construction of knowledge is a product of negotiation. In order to understand key ideas in subjects, students need to understand, and have access to, this process of negotiation. This suggests a need to examine critically the status of subject knowledge claims and whose cumulative wisdom is reflected in teachers' practice and in the curriculum guidelines within which they work. This examination needs to include gender, ethnicity, race and socio-economic class to determine which individuals and groups the knowledge is accessible to, and/or valuable for. In this perspective of learning, the teacher has the task of making cultural practices available to students for consideration. The implication of this is that reflection on the selection and sources of school knowledge should happen as part of the dialogue *between* teachers and students. Introducing examples of assessment practice for critical examination can help support this process by providing explicit examples of what is 'valued'. A further strategy involves teachers introducing controversial knowledge claims, e.g., hypothesized causal links between diet and cancer, as part of the subject curriculum. This provides opportunities for students to 'learn' about the nature of evidence while they examine the validity of such claims.

Kruse, in her chapter, refers to a strategy where everybody in a teaching group is given the opportunity to express their opinion about a subject matter. This, in her view, both 'strengthens symmetry and equality in communication' whilst countering 'hegemony and dominance'. Burton argues similarly for a shift from 'knowledge control by authorities external to the student, to the development of a community of voices with whom authority and indeed authorship rest'. In a classroom she sees this would consist of those 'children whose work was responsible for the derivation of some new understanding'. It then becomes part of the students' responsibility to judge the validity of their own understanding and to relate it to 'public', external understanding.

From these theories of learning and of knowledge there has emerged a different perception of the teacher–student relationship. This reflects both a different understanding of the significance of students' knowledge and ways of knowing and of the purpose of education, the latter now being seen as providing entry into different cultural practices and knowledges. In current theories the teacher's role is much more complex: the teacher has to find ways of helping students 'find, create and negotiate their meanings' (Lerman, 1993). This involves providing activities which are meaningful and purposeful from the students' perspective and which allow them to apply and develop their understandings in explicit relation to others. The focus on meaning and purpose in learning and assessment is a central feature of many of the interventions described in the chapters that follow. Common to these interventions is the need to create authenticity in tasks in order to engage girls' interests. Authenticity in tasks ensures that the links between school learning and out-of-school practices are explicit. That this is a need perceived by girls more than boys is a matter for concern. The literature on situated cognition shows that the activities from which students' knowledge is derived are intimately linked to that knowledge. Hence, if learning is focused on abstracted school tasks and rituals, what students will acquire is ritualistic knowledge applicable only to those situations in which it is learned. Consequently, authenticity in tasks is a prerequisite for developing knowledge that can be applied in the culture. It is therefore essential for *all* students' learning.

In current theories of learning, the responsibility for learning rests with students and teachers. Students are expected to engage in dialogue with each other, and with teachers, and to validate their own understandings rather than merely accept transmitted views. Students need particular study skills to participate in this type of learning. Interventions to enhance girls' learning typically involve collaborative ways of working. Girls more than boys prefer to cooperate and engage in dialogue with peers about their learning. Consequently, girls more than boys have the study skills that are needed for the type of pedagogy advocated. It is to be expected that many boys will need support to acquire these skills. A first step will be in establishing with them the significance of skills that hitherto have been devalued. The interventions described later in this volume (see Kruse, Chapter 13; Lewis, Chapter 14; Kenway *et al.*, Chapter 17) provide different approaches to this and document the types of resistance that such interventions receive from students. As Kenway points out, the resistance of students to pedagogic interventions needs to be reflected on when evaluating their effectiveness and future direction.

We turn next to consider how debates about pedagogy are being considered in the wider education arena and what key elements in the conceptualization of pedagogy are emerging from this debate.

Redefining Pedagogy

Didactics was a term introduced to bring coherence to the debate about pedagogy, it describes the study of the relationship between learners, teachers and educational subject knowledge. Didactics placed an emphasis on the uniqueness of school subjects and accorded them equal status with the *process* of presentation. Didactics is concerned with the processes of the person learning and the particular content to be learned (the knowledge and the know-how). However, the practical element of pedagogy, the putting into practice, was seen to be absent from such a description. Tochon and Munby (1993), in developing a wider definition of pedagogy, distinguish didactics from pedagogy in the following way:

> Pedagogy is concerned with our immediate image of the teaching situation. It is live processing developed in a practical and idiosyncratic situation. Didactic goals can be written down, but pedagogical experience cannot be easily theorised, owing to its unique interactive aspects. Though action research and reflection reveals the existence of basic principles underlying practical classroom experience, no matter what rules might be inferred, pedagogy still remains an adventure. (p. 207)

This move away from conceptions of pedagogy as the *science* of teaching, reflects a new epistemology of practice — an epistemology in which the notion of praxis is central. Praxis is a term used to describe the dialectical relationship between theory and practice in teaching — a form of reasoning informed by action. Schon (1987) describes this new epistemology of practice in the following way

> ... one that would stand the question of professional knowledge on its head by taking as its point of departure the competence and artistry already embedded in skilful practice — especially the reflection-in-action ... that practitioners sometimes bring to situations of uncertainty, uniqueness and conflict.

The reconceptualizing of pedagogy as art is not a small matter. The way professional knowledge is perceived as ambiguous and incomplete, a 'tacit knowledge that is hard to put into words, at the core of the practice of every highly regarded professional' (Schon, 1987) has led to a crisis of confidence in the profession of education.

It is for these reasons that reformists such as Shulman are currently attempting to articulate the knowledge base of teachers. He defines *pedagogical content knowledge* as 'that special amalgam of content and pedagogy that is uniquely the province of professional understanding' (1987, p. 8). He argues, as others do, that it is the *wisdom of practice* that is the 'least codified source of teacher knowledge'. What is challenged by those educationists examining Shulman's concept of pedagogical content knowledge is that it presumes subject knowledge is absolute, uncontestable, unidimensional and static (Meredith, 1995). Others argue the need to see the transposition of content knowledge to school knowledge as a didactic rather than pedagogic process. This didactic process involves change, alteration and restructuring if the knowledge is to be teachable (Chevellard, 1991, quoted in Banks, Bourdillon, Leach, Manning, Moon and Swarbrick, 1995). Hence a split between school knowledge and pedagogical school knowledge is envisioned to 'create a dynamic which leaves open to question curriculum constructs [such as subjects]' (Banks *et al.*, 1995, p. 8).

To reflect on this new epistemology of practice requires a discourse that Alexander refers to as 'dilemma-language' (Alexander, 1992). Dilemma-language is the articulation of 'Doubts, qualification, dilemma, consciousness of nuance, alertness to the affective dimension . . . [which] can indicate true insight . . . [and] inner strength rather than mere professional machismo.' Such a discourse, according to Alexander, has not yet been legitimized because of the imbalance in power between practitioners and others in the educational hierarchy. The dilemmas teachers face also need to be examined in the political, social and cultural contexts in which teachers practice. Osborn and Broadfoot (1992) observed in their study of French and English primary teachers that:

> . . . for English teachers the critical issue . . . [is] how to resolve the practical problems inherent in delivering an individualised pedagogy in the context of a range of external pressures and large class sizes. For French teachers the dilemma is providing equal justice under law with the assumption of a common cultural base. . . . given growing differentiation in the social context and individual values. (p. 12)

The redefinition of pedagogy as an art follows from the view that pedagogy is about the *interactions between teachers, students and the learning environment and learning tasks* — our working definition given in the introduction. However, we have argued that pedagogy cannot be disembedded from the wider educational system. So, in order to address what is an effective pedagogy, we must be agreed on the goals of education. In the context of the equity debate it is Freire's view that has been influential. In his liberatory pedagogy, Freire (1971) argues that education must help students develop an increasingly critical view of their reality. You will see many references in the chapters that follow to pedagogical practices that lead to critical thinking. It is appropriate, therefore, to now examine the feminist contribution to the debate about pedagogy. It was feminist research which first drew attention to inadequacies in pedagogy in relation to groups and individuals. Through feminist interventions and evaluations of these, we now have a much richer understanding of the nature of pedagogy.

Perspectives on Feminist Pedagogy

Feminist pedagogy grew out of concern about the absence of any discourses concerned with transformative and critical pedagogy in the debate about teaching and learning. Its aim is to create awareness of 'difference' and of the process by which social divisions such as race, sex and socio-economic class structure individual experiences and opportunities. Feminist pedagogy is based on an 'analysis of females' and males' multiple and different material realities and illuminates females' and males' multiple and different experiences' (Weiner, 1994, p. 130). To reveal the varying positions of students and teachers, pedagogy has to become a site of discourse.

A feminist pedagogy provides students with access to alternative discourses to help them understand how identities are shaped and meanings and truths constructed. As Janet White points out in her chapter, teachers need to understand the way 'language works to shape meaning and with it identity'. Pedagogy is, in Janet White's view, 'a set of cultural practices which are encoded in language, resulting in the creation of a set of texts no matter what the "subject" being taught.' Davies (1989) describes the way children acquire the discursive practices of their society and learn to position themselves as male or female. As in all human actions people are not passively shaped: each is active in taking up discourses through which he or she is shaped. For feminists, it is essential to reveal to students how meanings related to gender are produced and how these in turn influence the construction of femininity and masculinity. Gemma Moss (1992) describes her approach to reading which stresses the role that diverse social and cultural practices play in shaping how texts get read. For example, when looking at popular magazines she suggests issues that can be considered with students, such as the appeal of technical language in boys' magazines and the common requirement for 'expertise' on the part of the male reader. The application of different discourses offers students opportunities to see how individuals can be reconstructed in discourse, as different discourses offer different subject (i.e., individual) positions and points of view. Introducing students to concepts of discourse provides them with the means to deconstruct and reconstruct 'texts' both representational and 'lived', whatever the topic of study.

Feminist pedagogy advocates making students theorists by encouraging them to interrogate and analyse their own experiences in order to gain a critical understanding of them. In a similar way, students can become theorists about subject knowledge as it is presented. This theorizing starts with students' conceptualizing their own experiences and then, through action and dialogue on aspects of subjects, students gain new awareness and understanding, which, with the support of the teacher and peers, is analysed, organized and evaluated in relation to others' understandings. In this way, students and teachers can deconstruct the 'cultural wisdom' that shapes the curriculum and thus understand it.

Taking a critical stance to the curriculum and its processes not only empowers students, it provides them with a far more robust sense of the nature of knowledge and the status of subject knowledge claims. The knowledge they acquire is useful knowledge that can be applied outside of school. National surveys in the UK found that as students progressed through school they acquired more and more fragments of knowledge but *not* the ability to apply them to make sense of new situations and to solve problems (DES, 1988a, 1988b). Teachers have to help make explicit to students theirs' and others' ways of making sense to enable them to achieve a critical stance. As we have already noted there will be constraints on teachers' abilities to do this because of their own subjectivity and the various subjectivities of their students. Furthermore, such a pedagogy disrupts normative values that are deeply embedded in both teachers and students hence resistance to examining alternatives is to be expected. Kenway elaborates on this in her chapter. However, if movement towards such a pedagogy can be achieved, it opens up the potential for choice both in students' use of knowledge and in their desires to access alternative discourses and the 'truths' they produce in order to gain real insight into cultural knowledge.

A feminist pedagogy, as described here, reflects current theories about the nature of learning, of learners and of knowledge. This is evident in the practices it advocates and the relationships between teachers and students it aims to foster. Feminist research has provided a rich source of evidence about practice as interventions have been developed and revised as a result of experience. A major contribution to the general debate has been the exposition of the concepts of discourses. There is an emerging consensus about the socially constructed nature of knowledge and the need for students to understand this and to adopt a critical stance toward the curriculum. However, how this is to be achieved is less well articulated. Some of the chapters that follow provide both insights and practical examples to this end. Another major contribution of feminist practice has been the revelation and treatment of difference in classrooms. This has highlighted the necessity for continual reflection on practice by teachers. A further contribution has been the attention paid to the ramifications of such a pedagogy beyond the classroom door. It is essential to remember that the apparatuses of pedagogy are a site of production in their own right. We cannot therefore advocate a particular teacher–student relationship that ends abruptly at the classroom door. The relationships have to be seen to exist at all levels in a school. Students need to feel a sense of community in a school, a sense of a safe place — place not just in physical terms but in ideological terms as well. Furthermore, if we encourage students to adopt a critical stance to the curriculum then the same approach would have to hold for their engagement in the derivation of school policies and rules.

Many of the examples provided in the chapters that follow highlight the need for a range of ways of working to enable problem solving and cooperative learning. These ways of working have, it is argued, to be learnt and explored so that teachers and students engage in 'critical reflection on group processes' (American Association of University Women (AAUW), 1995). To put this into practice requires change in the organizations and apparatuses of schools. For example, if strong ongoing relationships between teachers and students are necessary for effective pedagogy, does the typical secondary school practice of many short timetabled sessions with different teachers allow for this? Research suggests that heterogeneous groupings where teaching takes careful account of individual knowledge and experience are the most appropriate for learning. How does this approach 'fit' in schools committed to tracking or streaming, working in the context of time-pressured lessons? Learning areas also need to be seen to support the ways of working advocated, in the arrangements and accessibility of furniture and resources etc. These few questions only touch on the issues that need to be considered in schools to enable an effective pedagogy to develop. They do, however, indicate the direction that needs to be taken if we treat seriously the demands of such a pedagogy.

Summary

In this chapter, attention has been paid to the relationship between understandings about pedagogy and views about learning and the purpose of education. Current theorizing has radically altered the way the teacher–student relationship is perceived and *gives* status to personal experiences as a source of knowledge. Feminist pedagogy similarly reflects these characteristics and has extended them to recognize overtly the issue of difference. In developing practice that is based on, and illuminative of, difference, feminist pedagogy has extended understanding of what constitutes effective pedagogy. Jan Harding (Chapter 9) refers to present and past pedagogy as a pedagogy for boys. This pedagogy was, however, premised on inadequate conceptions of learning and of knowledge which may go someway to explain recent patterns in boys' performance in schools and the current concern about 'male underachievement'.

Whilst significant steps have been taken in identifying and articulating effective pedagogic strategies we remain with an unresolved question and debate. We need to ask 'what is an educated person' in a world that recognizes difference and how do answers to this question help define a curriculum and pedagogy for equity. We need to continue to apply the principles of critical pedagogy enunciated here to reflect on subject knowledge in school in order to better understand what alternative forms exist and whose purposes they might serve. However, as has been pointed out, there is still a long way to go (Longino and Hammonds, 1990). Nor can we afford to develop pedagogic strategies that empower only some individuals within a group. We need to understand what is meaningful and relevant to working-class boys and girls, to ethnic minorities, for all groups who share an identity.

Any developments in pedagogic practice must rely on teacher involvement. A first step in ensuring that involvement is for teachers in their training to be helped to understand the problem and how it impacts on students' learning and teachers' expectations, behaviours and attitudes. The pedagogy advocated within schools should be mirrored in the pedagogy of teacher education. Unfortunately higher education institutions lag behind many schools in their commitment to, and understanding of, equity issues. Sue Lewis' description of the 'chilly learning environment' and the resistance to, and marginalization of, curriculum reform intervention programmes in higher education institutions testifies to this. This is a situation which needs to change if pedagogy in school is to become more effective for more students.

References

ALEXANDER, R. (1992) 'The problem of good primary practice', in ALEXANDER, R. (ed.) *Policy and Practice in the Primary Curriculum*, London, Routledge.

AMERICAN ASSOCIATION OF UNIVERSITY OF WOMEN (AAUW) (1995) *Growing Smart: What's Working for Girls in Schools*, Washington, AAUW.

BANKS, F., BOURDILLON, H., LEACH, J., MANNING, P., MOON, B. and SWARBRICK, A. (1995) 'Knowledge, school knowledge and pedagogy: Defining an agenda for teacher education', Paper presented at the first meeting of the European Educational Research Association, Bath, September.

BEST, F. (1988) 'The metamorphoses of the term "pedagogy"', *Prospects*, **XVIII**(2), pp. 157–66.

BROWN, J.S., COLLINS, A. and DUGUID, P. (1989) 'Situated cognition and the culture of learning', *Educational Researcher*, **18**(1), pp. 32–42.

BRUNER, J.S. (1985) 'Vygotsky: A historical and conceptual perspective', in WERTSCH, J.V. (ed.) *Culture, Communication and Cognition: Vygotskian Perspectives*, Cambridge, Cambridge University Press.

BRUNER, J.S. (1986) *Actual Minds, Possible Worlds*, Cambridge Massachusetts, Harvard University Press.

CHEVELLARD, Y. (1991) *La Transposition Didactique: Du Savoir Savant au Savoir Enseigné*, Paris, La Pensée Sauvage.

DAVIES, B. (1989) 'Education for sexism: A theoretical analysis of the sex/gender bias in education', *Educational Philosophy and Theory*, **21**(1), pp. 1–19.

DEPARTMENT OF EDUCATION AND SCIENCE (1988a) *Science at Age 11 — A Review of APU Survey Findings*, London, HMSO.

DEPARTMENT OF EDUCATION AND SCIENCE (1988b) *Science at Age 15 — A Review of APU Survey Findings*, London, HMSO.

EDWARDS, D. and MERCER, N. (1987) *Common Knowledge: The Development of Understanding in the Classroom*, London, Methuen.

FLETCHER, A.E. (ed.) (1889) *Cyclopedia of Education* (2nd edn), Swan Sonnenschein.

FREIRE, P. (1971) *Pedagogy of the Oppressed*, New York, Herden and Herden.

FREIRE, P. (1985) *The Politics of Education*, London, Macmillan.

GOULD, S.J. (1981) *The Mismeasure of Man*, New York, W.W. Norton.

HANSEN, S., WALKER, J. and FLOM, B. (1995) *Growing Smart: What's Working for Girls in School*, Washington American Association of University Women (AAUW).

LERMAN, S. (1993) 'The Problem of Intersubjectivity in Mathematics Learning: Extension or Rejection of the Constructivist Paradigm', London South Bank University Technical Report, SBU-CISM, pp. 93–3.

LONGINO, H.E. and HAMMONDS, E. (1990) 'Conflicts and tensions in the feminist study of gender and science', in HIRSCH, M. and FOX-KELLER, E. (eds) *Conflicts in Feminism*, London, Routledge.

MEREDITH, A. (1995) 'Terry's learning: Some limitations of Shulman's pedagogical content knowledge', *Cambridge Journal of Education*, **25**(2), pp. 175–87.

MOSS, G. (1992) 'Rewriting reading', in KIMBERLEY, K., MEEK, M. and MILLER, J. (eds) *New Readings: Contributions to an Understanding of Literacy*, London, A & C Black, pp. 183–93.

MURPHY, P. (1995) 'Sources of inequity: Understanding students' responses to assessment', *Assessment in Education*, **2**(3), pp. 249–70.

MURPHY, P. (1996) 'Assessment practices and gender in science', in PARKER, L.H., RENNIE, L.J. and FRASER, B.J. (eds) *Gender, Science and Mathematics: Shortening the Shadow*, Dordrecht, Kluwer Academic Publishers, pp. 105–17.

OAKES, J. (1994) 'More than misapplied technology: A normative and political response to Hallman on tracking', *Sociology of Education*, **67**, pp. 84–9.

OSBORN, M. and BROADFOOT, P. (1992) 'A lesson in progress? Primary classrooms observed in England and France', *Oxford Review of Education*, **18**(1), pp. 3–15.

PLOWDEN REPORT (1967) *Children and their Primary Schools*, London HMSO.

SCHON, D. (1987) *Educating the Reflective Practitioner*, San Francisco, Jossey-Bass.

SHULMAN, L.S. (1987) 'Knowledge and teaching: Foundations of the new reform', *Harvard Educational Review*, **57**(1), pp. 1–22.

SIMON, B. (1981) 'Why no pedagogy in England?', in SIMON, B. and TAYLOR, W. (eds) *Education in the Eighties*, London, Batsford Ltd.

SPEARMAN, C. (1927) *The Nature of 'Intelligence' and the Principles of Cognition*, London, Macmillan.

TOCHON, F. and MUNBY, H. (1993) 'Novice and expert teachers' time epistemology: A wave function from didactics to pedagogy', *Teacher and Teacher Education*, **9**(2), pp. 205–18.

VON GLASERSFELD, E. (1989) 'Learning as a constructive activity', in MURPHY, P. and MOON, B. (eds) *Developments in Learning and Assessment*, London, Hodder and Stoughton.

VYGOTSKY, L.S. (1978) *Mind in Society: The Development of Higher Psychological Processes*, Cambridge Massachusetts, Harvard University Press.

WALKERDINE, V. (1984) 'Developmental psychology and the child-centred pedagogy', in HENRIQUES, J., HOLLOWAY, W., UNWIN, C., VENN, C., and WALDERDINE, V. (eds) *Changing the Subject: Psychology, Social Regulation and Subjectivity*, London, Methuen.

WEINER, G. (1994) *Feminisms in Education: An Introduction*, Buckingham, Open University Press.

WOOD, D. (1988) *How Children Think and Learn*, Oxford, Blackwell.

2   A Girls' Pedagogy 'In Relationship'

Jane Roland Martin

A pedagogy for girls: when it has taken us well over a century to appropriate for our half of the species the educational treatment that western cultures give the male half? A pedagogy for girls: when females come in so many classes, races, and ethnicities? The case for a pedagogy of girls' own would have to be very strong, indeed. Besides demonstrating a compelling need, it would have to dispel fears that a gender-based educational system would inextricably be linked to a gender-based division of social roles and societal labor. It would also have to put to rest the inevitable charges of essentialism and false generalization. And supposing the case can be made: in view of western culture's education-gender system, is a pedagogy for girls enough?

The Compelling Need

Many will wonder why, in this day and age, anyone would even entertain the possibility of a pedagogy for girls. In Europe and North America was not the history of education in the nineteenth and twentieth centuries dominated by the struggle to extend to girls the education that was then limited to boys? Is not the one-track educational system that is embodied in the movements toward co-education an essential step in the march toward sex equality?

Before I began to study women and education, I was a firm believer in both co-education and the dictum that sex — or gender, as we would now say — is a difference that makes no difference to education. My research made me alter my position. I read the literature on the radically different socialization of males and females from infancy; on the higher valuation our culture assigns the traits and tasks it considers masculine; on the differential evaluation of traits that are associated with one sex when they are possessed by a member of the other; on the differing effects on the psychological development of boys and girls of the fact that women are their primary caretakers; on the different way of thinking about themselves and others that girls tend to exhibit far more than boys; on the chilly classroom climate for girls. In short order I became convinced that educators cannot ignore gender with impunity, and the work that has been published since I began my own work on women and education has only served to confirm that conclusion (see, for example, Clark, 1989; Orenstein, 1994; AAUW, 1992).

When I first came to the realization that in education gender makes a significant difference, my male colleagues were quick to say: For the sake of women, forget what you have learned! Assuming that equality is incompatible with difference, that the ideal of gender equality mandates the same educational treatment for girls and boys, and that the only alternative to a gender-blind form of education is one in which girls and boys are routed onto separate tracks leading to different destinations, they cautioned me against publicizing the workings of gender in education. But to accept their reasoning is to fall prey to a false dilemma. We do not face an either-or choice: gender blindness or outright gender bias. In the name of gender equality we can and should choose to be *gender-sensitive* — to adopt a policy that takes gender into account when and where it makes a difference and not otherwise (Martin, 1985, ch. 7; cf. Martin, 1994b, ch. 3).

A gender-sensitive approach allows us to explore the topic of a pedagogy for girls without being committed to a traditional two-track educational system such as the one that Rousseau designed for Sophie and Emile. It allows us to maintain — without being inconsistent — that gender is irrelevant to the question of, for instance, who should receive an education in critical thinking, who should study math and science, who should be computer literate, who should develop self-confidence and self-esteem, while insisting that gender does make a difference to the pedagogy one harnesses to those goals, and also to the ways in which the goals are defined. Indeed, it allows us to hold up a single overarching educational ideal for the two sexes — should we wish to — while designing different pedagogies for males and females.

A Pedagogy for Whom?

The ideal of sex or gender equality does not preclude a separate pedagogy for girls. Moreover, the facts of the case suggest that the different treatment of the two sexes might actually further this objective. The question remains, however, of whether it is possible to formulate a pedagogy for all girls when girls as a class are so diverse. Or rather, can we do so without losing sight of all the other differences that seem to make a difference to education?

When, in the 1980s, feminist scholars were accusing those who spoke of womanhood or used the category *women* of essentialism, some of the criticisms focused on the support that the positing of women's 'essential nature' seemed to lend to programs and policies considered inimical to women.[1] Others, however, singled out for criticism the denial of difference or diversity on which attributions of essences rest and the consequent illusion of uniformity amongst women implied.

There is no doubt that the search for the essence of things is a quest for unity or commonality. Whether the subject is justice, truth, piety, man, woman, or girl, essence talk focuses on sameness. Indeed, the concern for uniformity is often so pronounced that the diversity that first gives rise to the essence quest is forgotten.

Feminist scholarship unquestionably stands to gain from the reminder that essence talk masks differences. Yet the truth of the matter is that this danger is present even when talk of womanhood or woman 'as such' — and by extension girlhood or girl 'as such' — is assiduously avoided, for *all* naming and categorizing tends to call attention to similarities and to neglect differences.

One response of feminists to their realization that talk about women masks difference has been to recommend that we substitute talk about specific kinds of women: black women, white women, Asian women, Hispanic women; lesbians, heterosexual women, bisexual women; etc. This strategy can also, of course, be applied to girls. However, while it highlights at least some differences, the problem of masking diversity recurs at the more specific level of discourse. Although talk about, for example, black girls differentiates them from white, Hispanic, and Asian girls, it can serve to mask the considerable diversity among black girls. Granted, the specific terms or categories that feminist theorists recommend mask fewer differences than the general terms they replace.[2] But the argument that more specific categories are therefore better than more general ones can be used against the specific categories themselves. Just as the category of girls masks everything, the category black girls does and more; just as the category black girls masks everything, the category black Caribbean girls does and more. The same is true of the category black Caribbean girls in relation to black Jamaican girls; of the category black Jamaican women vis-à-vis twentieth-century black Jamaican women; and so on.

Taken to its logical extreme, the argument against general categories like girls and women — and also, of course, against the categories of gender, mothering, etc. — leaves not only those of us who are interested in pedagogy, but all feminist scholars, in the lurch. If categories exist that do not conceal difference, they will be so specific as to stultify intellectual inquiry.

Obviously, we do not have to travel to the extreme. Acknowledging that whatever categories we use to formulate a pedagogy will mask some differences, we can decide to use ones that uncover the differences we consider most important and that best fit our practical and theoretical purpose. The question of which categories we should highlight when developing a pedagogy — and, in particular, whether we should use the category *girls* — cannot, however, be answered in advance of inquiry or decided upon once and for all because the contexts of our investigations change over time and so do our interests and purposes. Further, everyone need not choose the same categories.

Feminist theorists have rejected those categories they call essentialist not merely because existing difference and diversity are obliterated, however. Although people's experiences and social practices differ from culture to culture and across historical periods, categories like *girls* and *women* seem to presuppose some fixed core — some 'essence' — that all members of the relevant class possess. Nevertheless, the *a priori* assumption that things that go by the same name share all or even some properties is mistaken. Consider the proceedings that we call 'games,' Ludwig Wittgenstein said, 'Similarities crop up and disappear' as we move from one group of games to the next, the result being that 'we see a complicated network of similarities overlapping and criss-crossing: sometimes overall similarities, sometimes similarities of detail' (Wittgenstein, 1953, para. 66). He called these 'family resemblances' (Wittgenstein, 1953, para. 67). Needless to say, Wittgenstein's approach to language does not replicate the search for essences. Demonstrating the availability of different kinds of definition, it teaches that even if scholars in the past defined *woman* and *girl* in essentialist ways, it does not follow that we all must. To be sure, no guarantee exists that an adequate definition of a given category or term can be constructed. But the possibility of failure in this endeavor does not vindicate a blanket rejection of the attempt.

The Education-Gender System

I think it extremely important to affirm — and continually reaffirm — that a pedagogy for girls is compatible with the ideal of gender equality and that it does not presuppose essentialism but, on the contrary, can accommodate difference and diversity. Nevertheless, education encompasses far more than pedagogy, and for the sake of both girls *and* boys this 'more' also cries out for transformation. For better or worse, a pedagogy is inevitably embedded in a larger educational system consisting of curricular goals and subject matter, institutional forms and structures, definitions of the function of school, conceptions of an educated person, and so on. Unfortunately, just as the dominant practices and ideology of western science constitute what Evelyn Fox Keller has called a 'science-gender system' (Keller, 1985, p. 8; cf. Harding, 1986), in western culture that larger context of educational practices and ideology represents an 'education-gender system.'[3]

Implicitly dividing social reality into the world of the private home, as Virginia Woolf called it (Woolf, 1938), and the world of work, commerce, politics, and the professions, just about all of us — parents, politicians, school teachers and administrators, and just plain citizens — take it for granted that the function of education is to transform children who have heretofore lived their lives in the one place into members of the other. Assuming that the private home is a natural institution and that, accordingly, membership in it is a given rather than something one must achieve, we see no reason to prepare people to carry out the tasks and activities associated with it. Perceiving the public world as a human creation and membership in it as something at which one can succeed or fail and therefore as problematic, we make the business of education preparation for carrying out the tasks and activities associated with it.

Now this in itself does not make our educational system gendered. That quality is conferred on it by the fact that, culturally speaking, the public world and the world of the private home are gender-coded. Given that the one is considered men's domain and the other is considered women's, and that education's ideology and practices are predicated on this dichotomy, gender becomes a basic dimension of the whole system.

To illustrate. The assumption we all make that becoming educated is a process of acquiring new ways of thinking, feeling, and acting might appear to be gender-neutral. Yet it is, in fact, gender-bound and biased. If the educational system is to be 'rational,' these new ways must be functional — or *at least they must be thought* to be functional — in relation to life in the public world. But this, in turn, is to say that they must be functional in a world that was, historically speaking, a male preserve and to this day reflects this fact. Furthermore, there is no need at all for the newly acquired ways of thinking, feeling, acting to be — or to be considered — functional in relation to the world of the private home, a world whose inhabitants are presumèd to be female. On the contrary, since these two worlds are culturally represented as polar opposites, there is no way that preparation for life in the one could foster ways of thinking, feeling, and acting that are functional in the other.

Woolf said in *Three Guineas* that life in the world across the bridge from the private home is competitive and that the people there have to be pugnacious and possessive in order to succeed. In our educational thought and practice, we in the west signify our agreement with her by assuming that the qualities or traits of love, nurturance, and the 3Cs of care, concern, and connection that are associated with the private home — and, of course, with women — run counter to education's *raison d'être*. Indeed, we take these to be such obstacles to the achievement of the objective of preparing children for life in the public world that we make one of primary school's main tasks that of casting off the attitudes and values, the patterns of thought and action associated with home, women, and domesticity (Martin, 1992).

It is surely no accident that the reports on the condition of American education published in the 1980s gave home the silent treatment. Viewing children as travelers to the public world, they saw school as the place children stop en route in order to acquire the knowledge, skill, attitudes, and values that they presumably will need when they reach their destination — a kind of wayside inn. Once children enter school when they do not go home again in this unexamined scenario; not ever, not even as adults. The authors of these volumes totally forgot that life is lived in both places and so do almost all of education's theorists and practitioners, critics and reformers.

A Girl-friendly Pedagogy and Girl-hostile Boys

Although there is a great deal more to say about the education-gender system, the question at issue here is: How much can one accomplish if one changes the way girls are taught without also taking a gender-sensitive approach to the other elements of their education?

In 1994, Peggy Orenstein reported hearing girls 'barraged by sexually explicit insults' and seeing boys 'grab girls' thighs, rears, and breasts' during her visits to classrooms in a California middle school (p. 148; cf. Stein and Sjostrom, 1994). Five years earlier, Clark reported (1989, pp. 25, 29, 40) that primary school girls in Australia have this to say on the subject:

There's a group of boys in our class who always tease us and call us — you know, dogs, aids, slut, moll and that.

This boy used to call us big-tits and period-bag and used to punch us in the breasts.

They take things off us and drag us into the boys' toilets.

They call us rabies, dogs, aids.

They reckon I'm a dog. My brother gave me to them. He said, 'Oh, come here, I've got a pet for you. Do you want my dog?' And he gave me to them as a pet dog.

Also in 1989, a US newspaper columnist told readers about sixth graders in a Boston public school who had been asked to tell the first word that came to mind about the other sex (Jackson, 1989). The girls said: 'Fine. Jerks. Conceited. Ugly. Crazy. Dressy. Sexy. Dirty minds. Boring. Rude. Cute. Stuck up. Desperate. Sexually abusive. Punks.' The boys said: 'Pumping ("big tits"). Nasty. Vagina. Dope bodies (big breasts and behinds). Door knob (breasts). Hooker. Skeezer ("a girl who will 'do it' with 50 guys").'

There is nothing idiosyncratic about those images the boys invoked. Nor do boys leave the images at the schoolhouse door. In the US, Australia — and, I presume, other countries too — girls of all ages are experiencing a degree of harassment and hostility in their in-school interactions with boys that is almost unimaginable to their elders. How could this not make a difference to both self-esteem and academic achievement? But supposing it has no deleterious effects, is it really in the interest of girls to educate them to deal with the boys' bad treatment without addressing the boys' misogyny directly? There is no doubt in my mind that it is not. Indeed, I would say that it is not even in boys' best interest — at least, not if one of the goals of everyone's education is the development of decent human beings who respect and have a concern for others.

Interestingly enough — and this point is generally ignored — the misogyny that young boys practise in school goes hand in hand with a quite precocious anti-domesticity. Here is what a second grade boy, vintage 1975, said to researcher Rafaela Best: 'I'll starve to death before I'll cook.' Over the course of four years, Best watched a group of elementary school children in the Central Atlantic region of the United States learn what she called the 'second curriculum' — the one that teaches each sex 'how to perform according to conventional gender norms.' Coming to know the children intimately, Best reported in *We've All Got Scars* that although most of the boys did not master this material by the end of first grade, in the next two years the majority became proficient in it. The ones who did not grasp the norms or were simply unable or unwilling to meet them were scorned by the other boys and excluded from their club. These outcasts were not necessarily shunned by the girls in the class but they were perceived as losers by themselves as well as by those who had passed the various tests of masculinity with flying colors. One of those tests was a scorn for things domestic. When asked how he planned to keep his house clean and have food to eat, the boy who would die rather than cook replied, 'I'll get a wife for that' (Best, 1983, p. 80).

Tracing the mastery of the second curriculum by those 6-, 7-, and 8-year-old boys, Best showed how closely the macho ideal to which they aspired was linked to a fear of feminization. The excluded boys 'were regarded as being like girls and not like real men,' she reported. For a third grader to be called a sissy 'was a fate worse than death.' To be a cry-baby or to be oriented to one's mother or female teacher was inexcusable. Kenny, one of the 'losers' in the class, liked doing house-keeping tasks in school for his teacher and enjoyed receiving her hugs in return. Jason, another loser, cried frequently. And Edward, whose behavior in school was far too perfect, was not good at games. Fighting, or at least the willingness to fight when challenged, was one essential ingredient of masculinity in the 'winner's' eyes. Playing well and playing rough was another. Engaging in 'anti-establishment' activities ranging from throwing mudballs at houses and cars to stuffing paper in the school lockers was a third. All three aspects of 7- and 8-year-old machismo were valued in large part because their opposites betokened femininity (Best, 1983, pp. 22, 24).

In the long run, the boys' 'domephobia' — their devaluation of and morbid anxiety about things domestic — has negative effects on girls' self-esteem and academic achievement. Let us not forget that the scorn that boys direct at domestic affairs extends to the girls and women whose responsibility these are assumed to be. In the long run — as the boys turn into grown men — the domephobia takes its toll on women and children. A US State Department of Revenue investigator told a news columnist: 'I've had 4,000 arrests on nonsupport, and this guy was the smoothest I've seen. All he talked about was how he loved sailing and couldn't wait to get back to it.' The man's ex-wife, who at one time held two jobs so as to stay off welfare, said, 'Now, I hope Chip can finish college. He's such a nice kid. I just do not understand how a father could leave a child like that' (English, 1989).

Anne Machung's revelations about the expectations of graduating seniors at the University of California Berkeley Campus bear directly on this depressing topic (Machung, 1989). In 1989, Machung reported that the overwhelming major-ity of those she studied hoped to marry, have children, and pursue a career. Of the women, nearly nine-tenths planned to acquire graduate degrees and half thought they would earn at least as much as their husbands. Few anticipated getting divorced or raising their youngsters alone. Each one believed she would rear two or three children and expected to interrupt her career for anywhere from six months to twelve years to do so. While in Machung's words the women were 'talking career but thinking job' in order to be in a position to take care of the children they wanted to have, the men were talking family but thinking career. They were willing to 'help out' at home but they did not want to be told what to do or have their con-tributions measured against their wives', let alone share housework equally. As for child care, most not only believed it to be the wife's responsibility, they could barely see themselves making day care arrangements or missing work when the children were sick.

Education for Living at Home and in the World

Those who care about girls need to rethink the education of both sexes. This is not a simple matter. One vital step in eradicating the boys' hostility and harassment is to combat the androcentrism of the disciplines of knowledge from which school's subject matter is drawn by integrating the study of women into the school curriculum. As members of the National S.E.E.D. Project on Inclusive Curriculum[4] and other groups attempting to transform the school curriculum well know, the task of subject matter inclusion is as challenging as any curriculum maker could wish. Yet even this is not enough. If we are to make school a place where girls as well as boys feel safe and secure enough to learn, another equally crucial step is to raise the misogyny to the level of consciousness by making it a *bona fide* subject of study in the school curriculum proper (Martin, 1994a, ch. 8, cf. Kruse, this volume, ch. 13).

Would that all this were sufficient! If, however, one is interested in women's equality — not to mention the well-being of both women and children — then, in view of the grossly inequitable division of domestic labor that obtains today, we must finally begin to make domesticity everyone's business. From the standpoint of education, this means teaching boys and girls alike that the tasks, functions, and duties culturally associated with society's private homes and families are as much the responsibility of men as they are of women.

Given our education-gender system, to achieve this end it will be necessary to redefine the function of school in particular, and of education more generally, so as to include preparation for life in our private homes as well as in the public world. To prevent misunderstanding, let me stress that in saying this I do *not* assume that all good homes must take the same form; in particular, I do *not* assume that they necessarily involve heterosexual pairings; and, furthermore, I do *not* have in mind preparation for life in traditional, patriarchal families. Rather, I believe that women stand to suffer as long as men fail to shoulder their fair share of domestic duties and responsibilities, and that children stand to suffer too. I am optimist enough to think that education has an important role to play in redressing the present imbalance.

Our work has just begun, however, when we redefine the function of education. For once this is done it becomes necessary to rethink our culture's very ideal of an educated person. The education-gender system presently defines that concept in relation to the goal of full-fledged membership in the public world. Since the two worlds — the world of our private homes and the public world — are culturally represented as polar opposites, our present ideal of an educated person excludes the very virtues that are culturally associated with domesticity — among other items, nurturance and the 3Cs of care, concern, and connection.

It might seem a simple matter to redefine our cultural ideal of an educated person by adding the missing traits or qualities to those we already include in it. However, in relation to the education-gender system, an additive approach would be tantamount to educating people to be divided selves. I do not doubt that a given girl or boy *could* acquire the set of traits currently associated with domesticity along with the set associated with the public world and learn to display the appropriate traits in the appropriate contexts. However, I am wary, to say the least, of replacing the old gender-based division of labor and the present inequitable division of domestic labor with a population of women and men who turn off their rationality when they get home at night and turn off their caring when they arrive at the office in the morning. Even if this policy is not psychologically damaging, and I should think it would be, it perpetuates the misleading and very dangerous stereotypes of a public world devoid of caring and of private homes devoid of reason. Thus, as we redefine our ideal, we must also replace the outmoded ideology of dichotomized spheres with new definitions of home, the world, and the connections between the two.

Having said all this, there is still the phenomenon of trait genderization to be reckoned with (Martin, 1985, ch. 2). As is well known, many attributes are appraised differently in males and females. Thus, for example, rationality is considered a highly desirable attribute of males — at least of white, middle- to upper-class males — but not of females. Conversely, caring is rated highly in females and not in males. An adequate pedagogy for girls faces the difficult task of dealing with the often devastating consequences for girls of the fact that the very qualities associated with success in fields like mathematics and science are genderized in favor of boys. If, besides helping girls excel in what were once considered to be boys' fields, we teach boys to make domesticity their business, we will also have to design a new gender-sensitive pedagogy for them. It, in turn, will face the possibly far more difficult task of dealing with the fact that traits such as nurturance and the 3Cs are genderized in favor of girls and that boys who exhibit these are all too often scorned and taunted.

Conclusion

It is tempting to try to develop a suitable pedagogy for girls without reference either to the education-gender system or to boys. For one thing, the task of dismantling that system is so enormous, so daunting, that prudence would seem to dictate that we should act as if it does not exist. For another, it will undoubtedly be easier to gain at least a modicum of public acceptance if one abstracts a girls' pedagogy from its systemic context. This precedent has already been set. Relating the androcentrism of the school curriculum to that entity's race, class, and ethic biases, more than a few who want to redress the gender bias proceed as if the problem bears no relationship to the education gender system; indeed, as if none such system exists. Connecting the sexual harassment of girls to violence in general, and more particularly to the homophobic behavior boys display toward other boys, many who want to improve the school climate do likewise.

Quite clearly, a similar path can be followed in the case of pedagogy. Focusing on girls' low self-esteem and similar issues, we can rely on what we know about women's and girls' development and ways of knowing, thinking, feeling, and acting to design a girls' pedagogy, all the while ignoring the education-gender system. Or rather, we can design pedago*gies* for girls without attending to the education-gender system, since, given the diversity of girls, there is no reason to assume that a single pedagogy will do.[5]

However, to take the path of least resistance is to repress what we know about the deep connections between gender and education. Given the deep connections between knowledge and power, to forget or deny our knowledge is, in turn, to disempower both ourselves and the girls we hope to serve. For to treat issues such as girls' low self-esteem, boy-hostile girls, and the curricular misrepresentations of women as unrelated, isolated phenomena instead of as interrelated byproducts of one and the same education-gender system, is to allow that large organization of beliefs and practices to remain hidden and to go unchallenged. And to do this is to invite the persistence of the very problems we wish to overcome, as well, I fear, as the emergence of new problems quite as damaging to girls as the old ones ever were.

In sum, then, just as feminist psychologists today perceive girls and women as 'in relationship' with others, I urge feminist educators to think of pedagogies for girls 'in relationship.' In the interests of realism we need to design girls' pedagogies in relation to our knowledge of the existing education-gender system. In the interests of moving forward into the twenty-first century, however, we also need to develop it in relation to a new philosophy of education for both sexes, one that dismantles the education-gender system and makes its main business teaching girls and boys, women and men to live and work together in safety and equality both at home and in the world.

Notes

1 For a fuller discussion of this and other points made in this section see Martin (1994b).
2 In this connection the problem of how to individuate or count differences does arise, however.
3 I have explicated the education-gender system without ever giving it this label in Martin (1985; 1992; 1994a, chs 1, 3, 5, 11, 13).
4 The project is based at the Wellesley College Center for Research on Women in Wellesley, Massachusetts. Peggy McIntosh and Emily Style are its co-directors. Orenstein (1994, ch. 12) gives a wonderful account of a California middle school teacher, a participant in the Seeking Educational Equity and Diversity (SEED) Project, who seems to have made astonishing progress toward this goal.
5 On the one hand, if we take a gender-sensitive approach to pedagogy that is also sensitive to race, class and ethnicity, we may well end up with a whole range of pedagogies for girls (on the possible need for plural pedagogies see Orenstein, 1994, pp. 160, 180, 210, 232). Furthermore, there is no reason whatsoever to suppose, *a priori*, that race, class and ethnicity are the only differences that make a difference to girls' learning, or even that they are the main differences (see Martin, 1994b).

References

AMERICAN ASSOCIATION OF UNIVERSITY WOMEN (AAUW) (1992) *How Schools Shortchange Girls*, Washington, AAUW.
BEST, R. (1983) *We've All Got Scars*, Bloomington, Indiana University Press.

CLARK, M. (1989) *The Great Divide*, Canberra, Curriculum Development Centre.

ENGLISH, B. (1989) 'No support, but nice tan', *Boston Globe*, May 15.

HARDING, S. (1986) *The Science Question in Feminism*, Ithaca, NY, Cornell University Press.

JACKSON, D.Z. (1989) 'Black studies: Why Harvard should blush,' *Boston Globe*, November 18.

KELLER, E.F. (1985) *Reflections on Gender and Science*, New Haven, Yale University Press.

MACHUNG, A. (1989) 'Talking career, thinking job', *Feminist Studies*, **15**(1), pp. 35–58.

MARTIN, J.R. (1985) *Reclaiming a Conversation*, New Haven, Yale University Press.

MARTIN, J.R. (1992) *The Schoolhome*, Cambridge, Harvard University Press.

MARTIN, J.R. (1994a) *Changing the Educational Landscape*, New York, Routledge.

MARTIN, J.R. (1994b) 'Methodological essentialism, false difference, and other dangerous traps', *Signs*, **19**(3), pp. 630–57.

ORENSTEIN, P. (1994) *School Girls*, New York, Doubleday.

STEIN, N. and SJOSTROM, L. (1994) *Flirting and Hurting*, Washington, National Education Association.

WITTGENSTEIN, L. (1953) *Philosophical Investigations* (trans. G.E.M. Anscombe), New York, Macmillan.

WOOLF, V. (1938) *Three Guineas*, New York, Harcourt Brace Jovanovich.

3 Citizenship, Difference and Marginality in Schools: Spatial and Embodied Aspects of Gender Construction[1]

Tuula Gordon

Introduction

The chapter begins by describing the context of the research and outlining the theoretical framework for the project. I then concentrate on two of the central concerns in our ongoing ethnographic study — these are spatiality and embodiment in schools. I explore how these are centrally implicated in gender construction in schools. The chapter concludes by arguing that any pedagogy for girls would need to take account of the *place* that 'girls' can *take* in schools. I use the expression 'girls' tentatively, because I argue that 'girls' are not a singular category.

In the project 'Citizenship Difference and Marginality in Schools', the focus of our research emerged through wanting to understand why boys get more attention in schools than girls, why their achievement is understood differently from that of girls, and why teachers find them more interesting than girls and treat them as *individuals* whose interests need to be engaged in order to motivate them in classroom activities. Hierarchical gender differentiation processes take place in schools, despite policies aimed at providing equal opportunities. Such processes are, however, not simple, mechanical or inevitable. Research conducted in Finland so far indicates that themes and issues uncovered in western gender and education research are largely applicable there as well. More research is needed to understand these *similarities* and to uncover *specificities* of gender and education, and the school processes which contribute to gender differentiation (Gordon, Lahelma and Tarmo, 1991). For these reasons, we decided to conduct a *cross-cultural, comparative* study of education and schooling which is theoretically framed, and moves from the macro- to the micro-level in two countries with different educational histories: Finland and Britain. We also wanted to place the study of gender differentiation in a broader theoretical context which involved an analysis of citizenship, and explored practices in schools which *normalize* school students from diverse structural and cultural backgrounds on the basis of the notion of an abstracted '*pupil*'. Fundamental to our approach is a conception of schools as microcosms of the social relations in society (Gordon, 1986). The research concentrates on the *official*, the *informal* and the *physical* school.

The Theoretical Framework

Citizenship and Individuality

Our research is framed by an analysis of *citizenship* in western democracies (cf. Gordon, 1992). The goal of education is to prepare pupils to take their place in a structurally and culturally framed adulthood. In western democracies such adulthood and citizenship are characterized by tensions and contradictions between egalitarianism and inequality. Formal equality is diffused by axes of structured inequalities: gender, social class, 'race' and ethnicity, age, disability and sexual orientation. These inequalities are both structurally and culturally constructed. A 'citizen' is an abstract norm, against which people are differentially positioned. A historical study of education indicates the crucial role allocated to, and played by, schools in this positioning. Schools have been expected to both confirm and challenge social divisions; to control and regulate, *and* to be sites of social change and emancipation (cf. Donald, 1992). We want to step outside the frames of regulation and emancipation, and view schools as sites of multiple levels and practices which may be contradictory.

The development of citizenship required the construction of modern *individuals* abstracted from their social locations. The social contract produced an inherently masculine notion of a citizen and an individual. Political theorists thought that the primary location of women was in the state of nature, whereas for men there was a rational separation between the state of culture and the state of nature (Pateman, 1988). Connected to this division are oppositions between mind and body, reason and emotions, rationality and irrationality, abstract and concrete, objective and subjective, public and private, masculine and feminine, male and female. 'Individuals' became citizens through a voluntary contract to maximize their own self-interest. The contract centred around the rights of men (cf. Yuval-Davies, 1991; Pateman, 1988; Bellah, Madsen, Sullivan, Swidler and Tipton, 1988). The 'individual' is a construction which marginalizes some groups as '*others*' within structures of power. The state of culture is the 'natural' habitat of the western white heterosexual, able-bodied male; hegemonic masculinity resides in this habitat (cf. Connell, 1987).

Liberal theories and social democratic policies have not been able to solve the contradictions and tensions in constructions of the 'individual' and 'the citizen'. Equal treatment is premised on *neutrality* which is accompanied by 'natural' attitudes towards gender, race and disability — dimensions that locate those designated as their bearers in the state of nature. Individuals are therefore faced with practices constituted on the basis of difference despite the 'sameness' rhetoric (cf. Eisenstein, 1988).

The discussion of individuality and otherness is relevant when analysing processes of schooling, where individualist doctrines are institutionalized (Meyer, 1986). The formal education system constructs girls and boys in schools as *pupils* with 'neutral' characteristics: as absolute individuals with equal opportunities. At this level the location of pupils in social relations is not relevant, because *absolute* individuals are formally equal; like citizens, pupils as *real* individuals are not socially, politically or economically equal. *Relativity* characterizes the individuation of women. The construction of neutral 'pupils' has different implications for girls and boys. Whilst liberal conceptions of education claim equal opportunities for all, pupils, as boys and girls, are perceived through 'natural' attitudes (Gordon, Lahelma and Tarmo, 1991). Citizenship, based on abstract notions of individuals, is mediated at the school level by abstract 'pupils', who, in the practices of schools, are differentiated. These processes of abstraction and differentiation have an effect on the formation of subjectivities of people in schools.

The Problem of Difference

The exploration of education in modern democracies that follows is based on a historical discussion of the production of citizenship, and attempts to desconstruct the concept of individual by considering structured *individuation*, cultural *individualism*, and the production of *subjectivities*. The focus of the discussion is on sex and gender, whilst avoiding essentialist notions of either. The intention is to disentangle and challenge binary opposites. Female/male is not taken for granted. Oppositional categorization, which directs attention to differences *between* groups, can be tautological. The problem of *difference* is posited as an analytical category in this research. The starting point for the discussion is gender *relations*, which place actual females and males in particular positions without foreclosing them. Differences *within* categories are therefore crucial. Thus the problem of difference is multifaceted and complex, and oppositional categorizations are not appropriate. Dimensions of inequality which intersect gender need to be considered. In the context of gender relations a working-class boy in a special education class enjoys a share of masculine privileges vis-à-vis girls, but in relation to hierarchical masculinities his privileges are contradictory, and deliver less than they promise (cf. Connell, 1987). An upper middle-class girl with economic and cultural advantages is placed differently and more obliquely, vis-à-vis the process of production of otherness, than a working-class girl with few financial and (recognized) cultural resources. The within-gender differences are located in the context of a sex-gender system which privileges the category 'male' over the category 'female' (cf. Gordon and Lahelma, 1994a).

Marginality

The production of otherness, and differential positioning of gendered subjects in that production, is connected to *marginality*. The term 'margin' is spatial. Shields (1991) connects conceptions of marginality to High/Low distinctions, where marginal is the other. Marginalities are multiple (Davies, 1991) social axes intertwined in structural and cultural power relations. Thus marginality does not signify powerlessness in any simple sense. Marginality is not a descriptive term, but an analytical concept.

Technologies of normalization (Ryan, 1991) in schools produce otherness and marginality, as it is not possible for all to attain absolute individuality in the cultural sphere. But the absolute/relative divide is challenged by people in their activities, and otherness and marginality are resisted. Thus schools do not foreclose all possibilities of power from marginal others. Education has been crucial as an avenue through which to challenge power/powerlessness. Yet these challenges are typically fragmented. Their success, if measured in relation to social change in structured inequalities, is at best contradictory and contentious. But the oppositional space (Gordon, 1986), opened up by lack of foreclosure, are nevertheless significant when problematizing thinking about education along the axes of regulation and emancipation. Educational policies (particularly during periods of recession) have addressed these spaces through processes of restructuring, which aim to redraw the map of possibilities and limitations of individual citizens.

Focusing Research on Education and Schools

On the basis of a theoretical framework concentrating on citizenship, individuality, difference, marginality and otherness, the following concerns emerge to be considered by the research (cf. Gordon, Lahelma and Tarmo, 1991):

- The average school achievement of girls surpasses that of boys in Finland and Britain (though there are some differences[2]).
- The participation of women in the labour market is considerable, but there are significant differences between Finland and Britain; the majority of Finnish women are engaged in full-time paid work.
- Equality of opportunity policies have been instituted in Finland and in Britain, but there are differences in the extent to which equal opportunity as an ideology is embedded in general rhetoric, and how it frames social policy.
- The gendered division of labour has nevertheless not broken down, or significantly altered, in Finland or Britain.
- There is a great deal of public debate about the feminization of education in Finland. The majority of teachers are women (though the majority of headteachers are men[3]), and as girls, on average, achieve better than boys in schools, concern is expressed about the problems of boys' achievement (cf. Gordon, 1992). This kind of discussion has only recently become prevalent in Britain; there, a critique of 'equality of opportunity' is emerging in education debates (cf. Mahony, 1992).

Anglo-American feminist education research has been conducted in a context where women participate less in the labour market than in Finland, are more likely to work part-time, and where public provision for child care is minimal. In this context, it seems that the participation of women in the labour market is crucial in providing them economic independence, and therefore would be expected to contribute to the equalization of the position of women and men. The case of Finland, however, illustrates that despite women's participation in the labour market gender inequalities have not been eradicated. The labour market is gender-segregated, and the pay and prospects of employees located in the predominantly male sectors are better than of those located in the predominantly female sectors. We are interested in understanding the processes in schools which are implicated in differentiating between and within genders.

Restructuring, Equal Opportunities and Individualization

We explore the processes of restructuring in education in order to contextualize our study. The focus of the exploration is on the implicit notions of citizenship that exist and on the shift in emphasis towards individualization and differentiation and away from equal opportunities. In our analysis, particular interest is directed at neo-conservative, neo-liberal and social-democratic elements in the constitution of educational politics and policies. The main comparison is between the Finnish model of a social-democratic welfare state, and the British model which has consistently contained conservative and liberal, but also social-democratic and radical elements.

Whilst in Britain, centralization of a decentralized education system is taking place, in Finland, decentralization of a tightly centralized system is occurring. Cuts in public spending have shaped the development of education in Britain since the 1970s; in Finland such cuts are more recent. Trends such as the increased demand for accountability, centralization, individualism, and for closer links between schools and industry can be found in both countries. These trends are evident in the 'market-speech' discernible in education policy and documents, for example, 'accountability', 'choice', 'customers', etc. In both countries, individual choice in relation to the educational paths to be pursued have been emphasized. Education is increasingly conceptualized by policy-makers as an economic, rather than a social, political or moral activity (Gordon and Lahelma, 1994a).

Curriculum, Equal Opportunities and Abstract Pupils

We next concentrate on the *curriculum* in order to illuminate the development of educational policies, and the differences and similarities between the two countries. The focus on curriculum also enables us to shift from the macro- to the micro-level: curriculum reports contain both general statements about broad educational aims, and more specific statements about teaching and learning at the school level. Different tendencies in Finland and Britain are contrasted. A decentralized curriculum in Britain has recently been replaced by a centralized national curriculum (Lahelma, 1993). In Finland, where the curriculum is traditionally centralized, the move has been in the other direction, towards decentralization. Considerable development work focusing on teaching and learning processes was conducted in schools in the 1960s in Britain, during a period of economic expansion. This work was hindered by public spending cuts which started during the late 1970s (Gordon, 1986), and continued through the 1980s. The major influence and restriction on curriculum development work was, however, the 1988 Education Reform Act which severely limited the possibilities for school-based initiatives. In Finland, such school-based curriculum development work has only very recently begun (as a mainstream, endorsed trend), and it too has now to contend with economic recession and cuts in public spending.

Everyday Processes in Schools

The empirical part of the project described here is an ethnographic study of two secondary schools in Helsinki. The data reported was gathered under such headings as teachers, students, the pedagogic relation, textbooks and teaching materials, lesson content, youth cultures, school–home relationships, and space and embodiment. In the Finnish project, students' activities outside the school and in the home were also followed.

In our study of schools, we distinguish three levels. The first level, *the official school*, includes the curriculum, teaching materials, teaching methods, and the disciplinary apparatus and formal hierarchies that exist. The second level, *the informal school*, includes the interaction in all areas of the school, the application and interpretation of school rules and the informal hierarchies that exist among teachers, and among students, etc. The third level is *the physical school*. Here we concentrate on embodiment and space.

Curriculum of the Body

Embodiment has received little attention in education research (cf. Shilling, 1991a), even though a great many of the practices in school are worked on and through the body. School rules stipulate permitted and forbidden movement. Discipline in the classroom has a substantial basis in regulated bodily comportment. Moreover, disruption and resistance by students in schools often carries bodily dimensions, for example, running when one should be walking, talking when one should be quiet, wearing hats and coats when they should not be worn, etc. Embodiment is implicated in differentiation in schools. Subjectivities assume visible signs; there is a sense in which students 'wear' their specific positioning in school hierarchies. We explore this by focusing on the *'curriculum of the body'* (Lesko, 1988) in schools.

Space

Spatial dimensions of social interaction in schools have also been neglected in educational research (Shilling, 1991b). The school as a physical space provides a context for the practices and processes that 'take place' there. But the spatiality of the physical school is more than a context; it is an aspect in the shaping of these practices and processes producing differentiation. Decisions about the use of space involve decisions about location and movement of bodies in specific areas of the school. 'Time–space paths' and 'stations' are constructed and routinized (Giddens, 1985). In this process, physical space becomes social.

Metaphors

School rules stipulate how students should conduct themselves. How specific they are varies. Further, their contextual interpretation and application varies. But every-day life in schools also consists of a number of small practices and customs which aim to maintain correct procedures. The situational interpretation and application maintains and produces gender differences in schools. A girl student in Mac an Ghaill's study (1994) expressed this in the following way:

> [The teachers] keep moaning about the way we dress or we're running down the corridor or if we're walking too slow ... [The deputy-head] has about a hundred rules just for girls. They're always trying to rule your life ... I'm sure we confuse them. But they wouldn't think they confuse us; one day do this, the next day the opposite, especially when they're in a mood. (p. 123)

A considerable number of school rules and practices are connected to spatiality and embodiment. There are fairly specific definitions about what particular spaces are used for, and when they are used. Part of the control exerted in schools is directed at maintaining correct use of space, and directing students to appropriate stations through specific time–space paths.

The development of our focus on the physical school started in the context of a collective venture by the Gender and Education Researchers' Network in Finland. In that context we asked school students to describe their school by using some metaphor. They were asked to complete the sentence: 'School is like a ...'. Some metaphors were recurrent — for example, a factory, a mental asylum, a torture chamber, a prison and an ant's nest. We intend to explore further what meanings students attach to these metaphors. So far we have focused on some of these metaphors by trying to deconstruct them as popular genre and reconstruct them in relation to the physical school. The metaphors seem to refer to the spatial and embodied control which symbolically constitute the school as a total institution.

Both spatiality and embodiment are social constructions. These social constructions contain assumptions about gender, and specifically about gender difference. There are different expectations about the use of space and conduct of bodies by girls and boys. These are communicated through rules and practices that constitute the curriculum of the body. These rules and practices learned at school indicate what kind of embodiment is acceptable (you must not run, you must not wear a cap, you must not eat chewing gum, etc.).

'A Hundred Rules for the Girls'

The physical school is a more spacious place for boys than for girls. For them, the schoolyard is larger, the corridors are wider, the classroom bigger, and the area surrounding their bodies greater. 'Boys' take their place. But some qualifications must be added to this generalization. Boys compete for their place in hierarchically structured masculinities. A boy who is not successful in this competition is marginalized. The space and place available for a boy who does not conform to conceptions of a heterosexual male is diminished. But, as noted above, space is not merely physical — it is socially constructed, shaped by human activities, whilst also shaping those activities.

For girls, the schoolyard is smaller, the corridors are narrower, the classrooms are tighter, and the space surrounding them smaller. Girls use less space when taking their places. They seem to conform to stereotypical conceptions of girls as more passive, boys as more active. But activity and passivity are also socially produced. What is considered as activity is gendered. Further, interpretations of the same activity can also be gender-specific. Different interpretations produce different reactions and practices. A boy who moves around the classroom, talks without putting his hand up, behaves 'like a boy'. Activity is connected to masculinity. In oppositional cultural understandings, descriptions connected to masculinity are seen as more positive. Our conceptions about what 'a girl' is like lead us to take more notice of a girl who uses space, moves about, uses her voice, etc.

Discipline in schools is not possible without a large proportion of students accepting the rules or accepting the need to follow them. But because school rules concentrate a great deal on correct embodiment, resistance by school students is typically also embodied. By running when one should be walking one can distance oneself from the control exerted in the school and assume more autonomy for one's body and one's space. In such a way, small victories are achieved over the prison, the factory, the torture chamber.

A running, shouting boy may be seen as his own master, an active, autonomous breaker of boundaries. If a girl is active and uses initiative in an embodied way she is likely to encounter control exerted by teachers but also by boys. When surrounded by 'a hundred rules', girls do tend to be more passive in the classrooms, in the corridors and in the schoolyard.

Having said that, we must question why activity and passivity is measured through embodied criteria. Why is a girl, who sits quietly and talks when she has been granted permission, seen as passive? In the school, acquisition of good manners and correct conduct is expected. But when girls learn such conduct it is seen as an indication of unthinking conformity and lack of imagination. We want to question such dichotomized assumptions about activity and passivity and to argue that a girl who sits passively may in fact be active (Gordon and Lahelma, 1994a).

In a Finnish chemistry book there is a definition of 'matter', which is illustrated by a picture of a boy eating an enormous portion of ice-cream. A girl next to him is not eating ice-cream — she imagines eating it, as is indicated by a thought bubble. The book explains that 'matter' requires space — thoughts are not matter, because they require no space. A girl who controls her body, her impulses and her desires, may be active in her mind, commanding wide spaces and inhabiting far-reaching fantasies. The restrictions on embodiment in classrooms lead to various attempts to escape — where boys tend to escape by having restless feet, the escape of girls is hidden under veiled eyes.

Behaviour that is considered disruptive in the school context is interpreted as fairly straightforward boisterousness when boys are involved. Teachers assess disruptive behaviour by considering to what extent it is a direct challenge to the authority of the teacher and to the discipline structure of the school. Where boys are thought to be letting off steam, unruly behaviour in girls may be thought of as 'nasty', or more indirect. When teachers do notice the veiled eyes of girls, they may find them irritating. A teacher in Mac an Ghaill's study (1994) comments:

> With the lads, most of them, you can have a good row and you both respect it in a way. You both know the rules. But with girls, it's hard to know what they're thinking.

Disruptive girls do not only confront school rules when they disrupt time–space paths or challenge the curriculum of the body. They also confront gendered meanings, because activity and passivity are constructed as binary opposites, and connected to masculinity and femininity.

In the course of our ongoing ethnographic study we have observed great differences in the gender balance in classrooms. In some groups, gender differentiation is very close to stereotypical conceptions. Boys make a lot of noise, move about, take space, and engage most of the teacher's attention. Girls sit quietly, dreamily or with a bored look while they wait and watch as the teacher is trying to settle boys. We see boys exerting control over these girls — for example, if they do talk, the boys may repeat what they say, and do so in a shrill, high-pitched voice. But we also see groups where girls move, talk and take space. They influence the pedagogic relationship by asking questions, or by diverting the teacher's agenda by telling stories which stretch the subject matter as defined by the teacher. They may sit very close together, comb each other's hair, etc. We have found such girls in groups where girls form the majority, and where their cooperation has shaped the classroom into a safe place for them.

Therefore, it is indeed the case that we should not generalize about girls and boys. Differences within gender are considerable. But at the same time, we must note that there are a great many processes and practices in school which emphasize gender difference. Further, all girls and boys have to deal with conceptions of masculinity and femininity and the power relations connected to these. They also have to deal with gendered meanings. The behaviour of girls may range from quiet to noisy, from still to mobile — but all of these girls have to deal with gendered notions of embodiment. They are more inclined to gaze than boys. Girls also have more tied up bodies — though the ties can be opened. Boys have more moving bodies — though the movement may be stopped.

Thus, in our ethnographic research it seems to us that one way of trying to understand and grasp the production of relatively fixed gender systems, both in Finland and in Britain, and the continuation of gender segregation in the labour market, is through the consideration of learned and internalized gendered embodiment. We want to see how abstract oppositional thinking becomes the space, place and voice girls are assumed to take, and the space, place and voice boys are assumed to take.

Pedagogic Implications

We argue that it is important that attention is paid to the curriculum of the body in schools, and to the extent to which students are expected to follow routinized time–space paths throughout the school space and school day. Developing an awareness of the significance of these is the first step towards tackling them pedagogically and confronting the control of bodies that students' metaphors refer to.

Our messages for practice are few at this point. For example, physical education (PE) can play an important role. In one of the schools I have participated in PE lessons for girls. Teachers typically use contact exercises which encourage initiative, improvisation, autonomy *and* cooperation. Participation in these has been experientially exhilarating and has helped me to develop skills required in exercises that are dependent on a confident use of the body. Iris Marion Young (1989) talks about 'throwing [a ball] like a girl'. She analyses why it is that girls are considered less capable of throwing a ball well. *Not* throwing like 'a girl' requires an assertive use of the body, a preparedness to extend one's bodily outlines and an ability to widen the space that surrounds one's own body. Thus learning to throw a ball well entails unlearning internalized gendered embodiment.

Careful thought must be given to the curriculum of the body and spatial control that is part of the disciplinary structure of the school. If this is done, embodied resistance is likely to become less important for students, and particularly for those (boys?) who take place and voice from others. Confident use of body and space is important for all students. We need to disrupt the body/mind dichotomy and its central role in the production of gender difference in order to provide broader learning opportunities for girls. Gendered meanings contained in embodiment and spatiality in schools have implications for citizenship. Schools prepare students for adult life. But taking one's place as a citizen who makes confident decisions about her or his life is difficult, if everyday life in schools limits independence by unduly restricting the use of space and the conduct of bodies.

Notes

1   The other members of the project are Elina Lahelma, Tuija Metso, Tarja Palmu, Tarja Tolonen and Pirkko Hynninen, all from the University of Helsinki. The first section of my paper 'Citizenship, Difference and Marginality' is based on a research proposal which I have written in collaboration with the project team. Janet Holland at the University of

London Institute of Education and Open University is going to conduct a similar, though smaller scale, project in two secondary schools in the London area.

2 For example, the achievement of Finnish girls in mathematics is better than that of British girls.

3 There are some differences between Finland and Britain. In Britain a larger proportion of teachers *and* headteachers are women in Britain. At the secondary level the proportion of men is larger in Britain than in Finland, where levels of women teachers (about 60 per cent) are similar at both primary and secondary levels.

References

BELLAH, R., MADSEN, R., SULLIVAN, W.M., SWIDLER, A. and TIPTON, S.M. (1988) *Habits of the Heart: Middle America Observed*, Hutchinson, London.

CONNELL, R.W. (1987) *Gender and Power: Society, the Person and Sexual Politics*, Cambridge, Polity Press.

DAVIES, C.B. (1991) 'Writing off marginality, minority and effacement', *Women's Studies International Forum*, **14**(4), pp. 249–63.

DONALD, J. (1992) *Sentimental Education: Schooling, Popular Culture and the Regulation of Liberty*, London, Verso.

EISENSTEIN, Z. (1988) *The Female Body and the Law*, University of California Press, Berkeley.

GIDDENS, A. (1985) 'Time, Space and Regionalisation', in GREGORY, D. and URRY, J. (eds) *Social Relations and Spatial Structures*, London, Macmillan.

GORDON, T. (1986) *Democracy in One School?: Progressive Education and Restructuring*, London, Falmer Press.

GORDON, T. (1992) 'Citizens and others: Gender, democracy and education', *International Studies in Sociology of Education*, **2**(1), pp. 43–55.

GORDON, T. and LAHELMA, E. (1994a) 'Being, having and doing gender in schools', Paper presented in Oslo 22–24 1994, Conference on 'Gender, Modernity and Postmodernity: New Perspectives on Development/Construction of Gender'.

GORDON, T. and LAHELMA, E. (1994b) 'Citizenship, difference and marginality in schools with special reference to gender: From restructuring of education to the physical school', Paper presented at 'European Conference on Ethnocentrism and Education', Delphi, 27–29 May.

GORDON, T., LAHELMA, E. and TARMO, M. (1991) 'Gender and education in Finland — Problems for research', *Nordisk Pedagogik*, No. 4, pp. 210–17.

LAHELMA, E. (1993) 'Policies of gender and equal opportunities in curriculum development — Discussing the situation in Finland and Britain', Research Bulletin 85, University of Helsinki, Department of Education.

LESKO, N. (1988) 'Curriculum of the body: Lessons from a Catholic high school', in ROMAN, L.G., CHRISTIAN-SMITH, L.K. and ELLSWORTH, E. (eds) *Becoming Feminine: The Politics of Popular Culture*, London, Falmer Press.

MAC AN GHAILL, M. (1994) *The Making of Men: Masculinities, Sexualities and Schooling*, Milton Keynes, Open University Press.

MAHONY, P. (1992) 'Which way forward?: Equality and schools in the 1990s', *Women's Studies International Forum*, No. 2, pp. 293–302.

MEYER, J.W. (1986) 'Myths of socialisation and of personality', in HELLER, T.C., SOSNA, M. and WELLBERY, D.E. (eds) *Reconstructing Individualism: Autonomy, Individuality, and the Self in Western Thought*, Stanford, Stanford University Press.

PATEMAN, C. (1988) *The Sexual Contract*, Cambridge, Polity Press.

RYAN, J. (1991) 'Observing and normalizing: Foucault, discipline and inequality of schooling', *Journal of Educational Thought*, **25**(2), pp. 104–19.

SHIELDS, R. (1991) *Places on the Margin: Alternative Geographies of Modernity*, London, Routledge.

SHILLING, C. (1991a) 'Educating the body: Physical capital and the production of social inequalities', *Sociology*, **25**(4), pp. 653–72.

SHILLING, C. (1991b) 'Social space, gender inequalities and educational differentiation', *British Journal of Sociology of Education*, **12**(1), pp. 23–44.

YOUNG, I.M. (1989) 'Throwing like a girl: A phenomenology of feminine body comportment, motility and spatiality', in JEFFNER, A. and YOUNG, I.M. (eds) *Thinking Muse: Feminism and Modern French Philosophy*, Indiana, Indiana University Press.

YUVAL-DAVIES, N. (1991) 'The citizenship debate: Women, ethnic processes and the state', *Feminist Review*, Special Issue No. 39, pp. 58–68.

4 The Pedagogy of Difference: An African Perspective

Sheila Parvyn Wamahiu

Introduction

As we approach the twenty-first century, education for all in most parts of Africa remain a distant dream. While education is problematic for both genders in systems largely characterized by authoritarian climates, irrelevant curricula, poor quality teaching, inadequate physical structures and learning resources, and an obsession with passing examinations, girls tend to be doubly disadvantaged. Female disadvantage manifests itself in the poorer enrolment rate, especially at the higher levels; precarious survival throughout the education ladder; lower examination performance in almost all subjects; and in the gender typing of subjects and careers.

It is generally supposed that the lack of equal facilities and opportunities, precipitated by limited financial and material resources, combine to produce the gender gap in formal education. However, there is evidence indicating that even when the education policy and official curriculum are gender neutral; even when girls and boys are exposed to the same facilities, textbooks and teachers; even when both genders come from similar socio-economic and cultural backgrounds, the results are not often the same.

Wamahiu and Njau (1995) argue that female participation in formal education 'is influenced by a complex interplay between macro-level policy (both international and national) and micro-level practices, beliefs and attitudes' (p. 2). The policy environment, whether at the international or national level, they note, is in turn influenced by dominant ideologies, including gender ideologies. To quote the authors: 'The national commitment to educating the female child derives largely from this, and in turn influences the availability, allocation and quality of resources at the State and community levels' (Wamahiu and Njau, 1995, p. 4).

This chapter examines gender ideology as a crucial causative factor in female disadvantage in formal education in sub-Saharan Africa. It traces the source of this disadvantage to a dominant patriarchal ideology perpetuated through the *pedagogy of difference*, operational both at home and in school. Despite the socio-cultural and historical diversity of the region, the pedagogy of difference characterizes all countries, influencing differential treatment and exposure of boys and girls in the education systems of Africa even when all other factors are seemingly equal. It is argued that unless we are able to replace the pedagogy of difference with a *pedagogy of empowerment*, the gender gap in African education will continue to widen.

The chapter is in four sections. In the first, the pedagogy of difference and of empowerment are conceptualized. The second and third examine the pedagogy of difference through the pre-colonial, colonial and post-colonial periods, citing examples mainly from the Kenyan context. It is important to note that the diversity of Kenyan cultures is assumed to be reflective of the immense diversity of sub-Saharan Africa. Finally, in the fourth section, adoption of a pedagogy of empowerment is advocated.

Conceptualizing the Pedagogy of Difference and Empowerment

Following feminist scholars such as Jordan, Hooks and Carly, the African educational philosopher, Bennaars (1994; 1995) defines the pedagogy of difference as 'a way of educating that stresses the differences ... rather than the similarities' (1994, p. 2) between the genders. It propagates the view that males and females are not only radically different, but that females are physically, and more significantly, intellectually inferior to males. Within the African context, the pedagogy of difference reflecting a social theory of silencing, domination and subjugation, is used to rationalize the continued disadvantage of women and girls in both the informal and formal education systems. Rooted in the pre-colonial era, it has been reinforced in the subsequent colonial and post-independence periods of African history.

From a feminist perspective, the pedagogy of difference is discriminative, inequitable and therefore totally undesirable. The question is, can it be transformed into a pedagogy that promotes gender equity and an egalitarian ideal? The answer, feminists contend, is yes. While acknowledging the biological differences between males and females, they argue that the pedagogy of difference is a socio-cultural construct. As such, it should, and can, be deconstructed in such a way that exposes the unjust political, social and economic relations established through it. It is only then that society can be reconstructed based on a new ethically inspired social vision that empowers both genders (Bennaars, 1995). The pedagogy of empowerment will make 'girls aware of their potential' and allow them to 'realise their abilities to the full'. It will equally change the attitudes and values of boys and make both genders socially responsible (Bennaars, 1994).

While adhering to the framework presented above, it is clear the impact of the pedagogy of difference on males, as practised in contemporary Africa, is paradoxical. It gives males 'power over' females but does not liberate them; it grants them freedom without endowing them with a sense of social responsibility; it creates a cycle of male dependency on the supposedly dependent females. It does not prepare them for the challenges of everyday living.

The Pedagogy of Difference in Pre-colonial and Colonial Africa

In pre-colonial Africa, life and education were so integrated that it became difficult to differentiate between the two (Kenyatta, 1938; Moumouni, 1964; Erny, 1981;

Wamahiu, 1992). Education was effective because it was relevant, utilitarian, participatory and reflective of the implicit and explicit goals of society. Society was characterized by the lack of written languages, relatively simple technologies, limited range of professional specializations, the emphasis on the social group rather than the individual, and a well-defined division of labour based primarily on gender and generation.

The implications of these characteristics for education were significant. Indigenous education was for the maintenance of the status quo, not for change. It was for the perpetuation of ethnic identities, and preservation of ethnic boundaries, and not for pan-ethnic unity. It was for the harmonious integration of individuals into their social groups, and for the glorification of the group and community living; it was not an education that encouraged individualistic values. It was for the preparation of individuals for their adult roles and status, for the production of culturally recognizable 'men' and 'women'. From the perspective of gender, indigenous education incorporated a pedagogy of difference.

The pedagogy of difference in traditional Africa was based on the following premises:

(a)   That men and women are biologically different.
(b)   They occupy distinct, though complementary, social worlds.
(c)   They, therefore, play separate though complementary roles in society.

Whether the pedagogy of difference also translated into differential status for the genders in the context of traditional African societies, is not very clear. Some feminist scholars contend that women in pre-colonial Africa constituted an oppressed class. They were beasts of burden, objects of exchange, and clearly occupied lower social status than men and boys (Kabira, 1992). Others disagree with this view. For example, Njau and Mulaki (1984) assert that 'most traditional societies recognised women of talent and allowed them to participate fully in society' (p. 4). Boserup (1970) maintains that where subsistence agricultural systems prevailed, using the hoe as the main tool of cultivation, females as the major producers and managers of food enjoyed relatively high status. The distinct male and female social worlds granted each gender their own spheres of activity and power (Boserup, 1970) and that '[E]galitarian relations or at least mutually respectful relations were a living reality in much of the world in pre-colonial time' (Etienne and Leacock, 1980, Preface).

The adherents of both schools of thought, however, do agree on one thing: whatever the status of women and girls in pre-colonial societies, gender differentiation began early in life, and was internalized by participation in daily life as well as in various rituals and practices. The following examples taken from several Kenyan communities serves to demonstrate this.

•   Among the Meru, the birth of female children was heralded by the mother and midwife repeating the traditional cry of joy (*nkemi*) three times as opposed to four times for boys.

- Though the Kamba baby boy received a cow from his maternal uncle, the baby girl was not given anything.
- The Mbeere would take a new born baby girl outside the house, and give the mother a small bundle of twigs symbolizing firewood. The mother carrying the baby would go around the compound, pretending that it was the female-child who was actually doing so. This bundle of twigs would then be hung by the baby's bed.
- Similarly, the Duruma women carried baby girls, straddled on the back, and a basket with a hoe in it, around the village. Returning home, a bunch of firewood was tied at the entrance to the house.
- The Digo placed a miniature *kaha* and *kuni* (frame for carrying the water container on the head, and firewood) on the door to signify the birth of a baby girl and her expected role in the future.
- Miniature bows and arrows were used to symbolize the birth of boys and their future roles among the Digo, Mbeere and Duruma.

Observation, imitation and participation were the key learning methodologies for both genders. The education of boys and girls, however, differed in terms of the gender of their teachers: while women were responsible for the education of both during early childhood, and continued with the education of girls even afterwards, men took over the education of boys after early childhood.

Boys and girls learnt early that they had different socio-economic roles to perform in society. The learning of roles involved acquiring knowledge of the physical and cultural environments, social and technical skills, morality and ethics including sex and religion, and the group's history. In all these areas, the pedagogy of difference was apparent. In many African communities, for example, girls were taught to recognize wild but edible roots and berries by the time they were 10- or 12-years-old. During times of famine, this knowledge was imperative for survival. Likewise, a herds-boy of a comparable age had to learn to differentiate between edible and inedible grass, vegetation, fruits and insects 'to ensure the health of the livestock entrusted to him' (Otiende, Wamahiu and Karugu, 1992, p. 12) and for his own survival.

Other cases can be cited. Among the Maasai, while circumcised boys were allowed to shake hands with elders, circumcised girls could shake hands only with members of their own age-sets. Gender differentiation among the Kamba was reflected in the fees paid to the male and the female circumcisers for services rendered; the circumcision of sixteen boys was equated to that of twenty girls and entitled the circumciser to one bull. While some of the practices do not, in themselves, suggest discrimination, others, like the examples cited above, do reflect the lower status of the female gender in culturally disparate groups such as the pastoral Nilotic Maasai and the sedentary Bantu-speaking Kamba.

The oral media was a vital tool in gender role stereotyping in essentially non-literate societies. Kabira (1992) argues that through the oral media not only did boys and girls learn that they were different, with different roles to perform, but among many ethnic groups, girls internalized negative self-images of themselves. They were socialized to take a back seat in the public affairs of their societies.

It is important to note that pre-colonial African society was marked by a complex network of social obligations and expectations based on the principle of reciprocity. The social and economic roles of males and females were closely interwoven. Reproduction of new members for the perpetuation of society was considered vital. Reproduction, however, had to be carried out within the institution of marriage. Thus, marriage, preceded by initiation rituals where they existed, was mandatory for both genders, marking the transition from adolescence to that of adulthood; from girl- and boyhood to woman- and manhood respectively. However, to be considered 'proper women' and 'proper men', individuals had to prove their fertility/potency soon after marriage. The birth of the first child elevated both parents to still higher status in the social hierarchy.

Traditional practices ensured that both boys and girls were well prepared for their lives as spouses and parents through sex and family life education. Traditional sex education 'included knowledge of bodily functions and hygiene, details of expected bedroom behaviour, male–female relationships (including sexual norms) and methods of family planning' (Otiende, Wamahiu and Karugu, 1992, p. 15). Njau (1992a) points out that traditional African society went beyond sex education to include: education on sexuality, incorporating its perceptions of sexual attitudes and behaviours; understanding of sexual feelings and desires; definition and expressability of these emotions; the context of expressing them; and the norms and the limitations and taboos related to sexual expressions. As she notes, pre-colonial Kenyan societies made a distinction between coital and non-coital forms of sexual expressions, actually encouraging and formalizing the latter in some communities but discouraging the former pre-maritally. She lists the non-coital methods generally acceptable as 'public dances where close body contact, petting and fondling was permissible' (Njau, 1992a, p. 5). Kenyatta (1938) records the existence of pre-marital sex play but not penetration, between circumcised Gikuyu males and females.

Sexual control was an integral part of the education in sexuality. Perhaps the most dramatic example of teaching in self-control can be cited from traditional Gusii culture: in a process known as *Ogosonia*, newly circumcised boys were intentionally provoked sexually to test for self-control. It is reported that sometimes the circumcision wounds would open up as the boys battled for self-control (Government of Kenya, Kenya, 1986).

Sex was considered to be normal and healthy in the traditional context, and much of the sex knowledge, including language, was learnt through the process of informal education (Njau, 1992a). Sex and sexual organs were not mystified, but were taken to be part and parcel of everyday life. Sexual language and values were transmitted through initiation songs, dances, proverbs, riddles and other forms of oral narratives (Njau, 1992a; Wamahiu and Bennaars, 1995).

In addition to the informal transmission media, specific institutions existed in various pre-colonial societies where sex education and education on sexuality were imparted deliberately. These were the initiation 'schools' of the Gikuyu, Meru, Kamba, Gusii, Maasai, Nandi and others, both within and outside Kenya. There were also 'youth dormitories' like the *unyago* of the East African coast and *siwindhi* for Luo girls. (A comparable institution for boys in Luoland was the *duol*).

It would be misleading to imply that these institutions were exclusively devoted to the teaching of sex education and education on sexuality. Initiation rituals symbolized a synthesis of all learning that had taken place before. To quote Erny (1981):

> The child does not usually learn anything new; he is simply made to understand that the technical motions already familiar to him have still another dimension . . . The child will return to his old environment, and apparently nothing has changed. In reality all has changed, the previous environment has become different because the individual has undergone a change. [Initiation] changes the meaning of the world by changing the meaning of life. (p. 143)

Though the author uses the masculine gender, he refers to both genders in the above extract. As *rites de passage* to adulthood, the initiation rituals were designed to test the initiates for endurance, bravery, perseverance, self-control, among other qualities. Here, too, gender differentiation was apparent as the following description of the Kamba initiation ceremony illustrates:

> It was the day when the courage of the initiates was tested. They confronted a frightening ritual monster called *mbusya* (lit. rhinoceros) . . . It was not possible to see the man who went in and made frightening noises imitating the roar of the rhinoceros. The purpose was to frighten the children and women . . . The paraphernalia used in the emission of this terrible noise included a small clay pot containing liquid. By blowing into it through a hollow tube, the cacophonous assortment of frightening noise came out producing the intended results — fear. (Ivulila, 1982, p. 16)

In comparison, the girls, perceived to be less courageous, had to undergo a less frightening ordeal involving 'the shaking of the gourd containing some seeds by an old woman' (Ivulila, 1982, p. 17).

Yet, circumcision ceremonies, where they were practised, tested for courage and endurance. Three types of female circumcision, viz clitoridectomy (or removal of the tip of the clitoris, comparable perhaps to the male circumcision), excision (or removal of the clitoris and other parts surrounding, like the labia majora) and infibulation (or removal of genitalia followed by the closure of the vagina by stitching, allowing only a small outlet for urine and menstrual flow) were practised throughout the continent by different ethnic groups. The distinction between the three types of circumcision, Armstrong (1991) points out, is 'often irrelevant since it depends on the sharpness of the instrument used, the struggling of the child, and the skill and eyesight of the operator' (p. 30). In the traditional context, the initiate was not expected to cry or show fear in the face of even extreme pain. However, the physical pain endured by the female child initiate was far more severe than that suffered by the male child who was circumcised. (Hence, in current usage female circumcision is referred to as female genital mutilation). Despite this, given the social significance of the practice, a girl was expected to be proud of being circumcised, and the community was expected to rejoice.

Another practice that was crucial to the status of the pre-colonial female was that of brideprice. The institution of brideprice was symbolic of the dominant patriarchal ideology of pre-colonial African societies. It signified the severance of the girl from her natal home, and entrance into a whole new world of being wife and mother. Brideprice, paid in several instalments, was multi-functional. First, it served to cement the social relationships between the families of the bride and groom. Second, and more importantly, it granted the husband and the husband's lineage rights over her productive and reproductive labour. Among the Gikuyu, to cite one example, social fatherhood was granted him who paid the brideprice specified for acquiring rights in the wife's reproductive labour, and not necessarily to the man who had sired the offsprings. (The practice of woman-to-woman marriages in many African communities draws attention to this dichotomy between social and biological fatherhood).

The advent of colonialism and Christianity, together with the imposition of a monetary economy and an education system to service them in the nineteenth century, had far-reaching consequences for the situation of African women. Feminist scholars have documented the extent of disorganization caused to African peoples in general, and to women and girls in particular, by these nineteenth-century influences (Boserup, 1970; Mutua, 1975; Smock, 1977; Wamahiu, 1988). Researchers have noted the added workload and a concomitant 'loss of status' suffered by the female gender throughout the sub-Saharan region (Bookman, 1973; Pala, 1976; Staudt, 1976). Specific colonial policies, including economic and educational ones, helped to widen the already existing gender gaps, robbing women of some traditional safeguards such as usufruct rights to land and security in their matrimonial homes.

In the colonial period, the pedagogy of difference continued, though its objectives had changed. The gender role ideology in colonial Africa propounded the view that male and female status and roles were divinely ordained and therefore immutable. Though there is a tendency by people to rationalize particular practices and behaviour patterns with reference to traditions, analysis of some African myths reveals that the concept of the divine origin of status and roles by gender was not inherent in them. Three examples, drawn from culturally diverse communities will suffice at this point:

- A well-known Gikuyu origin myth talks of female domination and male subordination in a mythical period in Gikuyu history. As the story goes, men frustrated by female oppression, conspired to take over political power. In a unique and unusual move, they impregnated all eligible females simultaneously, and when they were bogged down with the pressures of advanced pregnancies, the men staged a successful *coup-d'état*. Since then, men have ruled over the House of Mumbi (i.e., the Gikuyu).
- According to a Samburu myth, a long time ago, women were the owners

of cattle. However, they lost the cattle due to their own carelessness, prompting men to take charge of this very vital property.

• A Digo myth relates that men and women lived in harmony and performed similar roles a long time ago. Both genders liked to hunt, but women were the more successful hunters. The secret of women's success was a magical hunting dog. One day, the men borrowed this dog from the women and went out hunting. In the evening, they came home with a lot of game. Inspired by their success, the men kept on borrowing the dog for several days as the women remained at home. But suddenly, a misfortune occurred — the dog got lost! The men looked for it everywhere, but to no avail. They finally had to confess the loss to the women. The women, upset at losing their means of livelihood, decided to take the case before the Council of Elders. The Council of Elders, after hearing both parties, ruled that henceforth, as punishment for their carelessness, men would have to provide for women until such a time they are able to replace the hunting dog!

The myths summarized above look upon women's currently lower status as human constructs rather than divine or biological imperatives. They describe radical changes in gender relationships in the past, and point to the possibility of radical changes in the future.

Colonial education was used to propagate the view that a woman's place is exclusively at home, within the kitchen. While in pre-colonial societies, the female reproductive and socialization roles were considered to be vital, they were also recognized as producers of food and subsistence. The household was the key production-consumption unit, an integral part of the pre-colonial economy. Under the monetary colonial economy, the household came to be less valued. The female, economically dependent on male relatives for her sustenance, was presented as the ideal to strive for. For the first time, the African woman started to take pride in being just a 'housewife'.

The colonial education system gave a headstart to African males. The economic policies of the occupiers, on the one hand, and the colonial/Christian perception of female roles on the other, was instrumental in keeping the female child away from formal (western) education. The limited education offered to women by Christian missionaries and colonial administrators 'frequently taught them domestic skills appropriate for an English housewife rather than preparing them to go on to the higher levels of the educational system' (Smock, 1977, p. 202). Consequently, African females suffered a disadvantaged position in the employment market. Since colonial education was a gateway to cash employment, and higher status within an increasingly monetized economy, females were doubly marginalized.

Christian values were particularly instrumental in destroying vital aspects of indigenous education systems (Njau, 1992b). Sex education and education on sexuality were logical victims: traditional attitudes to sex were perceived by early Christians to be sinful and even satanic. Battle was waged against initiation rites, circumcision songs, modes of dressing, traditional ceremonies — in short, against traditional cultures with a view towards exorcizing the 'demon of promiscuity'. The consequences have been disastrous: pre-marital sex, especially at relatively young ages; unwanted adolescent pregnancies; child abandonment and infanticide; social irresponsibility especially among males; increasing alcoholism and violence against women — the list is long. Further, archival data indicate that the institution of brideprice became commercialized, with fathers 'selling off' their daughters at increasingly younger ages to rich old men in a bid to acquire additional cash and cattle.

While it is true that the colonial experience disorganized traditional African societies, and in the process, depressed female status further, we must be careful not to lose sight of the fact that the majority of pre-colonial African societies were, 'essentially patriarchal. Inherent in any form of patriarchy is sexism, subtle or blatant. Though most aspects of colonialism/Christianity did not "fit" in with traditional cultures, the one aspect that was reinforced was the dominant patriarchal culture' (Wamahiu and Njau, 1992, pp. 7–8).

The roots of gender discrimination in contemporary African societies, and its perpetuation through the pedagogy of difference, can thus be traced to both pre-colonial and colonial patriarchal ideologies. In contemporary African societies, the pedagogy of difference leads to an education that is problematic for both genders, but in disparate ways.

The Pedagogy of Difference in Contemporary African Society

Whatever the weaknesses of African indigenous education, it did manage to produce men and women with integrated personalities, well adapted to their cultural and economic contexts. Unfortunately, the same cannot be said of African education today. Neither the education that one receives at home, nor that received in school, prepares the individual for life as can be inferred from the growing crime rates and incidence of violence (individual and state sponsored) reported in the daily newspapers. Much of the violence appears to be directed towards women and girls both within and outside the school.

The pedagogy of difference seems to breed a culture of violence that begins at home and is continued into the school and workplace. At home, girls are socialized into the ethics of work and discipline by their mothers and other female relatives. From an early age, they learn by taking on some of the responsibilities of their mothers, like the care of younger siblings, cooking, fetching firewood and water, harvesting the fields and so on. In this respect, contemporary home learning reflects continuity with African traditional education (Wamahiu, 1988). Social responsibility is not accompanied with empowerment, however.

For boys, the opposite situation prevails. The father no longer takes over the education of his male children after the child attains the age of 5 or 6. The mother is either unsure, or reluctant to educate her sons into the ethics of social responsibility. He is given an enormous amount of freedom without accompanying checks and balances. Boys thus play and/or study for school as their sisters work and wait upon them. They begin to believe that the world owes them a living.

By the time children enter school (if and when they do), boys and girls have already begun to internalize different values and concepts of self-worth. The differential treatment of the genders in African textbooks reinforce feelings of superiority in boys and inferiority in girls. As Wamahiu (1990) observes in her evaluation of a secondary school textbook in Kenya, biological determinism is sometimes used to justify gender roles and status. The marginalization of women and girls in textbooks, and their portrayal as passive, dependent, weak, fragile and even mindless, engaged in non-remunerative, low prestige occupations are borne out by research conducted in many African countries like Zambia, Botswana and Ethiopia (Tembo, 1984; Tsayang, Ngwako, Zonneveld and Rasebotsa, 1989; Beyene, 1991; Obura, 1991; Nyati-Ramahobo and Mmolai, 1992). Women and girls are particularly absent from mathematics, science and technologically oriented textbooks.

The pedagogy of difference is transmitted not only through textbooks (both through the written word and pictorial illustrations), but by the teachers themselves. The teacher, in the highly authoritarian environment of the African classroom, acts as the mediator between the curriculum developers and textbook writers, and transmits the messages through monologuing, a talk-and-chalk teaching style, encouraging rote memorization and repetitious learning, and the frequent use of corporal punishment (Wamahiu, 1992) in stark contrast to the traditional participatory methods of learning. The teacher's worldview, in the majority of cases, an essentially patriarchal worldview, arising from many years of exposure to the pedagogy of difference in both formal and informal educational settings, influences the content of the messages that are transmitted.

Comparatively little research on gender differences in the classroom has been conducted in Africa. However, what has been done points towards implicit and explicit gender discrimination in the classroom. Research portrays girls in co-educational classrooms, especially in science classrooms, as displaying passive, quiet, subservient behaviour (Tsayang *et al.*, 1989; Mbilinyi and Mbughuni, 1991; Obura, personal communication, 1994). A study conducted in Rwanda revealed the silencing and subjugation of girls through deliberate discriminative behaviour in mathematics classrooms. The researcher found that the teacher (male) called the weaker girls to the blackboard more often than boys and brighter girls:

> If the girls called to the blackboard could not complete the work, comments were made by the teacher and male students alike concerning the girl's ability to complete the task. Commonly the teacher would then call upon another female student of comparatively low ability to assist the girls at the blackboard. Often the teacher would then call upon one of the more capable boys to complete the problem. (van Belle-Prouty, 1990, Annex I)

Teachers, it has been observed, not only denigrate female capability in academic achievement in general, and mathematics and the sciences in particular, but also transmit their perceptions of what constitute the correct behaviour and lifestyle for educated girls. Girls who deviate from the 'correct behaviour' risk being labelled 'abnormal' (Obonyo, personal communication). Masemann (1974), who conducted a study in a Ghanaian boarding school, concluded that teachers encourage girls to internalize the view that men have authority over women both at home and the workplace. It is no wonder then that many girls drop out of school to get married or because of pre-marital pregnancy.

The pedagogy of difference ensures that more African girls than boys remain outside the formal education systems of their countries. The survival chances for girls entering schools is slimmer than that of boys. (For example, the gender ratio for secondary school completion rate in sub-Saharan Africa is 0.64 per cent.) Girls' relatively poorer performance in almost all subjects, especially in mathematics and in the sciences, obstructs educational and career progression.

Towards a Pedagogy of Empowerment

As noted, the pedagogy of difference, incorporating a pedagogy of oppression, found in the classroom originates outside the school. The authoritarian climate of African classrooms provides the perfect breeding ground for it. Despite government rhetoric to the contrary, this kind of pedagogy legitimizes the subordinate position of females vis-à-vis that of males, both through, and in, the education system. It creates a vicious cycle of powerlessness and desperation for both boys and girls — the oppressors and the oppressed respectively. It is interesting to note that, despite the greater opportunities available to the African male for employment and economic empowerment, in many cases they become psychologically and, ironically, economically dependent on their womenfolk!

Education in the contemporary context, must be transformative. It must liberate all humankind and empower both genders through teaching them to 'advance their own development' (Bennaars, 1994). Both genders must learn that to be socially responsible is not incompatible with being free, that to be successful does not necessarily require aggressiveness, that a true leader does not rule with force. This can only happen within the context of a democratic school culture that replaces slavish allegiance to authority with critical thinking, creativity and flexibility.

The pedagogy of empowerment will be gender responsive. It will recognize the biological differences between males and females, but will reject biological or divine determinism of gender roles and status. It will accept women's rights as human rights.

Bennaars (1995) argues that gender education will be seriously hampered unless the pedagogy of difference is understood and appreciated as an ethical challenge. To replace this pedagogy with the pedagogy of empowerment will entail cataclysmic changes, including basic attitudinal and structural changes. Equally important, it will take commitment and concerted efforts by all interested parties; policy-makers, curriculum developers, educators, textbook publishers and writers, parents, girls and boys will all have to be catalysts of this change.

A truly African pedagogy of empowerment will synthesize the good, positive aspects of the old, with the good, positive aspects of the new. As Africans, we must be able to look back into the traditional pedagogy — the methods (e.g., freedom to explore the environment, the emphasis on participation, learning through living) and some of the content (e.g., sex education and education on sexuality, especially the frankness with which it was tackled; some values like respect for elders and for work). But most important of all, African mythology sets the precedence for change — a change from an oppressive system to an empowering one.

Notes

1 Preliminary observations from a field study conducted by Anna Obura, a leading African researcher in the area of gender and education.
2 Based on classroom observations in Kisii District of Kenya.

References

ARMSTRONG, S. (1991) 'Female circumcision: Fighting a cruel tradition', *New Scientist*, February.

BELLE-PROUTY, D. VAN (1990) 'Reproducers reproduced: Female resistance in Rwanda classroom', *Development*, pp. 74–9.

BENNAARS, G.A. (1994) *Girls' Education: An Agenda for Change*, Nairobi, Forum for African Women Educationalists (FAWE).

BENNAARS, G.A. (1995) 'Gender, education and the pedagogy of difference: The African predicament', *Basic Education Forum*, **6**, pp. 23–34.

BEYENE, A. (1991) 'Female participation and performance in rural primary schools in Ethiopia,' Research report presented to the Institute for Curriculum Development and Research, Ministry of Education, UNICEF and SIDA, Addis Ababa Ethiopia, August.

BOOKMAN, A.E. (1973) 'The changing economic role of Luo women: An historical and ethnographic approach' *Special Papers in Social Anthropology*, Harvard University.

BOSERUP, E. (1970) *Women's Role in Economic Development*, New York, St. Martin's Press.

ERNY, P. (1981) *The Child and His Environment in Black Africa*, (G. Wanjohi, trans.), Nairobi, Oxford University Press.

ETIENNE, M. and LEACOCK, E. (eds) (1980) *Women and Colonisation — Anthropological Perspectives*, New York, Berain Publishers.

IVULILA, P.N. (1982) 'The educational aspects in traditional rites of passage among the Akamba.' PGDE Major Project, Kenyatta University College, Nairobi, Kenya.

KABIRA, W. (1992) 'Gender ideology: The cultural context,' Paper presented at the AAWORD Seminar on Women and Democratisation, Nairobi, Kenya.

KENYA, GOVERNMENT OF (1986) *Kitui District Socio-Cultural Profile Institute of African Studies*, University of Nairobi and Ministry of Planning, Nairobi.

KENYATTA, J. (1938) *Facing Mt. Kenya*, London, Mercury Books.

MASEMANN, V.L. (1974) 'The "hidden curriculum" of a West African girls' boarding school', *Canadian Journal of African Studies* **8**(3), pp. 479–94.

MBILINYI, M. and MBUGHUNI, P. (ed.) (1991) *Education in Tanzania with a Gender Perspective: Summary*, Dar es Salaam, Swedish International Development Agency.

MOUMOUNI, A. (1964) *Education in Africa*, (P. Nouts, trans.), Andre Deutsch.

MUTUA, R. (1975) 'Women's education and their participation in changing societies of East Africa', *Kenya Education Review* **2**(2), Nairobi University of Nairobi.

NJAU, R. and MULAKI, G. (1984) *Kenyan Women Heroes and Their Mystical Power, Vol 1*, Nairobi, Risk Publications.

NJAU, W. (1992a) 'Traditional sex education in Africa: The case of Kenya', Paper presented at The First Inter-African Conference on Adolescent Health in Africa, Nairobi, Kenya, March.

NJAU, W. (1992b) 'Pre-marital teenage pregnancies and child bearing in Kenya', Paper presented at the 10th ISPOG Congress on Sexuality and Reproductive Life in Some Developing Countries, Stockholm, Sweden, June.

NYATI-RAMAHOBO, L. and MMOLAI, S. (1992) *Girl-child Study: Opportunities and Disparities in Education: Part II Published Study* UNICEF, FEMNET, ERNESA Collaborative, Gaberone, Botswana.

OBURA, A. (1991) *Changing Images: Portrayal of Girls and Women in Kenyan Textbooks*, Nairobi, African Centre for Technology Studies.

OTIENDE, J.E., WAMAHIU, S. and KARUGU, A. (1992) *Education and Development in Kenya: A Historical Perspective*, Nairobi, Oxford University Press.

PALA, A.O. (1976) 'A Preliminary Survey of the Avenues for the Constraints on Women in Development Process in Kenya', Institute of Development Studies, Discussion Paper No. 218, Nairobi Kenya, University of Nairobi.

SMOCK, A. (1977) 'The impact of modernisation on women's position in the family in Ghana', in SCHLEGEL, A. (ed.) *Sexual Stratification: A Cross-Cultural View*, New York, Columbia University Press.

STAUDT, K. (1976) 'Agricultural policy, political power and women in Western Kenya'. Doctoral Thesis, University of Michigan, USA.

TEMBO, L. (1984) 'A national survey on sex biases in Zambian textbooks in primary and junior secondary schools and their implications for education in Zambia,' Research report presented to UNESCO, Paris, France.

TSAYANG, G.T. and NGWAKO, A. with ZONNEVELD, M. and RASEBOTSA, N. (eds) (1989) 'Gender and Education'. Proceedings of a workshop at the University of Botswana, 27 February–1 March, Occasional Paper No. 2, Gaberone, Faculty of Education Research Committee, University of Botswana.

WAMAHIU, S.P. (1988) 'Continuity and change in Adigo women's roles, status and education: An exploratory anthropological study', Doctoral Thesis, Kenyatta University, Nairobi Kenya.

WAMAHIU, S.P. (1990) 'Writers, SEE and the social sciences' in BENNAARS, G.A., OTIENDE, J.E. and WAMAHIU, S.P. (eds) *Social Education and Ethics: Developing a New Area of Learning*, Nairobi, Professors of World Peace Academy.

WAMAHIU, S.P. (1992) 'The situation of the female-child in Kenya', Report submitted to the Kenya Alliance for the Advocacy for Children's Rights through the African Network for the Prevention and Protection against Child Abuse and Neglect, Nairobi, Kenya, November.

WAMAHIU, S.P. and NJAU, W. (1992) 'Towards the development of gender studies in Kenya', Paper presented at the Workshop on the Development of Academic Courses in Gender Studies in Eastern and Southern Africa, Entebbe, Uganda, September.

WAMAHIU, S.P. and NJAU, W. (1995) 'School girl drop-out and adolescent pregnancy: Counting the cost', *Basic Education Forum*, 6, pp. 1–22.

WAMAHIU, S.P. and BENNAARS, G. (1995) 'The current state of social education and ethics with special reference to selected gender issues among the Digo of Kwale District: A study in cultural anthropology and social philosophy', Research report submitted to the Organisation for Social Science Research in Eastern Africa, Nairobi, Kenya.

5   Gender Identity and Cognitive Style

John Head

Background

Introduction

Twenty years ago, research into cognitive styles was flourishing, e.g., Messick (1976) and Goldstein and Blackman (1977), including studies of gender differences, e.g., Kogan (1976). It might have been anticipated then that by now we should have an agreed body of knowledge in place to illuminate issues of gender and pedagogy.

Why has not this hope been realized? Two main factors were involved. One set of problems related to the nature of cognitive styles. Much of the activity of the 1960s and early 1970s did not stand up well to later scrutiny. The underlying constructs were often too vague and the psychological measures were unrefined. For example, much interest was shown in the field of creativity, but there was no agreed description of what the word creativity meant. Creativity tests were developed, but were clearly inadequate. In one well-known study, Getzels and Jackson (1962) used a battery of five creativity tests, but these only had a mean inter-test correlation of 0.30, which meant that only 9 per cent of the total variance could be allocated to the common factor. In terms of simple psychometrics this was clearly unsatisfactory and considerable test refinement was needed before creativity testing could be taken seriously. By about 1975, widespead disenchantment with research into cognitive styles set in, although a few workers quietly persisted in their studies, and only within the last few years have we witnessed a renewal of interest.

The second factor relates to the perception of gender differences. Central to much of feminist thinking in the 1960s and 1970s was the view that psychological differences were fairly trivial and the gender differences found in society could be attributed almost totally to discrimination and the denial of opportunity. The literature of cognitive abilities illustrates the point. Maccoby and Jacklin (1974) list some hundreds of studies into gender differences in abilities, a total which testified to the interest in the field in previous years. In a meta-analysis of such studies, Hyde (1981) demonstrated that measured cognitive differences were far too small to account for the lack of women in many parts of our educational systems. If cognitive differences contributed anything to the inequality between men and men, and that notion is debatable, then the contribution could only be very minor. In this climate of opinion, research on differences in cognitive styles seemed unimportant.

In the 1980s there was a major shift in feminist thought back to a belief that there might be some widespread psychological gender differences. Gilligan's (1982) work was both a symptom and a major contribution to this change. Her own work will be outlined later in this chapter and at this stage all that need be noted is that it was not cognitive abilities, but styles, which were being brought back into the limelight. It was still being argued that differences in abilities were minor but there might exist alongside that fact the possibility that men and women tended to use their abilities in different ways.

Against this background of changing ideas, both in respect to the study of cognitive styles and to the nature of gender differences, it is opportune to look again at the interaction between these fields and the possible contribution to notions of pedagogy.

Level and Style

One lesson can be learnt from the mistakes of the past twenty years; that is, the necessity of having a clear understanding of the constructs involved. In particular, cognitive abilities, or levels, need to be distinguished from cognitive styles.

Abilities are seen to be unipolar, starting from a zero position of not possessing the ability at all. Having a high level of an ability can only confer an advantage to the holder, although the extent of the advantage will depend on the task context. Consequently values can be attached to measures of cognitive abilities with the high scorers being favoured. A further characteristic, central to the concept of an ability, is that at a given time there is an upper limit to someone's ability and that is what we measure. They cannot perform above that measured level — if they do then clearly our measurement was at fault.

Styles are essentially bipolar. We postulate two contrasting ways of working, each being a viable and acceptable alternative, and locate people on a continuum according to their preference between the two options. According to the context, people at either end of the continuum might be advantaged, so values cannot be meaningfully attached to measures of style. There is no right or wrong in this situation. Futhermore, it is possible for people to display some flexibility and work in a different style should the task demand it. Under these conditions a person is said to display *coping behaviour*. The assumption is that such coping behaviour is not comfortable and the person will revert to their preferred style as soon as possible.

Measurements of cognitive styles should be orthogonal to those of cognitive abilities, that is, there should be no correlation between them, but as the preferences are a reflection of the personality we might anticipate significant correlations between measures of cognitive style and of personality. It is a test of the quality of cognitive style measures that correlations with other tests should conform to this pattern.

In the literature we can find references to cognitive styles, conceptual styles and thinking styles. No distinction is made between them in this chapter. They all address issues of the structure and process of thinking rather than the content of thought. They are all concerned with how individuals conceptually organize their environment and develop reasonably consistent strategies in dealing with unfamiliar tasks. They describe the ways individuals prefer to work.

With these qualities in mind we can move on to look at the evidence for there being gender differences in these various descriptions of styles.

The Evidence

Part of the confusion relating to cognitive styles is that more than twenty such styles are mentioned in the literature, too many to handle conveniently, and examination suggests that there might be considerable overlap between some of those listed. For example, authoritarianism, rigidity, intolerance of ambiguity and dogmatism are broadly similar in conceptualization and measurement, being associated with inflexibility and the assertion of beliefs. In this event methodological questions arise about which construct and measure is to be preferred as yielding the best understanding and data on the variables. For simplicity, in this chapter a number of possible style descriptions have been placed together into four main clusters and no attempt is being made to evaluate the relative value of the variables contributing to each cluster.

Males Extract, Females Embed

The best known style contributing to this cluster is that of field dependence and independence, which was originally described more than thirty years ago, e.g., by Witkin (1962). Surveys of the recent literature shows that the majority of journal articles describing gender differences in cognitive styles used measures of field independence, usually the Group Embedded Figures Test, as the principal research tool. However, there has been some controversy about the limitations of this concept and measure (e.g., McKenna, 1983; 1984) and for that reason Cohen's (1986) more neutral terms of extract or embed is used in this chapter to describe the cluster. Other similar style descriptions contained in this cluster would include the analytic versus holistic thinking preference (Riding and Cheema, 1991).

There is overwhelming evidence that females are more field dependent than males. This conclusion is reported by Kogan (1976) in surveying the evidence up until that year and has been repeatedly confirmed by subsequent studies. However, at this point the methodological problem, already mentioned, enters the picture. The Group Embedded Figures Test asks the respondent to identify a simple geometric shape which is hidden by being part of a more complex figure. The test, therefore, has a right answer, and thus resembles a test of ability rather than one of preferred style. In addition, there is some evidence of boys being better at solving spatial tests (Maccoby and Jacklin, 1974). The interaction of these two factors may suggest that all we are recording is a gendered difference in abilities, rather than one of cognitive style. More recent workers in this field, e.g., Riding and Cheema (1991), have developed tests which reward success both in extraction and embedding modes of working, so style can be measured independently of cognitive differences, such as intelligence (Riding and Pearson, 1994). In any event the gender differences with these various measures of style are greater in magnitude than the recorded differences in spatial abilities, so at least part of the gender variance must be attributed to something more than differences in ability.

One reason for valuing the model of extracting versus embedding is that it connects with certain other fields of psychological enquiry. Reference has already been made to the work of Gilligan (1982) in which she made two key points. She argued that males and females tended to adopt different approaches when considering moral issues, with the former opting for an analytical, legalistic stance while the latter exercised more empathy in a relational approach. Men tended to create precise rules and then used these rules to make moral judgments, e.g., driving at 30 miles an hour may be legal but at any greater speed is properly judged to be illegal. Women tended to consider the wider context of the situation, determining as far as possible the relationships and motivations of those concerned.

Gilligan's second point was that standard tests of moral development as developed by Kohlberg (e.g., 1973) were applicable to a typically male pattern of development but failed to describe the situation for females. Gilligan's first finding provided additional evidence, from a totally different source, of the gender differences in extracting and embedding in problem solving. Her second point, the criticism of the prevailing test methodology, exactly parallels the criticism of the field independency tests.

Thus reconceptualized field dependence and independence can be seen as value-free terms. In some contexts, e.g., locating which component of a car engine is malfunctioning, the extraction mode of thinking is needed. In other contexts, e.g., in enviromental biology, the embedding mode is better, as we would need to consider how a change in one part of the ecosystem affects other parts. Not least of the pedagogic implications of this work is the choice of assessment instruments. The so-called objective tests, such as multiple choice tests, employ the extraction mode and thus contain a gender bias.

Impulsiveness versus Reflection (Inhibition)

The second cluster of style measures describes the finding that males tend to be more hasty and impulsive in test situations while females exercise more care and deliberation (e.g., Maccoby and Jacklin, 1974). Helson (1967) argued that with males, 'The intellect functions as an organ for swift registration, development and organization . . . In matriarchal consciousness what is to be understood must first "enter" in the sense of fructification' (p. 214).

In different contexts either gender might be advantaged. The willingness of boys to take risks may help them in launching into a practical exercise even though they do not know what they are doing. In similar circumstances girls may feel inhibited from commencing the task. In essay writing the greater care and deliberation of girls is likely to pay off. Even when boys clearly have mastered the relevant concepts their work tends to be spoilt by careless mistakes. The speedier response rate of boys has to be traded against their greater error rate.

Reference has already been made to the use of multiple choice type tests. Generally boys do better at these tests as the need for a quick response does not worry them too much, but they make errors if the item has a complicated structure as they fail to read the words carefully enough. If a lesson is conducted at a fierce pace then girls may feel unable to contribute fully. There is research evidence that slowing down the pace a little, e.g., by allowing the pupil a few seconds to compose the reply to a verbal question, markedly improves the quantity and quality of the responses (Swift and Gooding, 1983).

In some situations the tendency of boys to enjoy the excitement of taking risks combined with the reluctance to lose face in front of the peer group leads to them displaying physical violence and other anti-social behaviour (Bell and Bell, 1993). More conventionally this combination of qualities can cause boys to be more disruptive and challenging of the teacher's authority.

The Locus of Control

The third cluster describes the boundaries of what individuals feel able to control, including descriptors such as locus of control, attribution, labelling, self-fulfilling prophecies and symbolic interactions. Again the concept is value-free as either extreme of attribution is likely to disadvantage a person. If someone accepts no responsibility for their behaviour and performance, believing that external factors solely determine outcomes, then they have little incentive to make an effort to improve. If, at the opposite extreme position, they feel personally responsible for every failure and injustice they encounter then they are likely to feel helpless and overwhelmed by a sense of guilt and the demands they make on themselves.

Males tend to develop a defence mechanism of attributing success to their own efforts and failure to external factors. Girls show the reverse tendency. Consequently boys will blame a fault in the apparatus, or in the teacher's explanation, if they experience failure in a practical class. Girls may blame themselves even if the problem lies with faulty apparatus.

The pedagogic implication is that girls may sink into the condition which Dweck (1986) describes as 'learned helplessness' in which the perception of personal failure inhibits subsequent performance. By contrast boys have to learn to accept responsibility for their poor work. This difference in self-valuation is largely independent of ability. The process of attribution, whether inter- or intra-personal, can be very powerful in creating the very qualities being attributed to a person. Peterson, Maier and Seligman (1993) describe how the extent of learned helplessness often experienced by women in a world still largely governed by men can be the precursor of clinical depression.

Dweck, Davidson, Nelson and Enna (1978) describe the importance of feedback from teachers in affecting feelings of learned helplessness. Teachers tend to give a wider range of feedback to boys, ranging from generous praise to sharp criticism, while girls receive bland praise, which is of little help to them. The intentions may be good, not to overwhelm girls with critical comments, but the pedagogic outcomes are likely to be unfortunate. To rescue someone from learned helplessness calls not simply for positive comments, although the reverse experience of unending criticism is demotivating, but for specific advice. The student needs to see precisely how an improvement can be made. We may recall Ausubel's (1968) famous comment: 'If I had to reduce all of educational psychology to just one principle, I would say this: the most important single factor influencing learning is what the learner already knows. Ascertain this and teach him [sic] accordingly.'

The work of the Russian psychologist Vygotsky introduces the notion of students needing 'scaffolding', that is appropriate support from a teacher, when they are operating in their 'zone of proximal development'. Vygotsky was arguing that learning occurs at a point just beyond the current understanding and competence of the learner, so they are operating in an area of some uncertainty and confusion. The learner needs to be given encouragement to go beyond that which is known and undertake the tentative exploration of new ideas. A gender-sensitive pedagogy has to combine a supportive environment with the provision of precise criticism, praise and guidance.

Cooperation or Competition

It may be argued that this title does not describe a cognitive style at all but a style of working. There are two reasons for its inclusion here. The preference for a way of working influences cognition as the social context provides a stimulus to thought. Secondly, there is a natural development of ideas which links this section to its predecessors.

Schools often employ a system of rewards and prizes in the belief that competition will act to motivate the learners. The evidence is that a sense of competition works more effectively with boys than girls. The interrelationships between boys are marked by competition, seen in contexts ranging from athletics through to the nature of their discourse, which is marked by boys tending to assert their own point-of-view and ignoring the contributions from others. The discourse of girls is more relational, in which one speaker refers back to the previous speaker, and in which stress is laid on similarities rather than differences.

Under these conditions it is arguable that girls may be more motivated by opportunities to work in cooperation with each other rather than in competition. Real problems can arise in co-educational contexts in which girls find it difficult to cope with the competitive ways of operating shown by the boys. Askew and Ross (1988) provide some amusing descriptions of these gender differences. If two girls are asked to cooperate in painting a picture together they negotiate an agreed plan. Under similar circumstances two boys may simply draw a line down the paper so each has half the page to complete and they then work quite independently.

It is a matter of fine judgment for a teacher to decide the extent of competitive spirit which should be introduced with a particular group of students, the extent to which the benefits are matched against the effects of learned helplessness already described.

It can be seen that the gender differences described under the four clusters of styles described in this section — field dependence and independence, impulsiveness versus reflection, the locus of control and, finally, the issues of cooperation and competition — have some common features. This similarity is not coincidental but a reflection of the underlying differences in gender identity.

Explanations and Implications

Causal Factors

A curious feature of the explanations offered during the past hundred years for gender differences is that biological determinist models keep coming up despite the lack of confirmatory evidence. As each suggestion, e.g., the possible influence of differences in brain size, has been dismissed new variants of the argument emerge. With respect to cognitive style the commonest contemporary example relates to brain hemisphere dominance. Sometimes it is argued that females have a more dominant left hemisphere, as the left side of the brain is associated with speech and the right side with visual-spatial skills. Others argue that women have a dominant right side of the brain as it is linked with more global and intuitive thinking while the left side is credited with logical, analytical thought. The stark contradiction between the claims, combined with the lack of empirical evidence for sex differences in hemisphere dominance, indicate that this hypothesis is no more valid than its predecessors.

We can analyse the social influences under three headings, one general and two specific to a given phase in the life of a person. The general influence is the all-pervasive gendered nature of our cultures and nations. Most languages are gendered, for example with English in the use of pronouns such as she or he. Most societies create different roles and expectations for boys and girls so that the roots of gender identity are established early on and are continuously being reinforced by experiences within and outside school. Even when parents make a conscious effort to treat their children equally, irrespective of their gender, this pervasive social influence is likely to thwart such effort.

The first age-specific factor is that boys and girls have an asymmetrical experience of being mothered (e.g., Lynn, 1962; Chodorow, 1978). Usually it is the mother or another female who acts as the primary caretaker for the child. Thus girls can learn their gender identity by identification with the mother whereas a boy has to acquire his identity by being different, by breaking away from the mother.

Observations reveal that young children are treated very differently according to their perceived sex. Smith and Lloyd (1978) describe a study of women being asked to look after a young child who was sometimes described as a boy and on other occasions as a girl. If perceived to be a boy it was stimulated when it cried while a perceived girl was comforted. At the crawling stage a boy was allowed to crawl further away from the women before being brought back. Girls were talked to more. Studies show mother–daughter talk contains more sharing, as women talking together about common interests, while talk with sons is less and has a different quality of negotiation between unlike beings.

The links between these early childhood experiences and differences in cognitive style are obvious. Young girls are inducted into a relational mode in which they are encouraged to be conscious of the needs and concerns of others. Child rearing requires this capacity — hence Chodorow's clever choice of title for her book: *The Reproduction of Mothering*. This awareness of others acts as a foundation for the more cooperative way of working and global way of thinking associated with women.

Young boys are encouraged to be autonomous and it is suggested, e.g., by Hudson and Jacot (1991), that if the separation from the female primary caretaker is too abrupt or premature it can inflict a 'male wound' characterized by an inability to relate to others. Boys may compensate for their poor social skills be investing their time in the world of material objects, hence their liking for science and computers. As boys have to achieve their sense of identity on their own they tend to be egocentric and selfish. This predisposition leads to the competitive interactions between boys. In order to contain this competition males set up rules to govern these interactions and hence males operate within a legalistic rule-bound social environment which leads to the legalistic, analytical, extraction mode of thinking.

The second age-specific factor is that of puberty which provides a very different experience for boys and girls for three reasons. Girls mature at an earlier age. The physical experience of puberty is not usually a problem in itself for boys while a high proportion of adolescent girls report considerable distress with menstruation (Prendergast, 1992). Finally, girls are very conscious of the possibility and consequences of pregnancy while boys see sexual activity simply as a pleasurable adjunct to living. The consequences of these differences is that boys and girls tend to cling to the same-sex peer group in early adolescence and gain their sense of personal identity from a gender-specific stereotypical set of beliefs and values. Early adolescence represents the time when boys and girls display the least understanding of each other. Although the evidence with adults shows that those displaying psychological androgyny are advantaged (Bem, 1975), it is difficult for those in early adolescence to behave other than within the constraints of the peer group.

One criticism of any explanation based on social factors is that it may only hold true for a specific type of society. It might be argued that the models outlined above relate to western democracies, e.g., with Chodorow describing the situation in the United States and Smith and Lloyd conducting their research in Britain. To evaluate this reservation we need to look at the extent of common practice and experience between countries.

Although there is no biological necessity for child bearing and child rearing to be carried out by the same person we find that in most societies women perform the primary caretaker role with young children and thus Chodorow's model should have widespread validity. Similarly the different experiences of puberty are not specific to a given culture. The distribution of gendered roles in the workplace shows broad similarities across many cultures. Although there may be regional variations in social practices in detail, nevertheless there are enough underlying structural similarities for the explanatory models to have widespread credence.

We might, therefore, expect both gender identities and preferences in cognitive and learning styles to be broadly similar in most cultures. Certainly my own experience in visiting schools in more than a dozen countries in four continents confirms the view that comparable gender differences can be observed within widely differing political and social contexts.

Pedagogic Implications

Do these cognitive style differences matter? To what extent do they contribute to the known inequalities in schooling? Gender effects are cumulative. Cognitive style differences in isolation may not be crucial, but, combined with other factors which produce similar effects, they may appreciably affect outcomes. In many countries girls do not participate equally with boys in science and technology education. In such instances a number of variables act together, including social expectations, images of the subjects, the curriculum content and the classroom interactions. If, when girls find themselves disadvantaged in several ways, there is an additional problem relating to their preferred learning and cognitive styles not being matched by the teaching tactics then the situation is made worse. Some of the contributing variables, such as social attitudes, cannot be changed by teachers within a short time. Awareness of differing cognitive styles gives teachers something to act on in the immediate future.

In a controlled experiment Head and Ramsden (1990) found that altering the organization and context of learning, without altering the actual curriculum content, could make both quantitative and qualitative differences to the uptake of physics by girls. More girls opted for the subject and personality measures suggested that a wider spread of psychological type made this choice. This finding confirms the belief that teachers can bring about significant changes in educational outcomes.

What does work on cognitive styles suggest for a more gender-sensitive pedagogy? Initial impressions of a classroom convey powerful images. Think of the reaction of a girl entering a science laboratory, which she may already perceive as being a male domain, and meeting male teachers who talk about the male heroes of science, such as Newton and Darwin, and illustrate the curriculum with examples of rockets, engines and football. All her sense of gender identity would indicate that this is an inappropriate place for her. It should not be difficult for teachers to find a variety of images and examples so that any student can identify with some of them.

There may be a mismatch between the cognitive styles of the teacher and the student. One of the most well-developed models and measures of cognitive style in recent years has been that of Kirton (1994) on adaption-innovation. Kirton postulates that when confronted by a novel type of problem people display a difference in style. Those at the adaptor end of the continuum attempt to solve the problem by making small adaptions to existing and tried procedures. Those at the innovative end of the spectrum tend to seek a totally novel approach to the problem. This body of work has been developed within the fields on personnel selection and management training and has not yet been extensively used in educational contexts, but one finding does appear significant. If two people have widely differing scores on the adaption-innovation test, something in excess of one standard deviation between them, then they tend not to communicate effectively with each other. In this event management team building may involve introducing a third position with an intermediate test score who acts as an interpreter between the other two.

What happens if there is a similar mismatch between the teacher and student? The only way out might be for one of them to adopt *coping behaviour*, that is take on an unfamiliar thinking style for the duration of the exchange between them. It is difficult for the student to act out of role in this fashion as the student already has to cope with the learning task. It should be much easier for the teacher, who ought to be in strong command of the subject content, to act in this way. As there will likely to be considerable diversity within a given class the teacher should seek to present a new idea in a variety of ways, so that students have a choice in the mode with which they access the material to be learnt. For example, a teacher may start with a general overview and then deal with specific examples, but at a later time the reverse procedure could be followed. Holist or embedded thinkers may prefer the former procedure while extractors may prefer the latter.

If the classroom dynamics are such that a girl faces competition with boys, for gaining access to both apparatus and the teacher, then her confidence may be eroded. If the teacher relies heavily on multiple choice assessment tests then she may experience further difficulties. If the teacher fails to place the science content into a humanistic context and uses a pedagogy which rewards the competitive quick response risk-taking boys, then the disillusionment will be complete.

If boys and girls prefer different learning procedures then teachers in co-educational schools should be flexible in their choice of teaching and assessment methods. But these gender differences are not absolute, there is considerable overlap between the two sexes and considerable variation within one group. A flexible approach to pedagogy should, therefore, be of general benefit to the school population. The real criticism of a pedagogy based on stereotypical male values and practices is not that it is totally valueless, but that it is too limited. It is not merely aimed at one gender but at one sub-group within that gender, that is those boys who conform to the stereotypical male behaviour pattern. The value of feminist thought and methods in many fields has been to open up practice to a wider range of possibilities, yielding a more flexible and responsive system. If such reform can be carried out within our classrooms then all, boys and girls, should benefit.

References

ASKEW, S. and ROSS, C. (1988) *Boys Don't Cry*, Milton Keynes, Open University Press.
AUSUBEL, D.P. (1968) *Educational Psychology: A Cognitive View*, New York, Holt, Rinehart and Winston.

BELL, N.J. and BELL, R.W. (1993) *Adolescent Risk Taking*, Newbury Park, Sage.

BEM, S.L. (1975) 'Sex-role adaptability: One consequence of psychological androgyny', *Journal of Personal and Social Psychology*, **31**, pp. 634–43.

CHODOROW, N. (1978) *The Reproduction of Mothering*, Berkeley, University of California Press.

COHEN, R. (1986) *Conceptual Styles and Social Change*, Acton, M.A., Copley.

DWECK, C.S., DAVIDSON, W., NELSON, S. and ENNA, B. (1978) 'Sex differences in learned helplessness: II, The contingencies of evaluative feedback in the classroom', *Developmental Psychology*, **14**, pp. 268–76.

DWECK, C.S. (1986) 'Motivational processes affecting learning', *American Psychologist*, **41**, pp. 1040–8.

GETZELS, J.W. and JACKSON, P.W. (1962) *Creativity and Intelligence*, New York, Wiley.

GILLIGAN, C. (1982) *In a Different Voice*, Cambridge, Mass., Harvard University Press.

GOLDSTEIN, K.M. and BLACKMAN, S. (1977) 'Assessment of cognitive style', in MCREYNOLDS, P. (ed.) *Advances in Psychological Assessment*, **4**, San Francisco, Jossey-Bass.

HEAD, J. and RAMSDEN, J. (1990) 'Gender, psychological type and science', *International Journal of Science Education*, **12**, pp. 115–21.

HELSON, R. (1967) 'Sex differences in creative style', *Journal of Personality*, **35**, pp. 214–33.

HUDSON, L. and JACOT, B. (1991) *The Way Men Think*, New Haven, Yale University Press.

HYDE, J.S. (1981) 'How large are cognitive gender differences?', *American Psycholgist*, **36**, pp. 892–901.

KIRTON, M. (1994) *Adaptors and Innovators*, London, Routledge.

KOGAN, N. (1976) 'Sex differences in creativity and cognitive styles', in MESSICK, S. (ed.) *Individuality in Learning*, San Francisco, Jossey-Bass.

KOHLBERG, L. (1973) 'Continuities and discontinuities in childhood and adult moral development revisited', *Collected Papers on Moral Development and Moral Education*, Cambridge, Harvard University Press.

LYNN, D.B. (1962) 'Sex-role and parental identification', *Child Development*, **33**, pp. 555–64.

MACCOBY, E.M. and JACKLIN, C.N. (1974) *The Psychology of Sex Differences*, Stanford, Stanford University Press.

MCKENNA, F.P. (1983) 'Field dependence and personality: A re-examination', *Social Behavior and Personality*, **11**, pp. 51–5.

MCKENNA, F.P. (1984) 'Measures of field dependence: Cognitive style or cognitive ability?', *Journal of Personality and Social Psychology*, **47**, pp. 593–603.

MESSICK, S. (ed.) (1976) *Individuality in Learning*, San Francisco, Jossey-Bass.

PETERSON, C., MAIER, S.F. and SELIGMAN, M.E.P. (1993) *Learned Helplessness*, New York, Oxford University Press.

PRENDERGAST, S. (1992) *This is the Time to Grow Up: Girls' Experience of Menstruation in School*, Cambridge, Centre for Family Research.

RIDING, R. and CHEEMA, I. (1991) 'Cognitive styles — An overview and integration', *Educational Psychology*, **11**, pp. 193–215.

RIDING, R. and PEARSON, F. (1994) 'The relationship between cognitive style and intelligence', *Educational Psychology*, **14**, pp. 413–25.

SMITH, C. and LLOYD, B.B. (1978) 'Maternal behaviour and perceived sex of infant', *Child Development*, **49**, pp. 1263–5.

SWIFT, J.N. and GOODING, C.T. (1983) 'Interaction of wait time, feedback and questioning instruction in middle school science teaching', *Journal of Research in Science Teaching*, **20**, pp. 721–30.

WITKIN, H.A. (1962) *Psychological Differentiation*, New York, Wiley.

II

Differential Learning and Performance

6   Scholarship, Gender and Mathematics

Elizabeth Fennema

Since the early 1970s I have been studying and wondering about gender differences in mathematics. My first article was published in 1974 and was a review of extant work that had been done on sex difference in mathematics. I concluded that there was evidence to support the idea that there were differences between girls' and boys' learning of mathematics, particularly in items that required complex reasoning; that these differences increased at about the onset of adolescence; and that these differences were recognized by many leading mathematics educators. As an aside, it was really the writing of that 1974 article that turned me into an active feminist, compelling me to recognize the bias that existed toward females, which was exemplified by the recognition and acceptance by the mathematics education community at large of gender differences in mathematics as legitimate.

In 1990 (and I still believe this in 1995), I concluded that research indicated that:

1   Gender differences in mathematics may be decreasing.
2   Gender differences in mathematics still exist in learning complex mathematics, personal beliefs in mathematics, and career choice that involves mathematics.
3   Gender differences in mathematics vary by socio-economic status, by ethnicity, by school, and by teacher.
4   Teachers tend to structure their classrooms to favor male learning.
5   Interventions have sometimes resulted in smaller gender differences in mathematics.

It is clear that in the two decades following my original review in 1974, my understanding of gender and mathematics has grown as far as related variables are concerned, but the same gender differences, *albeit* perhaps smaller, still exist. I now can describe the problem more precisely. I know that large variations between groups of females exist; I know that there are differences among schools and teachers with respect to gender and mathematics issues; I know that females and males differ with respect to personal beliefs about mathematics; and I know that interventions can make a difference. I understand that the issue of gender and mathematics is extremely complex. I accept without question the basic promise of the International Commission on Mathematical Instruction Study Conference on Gender and Mathematics

(1992), that 'there is no physical or intellectual barrier to the participation of women in mathematics'. But in spite of all the work done by many dedicated educators, mathematicians, and others, the 'problem' still exists in much the same form that it did in 1974.

Now, before I sound too pessimistic, it should be noted that there are many females who are achieving in mathematics and are pursuing mathematics-related careers. However, let me reiterate that in spite of some indications that achievement differences are becoming smaller, and they were never very large anyway, they still exist in those areas involving the most complex mathematical tasks, particularly as students progress to middle and secondary schools. There are also major differences in participation in mathematics-related careers. Many women, capable of learning the mathematics required, choose to limit their options by not learning mathematics. And while I have no direct data, I strongly suspect that the learning and participation of many women, who might be in the lower two-thirds of the achievement distribution, have not progressed at all. I must conclude that many of the differences that were reported in the 1970s, while smaller overall than they were then, still exist in 1995.

What specifically does the research literature have to say about pedagogy, gender, and mathematics? The series of studies dealing with educational variables, reported and summarized in the book Gilah Leder and I edited (Fennema and Leder, 1990), suggested that it is relatively easy to identify differential teacher interactions with girls and boys: in particular, teachers interact more with boys than with girls, praise and scold boys more than girls, and call on boys more than girls. However, the impact of this differential treatment is unclear and difficult to ascertain. There are few data that support the premise that differential teacher treatment of boys and girls causes gender differences in mathematics (Koehler, 1990; Leder, 1982; Eccles and Blumenfeld, 1985). *In 1995, there is still not sufficient evidence to allow us to conclude that interacting more or differently with girls and boys is a major contributor to the development of gender differences in mathematics.* I believe that differential teacher treatment of boys and girls is merely a symptom of many other causes of gender differences in mathematics and that, as in medical practice, treating the symptom is not sufficient to change the underlying cause.

Identifying behaviours in classrooms that influence gender differences in learning and patterns in how students elect to study mathematics has been difficult. Factors that many believed to be self-evident have not been shown to be particularly important. Consider the sexist behaviours, such as those indicating that mathematics is more important for boys than for girls. No one would deny that such behaviours exist. However, Peterson and I (Peterson and Fennema, 1985; Fennema and Peterson, 1986) did not find major examples of overall sexist behaviours on the part of teachers, but rather small differences in teacher behaviour, which, when combined with the organization and instruction, made up a pattern of classroom organization that appeared to favor males. We also found patterns of teacher behaviour and classroom organization that influenced boys and girls differently. For example, competitive activities encouraged boys' learning and had a negative influence on girls' learning, while the opposite was true with cooperative learning.

Since competitive activities were much more prevalent than cooperative activities, it appeared that classrooms we studied were more often favourable to boys' learning than to girls' learning.

In connection with this series of studies, Peterson and I proposed the Autonomous Learning Behavior model, which suggested that because of societal influences (of which teachers and classrooms were main components) and personal belief systems (lowered confidence, attributional style, belief usefulness), females do not participate in learning activities that enable them to become independent learners in mathematics (Fennema and Peterson, 1985). This model still appears valid, although my understanding of what independence is has grown, and I believe that independence in mathematical thinking may be learned through working in cooperation to solve mathematical problems.

Another line of enquiry, which has added a significant dimension and more complexity to the study of gender and mathematics, is the work that has divided the universe of females into smaller groups. In particular, the work of the High School and Beyond Project (a large multi-year project that documented gender differences in mathematics as well as many other areas) as interpreted by Secada (1992), and the work of Reyes (was Hart) and Stanic (1988) has investigated how socio-economic status and ethnicity interacts with gender to influence mathematics learning. Most countries are highly heterogeneous societies, made up of many layers, divisions, and cultures. The pattern of female differences in mathematics varies across these layers and must be considered.

One finding which has not been systematically studied is the variation in gender differences in mathematics across schools and across teachers. Casserly (1980) reported that some US schools were much more successful in attracting females to the most advanced mathematics classes than other schools. The Fennema-Sherman studies reported variations in the size of the differences between schools. And one large urban school system in the US reported substantial discrepancies in gender difference scores by high school on the SAT, a college entrance examination that is recognized as being a good test of mathematical reasoning. Confirming this variation between schools and teachers, recent unpublished work of mine has identified certain teachers whose classes consistently show greater gender differences in favour of males than do the classes of other teachers.

New Scholarship on Gender and Mathematics

Much of what we know about gender and mathematics has been derived from scholarship that has been conducted using a positivist approach that has looked basically at overt behaviours such as answers on a mathematics test, the amount one agrees with an item that is part of a confidence scale, interactions between a teacher and a student, or the career decisions that students make. While studies conducted from a positivist perspective have provided powerful and rich information about gender and mathematics, I do not believe that we shall understand gender and mathematics until such studies are complemented with scholarly efforts that utilize other perspectives. I believe that research conducted within two new perspectives would provide important insights into the issues involving gender and mathematics.

I will discuss and provide examples of research from a cognitive science perspective, which emphasize the irrelevance of female–male differences; and feminist perspectives, which emphasize that female–male differences are critical to the learning of mathematics.

Cognitive Science Perspective

Central to this perspective is the idea that much of behaviour is guided by mental activity or cognitions. Cognitive science research has provided insights into teachers' behaviours, knowledge, and beliefs, although little has been done related to teachers' cognitions about gender. Such studies may lead to deeper understanding of gender differences in mathematics as understanding is gained about the mental life of students, teachers, and others, and how it influences daily decisions about learning mathematics. Unfortunately, there are not many studies related to gender that have been done using this perspective and I must rely on my own and my colleagues' work. One study concerned teachers' knowledge of and beliefs about boys' and girls' successes in mathematics (Fennema, Peterson, Carpenter and Lubinski, 1990). Although teachers thought the attributes of girls and boys who succeeded in mathematics were basically similar, teachers' knowledge about which boys were successful was more accurate than teachers' knowledge about which girls were successful; and teachers attributed boys' successes more to ability and girls' successes more to effort. Weisbeck (1992) found that during stimulated recall interviews, teachers reported that they thought more about boys than about girls during instruction. However, the characteristics they used to describe girls and boys were very similar.

It appears that teachers are very aware of whether the child they are interacting with is a boy or a girl. However, they do not think that there are important differences between girls and boys that should be attended to as they make instructional decisions. Boys are apparently just more salient in the teachers' minds. Teachers appear to react to pressure from students, and they get more pressure from boys.

Carolyn Hopp (1994) was concerned with what happens in cooperative small groups that influences the learning of mathematics, particularly the learning of complex mathematics like problem solving. Her study suggests boys and girls engage in different mental activities during cooperative problem solving, and the impact of working in cooperative groups on their learning may be quite different depending on what mental activity they engage in during the cooperative activity. Just working in small groups does not ensure that girls will learn mathematics. It depends upon what the girls think about as they engage in cooperative activity.

Thus, while research conducted from a cognitive science perspective is still in its infancy as far as gender and mathematics are concerned, such studies can provide knowledge that will help us understand the underlying mechanisms that have resulted in gender differences in mathematics. Consider the case of the relationship between confidence in learning mathematics and the actual learning of mathematics.

It has been assumed for at least two decades that lower confidence contributes to gender differences in mathematics. Perhaps, a careful study of males' and females' perception of what has influenced their development of confidence in doing mathematics, and how their confidence has impacted on their study and learning of mathematics, might give us better insight into the relationship of the two. Or, studying the impact that teachers' perception of the confidence of their students has on decisions that teachers make during mathematics instruction might provide deeper insight into teacher–student interactions.

Knowledge derived from a cognitive science perspective has enabled some teachers to eliminate gender differences in mathematics. Carpenter and I have been investigating how knowledge of the universals of children's thinking about whole-number arithmetic could be used in classrooms and whether this knowledge would make a difference in what teachers did and how children learned (Carpenter and Fennema, 1992). We called the project Cognitively Guided Instruction (CGI) and we continue to investigate it today. Basically, we shared with teachers what we knew about the universals of children's learning, enabled them to become secure in that knowledge, and supported them as they applied the knowledge in their primary classrooms. Briefly, we found that teachers could acquire this knowledge of universals and use it in classrooms to make instructional decisions about individual children. CGI teachers' beliefs about children changed and children in CGI classrooms have learned mathematics in excess of anything we expected.

At the beginning of our first study, before teachers had learned about children's thinking, we found that first-grade boys were better problem solvers than first-grade girls. In succeeding studies of children in Grade 1–3, who have spent a year with teachers who know and understand children's thinking, we have found variable gender differences. Often, no differences exist; sometimes they are in boys' favor, and at other times they are in girls' favor. It appears that when teachers make instructional decisions based on their knowledge of individual children, overall gender differences are not found. It also appears that among certain teachers, although they are few in number, gender differences in favour of boys usually exist across classrooms and years; and among even fewer teachers, differences in favour of girls are found across years. We are just beginning to try to ascertain whether we can identify components of their classrooms or cognitions that encourage the development of these gender differences in certain teachers' classrooms.

Thus, it appears that research utilizing a cognitive science perspective can be helpful in gaining an understanding of gender and mathematics. It enables us to go beyond surface knowledge and our behaviour, to develop an understanding of underlying mechanisms. When we understand more, future educational directions can be identified.

Feminist Perspectives

While within the work of scholars included in the feminist tradition there are marked differences that go beyond the purview of this paper, they do share a commonality.

Without exception, they focus on interpreting the world and its components from a feminine point of view, and the resulting interpretations are dramatically different from what exists in most places today.

Feminist scholars argue very convincingly that most of our beliefs, perceptions, and scholarship, including most of our scientific methodologies and findings, are dominated by male perspectives or interpreted through masculine eyes. According to feminist scholars, because females have been omitted, the view of the world as interpreted through masculine perspectives is incomplete at best, and often wrong. If women's actions and points of view had been considered over the last few centuries, according to many of these feminist scholars, our perceptions of life would be much different today.

A basic assumption of feminist work is that there are basic differences between females and males that are more prevalent than the obvious biological ones and these differences result in males and females experiencing and interpreting the world differently. The idea of masculine-based interpretations in areas like history or literature, and even in medical science, is not too difficult to illustrate, nor even to accept. Does the prevalence of this attitude apply to mathematics and if so, how? Can mathematics be seen as masculine and feminine? Is not mathematics a logical, value-free field? The ideas of a masculine or a feminine mathematics is difficult to accept and to understand, even to many who have been concerned about gender and mathematics. A few people are working to explicate what a gendered mathematics might be — in particular, Suzanne Damarin (1995), Zelda Issacson (1986), and Judith Jacobs (in press), who are struggling to define what a feminist approach to the study of mathematics education might be.

One way to approach the problem of a gendered mathematics is not to look at the subject directly, but to examine the way that people think and learn within the subject. Many who work in the field of gender and mathematics have suggested that we have to identify a pedagogy which is unique to females before we can ensure equity in mathematics, e.g., the greater inclusion of cooperation rather than of competition in classrooms. Others have argued for single-sex schools oriented to the mathematics instruction of females. Running through these suggestions, it seems to me, is a basic belief that females learn differently and perform differently in mathematics than do males.

It is too early to be able to assess the impact that studies using feminist methodologies will have on our understanding of pedagogy, gender, and mathematics. However, it appears that viewing the gender differences that exist from a feminist standpoint redefines the issues related to gender and mathematics. Instead of interpreting the challenges related to gender and mathematics as involving problems associated with females and mathematics, we should look at how a male view of mathematics has been destructive to females. The problem lies in our current views of mathematics and its teaching. I am coming to believe that females have recognized that mathematics, as currently taught and learned, restricts their lives rather than enriches them.

I believe that we need to examine carefully how feminist perspectives can add enriched understanding to our knowledge of mathematics education. And indeed, we should be open to the possibility that we have been so enculturated by the masculine dominated society we live in that our belief about the neutrality of subjects such as mathematics is inaccurate and, at the very least, incomplete. Perhaps we have been asking the wrong questions as we have studied gender and mathematics. Could there be a better set of questions, studied from feminist perspectives, that would help us understand gender issues in mathematics? What would a feminist mathematics look like? Is there a female way of thinking about mathematics? Would mathematics education, organized from a feminist perspective, be different from the mathematics education we currently have? Suzanne Damarin (1995) has stated that we need to 'create a radical reorganization of the way that we think about and interpret issues and studies of gender and mathematics.' Many scholars believe that only as we do this will we be fully able to understand gender issues in mathematics. Perhaps my beginning to believe that the decision by females not to learn mathematics because it has not offered them a life they wish to lead, is an indication that my old view about learning and teaching mathematics, as well as about gender and mathematics, was immature and incomplete. I am beginning to believe that an examination of what the female voices in the new research are saying will help me — and perhaps others — to understand teaching, learning, gender, and mathematics better.

New Research Perspectives: Some Contrasts

Cognitive science and feminist perspectives, while sharing surface similarities, are based on dramatically different assumptions about females and males. These assumptions dictate the questions that are addressed, how studies are designed, and how evidence is interpreted. They are assumptions that are more far-reaching than issues of scholarship; they influence how we view the entire issue of gender and mathematics. What is the magnitude and impact of differences between females and males? Are males and females fundamentally different, so that all decisions about mathematics and understanding gender and mathematics need to be made on the basis of these differences? Or, with the exception of their biological differences, are males and females fundamentally the same, and are these differences irrelevant with respect to mathematics? Cognitive science research, as it identifies universals, would suggest that looking at the world through either feminine or masculine eyes does not make sense. Feminist perspectives suggest just the opposite: female–male differences permeate the entirety of life and must be considered whenever scholarship is planned.

The implications of these assumptions are dramatic in both doing and understanding research, as well as work in the field of gender and mathematics. Each individual should think deeply about his or her own beliefs and reinterpret knowledge about gender and mathematics in relation to these beliefs or assumptions.

References

CARPENTER, T.P. and FENNEMA, E. (1992) 'Cognitively Guided Instruction: Building on the knowledge of students and teachers', *International Journal of Educational Research*, **17**(5), pp. 457–70.

CASSERLY, P. (1980) 'Factors affecting female participation in advanced placement programs in mathematics, chemistry, and physics', in FOX, L., BRODY, L. and TOBIN, T. (eds) *Women and the Mathematical Mystique*, Baltimore, John Hopkins University Press.

DAMARIN, S. (1995) 'Gender and mathematics from a feminist standpoint', in SECADA, W.S., FENNEMA, E. and BYRD, L. (eds) *New Directions for Equity in Mathematics Education*, New York, Cambridge University Press, pp. 242–57.

ECCLES, J.S. and BLUMENFELD, P. (1985) 'Classroom experiences and student gender: Are there differences and do they matter?', in WILKINSON, L.C. and MARRETT, C.B. (eds) *Gender Influences in Classroom Interaction*, New York, Academic Press.

FENNEMA, E. and LEDER, G. (eds) (1990) *Mathematics and Gender: Influences on Teachers and Students*, New York, Teachers College Press.

FENNEMA, E. and PETERSON, P. (1985) 'Autonomous learning behavior: A possible explanation of gender-related differences in mathematics', in WILKINSON, L.C. and MARRETT, C.B. (eds) *Gender-related Differences in Classroom Interaction*, Orlando, Florida, Academic Press, pp. 17–35.

FENNEMA, E. and PETERSON, P. (1986) 'Teacher-student interactions and sex-related differences in learning mathematics', *Teaching and Teacher Education*, **2**(1), pp. 19–42.

FENNEMA, E., PETERSON, P., CARPENTER, T.P. and LUBINSKI, C.A. (1990) 'Teachers' attributions and beliefs about girls, boys, and mathematics', *Educational Studies in Mathematics*, **21**(1), pp. 55–65.

HOPP, C. (1994) 'Cooperative learning and the influence of task on learning of mathematics', Unpublished doctoral dissertation, University of Wisconsin-Madison.

INTERNATIONAL COMMISSION ON MATHEMATICS INSTRUCTION (1992) Study Document for Gender and Mathematics Conference.

ISSACSON, Z. (1986) 'Freedom and girls' education: A philosophical discussion with particular reference to mathematics', in BURTON, L. (ed.) *Girls into Maths Can Go*, London, Holt, Rinehart & Winston.

JACOBS, J. (in press) 'Feminist pedagogy and mathematics', *International Review on Mathematical Education*.

KOEHLER, M.S. (1990) 'Classrooms, teachers and gender differences in mathematics', in FENNEMA, E. and LEDER, G. (eds) *Mathematics and Gender*, New York, Teachers College Press.

LEDER, G.C. (1982) 'Mathematics achievement and fear of success', *Journal for Research in Mathematics Education*, **13**(2), pp. 124–35.

PETERSON, P. and FENNEMA, E. (1985) 'Effective teaching, student engagement in classroom activities, and sex-related differences in learning mathematics', *American Educational Research Journal*, **22**(3), pp. 309–35.

REYES, L.H. and STANIC, G.M.A. (1988) 'Race, sex, socioeconomic status and mathematics', *Journal for Research in Mathematics Education*, **19**(1), pp. 26–43.

SECADA, W. (1992) 'Race, ethnicity, social class, language, and achievement in mathematics', in GROUWS, D.A. (ed.) *Handbook of Research on Mathematics Teaching and Learning*, New York, Macmillan.

WEISBECK, L. (1992) 'Teachers' thoughts about children during mathematics instruction', Unpublished doctoral dissertation, University of Wisconsin-Madison.

7   Girls and Information Technology

Karen Littleton

Introduction

The notion that the computer could influence 'the shape of minds to come' has considerable currency, and much has been written about the potential of the computer to provide new environments in which children can be educated (Crook, 1992; Scrimshaw, 1993). However, educationalists and psychologists alike are becoming increasingly concerned that the use of computer technology in schools could serve to amplify pre-existing patterns of social inequality (Littleton, Light, Barnes, Messer and Joiner, 1993). Enthusiasm for the use of computers in the classroom is thus being moderated by a growing awareness that the social and educational effects of this technology could potentially be divisive (e.g., Laboratory of Comparative Human Cognition, 1989; Olson, 1988). Issues of equality of opportunity and access arise for various groups of children, including those of low socio-economic status and ethnic minorities. The particular concern of this paper, however, is with gender differences in response to computer-based learning, for it has been noted that the increasing deployment of computers in schools could place girls at a serious disadvantage relative to boys (e.g., DES, 1989; Evans and Hall, 1988; Hoyles, 1988). This concern arises from the growing body of research revealing that male and female students differ in terms of their expressed enthusiasm for, their access to, and participation in, computer-related activities (Littleton *et al.*, 1993).

The aim of this paper, then, is to document the research which has prompted the concern over girls' lack of engagement with computer technology; identify some of the factors which may underpin gendered responses to computers and; highlight intervention strategies designed to ameliorate the situation. The material under discussion is drawn from diverse sources spanning several different disciplines. At times I have drawn upon my own research, allowing myself a little more detail in the case of material which is yet to be published.

The Evidence

Attitudes Towards Computers

Data spanning the entire age range of compulsory schooling reveal that girls are often less positive about computer-use than boys (e.g., Martin, 1991; Todman and Dick,

1993). While they may generally regard males and females as equally competent, girls often report more negative feelings concerning their own personal involvement with computers (Chen, 1986). We should not, however, simply conclude that girls are not interested in using computer technology. Rather, it would appear that girls' responses to computers are more polarized than those of boys (Culley, 1993). For example, a survey of attitudes to computers conducted in Australian schools revealed that whilst as many girls as boys enjoyed using computers, many more girls than boys ardently disliked them (Hattie and Fitzgerald, 1988). Boys and girls tend to see the use of the computer as an activity that is somehow more 'appropriate' for boys than for girls (Wilder, Mackie and Cooper, 1985). It is also apparent that in some schools the computer is regarded as a 'machine for men and boys' (EOC, 1983) and even where girls and boys express equally positive attitudes, both believe that boys like and use computers more than girls do (Hughes, Brackenridge and MacLeod, 1987). This belief may well be justified since there is some evidence to suggest that more boys than girls actually report liking computers (Wilder, Mackie and Cooper, 1985). Moreover, males perceive computers as having a larger part to play in their future lives and career aspirations (Hattie and Fitzgerald, 1988; Culley, 1993).

Computer Use in School

With respect to actual computer use, levels of participation in computer-related activities amongst girls in UK secondary education tend to be low. A detailed investigation of eight secondary schools in three local education authorities revealed that:

> In most schools fewer girls than boys participate in optional computing activities such as computer clubs, where girls were less than 10% of regular attenders. Computer rooms in most schools were regarded as male territory and girls report being made to feel very uncomfortable by the attitudes and behaviour of the boys. Several schools had recognised this problem and responded by establishing certain times as 'girls-only'. Such schemes were only partly successful, however. The tendency was for the open sessions to become the boys' sessions and thus reduce even further the access of girls to computers. In one school the 'open sessions' were overseen by a male computer teacher, while the 'girls-only' sessions was staffed by a female teacher who had no computing expertise. (Culley, 1988, p. 4)

A further indicator of these low levels of participation is the relative number of girls and boys being entered for public examinations in computer studies and computer science. In the UK at least, there is a very marked gender bias in the numbers of girls and boys being examined in these subjects (Hughes, 1990; Culley, 1993) and the gap appears to be becoming increasingly pronounced over time as the proportion of girls studying computer science declines (Buckley and Smith, 1991). Applications by girls to study computer science at university dropped by 50 per cent between 1978 and 1988, as did acceptances (Hoyles, 1988).

The problem of low levels of female participation in computer-related activities is not, however, restricted to children of secondary school age. Straker cites a report on computer-use in the British primary curriculum which concludes that '... there are increasing signs that computers are being used more by boys and male teachers than by girls and female teachers. Primary schools may need to take positive steps to ensure that both sexes have equal opportunities ...' (Straker, 1989, p. 230). Somekh (1988) talks about girls becoming hesitant computer users in their junior school years. But the problem is not restricted to the school domain. Gender disparities in home computer-use have long been noted and it is clear that differential access of boys and girls to computer technology in the home is significant (Culley, 1988; Evans and Hall, 1988; Hoyles, 1988).

Computer Use Outside School

It has often been documented that parents are more likely to encourage boys than girls to use computers (e.g., Hoyles, 1988) and there is evidence to suggest that parents more frequently buy computers for boys than for girls (Mohamedali, Messer and Fletcher, 1987). Boys make more use of computers in the home than girls (Fife-Schaw, Breakwell, Lee and Spencer, 1986; Lockheed, 1985; Robertson, Calder, Fung, Jones and O'Shea, 1995) and whilst this is primarily for games, gender differences in use are reported in all home computer activities (Martin, 1991). These differences in home experience seem likely to impact on children's response to computers at school. Beynon (1993) argues that 'Boys are far more likely to enter into formal schooling culturally and practically positioned to accept and be motivated by computers' (p. 167). It has also been suggested (Crawford, Groundwater-Smith and Millan, 1989) that, because of their lack of experience of computers within the home, girls are more likely to perceive themselves as lacking expertise and this in turn contributes to their relative passivity in the computing classroom. Hoyles (1988) further notes that girls taking computer studies examinations are less likely than boys to have access to a home computer — a position which inevitably places the girls at a disadvantage.

In addition to the disparity in levels of home and school computer use, it is also apparent that boys are more likely to use computers in clubs and engage in extra-curricular computer activities than girls. Hess (1985), for example, reported data from the US which revealed that three times fewer girls than boys were enrolled in summer camp programmes and that the ratio of females to males decreased as a function of grade, cost and level of difficulty of the programme.

Explanations and Interventions

A variety of factors are thought to underpin gender differences in response to computers and it is widely acknowledged that these factors are likely to interact in complex and subtle ways. For ease of presentation, however, each of these factors, together with any associated implications for intervention, will be considered independently. A basic premise is that the currently observed gendered patterns of response to computer technology are neither inevitable or immutable. First, the public image of computers and computing is examined, then the organization of computer activities in schools is considered.

In attempting to account for gendered patterns of response to computer technology, researchers often point to the image that the computer has within our society, where the computer seems to be defined as a 'machine for men'. Hoyles argues that 'the control of computers tends to call up a default image of a man rather than a woman' (Hoyles, 1988, p. 2). Moreover, the type of software aimed at the home computing market both reflects and reinforces this situation. Many of the games involve war scenarios or physical adventures and the titles as well as the themes exhibit gender bias. As Crawford, Groundwater-Smith and Millan (1989) note, many girls seem to resist engagement with the 'male toy' at home. Computer games, which girls often deem sexist or offensively violent, are seen as an extension of arcade games and thus part of the 'macho male domain'. For boys, then, computer games appear to provide an initial motivation to become more acquainted with both computers and computer programming. As Culley notes: 'Games form a key part of an important social network outside schools from which girls are excluded' (Culley, 1993, p. 151).

What, then, is the image of a successful computer user? Ware and Stuck (1985) investigated this in their exploration of the pictorial representation of males and females in popular computer magazines. Overwhelmingly, men were represented as experts and managers, while women were depicted in supportive and decorative roles. Only women were shown as 'computer-phobes'. In some respects, however, these images provide quite an accurate reflection of the current employment situation where 'women occupy the lower strata of computing jobs and therein are often victims of sexism' (Beynon, 1993, p. 167).

If school teachers are asked to account for girls' negative response to computers many point to 'forces in wider society' and highlight some of the factors raised above. Others, however, see girls' lack of enthusiasm as something inherent in girls or in computing:

> *Teacher:* The computers themselves just don't seem to attract girls and I don't see any way of improving that. I mean computers are computers and they are not suddenly going to start doing something interesting to girls. (Culley, 1993, p. 154)

Willis (1987), in her review of Australian evidence, notes that girls' lack of interest in computers was widely seen by teachers as a reflection of boys' and girls' different interests. The implication here is that there is little that can be done about it. However, there is evidence to suggest that girls in single-sex schools are less likely to be influenced by gender stereotypes in their attitudes to computers than their counterparts in co-educational schools (Gardner, McEwen and Curry, 1985).

There is also some indication that '. . . in girl-only schools there is no shortage of enthusiasm for computing; that computer studies is a popular option; and that computer clubs thrive' (Culley, 1988, p. 7). This raises the possibility that:

> Since outside influences are unlikely to be radically different for girls attending single-sex schools, the processes involved in the organisation of teaching with and about computers in a co-educational setting must be significant. (Culley, 1988, p. 7)

Mixed Gender Interactions and Computer-use

Culley's detailed observations of computer awareness classes revealed that not only do girls tend to get less time on machines than boys but when they do work on the computers they tend to get less assistance from the teachers because the boys dominate both machine and teacher resources:

> In the discussion part of lessons boys dominated the lesson, consistently asking more questions of the teacher and making more comments on the content of the lesson. Girls were also marginal to the classes in the physical sense, often seated at the back or sides of the room. In the practical part of the lessons boys would typically acquire the newest computers, those with disk drives and *colour* monitors. Often girls would be elbowed out the way and left standing in the rush, without access to a computer at all. (Culley, 1988, p. 6)

Thus, through their greater familiarity and their general physical and social power, the boys managed to secure for themselves a greater share of resources and teacher attention than did the girls. A similar pattern of interaction between pupils and teacher was also seen in computer studies options classes. In both cases, few teachers seemed to make any effort to counteract the tendency of boys to dominate the lessons, although some at least acknowledged this as a problem. Culley (1993) also found that:

> Pupils usually worked in single-sex groups. The female groups tended to share the facilities they were using quite well, and adopted a more co-operative approach to the working out of problems and entering data. The male groups tended to generate more arguments about 'turns', more competition and more concern about individual and group performance. This generated more noise and attention from the teacher. Mixed sex working groups were relatively rare and only entered into when unavoidable. In these groups, almost without exception, boys would dominate the keyboard whilst the girls looked on. On the few occasions when teachers insisted that a boy give over control of the computer to the girl there was considerable resentment expressed. Male groups tended to demand the teachers' attention more

than the female groups and did this by waving hands and by calling out. Consequently, more attention was given to the boys' needs. (p. 152)

This tendency for boys to dominate both computer and teacher resources can also be seen amongst children of primary school age. Here, too, it is the boys who take over the computers in the free periods (Carmichael, Burnett, Higginson, Moore and Pollard, 1986). It is also apparent that in class time girls are less willing to volunteer to use the computer. Moore (1986) documents the activity in one Grade 7 class where the boys had gained complete control over the five computers. Perhaps not surprisingly their confidence increased, while that of the girls declined. By the end of the year the girls believed that they had fallen so far behind that they could never make up the lost ground. They also remarked that they never wanted a computer in their classroom ever again (Moore, 1986). There is also evidence of boys in mixed-sex groups dominating computer-based activities. Barbieri and Light (1992), for example, found that boys in mixed-gender pairs typically sat themselves in such a way so as to ensure that it was they who gained immediate control of the mouse.

These kinds of observation have raised the possibility that girls' lack of engagement with computer-related activities may, at least in part, stem from their often unsatisfactory experiences of computer use within the classroom. Taken together with the positive engagement with computers to be found with pupils in girls-only schools, such observations have prompted enthusiasm in some quarters for segregating girls from boys in the context of computer use in the hope that girls in girls-only groups will be less inhibited and will thus learn more. Experimental research designed to investigate whether girls learn less when working with boys has sometimes indicated that girls are particularly disadvantaged by working with boys (e.g., Underwood, McCaffrey and Underwood, 1990), but this is by no means always the case (e.g., Hughes, Brackenridge, Bibby and Greenhough, 1988; Littleton, Light, Joiner, Messer and Barnes, 1992). We should, however, be wary about concluding that it often makes no difference whether girls work in same or mixed-gender groupings. The focus of these research studies is clearly on whether children's performance and learning vary as a consequence of working either as part of a mixed or same gender pair. What they often fail to consider is whether children's attitudes and feelings about computers and computer work alter as a function of the gender of their working partner. It may well be that the crucial impact of mixed or same gender working conditions is reflected, not in terms of learning and performance, rather in terms of confidence, attitudes and motivation. My colleagues and I have suggested that this could indeed be the case (Littleton, Joiner, Light, Messer, Riley, Barnes and Agiobu-Kemmer, 1991). In our work we found that girls' experience in a single-gender pair had a more positive effect on their attitudes than experience in a mixed-gender pair, even though their *performance* was, if anything slightly better in the *mixed* pairs.

It is fair to say, though, that the effectiveness of single-gender grouping as an appropriate strategy has yet to be established. Some, for example, Willis and Kenway (1986) point to the inherent dangers in such a course of action. It is, for instance, possible that the teaching staff would regard the girls' classes as being lower interest/ability classes and consequently have lower expectations of them. They argue that:

> ... separating out girls from boys (boys from girls) will not, in itself, change the perceptions of the teachers and administrators in the schools, any more than it will automatically change the attitudes of the students themselves. (Willis and Kenway, 1986, p. 145)

Willis and Kenway also comment that whilst the strategy of segregating boys and girls for computer-based work possesses some superficial appeal, it could result in resources being diverted away from the important issue of curriculum reform. Thus, it is argued, if schools are to consider adopting such a strategy it is vital that they ensure that a change in the gender structure of the classes is not a substitute for an examination of curriculum content, teaching methodologies and assessment practices.

Culley (1993), mindful of the comments of Willis and Kenway, is tentative about advocating segregation as an effective intervention strategy for lesson-based computer work. She sees the need for teachers to develop an understanding of classroom dynamics and the ways in which boys may come to dominate the computer classroom. Classroom management strategies, she argues, need to involve girls more centrally and pupils need to be involved in discussion of patterns of gender interaction. Culley does, however, believe that there is a much stronger case to be made for ensuring that girls have access to free-time use of computers in 'girls-only' settings, where they are free to develop skills and 'tinker' in a supportive environment. She adds that any such 'girls-only' sessions should be supervised by teachers who are both competent in computing and sensitive to gender issues.

A note of caution regarding the potential problems associated with a reduction in the opportunities for interaction between boys and girls is raised by some recent experimental work conducted by my colleagues and I (Light, Littleton and Bales, 1994). We studied 11-year-old children working on a computer-based problem-solving task either in 'co-active' or 'interactive' pairs, in either girl–girl, girl–boy or boy–boy pairings. In the case of the 'co-active' pairs, whilst the children entered the room together, each child worked individually at one of two machines. There was no verbal interaction, and the children were unable to see one another's screens. In the case of the 'interactive' pairs, the children entered the room together and then proceeded to work together on the problem at one computer. The children were matched on the basis of an individual on-task pre-test, both within the particular pairs and across the conditions. Our data revealed that, while they were actually working together, the children in the interaction condition performed slightly better than the children in the co-action condition. However, this advantage disappeared when the children were post-tested individually on a slight variant of the task just one week later.

More interestingly, however, in the *interaction* condition the boys and girls performed equally well, and it made no apparent difference to their performance whether they were working in same or mixed-gender pairs. In the *co-action* condition, however, where the children had no opportunity to interact with one another, the mixed gender pairs produced a marked and statistically significant polarization of performance, with the girls in the mixed pairs performing worse at post-test than the girls in the other conditions and the boys in the mixed pairs performing much better than boys in other conditions. The absence of gender polarization of performance in mixed pairs in the interaction condition was consistent with previous findings using this software (e.g., Littleton *et al.*, 1992). The discovery of such polarization in the 'co-action' condition was all the more unexpected.

As a check on the result, we ran a further study (Light, Littleton and Bales, 1994). Using exactly the same software, we examined the performance of pairs of 11-year-old children working on the task during a single session under 'co-action' conditions. One third of the pairings were girl–girl, one third boy–girl and one third boy–boy. Once more, as seen in the previous study, a gender by pair-type interaction emerged, with boys performing markedly better than girls only in the mixed-gender pairings. It would appear, then, that the effect which a number of educationalists have been concerned about, namely the fostering of gender differences in performance in mixed-gender groupings, does occur, quite markedly, but only when the children work alongside one another without interaction. When they are actually collaborating, the same polarization does not seem to occur.

Explaining these results is far from easy. We know from their responses to attitude questionnaires and interviews that the children do subscribe to the view that boys are generally more interested in and more capable with computers than girls. However, we also know that with this software the girls are actually at least as good as the boys, and, in the first study of the two studies, the children had been paired so that (while they did not know it) the partners always had the same pre-test scores. We might speculate, then, that the opportunity for interaction provides some feedback to the children on how well they are performing relative to their partner; and that this feedback has a tendency to undermine their gender stereotypes. In the case of the 'co-active' pairs, however, these stereotypes may be evoked by the situation of working alongside a partner of the opposite sex and cannot be ameliorated by feedback. In the first of these studies the two children came from different school classes so that their particular knowledge of one another's abilities was limited. The situation was such that they were well aware of one another's presence, and there was perhaps a tacit expectation that their relative achievements on the task would be made visible to one another at the end (though actually they were not). Thus the partners constitute both an audience for one another and potential competitors for one another. The absence of feedback during the session serves to maintain these relations throughout the session. In the mixed-gender situation, therefore, boys are particularly challenged to achieve well, while girls may be inhibited by low expectations of their own likely relative performance.

Such an interpretation remains speculative and these results obviously need exploring further. But for now the message might be that there may well be potential costs associated with reducing opportunities for interaction between boys and girls when they are working with computers.

Computers and Mathematics

When making decisions about whether to accept pupils onto computing courses many schools consider the pupils' ability in mathematics, even though it is generally acknowledged that such 'ability' is not indicative of future success on the course. The rationale for adopting mathematics ability as one of the key criteria seems to be that it provides an easy means of selection. This is nevertheless a good illustration of the strength of the association between mathematics and computing — an association which many argue is instrumental in deterring many girls from choosing to study computing. In a great many schools responsibility for computer studies still lies within the remit of the mathematics department and even as this tendency declines, the linkage still persists (Hoyles, 1988; Culley, 1993). Thus computers tend to be 'conceptually assimilated into the category of science, mathematics and technology and acquire some of the traditional qualities of differentiated interest amongst boys and girls' (Hoyles, 1988, p. 10).

As Beynon notes computers are still 'ideologically locked inside mathematics departments, and the huge aversion felt by many girls towards mathematics is transferred to computer studies' (Beynon, 1993, p. 167). This is regrettable since professional use of computers typically has few links with science and mathematics (Hoyles, 1988). Many have thus argued that there is a need to break the historical link between computing and maths/science. Suggestions regarding ways to do this have included locating the school computer room in a 'neutral' space, regarding it as part of the school's information management service in a similar way to that of the school library. The overall coordination of school computer use could be the joint responsibility of many different departments. Moreover, teachers of all subjects should be encouraged to explore the way in which computers may aid their teaching and given opportunities to develop confidence and competence in handling computers (Culley, 1993). One should also ensure that female teachers are amongst those becoming more involved in the use of computer technology. For, as Hoyles notes: 'Girls need to see females as competent, confident and enthusiastic computer users, although of course it must be recognised that the sex of the teacher is not a predictor of non-sexist practice!' (Hoyles, 1988, p. 11).

Modes and Styles of Working with IT

A key factor in considering gendered patterns of computer use is the mode of working. Hoyles (1988) notes that the use of the computer is often regarded as a solitary and isolating activity devoid of social interaction. Moreover, she argues that when the use of the computer is associated with an individual or perhaps even competitive mode of working, girls tend to find the experience alienating. This contrasts sharply with their experience when the computer is associated with a genuinely collaborative mode of working. Under these conditions girls are typically just as enthusiastic as boys in their response to computer technology (Hawkins, 1984; Hattie and Fitzgerald, 1988; Hoyles, Sutherland and Healy, 1991). On the basis of observational evidence from the Logo Maths Project, Hoyles suggests that for many boys discussion with peers is a time consuming diversion. Girls, however, seem to value the sharing of ideas and mutual assistance which interaction with a partner allows:

> Boys not only tend to monopolise computer hardware but also find it difficult to share interactions at the keyboard and see arguments with peers as time consuming and diversionary. Girls on the other hand, tend to appreciate the opportunity available in computer-based groupwork for mutual help and the sharing of ideas. (Hoyles, Sutherland and Healy, 1991)

A similar picture emerges from classroom accounts gathered during an ILEA (Inner London Education Authority) project (Burke, Edwards, Jeffries, Jones, Miln, Mongomery, Perkins, Seager and Wright, 1988) lending support to the idea that a collaborative mode of working may be crucial to girls' effective use of computers. An early study by Char and colleagues (Char, Hawkins, Wooten, Sheingold, and Roberts, 1983) looked at three pieces of software being tested in American elementary school classrooms. One provoked greater interest and superior performance from boys than girls; the other two did not. Both of the latter typically educed a collaborative mode of working, whilst the former was essentially a solo task. The implication here is that if girls are to engage with computer technology then we must 'allow flexible working arrangements which cater for peer collaboration as well as individual work' (Hoyles, 1988, p. 10). This then raises all sorts of thorny issues concerning what makes for effective working partnerships (Light and Littleton, 1994). It also raises questions concerning what is valued by the teacher (Hoyles, 1988). Carmichael *et al.*, (1986) found that boys enjoyed working speedily to achieve the challenges set, but that girls' interest declined as their efforts were not acknowledged: 'Boys get commended for things that girls can do, but we complete it half an hour later and it doesn't matter then' (Moore, 1986, p. 7).

In addition to thinking about how we organize the activity around the computer we also need to be sensitive to issues concerning 'learning style' and be aware that boys and girls may favour different approaches to the same educational task. Sutherland and Hoyles' (1988) work, for example, suggests that there are differences in programming 'style' between boys and girls using Logo, with boys adopting a more formal and closed approach compared to the open-ended and exploratory style favoured by girls. Both approaches should be valued. This issue is picked up by Turkle (1984; Turkle and Papert, 1990) who argues that there may be fundamental differences in the cognitive styles of males and females which affect the ways in which they relate to computers. Turkle notes that many women find the experience of computer use aversive and argues that this is because the prevailing computer culture imposes on them a masculine, 'top-down', formal-analytical method of working. According to this account, if women and girls are to become full users of computer technology then they must reject the emerging conventions concerning how computing is done, and negotiate with the computer in ways they find convivial (Kirkup, 1992).

Gender and Educational Software

While there are these gender-related differences in style of computer use, and level of participation in and attitudes towards computer-related activities, this pattern tends not to extend to *performance* on computer-based learning tasks and programming activities (Underwood and Underwood, 1990). There is a long series of studies which have found no gender differences on computer-based learning and programming tasks. For example, studies have found that girls work as effectively as boys on programming tasks (e.g., Finlayson, 1984; Webb, 1984; Light and Colbourn, 1987), electronic database search tasks (e.g., Eastman and Krendl, 1987), on simulation exercises (e.g., Johnson, Johnson and Stanne, 1985; Cummings, 1985) and on science tasks (Issroff, 1994). However, an exception to this trend was reported by Barbieri and Light (1992) who studied children's computer-based problem solving using a route planning task known as 'King and Crown' and found marked differences in performance (how far they got towards the correct solution within a fixed period of time) favouring boys.

Similar differences were not evident, however, when my colleagues and I (Littleton, Light, Joiner, Messer and Barnes, 1992) examined the relative performance of boys and girls using a structurally identical, but apparently less gender-stereotyped, version of the same task known as 'Honeybears'. Since the structure and the cognitive demands of the two tasks were identical, the reduced gender differentiation shown with 'Honeybears' suggested that the setting of the task and the gender of the characters may have had a crucial bearing on the relative performance of boys and girls. There were, however, other design differences between the two studies which meant that we were unable to draw this conclusion with confidence, so we went on to make a direct comparison of the performance of girls and boys working with the two versions. The study involved 11–12-year-olds working individually either on the 'King and Crown' or the 'Honeybears' problem for half an hour. The boys' performance was little affected by the version of the software they were using. The girls' performance, however, was substantially affected by the version of the software in use, it being far superior for 'Honeybears'. We repeated the study with a new sample of children, and with an even closer isomorphism of the two versions ('Pirates' vs 'Honeybears') and the results show a close replication of the previous study's findings (Littleton *et al.*, 1993). A not dissimilar pattern of responses also emerges from a recently completed study (Littleton and Light, 1994) in which we looked at the performance of girl–girl and boy–boy pairs working for one half-hour session on either the 'Pirates' or the 'Honeybears' software. Here again the girl–girl pairs showed markedly superior performance on the 'Honeybears' while the boy–boys responded similarly to the two software types.

The reason for the girls' greater responsiveness to the 'Honeybears' version is difficult to articulate precisely. From observing the children working on the different versions, it appeared that whilst the boys found both versions equally appealing, the girls appeared to find the 'King and Crown/Pirates' software less motivating and enjoyable than the 'Honeybears' version. It was apparent that many of the girls identified with the characters, and afterwards spontaneously talked about which bear was their favourite. More than one talked about taking particular bears on their journey to get the honey because 'they wouldn't want to be left behind'. This kind of identification with the characters was not apparent amongst the boys, or with the 'King and Crown/Pirates' version. It seems that these software 'hooks' served to engage the girls with the 'Honeybears' software. In themselves, these kinds of identification and projection will not help to solve the task — indeed, they could potentially hinder solution. However, it is apparent that, given an initial motivation to engage with the task, the girls were every bit as capable of handling the interface and thinking their way through the problem as the boys.

Whatever the precise explanation for these findings, the results offer a caution to software designers developing programs for children, be this for home or school use. Gender differences in response can be massive, but they are far from immutable. The metaphors and images used in the presentation of the task can have an influence out of all proportion to their significance to the designer. Here, as elsewhere, context effects exert a critical influence on cognitive performance, and can affect not just the absolute difficulty of a task, but also its relative difficulty for different groups of children. Vehicles for task presentation are rarely, if ever, neutral in their effects. We need to be aware of the nature of the software we are deploying in classrooms and Culley offers the following recommendations:

> The software that teachers use should be carefully selected and examined for the way it constructs males and females. Teachers could collaborate to develop checklists for use in software evaluation to ensure that it reflects their educational objectives in a non-sexist way. For example, how are males and females presented? Is the language sexually inclusive? Is the software motivating for all pupils? Do examples build equally on the experiences of girls and boys? Does the software provide the opportunity for groupwork and co-operative learning and is it likely to develop the confidence of pupils? (Culley, 1993, p. 157)

Concluding Remarks

The material discussed in this chapter clearly highlights that the contexts for development provided by the computer are by no means equivalent, in terms of their cultural connotations or accessibility for all children. IT shares with science a problem in terms of girls' restricted access to machines and equipment, both outside and inside the school. Girls have fewer opportunities than boys to learn about computers. It is hardly surprising, then, that they are often characterized as under-confident users of computer technology. Any problems associated with girls' lack of access to computers may well be compounded by the kinds of computer-based activities they engage in. As is the case with other masculine domains, computer tasks are typically either abstracted from context, or are set in overtly masculine settings and styles. The result is alienation, underachievement and a rejection of the domain. Within IT this is particularly worrying as efforts are currently being made to extend its use across the curriculum and down to the youngest ages. Moreover, in many of the major school-based reforms the use of IT is being given priority in establishing a 'community of learners'. Yet without attention to gender effects such reforms could work to the advantage of some children but to the disadvantage of many others. Technologies inevitably arise in the context of existing social relations and for this reason are highly likely to result in the reproduction of these forms of relationship. Nonetheless the same technologies may open up possibilities for the transformation of these social relations. In the case of IT it is imperative that we seek out and create the conditions for achieving such a transformation.

Acknowledgment

The author wishes to thank Patricia Murphy, Paul Light, Annerieke Oosterwegel and Madeleine Watson for their comments on previous versions of this chapter.

References

BARBIERI, M.S. and LIGHT, P. (1992) 'Interaction, gender and performance on a computer-based problem solving task', *Learning and Instruction*, **2**, pp. 199–213.

BEYNON, J. (1993) 'Computers, dominant boys and invisible girls: Or Hannah, it's not a toaster, it's a computer!', in BEYNON, J. and MACKAY, H. (eds) *Computers into Classrooms: More Questions than Answers*, London, Falmer Press.

BUCKLEY, P. and SMITH, B. (1991) 'Opting out of technology: A study of girls' GCSE choices', in LOVEGROVE, G. and SEGAL, B. (eds) *Women into Computing: Selected Papers 1988–1990*, Heidelberg, Springer-Verlag.

BURKE, J., EDWARDS, J., JEFFRIES, J., JONES, K., MILN, J., MONGOMERY, M., PERKINGS, B., SEAGER, A. and WRIGHT, H. (1988) 'My mum uses a computer too', in HOYLES, C. (ed.) *Girls and Computers*, London, University of London, Institute of Education, Bedford Way Papers, No. 34.

CARMICHAEL, H., BURNETT, J., HIGGINSON, W., MOORE, B. and POLLARD, P. (1986) *Computers, Children and Classrooms: A Multisite Evaluation of the Creative Use of Microcomputers by Elementary School Children*, Ontario, Canada, Queen's Printer.

CHEN, M. (1986) 'Gender and computers: The beneficial effects of experience on attitudes', *Journal of Educational Computing Research*, **2**(3).

CHAR, C., HAWKINS, J., WOOTEN, J., SHEINGOLD, K. and ROBERTS, T. (1983) 'Classroom case studies of software, video and print materials,' Report to the US Department of Education, New York, Bank Street College of Education.

CRAWFORD, K., GROUNDWATER-SMITH, S. and MILLAN, M. (1989) *Gender and the Evolution of Computer Literacy*, School of Teaching and Curriculum Studies, University of Sydney, Australia.

CROOK, C. (1992) 'Cultural artefacts in social development: The case of computers', in McGURK, H. (ed.) *Childhood Social Development: Contemporary Perspectives*, Hove, Lawrence Erlbaum Associates Ltd.

CULLEY, L. (1988) 'Girls, boys and computers', *Educational Studies*, **14**, pp. 3–8.

CULLEY, L. (1993) 'Gender equity and computing in secondary schools: Issues and strategies for teachers', in BEYNON, J. and MACKAY, H. (eds) *Computers into Classrooms: More Questions than Answers*, London, Falmer Press.

CUMMINGS, R. (1985) 'Small group discussions and the microcomputer', *Journal of Computer Assisted Learning*, 1, pp. 149–58.

DES (1989) *Information Technology from 5 to 16*, London, HMSO.

EASTMAN, S. and KRENDL, K. (1987) 'Computers and gender: Differential effects of electronic search on students' achievement and attitudes', *Journal of Research and Development in Education*, **20**(3), pp. 41–8.

EQUAL OPPORTUNITIES COMMISSION (1983) *Information Technology in Schools*, Manchester, EOC.

EVANS, A. and HALL, W. (1988) 'Computer education and gender inequality', *National Union of Teachers' Education Review*, **2**(1), Spring.

FIFE-SCHAW C.R., BREAKWELL, G.M., LEE, T. and SPENCER, J. (1986) 'Patterns of teenage computer usage', *Journal of Computer Assisted Learning*, 2, pp. 152–61.

FINLAYSON, H. (1984) 'The transfer of mathematical problem solving skills from LOGO experience,' Research Paper Number 238, Department of Artificial Intelligence, University of Edinburgh.

GARDNER, J., McEWEN, A. and CURRY, C. (1985) 'A sample survey of attitudes to computer studies', *Computers and Education*, **10**(2), pp. 293–8.

HATTIE, J. and FITZGERALD, D. (1988) 'Sex differences in attitudes, achievement and use of computers', *Australian Journal of Education*, **31**(1), pp. 3–26.

HAWKINS, J. (1984) *Computers and Girls: Rethinking the Issue*, Technical Report 24, New York, Bank Street College of Education.

HESS, R. (1985) 'Gender differences in enrolment in computer camps and classes', *Sex Roles*, **13**(3/4), pp. 193–203.

HOYLES, C. (ed.) (1988) *Girls and Computers*, London, University of London, Institute of Education, Bedford Way Papers, No. 34.

HOYLES, C., SUTHERLAND, R. and HEALY, L. (1991) 'Children talking in computer environments: New insights on the role of discussion in mathematics learning', in DURKIN, K. and SHIRE, B. (eds) *Language in Mathematical Education: Research and Practice*, Milton Keynes, Open University Press.

HUGHES, M. (1990) 'Children's computation', in GRIEVE, R. and HUGHES, M. (eds) *Understanding Children*, Oxford, Basil Blackwell.

HUGHES, M., BRACKENRIDGE, A., BIBBY, A. and GREENOUGH, P. (1988), 'Girls, boys and turtles', in HOYLES, C. (ed.) *Girls and Computers*, London, University of London, Institute of Education, Bedford Way Papers, No. 34.

HUGHES, M., BRACKENRIDGE, A. and MACLEOD, H. (1987) 'Children's ideas about computers', in RUTKOWSKA, J. and CROOK, C. (eds) *Computers, Cognition and Development*, London, Wiley.

ISSROFF, K. (1994) 'Gender and cognitive and affective aspects of co-operative learning', in FOOT, H., HOWE, C., ANDERSON, A., TOLMIE, A. and WARDEN, D. (eds) *Group and Interactive Learning*, Southampton, Boston, Computational Mechanics.

JOHNSON, R., JOHNSON, D. and STANNE, M. (1985) 'Effects of co-operative, competitive and individualistic goal structures on computer-assisted instruction', *Journal of Educational Psychology*, **77**, pp. 668–77.

KIRKUP, G. (1992) 'The social construction of computers', in KIRKUP, G. and KELLER, S. (eds) *Inventing Women: Science, Gender and Technology*, Oxford, Polity Press.

LABORATORY OF COMPARATIVE HUMAN COGNITION (LCHC) (1989) 'Kids and Computers: A positive vision of the future', *Harvard Educational Review*, **59**(1), pp. 73–86.

LIGHT, P. and COLBOURN, C. (1987) 'The role of social processes in children's microcomputer use', in KENT, W. and LEWIS, R. (eds) *Computer Assisted Learning in the Social Sciences and Humanities*, Oxford, Basil Blackwell.

LIGHT, P. and LITTLETON, K. (1994) 'Cognitive approaches to groupwork', in KUTNICK, P. and ROGERS, C. (eds) *Groups in Schools*, London, Cassell.

LIGHT, P., LITTLETON, K. and BALES, S. (1994) 'Children solving problems in mixed gender pairs', Paper presented at the British Psychological Society Developmental Section Annual Conference, University of Portsmouth, September.

LITTLETON, K., JOINER, R., LIGHT, P., MESSER, D., RILEY, S., BARNES, P. and AGIOBU-KEMMER, I. (1991) 'Peer interaction, gender and computer use,' Paper presented at the Fourth meeting of the European Association for Research in Learning and Instruction, University of Turku, Finland, August.

LITTLETON, K. and LIGHT, P. (1994) 'Gender and software effects in children's computer-based problem solving: Analysing interaction', Paper presented at the International Conference on Group and Interactive Learning, University of Strathclyde, September.

LITTLETON, K., LIGHT, P., BARNES, P., MESSER, D. and JOINER, R. (1993) 'Gender and software effects on children's computer-based problem-solving', Poster presented at the Society for Research in Child Development Annual Convention, New Orleans, USA, March.

LITTLETON, K., LIGHT, P., JOINER, R., MESSER, D. and BARNES, P. (1992) 'Pairing and gender effects on children's computer-based learning', *European Journal of Psychology of Eduction*, **7**, pp. 309–23.

LOCKHEED, M.E. (1985) 'Women, girls and computers: A first look at the evidence', *Sex Roles*, **13**, pp. 115–22.

MARTIN, R. (1991) 'School children's attitudes towards computers as a function of gender, course subjects and availability of home computers', *Journal of Computer Assisted Learning*, **7**, pp. 187–94.

MOHAMEDALI, M., MESSER, D. and FLETCHER, B. (1987) 'Factors affecting micro-computer use and programming ability of secondary school children', *Journal of Computer Assisted Learning*, **3**, pp. 224–39.

MOORE, B. (1986) *Equity in Education: Gender Issues in the Use of Computers. A Review and Bibliography*. Ontario, Canada: Review and Evaluation Bulletins, Ministry of Education, Vol. 6, No. 1.

OLSON, C.P. (1988) 'Who computes?', in LIVINGSTONE, D.W. (ed.) *Critical Pedagogy and Cultural Power*, Massachusetts, Bergin and Garvey.

ROBERTSON, I., CALDER, J., FUNG, P., JONES, A. and O'SHEA, T. (1995) 'Computer attitudes in an English secondary school', *Computers and Education*, **24**, pp. 73–81.

SCRIMSHAW, P. (ed.) (1993) *Language, Classrooms and Computers*, London, Routledge.

SOMEKH, B. (1988) 'Micro-reflections,' Paper presented at the BERA Symposium on IT/Education, University of East Anglia, September.

STRAKER, A. (1989) *Children Using Computers*, Oxford, Blackwell.

SUTHERLAND, R. and HOYLES, C. (1988) 'Gender perspectives on Logo programming in the mathematics curriculum', in HOYLES, C. (ed.) *Girls and Computers*, London, University of London, Institute of Education, Bedford Way Papers, No. 34.

TODMAN, J. and DICK, G. (1993) 'Primary children and teachers' attitudes to computers', *Computers in Education*, **20**(2), pp. 199–203.

TURKLE, S. (1984) *The Second Self: Computers and the Human Spirit*, London, Granada.

TURKLE, S. and PAPERT, S. (1990) 'Epistemological pluralism: Styles and voices within the computer culture', *Signs: Journal of Women in Culture and Society*, **16**, pp. 128–57.

UNDERWOOD, G., MCCAFFREY, M. and UNDERWOOD, J. (1990) 'Gender differences in a co-operative computer-based language task', *Educational Research*, **32**, pp. 16–21.

UNDERWOOD, J. and UNDERWOOD, G. (1990) *Computers and Learning: Helping Children Acquire Thinking Skills*, Oxford, Basil Blackwell.

WARE, M.C. and STUCK, M.F. (1985) 'Sex-role messages vis-à-vis microcomputer use: A look at the pictures', *Sex Roles*, **13**(3/4), pp. 205–14.

WEBB, N. (1984) 'Microcomputer learning in small groups: Cognitive requirements and group processes', *Journal of Educational Psychology*, **76**, 1076–88.

WILDER, G., MACKIE, D. and COOPER, J. (1985) 'Gender and computers: Two surveys of computer-related attitudes', *Sex Roles*, **13**(3/4), pp. 215–28.

WILLIS, S. (1987) 'Access to the program by girls and disadvantaged groups', in BIGUM, C. et al. *Coming to Terms with Computers in Schools: Report to Commonwealth Schools Commission*, Deakin Institute for Studies in Education, Australia, September.

WILLIS, S. and KENWAY, J. (1986) 'On overcoming sexism in schooling: To marginalise or mainstream', *Australian Journal of Education*, **30**(2).

8   Research on English and the Teaching of Girls[1]

Janet White

Introduction

What is the Nature of Girls' Success in English?

There is an accumulated weight of research evidence to suggest that of all the areas of the curriculum, English is the one in which girls excel, and the one which they most enjoy. Results from the earliest years of formal schooling in the UK right up to those from examinations at school leaving age, indicate that girls as a group do better than boys in English. This finding holds true across different modes of language use, within aspects of one or other mode of language, and seems little affected by the context or style of assessment. Similar findings are reported from international studies which have sought to measure performance in reading and writing the language of instruction of other school systems. Perhaps, then, an examination of some of the ways in which English is taught and learned might reveal the distinctive features of an effective pedagogy for girls?

There are, however, various discomforting paradoxes surrounding girls' success in English (and by extension, in literacy in other major instructional languages), which make it problematic to simply aim to extrapolate from the domain of 'English teaching' such features which might be assumed to be 'girl friendly' and apply these to other areas of the curriculum. English language and literacy are not neutral serviceable tools: within the context of schooling, girls and boys learn ways of doing English which is fundamental to a much larger process of differentiation by gender in the outcome of education as a whole.

Typically, girls do well at English, but how empowering is their specific success? And why is it that the comparative lack of success on the part of boys ultimately seems so little of a hindrance, despite high public valuation placed on standards in English/literacy in all walks of life?

The case of English shows very clearly that far more is learnt in a 'subject' than subject content. If we acknowledge that the generic structures of speech and writing shape and create the knowledge of school subjects, we need also to take heed of the ways in which they simultaneously shape the identities of young speakers and writers. Despite an apparent equality of provision, girls and boys learn to be literate in different ways and with very different degrees of proficiency.

97

Learning Different Literacies

In the UK, for example, a series of Assessment of Performance Unit (APU) language surveys conducted between 1979 and 1983 (Gorman, White, Orchard and Tate 1981; 1982a; 1982b; 1983) provided a clear picture of the literacy orientations of pupils aged 11 and 15, specifically connecting reading and writing habits. This research noted that both boys and girls enjoy reading various kinds of fiction in the primary school (with preferences differing along gender lines), but that boys rather than girls have clearly developed interest in a range of 'hobbyist' magazines (for example, fishing, cycling, model making, stamp collecting, etc.). Girls are, in general, more avid readers, whereas boys prefer to watch television, and both have positive cases to put for their preferred medium.

By age 15, these differences are accentuated, with many more boys than girls stating a preference for books and magazines 'which give accurate facts about hobbies or how things work'. It is clear that boys and girls are looking to reading material to provide different forms of knowledge, with girls stating that they read to 'help understand their own and other people's problems' such as those to do with sex, love and marriage. While a great deal of this reading material (love stories, comics, specialist magazines) is not the subject of official study at school, there is more coincidence between the themes of girls' preferred reading and courses in English literature. There are, similarly, direct links between the technical reading consumed by boys and scientific/mathematical areas of the curriculum. (See also national survey data from both the UK and the USA which relate pupils' leisure interests to their take-up of science subjects, Johnson and Murphy, 1986.)

The reading predilections of each sex group are equally evident in their writing. The voluntary writing of girls in primary school comprises often quite voluminous correspondence with pen friends, contrasted with boys who write the 'odd letter' or, in about one in three cases, never put pen to paper outside school (White, 1987). Boys who do write fiction for their own enjoyment choose themes such as plane crashes, murders, thrillers or war exploits — poles apart from girls' interests in 'things I would like to happen to me', fairy stories or stories about horses. At age 15, girls continue to give preference to writing which is self-reflective or empathetic in character, in contrast to the practical, informative bias of boys' writing. Increasingly, boys' self-directed literacy is associated with the microcomputer, further extending earlier interests in graphics, tables and symbolic displays (EOC, 1985).

Who is Disadvantaged?

These seems to be a general consensus that the narrowing of girls' interests to genres of writing which are easily marginalized puts them at a disadvantage educationally:

> Telling fairy stories, even telling good fairy stories very well, for all that has
> been said about the importance of fantasy in psychological development,

simply doesn't count. The real positions of power and influence in our society necessitate command of genres for which boys' educational experience provides an appropriate preparation and girls' does not. (Poynton, 1985, p. 36)

In fact, girls have far more flexibility in written language than is generally assumed; the question remains, though, to what extent could they do better if their abilities as writers were recognized and developed across a full range of subject areas? And how would the technocratic subjects have to change in order to accommodate the humanistic and socially responsive interests of girls, assuming girls continue to be a pressure group to be reckoned with? Notwithstanding the longer term discussion that Poynton signals, the contrast between the school-based performance of boys measured in relation to that of girls indicates underachievement on a scale that would be utterly disabling were it not for two factors in their language development experience: promotion of competence in oral language and the nature of their out-of-school reading. The trade-off between oral and written language modes serves not merely to excuse boys' indifference to school standards of literacy, but actually operates to ensure a different kind of success and power in the dynamics of the classroom (Swann and Graddol, 1988; Mahoney, 1988).

Voluntary Reading and Involuntary Learning

The most cursory glance at the range of comics and magazines which are voluntarily consumed by children reveals fundamental differences in the uses of language favoured by the writers of girl- and boy-directed material. Of course, the private reading of any group of children can only be one of many factors in a complex web of factors implicated in different educational outcomes, but because of its relative invisibility it is worth more attention.

Boys of primary school age and beyond who are keen consumers of comics are practising reading on texts very different from conventional reading material. Many types of boys' comics are distinguished not simply by their themes of violence and terror, but also by their complex visual formats in which explosive actions interrupt the linearity of narrative sequence, and stylized representations of sound effects engage a more sensory, if less reflective, reading than is the case with 'classical' descriptive narration. The fantastic world of science fiction, with its attendant tales of mythical quests, introduces a distinctive and at times untranslatable vocabulary: Blusteroids, Chelnov, Excisus, Shinobo, Gryznov, The Monad, etc. (examples taken from *Masters of the Universe*). Such vocabulary, however ludicrous to the adult eye, has a pedigree of scientism about it, and arguably plays its part in familiarizing the young reader with a whole range of textbooks in which the vocabulary is similarly opaque but just as authoritative. Even when there is resistance to reading such textbooks, we might assume they will be more tolerable to readers accustomed to de-personalized use of language than to those who have been led to anticipate meaning and personal relevance from the printed page.

Very helpfully, the writers of boys' comics print in bold their 'technical terms': 'My **mystic explosion** has trapped the fool on that plant world. The plants have no machines so he-man will not be able to **rebuild a teleportation machine**.' Conventions of capitalization are used in standard expository texts to highlight key words and concepts: on this level too, reading comics may be a useful preparation for learning some of the conventions of school textbooks.

A variety of reading positions is available within a comic which might comprise an adventure story, a detachable subtext of mechanisms of conquest, a riot of graphic elaboration, and a form of dialogue — or speechifying — which is archaic, formal and coded in a way the vernacular of interpersonal relations is not, this latter offering another possibility of distance from the narrative. These are not modes of reading which are emphasized in initial literacy schemes, nor indeed in traditional English literature classes (Barnes, 1987; Belsey, 1980). They are important though in coping with a mass of texts, literary or not, in subjects other than English and in the world beyond school. Indubitably, these modes of reading are hard to acquire and rarely taught explicitly, but they are some of the 'advantages' which boys may derive from their out-of-school reading — in the long term. In the short term, boys swell the ranks of remedial readers, unable to cope with such texts as schools insist they do read, and presumably struggling with portions of unsupervised reading as well.

The *disadvantages* of such a diet of reading material lie in its power to generate and validate a view of experience which gives short shrift to matters of personal reflection, humane responsibilities, or the exigencies of living in a social context — areas of experience which are borne in upon girls through their 'chosen' leisure reading as much as by their school work.

Boys' and Girls' Achievements in English: The Extent of the Difference

I would like to start this section by mentioning the most recent piece of research I have been involved with, namely a study of Differential Performance in English and Mathematics carried out in 1991–92, under tho joint sponsorship of University of London Examinations and Assessment Council (ULEAC) and the National Foundation of Educational Research (NFER) (Stobart et al., 1992). This project sought to document and explain the differences in performance between boys and girls in GCSE English and mathematics. We used results from public examinations in combination with questionnaire and case-study data. Although I will only deal here with some of the findings for English, it is worth bearing in mind the 'mirror image' of another core subject in the shaping of gendered outcomes. (Mathematics has for a long time been held to be the subject area in which boys, not girls, excel. However, in recent years, girls' achievements at GCSE have risen to a point where there is virtually no difference overall between the sexes, yet the perception remains that boys are much better at maths than girls — this a compensatory belief that is due for a challenge.)

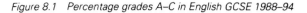

Figure 8.1   Percentage grades A–C in English GCSE 1988–94

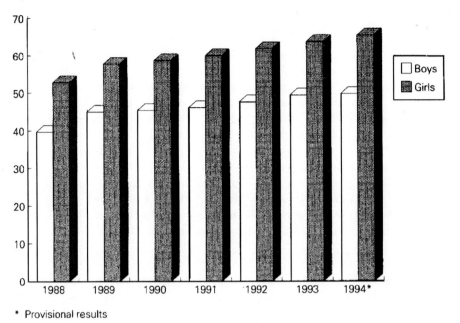

* Provisional results

In 1992, we looked at the percentages of boys and girls gaining GCSE grades A–C in English in the period 1988–91, the first four years of the GCSE. Evidence as to the difference in performance drawn from the percentages of grades A–C may be an oversimplified approach, but it provides a widely understood yardstick. Figure 8.1 continues the tabulation up to the 1994 examination.

A caveat should be added to these national statistics. In 1991 these involved combining the results of fifty-three English syllabuses. The variety of approaches and styles of assessment within individual syllabuses should caution against treating the subject of English as monolithic, either its assessment or its pedagogy. We were especially concerned to explore where and whether syllabuses generated gender-related variations, and there is much work still to be done on these questions.

Nevertheless, even at this level of generality several features are immediately apparent:

- The gap in English is substantial and shows no sign of narrowing (a much narrower gap in mathematics by contrast has been the stimulus for both intensive research and positive action campaigns). Between the years 1988–93, the proportion of boys and girls gaining grades A–C increased by 5 per cent, since when the increases have been relatively slight. The interval between the scores of both groups has remained relatively steady at about 14 per cent.
- The provisional figures for 1994, however, show that about 66 per cent of

girls gained grades A–C compared to about 50 per cent of the boys. This finding is particularly interesting, given the radical change in the examination system, and the demise of coursework, so often alluded to as the reason for girls' greater success in English (girls' ability to cope with examinations will be referred to again below).

A further point of interest, not visible in the table, concerns *spoken language*. The GCSE data from the spoken language component on two major syllabuses in 1991 showed a significant advantage for girls; although in the course of national language surveys throughout the 1980s few differences of significance in favour of girls had been found in oracy. Such differences or trends as there were tended to favour boys. So there are perhaps signs of a sea-change in language practices in this area. But because the oral component in GCSE was given as an endorsement on the final grade, rather than an achievement in its own right, such changes tend to be unnoticed. Now that Speaking and Listening contributes directly to the coursework element, perhaps it will be seen as meriting more attention.

Are GCSE Results Typical of Other Findings about Pupils of Different Age Groups?

Girls have consistently been found to out-perform boys in both reading and writing across the entire 5–16 age range.

The evidence on 7-year-olds comes from the results of standard assessment tasks taken at the end of Key Stage 1 in Reading, Writing, Spelling and Handwriting. The results from National Curriculum assessments in 1994 showed significant differences between girls and boys in all these components (DFE, 1994). At Key Stage 1, Level 2 is the expected level of achievement. In Reading, 9 per cent more girls than boys attained this level or above; in Writing, the difference in favour of girls was 13 per cent. Conversely, 12 per cent more boys than girls attained Level 1 or below for Reading and Writing. In Writing, the most difficult attainment target, over one third of boys' work was assessed as being Level 1 or below.

National assessment in English at other key stages has provided data on the performance of 11-year-olds and 14-year-olds, *albeit* on a less-than-national scale, because of test boycotts and the smaller samples used for pilot trials. Such data as are publicly available point to similar patterns of advantage for girls. For example, results from the testing of 14-year-olds in 1994 show that 17 per cent more girls than boys attained Level 5 or above in English (a composite measure of reading, writing and response to Shakespeare).

These patterns are in line with evidence from a study of initial literacy development carried out by the NFER in the late 1980s, as well as with international studies of written composition amongst school populations. Apart from these studies, the most extensive comparative data on the performance of boys and girls in English in the UK comes from the series of language surveys conducted throughout the 1980s on behalf of the Assessment of Performance Unit (APU) with children aged

Figure 8.2   APU Language 1988: Differential performance by categories

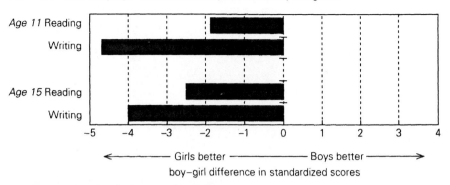

Note: All differences are statistically significant

11 and 15. The summary in Figure 8.2 indicates the scale of difference in favour of girls in both APU reading and writing assessments.

What was the Scope of APU Assessment in English?

The APU assessment tasks were devised in the light of curriculum framework not dissimilar from that used by the GCSE Groups. However, unlike the recording of examination results, the APU findings were given in terms of specific types of task, and in relation to different forms of marking. Thus, it was possible to look more particularly at the performance of groups of pupils in terms of the differing demands of different tasks. As we can see from Figures 8.3 and 8.4 below, there are marked task and gender interactions on both the writing and reading materials.

APU Assessment of reading

Differences in performance were most evident in the reading surveys which, like GCSE, included both expository and narrative texts. Unlike GCSE, responses were scored primarily for content, and although a pupil's ability to write can never be discounted in pencil and paper tests, the results suggest that when a diverse range of questions are posed, and when extended amounts of writing are not demanded, the performance of candidates shows just as much of a task as a gender effect.

In the GCSE study, we noted that examining groups differed in their approaches to the assessment of reading: some used all the written responses as evidence of both reading and writing performance; others allowed some parts of the paper to count as responses to reading only. If it had been possible to disentangle the scores of candidates from these contrasting assessment contexts, a more diverse picture of boy–girl differences might have been revealed at age 16. There is an implication here for pedagogy: informed interventions in the reading and writing practices of

Figure 8.3   APU Secondary reading survey 1988: Gender differences

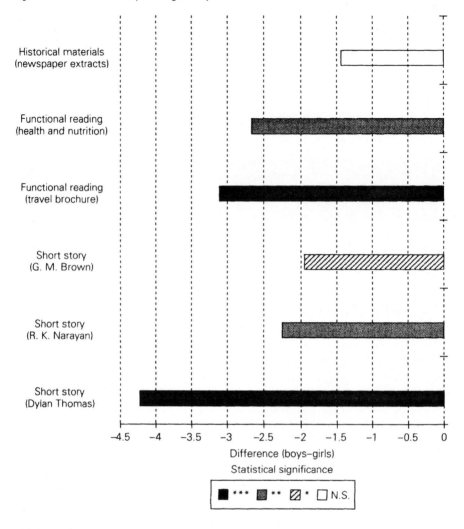

pupils assume a degree of analytical knowledge of strengths and weaknesses such as the results above reveal.

APU Assessment of writing

With regard to APU assessment of writing, the boy–girl differences are solid across tasks and irrespective of system of marking employed. Our investigations of GCSE performance pointed in the same direction, namely that the single most important factor in 'explaining' girls' superior performance in English was that of their control of written language.

The APU task types on which the performance gap lessened were those which

Figure 8.4   APU Secondary writing survey 1988: Gender differences

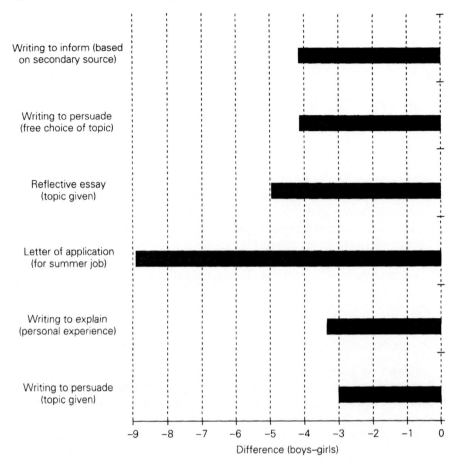

either drew directly on the pupil's recent experience or offered some support for the writer in terms of relevant source material. In the APU surveys, these tasks also had specified readers. The tasks for which the pupil had responsibility to devise and shape subject matter, as well as to define the readership, proved to be the ones on which girls did considerably better than boys.

Arguably, these aspects of writing might be considered 'higher order skills', and at any rate are a far cry from the 'merely' secretarial features of writing which are traditionally allowed to be amongst girls' strengths in English.

Results from Previous O-level and CSE Examinations in English

Girls' success in English is not a recent phenomenon, nor one which is uniquely associated with a particular ethos of teaching and examining. A 'case study' of the

Figure 8.5   Patterns of differential achievement in English examination at age 16

	ULSEB	WJEC
YEAR	% difference grades A–C, girls–boys	% difference grades A–C, girls–boys
1970	22.2	11.8
1975	15.4	10.2
1980	9.7	11.3
1985	3.7	13.4
1991	18.3	13.8

results of examinations in English at 16+ over the past twenty years for two groups (the Welsh Joint Education Committee, WJEC, and the University of London School Examinations Board, ULSEB) puts paid to easy assumptions. Figure 8.5 shows very clearly that the gender gap in English is not something which has arrived with GCSE and which can be simply attributed — as is sometimes alleged — to factors such as the rise of coursework. At different times over the past two decades the gender gap has actually been greater in O-level examinations. What is constant across numerous examinations in English is the premium placed on written language, and in that mode girls typically excel.

Entry patterns and expectations in English/English Literature

In English, despite the recent moves towards setting tiered papers, the assessment philosophy is one of differentiation by outcome rather than by task. However, the options of single, dual or separately certified English/English Literature would seem to have a role to play in differentiation by gender.

As an aside, it is too early to say what the effects of recently introduced tiering will have in English GCSEs. Indications from the 1994 examination suggest that the vast majority of the age group, boys and girls alike, were entered for the higher of the two tiers on offer. However, of the 10–20 per cent who sat the lower tier paper, there were about twice as many boys as girls.

Although an older divide within English, that between 'language' and literature, has been largely dissolved by Dual Certification syllabuses, English Literature as a separate subject maintains a higher entry from girls (around 20,000 more girls than boys sat papers in English Literature in the 1991 examinations).

Within the subject as a whole, fewer boys than girls pursue both strands of the subject. This is possibly one factor — both cause and effect — in their lower performance relative to girls: boys simply do less reading and writing in the subject. And as is the case for those pupils (typically girls) without higher-tier qualifications in mathematics, pupils (typically boys) without GCSE English Literature or a good pass in English are neither expected or encouraged to take the subject on to A-level.

However, the seeking to address the issue of the overall rise in *boys'* scores in English since the introduction of GCSE, the significance of Dual Certification courses cannot be overlooked. A majority of pupils doing GCSE English follow such courses. The salient feature might reside not so much in the manner of assessment prevalent in 1991 (100 per cent coursework), as in the fact that these syllabuses demand a wider range of reading and writing, and at best promote an integrated approach to language and literature. The structured access thus offered to the subject in its broadest sense is likely to be particularly advantageous to those pupils (typically boys) who otherwise would spend less time and effort on English-related activities. Teachers and pupils in the case studies certainly testified to the motivating aspects of these courses of study.

Again, there are implications concerning 'effective' pedagogy which have to do with the provision of a wide and challenging range of reading as a necessary factor in developing writing.

The effect of coursework

In the GCSE study, statistical analyses were carried out to investigate the relative contribution of coursework and terminal papers in combination syllabuses. When the achieved weight of these components was computed for English, it was found that for girls the coursework/examination components were closer to the intended weighting (50/50) than was the case for boys. Coursework made a slightly larger contribution to the final subject mark for boys than did the examination.

This was part of a wider picture whereby coursework was seen to contribute increasingly to the total mark as the grades decreased. While this was true for both boys and girls, the fact of more boys being in the lower grade bands indicates that as a group they benefit slightly more from coursework than do girls. Such a finding runs counter to many assumptions about coursework being of greater advantage to girls, on account of their supposed greater diligence, consistent application to task, fear of the unknown which an examination enshrines, etc., etc. These attributes are contrasted with the 'flair' of boys, their presumed ability to rise to a challenge, to get it together on a shoe-string. These stereotypical assumptions are not supported by the evidence, but they chime with other judgments about the 'quiet girl' reading and writing with untroubled competence who is thought to be merely passive and probably dull, while the boy who can barely write his own name is excused on the basis of having 'flair', of being 'bored . . . not because he is not clever, but because he just cannot sit still, he has got no concentration . . . very disruptive . . . but quite bright' (ESRC, 1988).

Qualitative analysis of written coursework

There is, however, another dimension to coursework which deserves attention in estimating the benefits of the system to pupils of either sex. A review of candidates' work from different grade levels on one syllabus showed a strong school effect in terms of the ways in which the assessment objectives were realized in classroom practice. Overall, what was not well covered were two types of writing which were described in the syllabus respectively as 'objective descriptions or explanations of processes', and 'accounts or explanations of how problems might be solved or tasks performed.'

Such genres of writing have been shown to be well responded to by both boys and girls in the context of APU surveys. Unlike much else on the English syllabus, the models for writing in these ways occur in other curriculum areas, or outside school itself. Thus they have the potential for readers and writers of a non-traditional kind to produce good work which is less dependent on the study of narrative fiction, a known strong interest for girls.

The underrepresentation of non-narrative genres in coursework folders served to emphasize what were apparently more valued genres of writing: those concerned with descriptive narrative. Pupils implicitly confirmed this valuation by placing their narrative pieces first in their folders, with the more discursive or factual piece(s) at the end. Girls' folders tended to contain a majority of imaginatively based pieces, while boys' contained more discursive writing.

Typically, girls' narrative/descriptive work was superior to any other type of writing. Teachers seemed by their comments to reward and encourage narrative and descriptive writing more than they encouraged factual and analytical work. Some discursive pieces had elicited no written comments from teachers at all, in contrast with the often warm responses on obviously personal writing. Overall, it seemed to be the case that writing which drew on the field of personal affection and emotions was more highly valued than that which drew its inspiration from a public or political domain. While girls were able to activate these areas of experience when prompted, there was less incentive for them to do so. When boys' personal writing arose from a less intimate domain than girls', its perceived impersonality may have lead to an under-valuation.

The case-study observations and interviews in schools indicated the consequences of a perceived lack of success, if not underachievement in English. On the part of boys who were not doing particularly well in the subject, there was a defensive attitude about the subject being mainly to do with onerous demands of reading and writing fiction — which were things that girls were good at. A laddish attitude was frequently expressed to the effect that a bare pass in the subject would be sufficient. Some teachers took a resigned view that they were bound to lose their more able boys to maths and science A-levels anyway, thus confirming a more pervasive under-valuing of the subject English within the curriculum as a whole.

Conclusion

I have argued that for teachers to begin to counter the gendered outcomes of schooling, they need to be prepared to intervene in the literacy development of pupils with a clear, explicit knowledge of the way language works to shape meaning and, with it, identity. The generic structures of speech and writing shape and create the knowledge of school subjects, and they simultaneously shape the identities of pupils as speakers and writers. In this respect it is important that we understand 'pedagogy' itself as a set of cultural practices which are encoded in language, resulting in the creation of a set of texts — no matter what the 'subject' being taught — whose emphases and omissions help to construct what a subject means and what it means to know it. Societies do not as a rule educate young people to assume androgenous personalities. The pedagogies of a school are part of a wider process by which language shapes the identities of its users, inasmuch as it gives them frameworks of explanation and reference, and the means for imagining past and future worlds.

For there to be any fundamental change in the outcomes for girls and boys in courses in English, there would need to be something of a revaluation of the position and status of the subject overall. Why is it acceptable in so many classrooms that English 'doesn't matter for boys', so their poor performance can be excused, or that because girls are 'naturally good at' English, their considerable achievements are taken for granted, or even down-played? Only by changing the set of expectations schools hold for pupils is it realistic to expect that outcomes for different groups will alter. These expectations would need to be evident in the language practices in the daily work of every classroom, not just within the confines of English lessons.

Beyond the school and its pedagogies, of course, are numerous other language practices which may contrast or collude with those of the educational system in shaping 'subjects' both human and abstract. While the reflective practice of a school and its teachers can make a difference to outcomes within an institution, we do well to pay attention to the many less visible, but possibly more powerful, influences on the language and literacies we aim to teach.

Note

1 The views expressed in this paper are those of the author and not necessarily those of SCAA.

References

BARNES, D. (1987) 'The politics of oracy', in MACLURE, M., PHILLIPS, T. and WILKINSON, A. (eds) *Oracy Matters: The Development of Talking and Listening*, Milton Keynes, Open University Press.

BELSEY, C. (1980) *Critical Practice*, London, Methuen.

DFE (DEPARTMENT FOR EDUCATION) (1994) *Testing 7-year-olds in 1994: Results of National Curriculum Assessments in England*, London, HMSO.

EOC (EQUAL OPPORTUNITIES COMMISSION) (1985) *Girls and Information Technology*, Report of a project in Croydon to evaluate guidelines for good practice in the IT curriculum, Overseas House, Manchester.

ESRC (ECONOMIC AND SOCIAL RESEARCH COUNCIL) (1989) *Girls and Mathematics: Some Lessons for the Classroom*, London, Girls and Mathematics Unit, Institute of Education, University of London.

GORMAN, T.P., WHITE, J., ORCHARD, L. and TATE, A. (1981) *Language Performance in Schools: Primary Survey Report No. 1*, London, HMSO.

GORMAN, T.P., WHITE, J., ORCHARD, L. and TATE, A. (1982a) *Language Performance in Schools: Primary Survey Report No. 2*, London, HMSO.

GORMAN, T.P., WHITE, J., ORCHARD, L. and TATE, A. (1982b) *Language Performance in Schools: Secondary Survey Report No. 1*, London, HMSO.

GORMAN, T.P., WHITE, J., ORCHARD, L. and TATE, A. (1983) *Language Performance in Schools: Secondary Survey Report No. 2*, London, HMSO.

GORMAN, T.P., WHITE, J., HARGREAVES, M., MacLURE, M. and TATE A. (1984) *Language Performance in Schools: 1982 Primary Survey Report*, London, DES.

GORMAN, T.P., WHITE, J., and BROOKS, G. (1984) *Language Performance in Schools: 1982 Secondary Survey Report*, London, DES.

GORMAN, T.P., WHITE, J., and BROOKS, G., MacLURE, M. and KISPAL, A. (1988) *Language Performance in Schools: A Review of APU Language Monitoring, 1979–83*, London, HMSO.

JOHNSON, S. and MURPHY, P. (1986) *Girls and Physics: Reflections on APU Survey Findings*, APU (Assessment of Performance Unit) Occasional Paper NO. 4, London, DES.

MAHONEY, P. (1988) *Schools for the Boys? Co-education Reassessed*, London, Heinemann Educational Books.

McNARMARA, J. (1989) 'The writing in science and history project: The research questions and implications for teachers', in CHRISTIE, F. (ed.) *Writing in Schools* (BEd course reader) Geelong, Victoria, Deakin University Press.

POYNTON, C. (1985) *Language and Gender: Making the Difference*, Oxford, Oxford University Press.

STOBART, G., WHITE, J., ELWOOD, J., MASON, K. and HAYDEN, M. (1992) *Differential Performance in Examination at 16+ English and Mathematics*, Report Submitted to School Examination and Assessment Council.

SWANN, J. and GRADDOL, D. (1988) 'Gender inequalities in the classroom', *English in Education*, **22**(1), pp. 48–65.

WHITE, J. (1987) *Pupils' Attitudes to Writing*, Windsor, NFER-Nelson.

9 Girls' Achievement in Science and Technology — Implications for Pedagogy?

Jan Harding

Introduction

A dictionary definition for 'pedagogy' is 'the science of teaching' with the given derivation from the Greek 'to lead a boy'! This chapter will focus on the conditions in schooling which, seemingly, lead girls to learn effectively and with commitment in science and technology education, to their own personal enrichment and to the benefit of the society to which they belong.

In discussing schooling, however, one must bear in mind the influence of cultural contexts in which schools exist. In western cultures the rise of modern science and technology has been associated with males. Scientists and technologists or engineers are expected to be male. Science education, despite rhetoric claiming a cultural purpose, has included a strong vocational element: young people choose to study science subjects in school if they need them for a future job. Within this process the sciences are differentiated, with boys, given the choice, choosing physics and chemistry; and girls, biology, seen to be appropriate for their child-bearing and household roles, as well as to careers in health care.

Technology education in schools is not yet well defined. The increasing dependence of modern society on technology claims a place for it in the curriculum. Its antecedents may be high status applied science or low status handicrafts based in the workshop (boys' craft rather than girls'). McCulloch, Jenkins and Layton (1985) describe how developments in both areas were in competition for control of the emergent technology curriculum in the UK after World War II. They point out the invisibility of girls in these developments which focused on the perceived needs of boys and of industry. In some education systems technology is synonymous with computing or information technology. Although this area does not carry an historical weight of sex-stereotyping, in some cultures, including the UK, it has acquired a strong masculine image (Culley, 1986; Burke, et al., 1988).

In western cultures all three potential forms of technology are biased to the male. As a result, science and technology emerge as some of the most strongly sex-stereotyped areas of the curriculum. In seeking effective pedagogies we must recognize that within science and technology there exists a pedagogy for boys. Kelly (1985), drawing on observations made in the course of the GIST project (Girls into Science and Technology), demonstrated how school science is masculinized: through the overwhelming number of scientists who are males; through illustrations and examples used in teaching; through the world views, experiences and ways of working that are assumed; and the way in which students and teachers use the laboratory context to reconstitute gender within the interactions of teaching and learning. Pedagogy is leading the boys!

Against this background the question to ask is 'What must change so that pedagogy meets the needs of girls?'

In what follows, a number of research studies that provide insights into the factors which are associated with girls' choice of, and success in, science and technology will be discussed.

Factors Associating with Girls' Success in Science and Technology

Expectations

The expectations of teachers can be powerful stimulants to girls' success. That teachers' expectations in science can be biased against girls was dramatically demonstrated by Spear (1984) who showed that teachers gave a lower grade to a piece of work if they thought a girl had produced it than if they assumed a boy was the author. On the other hand, positive expectations from teachers can result in participation and success for girls in science and technology. The author has worked with an annual County Technology Fair which has shown increasing entries from girls in Infant and Junior Schools since technology has been established in primary schools in the UK. Interviews with teachers have shown that many expect (and get) just as much interest and enthusiasm for projects from girls as from boys. However, entries from girls fall off as they progress through secondary schools in the area, an exception being one girls' school which consistently enters teams, one of which has been awarded the major prize in several years. They have an enthusiastic male technology teacher, but the absence of boys is probably a factor in the high levels of girls' participation and success, indicating the need to work with boys in order to achieve a gender-inclusive context in which girls can work.

This is how a group of Year 10 girls described their experiences in a class where the teacher encouraged the students to explore new ideas in mathematics, working collaboratively and with Logo.

> Everyday we have learned something new ... It makes it a little more adventurous and exciting and makes you really want to do maths ... Boys are always encouraged to do special projects ... Most girls just do the work that has been set and don't bother to explore new ideas. This is because they haven't had enough encouragement. Our teacher praises us every time we do something different. With her encouragement we could do anything. (Sutherland and Hoyles, 1988, pp. 17, 18)

Expectations are mediated to students if they are offered a choice within the curriculum: they do not need to follow all alternatives, and sex-stereotyping present in their culture will influence their choices.

When the separate sciences were among a menu of subjects from which pupils, at the age of 13/14, put together a course for the last two years of compulsory schooling in England, inspectors reported that only 12 per cent of girls continued with the study of physics, although 50 per cent of boys did so (HMI, 1979). Since then two changes have occurred: a General Certificate of Secondary Education (GCSE), in which coursework made a significant contribution to assessment, replaced the two separate examinations at 16+; and a National Curriculum has been introduced with 'a broad and balanced' science joining English and mathematics as core subjects for all from 5–16. Although this was introduced for 14–16-year-olds in 1994 only, examination boards and schools had already moved some way towards offering broad and balanced science courses. The figures for 1992 showed entries for 'double science' were around five times those for the separate sciences and that nearly as many girls were studying the same amount of science (including physics) as boys were (they formed 49.5 per cent of entries). Moreover, girls were as successful as boys: 44.1 per cent of them achieving double certification with top grades, to boys' 44.7 per cent. However, this does not appear to increase girls' readiness to pursue the study of physics further. The 1992 data for A-level entries show a decrease in proportion of girls when compared to 1982. A similar decrease in proportion of boys is apparent in biology. Only in chemistry do entries show a reduction in sex differentiation.

Science has formed a compulsory element in Thai schools for many years. Although only 15 per cent of the 15–18 age group participates in the senior high school programme rather more than half of these are girls (Keeves and Kotte, 1992). They are able to choose a science or humanities course. About half, with roughly equal numbers of girls and boys, go into each course. The humanities course contains a sizeable compulsory science module and there is no choice between the separate sciences in the science line: all students study physics, chemistry and biology. A project that examined achievement across theory and practical work, and students' perceptions of science, showed that girls scored higher than boys in chemistry, and equal to them in physics. The course was judged to be 'traditional' with no attempt to include social implications of science, but it was based firmly in practical investigations. Both males and females associated the practical techniques of chemistry with women's work in the kitchen. However, the same was not true of physics practical work which was associated with boys and men (Klainin, Fensham and West, 1987).

While cultural expectations appear to support young women's participation in physical sciences education, women are poorly represented in science-based employment except in the field of education. A high proportion of all high school science teachers in Thailand are women, which may provide a role model function for girls and therefore contribute to the expectation effect.

Teaching Style

A study in the UK in the 1970s enquired into teaching styles and associations with achievement and attitudes to science of the Year 10 students involved. Three styles were identified: I, the Problem Solvers; II, the Informers; III, the Enquirers (Galton, 1981).

The study comprised ninety-four teachers: sixty-nine men and twenty-five women. Style I, a teacher-directed style in which students were challenged to generate hypotheses and solve problems, was used by nearly half the sample and more by physical science teachers than biologists, of whom more than half used Style II which focused on recall and application of facts. For both sexes Style I resulted in the greatest achievement. Style III, which was characterized as pupil-centred enquiry, gave the highest mean scores on data manipulation and problem solving. A higher proportion of men teachers used Style I, while the reverse was true for Style III. This latter style was the only one in which a more positive attitude developed on the part of the students, especially for girls with negative initial attitudes.

Girls did not like Style I, preferring Styles II or III. Since these are very different contrasting styles this may appear puzzling, but Galton (1981) points out both require minimal public interaction with the teacher. The aggressive, public exposure associated with Style I, where the teacher (often male) may expect a single correct answer related to his own experiences, is likely to deter girls who attempt to answer from a different experiential base and with a different perception of the problem in mind.

Similarly in a study of students' reactions to the introduction of a thematic approach to the teaching of physics in Danish gymnasia (16–19), Blegaa and Reich (1987) report that girls preferred a learning process where they themselves, rather than the teacher, were active participants.

Content, Context and Presentation

The importance to girls of placing the teaching of science and technology in the social context has been identified by many researchers. Ormerod (1971) showed that the recognition that science had social implications correlated with girls' choice of physical science subjects, but not boys'.

The Education Department of Tasmania, Australia, exploited this association when introducing computing into schools in 1986. Personnel were aware of the masculine image computing assumed elsewhere, so initial in-service programmes were provided for humanities and social science teachers, not for those of mathematics and science which were already male-stereotyped. The social science curriculum drew upon the detailed database available for the convicts who were transported from Britain to Van Dieman's Isle (Tasmania) in the nineteenth century. Girls became enthusiastically involved in using programs to question the databases. When it was observed that boys attempted aggressively to monopolize computers, these were 'sexed': equal numbers were allocated for use by girls and by boys (personal communication).

It seems that to place learning in a social context provides a strong motivating factor for girls to work with science and technology. When boys' and girls' entries over a three-year period to a UK National Design Competition were analysed, gender differences were apparent. Although they worked on similar devices, a clear difference emerged when they were required to define the problem they were working on. For the boys the problem was technical, the improvement of a device, but for the girls the problem lay in the social context. They were working on a device to help a young child learn, an elderly or disabled person to be more independent and so on. If this required the use of micro-electronics girls showed no reservations about developing skills in this area (Grant and Harding, 1987).

It has been common practice in workshop-based courses to establish technical skills and knowledge bases before moving to problem-orientated work. This may be unhelpful for girls as they see no justification for their involvement in the skills and content in an area which has been traditionally male dominated. A conclusion from the evidence above is that, given the opportunity to define a problem within their own set of values and frameworks, girls are able to work towards effective and realistic solutions. Within the GATE (Girls and Technology Education) project such an opportunity was provided for 12-year-olds in an introductory technology course developed from the issue of safety in children's playgrounds (Grant and Givens, 1984). Girls and boys were both enthusiastically involved.

Familiarity with a context, or even a perception that the context may have a personal significance, increases commitment and performance. The Assessment of Performance Unit (APU) within the Department of Education in England and Wales in the 1980s surveyed standards of achievement in science at age 11, 13 and 15 and in technology at age 15. If a problem was set in an industrial or laboratory context, or involved vehicles in some way, the performance of boys was enhanced. If, on the other hand, the task was based in the kitchen or the office, or involved children's toys, girls appeared to have an advantage (Murphy, 1993; SEAC, 1991). Murphy, who worked within the Assessment of Performance Unit in Science (a ten-year programme which sampled and tested performance in science at ages 11, 13 and 15 across the UK), concluded that girls and boys tended to identify different problems within a set task. Typically girls took into account the circumstances within which the task was set, whereas boys, as a group, considered the task in isolation, apart from its context. Girls were better able to tolerate ambiguity since they were not seeking a single 'right' answer which would be inappropriate to the complexity of the problem they had identified (Murphy, 1993).

The valuing of their personal experience and an acceptance of feelings provide means for integrating girls into the study of physics. Vedelsby (1987) drew on 'confluent education' in a project involving teachers in Danish gymnasia. In this approach affective and cognitive aspects of learning are directed to the same goal of understanding. For the first session of a new topic (electricity), music related to the theme was playing as the students entered the room. They were asked to listen quietly and were then required to write down all their experiences and feelings relating to electricity. They shared these accounts, some of them humorous, in small group discussions, during which each group had to agree on the definition of electric current. The teacher developed the course from these definitions. The approach has also been used successfully with other topics and with unemployed women with minimal formal education.

Teachers in Victoria, Australia, have worked together in a collective to develop strategies for teaching science and mathematics that are more gender-inclusive. Approaches which encourage girls were found to include the use of creative writing, drama, role modelling, and values clarification (Hildebrand, 1989). These strategies have been published (Gianello, 1988) and a professional development manual produced for teacher education (Lewis and Davies, 1988).

Maturation and Personality

Head (1980) has shown that maturation interacts with gender in the choice of science. Using Loevinger's Sentence Completion Tests for Ego Development, he demonstrated that among girls who chose science at the age of 13/14 was a high proportion of the most mature girls, according to this test, while the boy scientists contained a high proportion of the least mature boys.

Collings and Smithers (1984), surveying young people in school sixth forms with a person orientation test, found that those who had chosen science were less person orientated than their peers within the same sex. However, girl scientists were still more person orientated, according to the test, than boys who chose arts subjects.

Head went on to review studies of the personality of practising scientists (all with male samples) and showed that they tend to be less person orientated, more emotionally reticent and authoritarian and with a greater commitment to what may be termed a 'Puritan work ethic' than their peers (Head, 1985). It appears that, in some measure, personality acts as filter in science choice.

If, within science education, science is presented as impersonal, detached (objective), abstract, law bound and enabling control, then it, especially, matches the needs of immature or emotionally reticent males and enables these, in larger numbers than from other groups, to progress through its study. The greater maturity of some girls choosing science had possibly enabled them to reject the sex-stereotyped image of science and to recognize how it might serve a purpose for them in the future. By changing the way science is packaged and presented it should be possible to attract to its study a wider range of people, female and male, with different needs.

Cognitive Style

Head's analysis of the literature on cognitive style in Chapter 5 of this volume shows many parallels with the empirical studies reviewed in this chapter. The controlled experiment carried out in a girls' school to which he refers demonstrates that the packaging of science can, indeed, alter the range of personality types, in terms of choosing physics.

Other studies also point to differences in preferred learning styles of girls and boys. Within APU Science Surveys in the UK it was found that girls had a greater ability to identify, and take into account, a wide variety of factors relating to an issue (Murphy, 1993). A similar effect occurred in APU Technology modelling tasks, one supervisor commenting:

> Girls appeared to work fundamentally from human needs, dealing predominantly with issues. They were often cautious in their entry to a situation, wanting to know how, why and whom it was for. While studying and designing the minutiae they were constantly seeking to keep the implications of the whole in view, and for some this complexity became intolerable to the point where they capitulated. Boys, on the other hand, seemed able, not only to start into the activity without knowing much, but were prepared to work on specific parts of it without considering the whole ... possibly to lose sight of it altogether. (SEAC, 1991, p. 120)

The interaction of perception of the complexity of an issue with responses to an 'attitude to science and technology' survey was apparent within the GATE project. Boys' attitudes formed a bipolar distribution — they were either enthusiastically *for* the uses and effects of science and technology, or disparaging. The girls made much greater use of the mid-point of the scale (not sure). This latter effect has been found for females in other studies, where it has been speculated that the result arises from poorer decision-making skills. However, when the researcher interviewed girls who had made frequent use of the 'unsure' category, he found their responses had been prompted by a recognition of complexity in the statements provided which made unequivocal agreement or disagreement difficult. The girls were saying 'you didn't give me enough information' (Grant and Harding, 1987).

In APU Technology tasks girls were found to excel in those requiring reflective skills: assessment of needs and evaluation of products. They impressed a supervisor with the way the 'were more concerned than boys to really understand the task' (SEAC, 1991, p. 123).

Burns and Bird (1987) also found gender differences when exploring the concept 'understanding' in chemistry with Year 11 students in six New Zealand schools. Girls were more concerned to understand as much as possible, while boys' first concern was to pass the examination, if possible with top grades. High achievers and girls identified 'understanding' as a recognition of order among concepts, while for low achievers and boys the accumulation of knowledge represented understanding. From the students' responses four ways of achieving understanding were identified. They preferred: working alone (30 per cent boys but no girls); asking the teacher (but 40 per cent had reservations and for 25 per cent of boys this was a last resort); consultation with classmates (65 per cent girls, but 25 per cent of boys rejected it outright); consulting sources outside school (an option used by high achievers, but 30 per cent of girls and only one boy made use of other people). Referring to opportunities provided in formal schooling, 85 per cent of boys and 60 per cent of girls said they had to work on their own as a first course of action, an option no girl preferred.

The authors identified a task orientation among girls which, together with a focus on relationships between ideas, could lead to a 'deep' approach to learning.

It was found, however, that the girls had less confidence in their understanding than boys had. This was attributed to the negative experiences of girls in the competitive ways of secondary school. The authors comment: 'These young women's ability to work co-operatively may signal some unusual strengths which could be better used to enhance their learning' (Burns and Bird, 1987, p. 24).

Girls' preference for working collaboratively and through discussion with others was identified in the APU Technology surveys. Girls were observed displaying 'an ability to take on a wide range of issues in discussion' and acting as facilitators to the boys' ideas, 'being able to give them lots of support and to point out the strengths and weaknesses of their ideas' (SEAC, 1991, p. 126).

A Danish study of 10-year-olds working on a computer task found that boys negotiated time on the computer, then worked independently, while girls worked in groups, exploring verbally a great many tangential ideas (Nielsen and Ropstorf, 1985).

Assessment Effects

For girls to experience success in science and technology it is important that assessment instruments are not biased against them. Evidence that there may be a gender interaction with mode of assessment emerged in the 1970s. Harding (1979) and Murphy (1982) have shown that multiple choice, or so-called objective, tests favour boys. This is probably because the mode does not allow for girls to express the complexity they see in a problem. In addition, a report from the US (David, 1981) throws doubt on the educational value of multiple choice and short-answer tests, as they discourage the ability to reflect — a characteristic which we have seen correlates with girls' success. The use of an assessment mode that allows candidates control over how they respond (e.g., coursework or project work) is likely to be more gender-fair than others (Murphy, 1993). It is of interest that during the period that coursework formed a substantial element of GCSE assessment, girls' achievement in science and mathematics increased to match that of boys. And it is of concern that politicians have recently placed arbitrary limits on the contribution of coursework to assessment in public examinations.

As Hildebrand reports in Chapter 12 of this volume, when assessment methods were used innovatively in physics in the Victorian Certificate of Education, there was a marked increase in pupil success rates overall, but especially in the higher grades for girls. The assessments tasks required the physics curriculum, which looked quite traditional, to be learnt in the context of real-life interactions, meaningful to the young people involved. However, not all girls benefited: '. . . girls from lower socio-economic backgrounds actively resist pedagogical and assessment practices based on interpretation, exposition and independent work' (Hildebrand and Allard, 1993). Again, with a change of government to a more right-wing administration, some of the innovations which particularly supported girls' performance have been discontinued. A general paper composed of mainly multiple choice questions has been introduced to moderate grades in all subjects, but Hildebrand reports that this has not diminished the newly discovered excellence of girls in physics.

Girls as Deficient Learners

So far in this paper most of the research quoted has focused on girls successfully learning science and technology when conditions are favourable. However, the literature on sex or gender differences abounds with studies which appear to demonstrate that girls possess inadequate learning skills. Just two have been selected for comment.

An Israeli study, using data from the second International Association for the Evaluation of Educational (IEA) survey (1983–84) found that boys out-scored girls in all four science areas, with the smallest differences in biology and the largest in physics. The assessment throughout used multiple choice tests. They report that girls were more likely to choose a distractor which presented valid and related information or were influenced by a key word or graphical distractor. Although they comment that 'Boys' advantage was achieved through a number of items which were highly related to activities more usually encountered by boys than by girls', they go on to conclude that 'Girls' errors seem to reflect the hesitant, dependent, anxious, unmotivated help-searcher learner typical of feminine affective profile' (Levin, Sabar and Libman, 1987, p. 111). They imply that girls' problems in learning science lie in their lack of affective readiness.

The other study was part of the project based in Danish gymnasia to which reference has already been made. Mainly qualitative methods were used in following the physics experiences of some eighty pupils in three schools over more than a year. The researchers identified the need to integrate affective and cognitive elements in the teaching of physics and this was addressed in another part of the project (Vedelsby, 1987). This particular study focused on sex differences which emerged in problem solving and the understanding of physics concepts.

Difficulties arose when the physics was based in everyday phenomena not seen as problematic. Although motivation increased, students, particularly girls, seemed unable to move beyond everyday explanations to seek out the physics involved. Some 'bright' pupils expressed a preference for 'pure physics problems'. It seems that few had the skills required to reformulate the problem so that the physics concepts were exposed and standard methods of resolution could be used. The authors' view is that the learning of concepts does not take place by simple assimilation, rather the learner has to live through a crisis and take risks. They refer to girls' need, not so imperative for boys, to have a thorough understanding of one subject before going on to another. When the pace of teaching does not allow for this, girls revert to rote learning with loss of understanding. Girls' learning style (as a result of their socialization) 'is characterised by less self-confidence and less perseverance' (Beyer and Reich, 1987, p. 60). The solution recommended is one of making teachers aware of sex differences in learning styles and encouraging them to provide contexts where girls are given experiences of success (if only partial).

In an intervention with UK A-level students (pre-university level) to examine the effect of using computers with a Logo program to develop understanding of Newtonian mechanics, it was girls who showed interest and volunteered to continue work in extra sessions (less self-confidence, or wanting to understand?). Most of them showed the kind of 'everyday' explanations or misconceptions that Beyer and Reich reported, but by working collaboratively and interacting with the Logo turtle they were able to work through their misconceptions. Burns and Smart (1988) describe the interactions whereby a number of girls resolved their difficulties, commenting: 'They were emotionally as well as intellectually involved and frequently talked about their feelings of excitement, frustration and fun . . . They went away with a sense of achievement and a new confidence' (p. 73).

Discussion

It appears that pedagogy which enables girls to achieve at least as much success as boys do in science and technology is culture dependent. The Thai experiences of an able élite suggests no special pedagogy is required in science. However, the components of the pedagogy used included a high status and positive image of science, a foundation in practical investigations and a high proportion of female teachers. But equality exists in Thailand within narrow limits, vocational education is more differentiated, providing more for boys, which accounts for the greater number of girls in school education at this stage (Keeves and Kotte, 1992). Cultural norms prevent women working in science-based employment other than teaching science. In India, also, it appears that cultural norms may both provide support *and* create barriers in science for young women from privileged families. They are entering university science departments and achieving more than young men. One group of young women attributed success to their habits of obedience and deference to authority which they found protective and supportive (Chandra, 1987). Should one question the pedagogy that generated resonance with these characteristics? In general, young women proceed no further than a good degree (Gangal, 1993).

In 'western'-style culture, where modern science developed alongside extreme gender-stereotyping, women were effectively excluded from science for many years. Gender roles continue to be markedly sex-stereotyped. In this context broad differences in preferred learning styles have been identified between girls and boys. The girls generally work most effectively within a philosophy of care, recognizing human need. They perceive, and are reluctant to discard, complexity, thereby opening themselves to charges of hesitancy and irrationality. They seek collaboration and value discussion in order to achieve real understanding, but are judged to be dependent and 'help-searchers'. If learning is presented in a style alien to them they will appear anxious and may resort to dependency or rote learning. The qualities that girls display as learners have too often, in science, been interpreted negatively instead of looking for a mismatch in the pedagogical system.

The skills that girls display are ones that are becoming more valued in a rapidly changing, technologically-based society which is developing a consciousness of the damage wrought on a fragile global system. They should be matched by a relevant pedagogy or range of pedagogies, for difference exists among girls within subcultures related to ethnicity, socio-economic position and even the school ethos of a co-educational or single-sex community. We need to identify their needs and skills as learners and foster the ones that lead them to confident, deep understanding. In this we will apply value judgments and our understanding of educational processes. The emergent pedagogies will undoubtedly be student centred. It is to be deplored that in too many more 'traditional' political systems, weight is being given to didactic methods of teaching which do not allow for collaboration and discussion, and that commitment to accountability leads to frequent external testing which can only be satisfied in terms of cost by the ubiquitous, but inadequate and invalid, multiple choice instrument.

Conclusion

If our objective is only to involve more girls fully and successfully in science and technology education, then, it seems, no single pedagogical approach will be required. Much will depend on cultural context.

In western-style cultures, a successful pedagogy in science and technology, different from the traditional approach used mainly for males, has been identified. This places teaching/learning in a social context, relating to human need and real problems; allows for collaborative ways of learning, including discussion-based exploration of understanding, and; provides assessment procedures that allow for the recognition of complexity and the identification of a range of problems.

But if the objective is to enable women in any culture to make a full contribution to the development and uses of science and technology, the following approach is required:

- the questioning of pedagogies already in place, with gender as an analytical tool;
- the inclusion of the dimensions of ethnicity and socio-economic categories in that questioning;
- the identification of skills and qualities displayed by girls and women as learners;
- the identification of skills and qualities needed for development in a rapidly changing world, again using gender as a tool for analysis;
- the use of pedagogies that take account of both the needs of development and the skills of women — only then may they be regarded as 'effective';
- the removal of cultural constraints that prevent women from making a full contribution to the development and uses of science and technology as adult workers and decision-makers.

References

BLEGAA, S. and REICH, J. (1987) 'Is a girl-friendly physics curriculum organised around themes?', *Contributions to the Fourth GASAT Conference Vol. 2*, Ann Arbor, Michigan, USA, pp. 34–40.

BEYER, K. and REICH, J. (1987) 'Why are many girls inhibited from learning scientific concepts in physics?', *Contributions to the Fourth GASAT Conference Vol. 1*, Ann Arbor, Michigan, USA, pp. 53–61.

BURKE, J., EDWARDS, J., JEFFRIES, J., JONES, K., MILN, J., MONTGOMERY, M., PERKINS, B., SEAGER, A. and WRIGHT, H. (1988) 'My mum uses a computer, too!', in HOYLES, C. (ed.) *Girls and Computing*, Bedford Way Paper 34, Institute of Education, University of London.

BURNS, J. and BIRD, L. (1987) 'Girls' co-operation and boys' isolation in achieving understanding in chemistry', *Contributions to the Fourth GASAT Conference Vol. 2*, Ann Arbor, Michigan, USA, pp. 16–25.

BURNS, S. and SMART, T. (1988) 'Sixth form girls using computers to explore Newtonian mechanics', in HOYLES, C. (ed.) *Girls and Computing*, Bedford Way Paper 34, Institute of Education, University of London.

CHANDRA, D. (1987) 'Are cultural barriers the promoters of success of girls in science and technology in India?', *Contributions to the Fourth GASAT Conference Vol. 2*, Ann Arbor, Michigan, USA, pp. 41–8.

COLLINGS, J. and SMITHERS, A. (1984) 'Person orientation and science choice', *European Journal of Science Education*, 6(1), pp. 55–65.

CULLEY, L. (1986) *Gender Differences in Computing in Secondary Schools*, Loughborough University of Technology, Leicester, UK.

DAVID, P. (1981) 'Multiple-choice under fire', *Times Educational Supplement*, 27 November.

GALTON, M. (1981) 'Differential treatment of boy and girl pupils during science lessons', in KELLY, A. (ed.) *The Missing Half*, Manchester University Press, England, pp. 180–91.

GANGAL, S. (1993) 'Science education and science careers for Indian women from metropolitan cities', *Proceedings of the Seventh GASAT Conference*, Waterloo, Ontario, Canada.

GIANELLO, L. (1988) *Getting into Gear: Gender-inclusive Teaching Strategies in Science*, Canberra, CDC, developed by the McClincock Collective.

GRANT, M. and GIVENS, N. (1984) 'A sense of purpose: Approaching CDT through social issues', *Studies in Design Education, Craft and Technology*, 16(2).

GRANT, M. and HARDING, J. (1987) 'Changing the polarity', *International Journal of Science Education*, 9(3), pp. 335–42.

HARDING, J. (1979) 'Sex differences in performance in examinations at 16+', *Physics Education*, 14(5), pp. 280–4.

HEAD, J. (1980) 'A model to link personality characteristics to performance in science', *European Journal of Science Education*, 2, pp. 295–300.

HEAD, J. (1985) *The Personal Response to Science*, Cambridge Science Education Series, Cambridge University Press.

HILDEBRAND, G. (1989) 'Creating a gender-inclusive science education', *The Australian Science Teachers' Journal*, 18(3), pp. 7–16.

HILDEBRAND, G. and ALLARD, A. (1993) 'Transforming the curriculum through changing assessment practices', *Contributions to the Seventh GASAT Conference, Vol. 1*, Waterloo, Ontario, Canada, pp. 254–62.

HMI (1979) *Aspects of Secondary Education in England*, HMSO, London.

KEEVES, J. and KOTTE, D. (1992) 'Disparities between the sexes in science education: 1970–84', in KEEVES, J. (ed.) *The IEA Study of Science III*, Oxford, Pergamon Press.

KELLY, A. (1985) 'The construction of masculine science', *British Journal of Sociology of Education*, 6, pp. 133–54.

KLAININ, S., FENSHAM, P. and WEST, L. (1987) 'Some remarkable findings about learning the physical sciences in Thailand', *Contributions to the Fourth GASAT Conference Vol. 2*, Ann Arbor, Michigan, US, pp. 66–87.

LEVIN, T., SABAR, N. and LIBMAN, Z. (1987) 'Girls understanding of science: A problem of cognitive or affective readiness?', *Contributions to the Fourth GASAT Conference Vol. 2*, Ann Arbor, Michigan, USA, pp. 104–12.

LEWIS, S. and DAVIES, A. (1988) *Gender Equity in Mathematics and Science*, GAMSAT Professional Development Manual, Canberra, CDC.

McCULLOCH, G., JENKINS, E. and LAYTON, D. (1985) *Technological Revolution? The Politics of School Science and Technology in England and Wales Since 1945*, London, Falmer Press.

MURPHY, R. (1982) 'Sex differences in objective test performance', *British Journal of Education Psychology*, **52**, pp. 213–19.

MURPHY, P. (1993) 'Assessment and gender', in BOURNE, J.G. (ed.) *Thinking Through Primary Practice*, London, Routledge.

NIELSEN, J. and ROPSTORF, L. (1985) 'Girls and computers — Delight or necessity?', *Contributions to the Third GASAT Conference*, Chelsea College, University of London.

ORMEROD, M.B. (1971) 'The social implications factor in attitudes to science', *British Journal of Education Psychology*, **41**(3), pp. 335–8.

SEAC (1991) *The Assessment of Performance in Design and Technology*, London, Schools Examination and Assessment Council.

SPEAR, M. (1984) 'The biasing influence of pupil sex in a science marking exercise', *Research in Science and Technology Education*, **2**, pp. 56–60.

SUTHERLAND, R. and HOYLES, C. (1988) 'Gender perspectives on Logo programming in the mathematics curriculum', in HOYLES, C. (ed.) *Girls and Computing*, Bedford Way Paper 34, Institute Of Education, University of London.

VEDELSBY, M. (1987) 'Some proposals for integration of affective and cognitive aspects in physics education', *Contributions to the Fourth GASAT Conference Vol. 1*, Ann Arbor, Michigan, USA, pp. 171–6.

10   Is There a Space for the Achieving Girl?[1]

Michèle Cohen

> When we so often see a *French*-Woman teach an *English*-girl to speak and
> read *French* perfectly in a Year or Two, without any Rule of Grammar,
> or anything else but pratling to her I cannot but wonder, how Gentlemen
> have over-seen this way for their Sons, and thought them more dull or
> incapable than their Daughters. (Locke, 1989, p. 218)

This remark of John Locke's encapsulates the main issue I want to address in this
chapter: girls' achievement and how it is constructed. In *Some Thoughts Concerning Education* (1693), Locke was interested in discussing how to educate young
gentlemen, not how clever little girls were. He wanted to promote the conversational method to teach boys Latin, and his reference to girls was merely to show
how *easily* languages were learned by conversation rather than by rules (Locke,
1989, p. 218). By attributing girls' success to the *method*, he was able to correct
gentlemen's misapprehension that their daughters might be brighter than their sons.
For Locke, as one concerned with the education of gentlemen, it was inconceivable
that boys might be less able than girls.

Nevertheless, Locke's remark also shows that he did not fail to notice
girls' attainment. This is the main argument of this chapter: it is not so much that
girls' achievement has been ignored or overlooked throughout history, it is rather
that the often visible evidence of this achievement has served to construct female
minds as inferior. Conversely, lack of achievement has produced what have been
construed as the superior mental power and, especially, the boundless potential of
boys. The issue, then, is not the visibility of girls' achievement but the way this
performance has been inserted into other discourses — discourses on sex difference
and education.

To illustrate my argument, I have chosen to discuss the study of French in
England in the past three hundred years. There are several reasons why French is
a useful tool for research into gendered achievement. The first is historical. Because
French was the only 'serious' subject learned by both sexes throughout the period
I will be discussing — from the late seventeenth century to the present — it provides a unique point of entry into the history of boys' and girls' education, and a
vantage point from which to look at achievement from the perspective of gender.
The second is contemporary. In English secondary schools, not only is French
perceived to be a 'female subject' but this femaleness of French is itself intricately

interwoven with the issue of gendered achievement. For it is the 'femaleness' of French (and/or of its teachers) that is still held to account for both boys' inferior performance and girls' superior attainment in the language (Powell, 1985). However, while this explanation may attempt to excuse boys' failure, it undermines girls' success. The third reason is both historical and contemporary. Because the study of French has been associated with 'female' accomplishments, it has become a metonym for the education girls have received throughout the ages, i.e., frivolous and superficial.[2] As a result, while girls' underrepresentation and underachievement in maths and sciences have been cause for concern to feminist educationists (Kelly, Whyte and Smail, 1984; Walkerdine, 1989) girls' success in French has been uncomfortable. The site where one would expect a celebration of girls' achievement is precisely the site where it is never spoken of.

In a book concerned mainly with girls in maths and science, French thus presents a useful contrast, for it points to questions that must be asked, and it may warn us to be cautious about solutions. In the first place, French is one subject where interventions have not been necessary to encourage girls to do well. Quite the opposite. Addressing a Symposium on Language Teaching at St Paul's Girls School in June 1987, Michael Buckby read a paper discussing the relative merits of a particular method on boys' motivation. Asked by a member of the audience 'and what about the girls?', Buckby, a member of the modern language establishment replied: 'Unfortunately, their attainment keeps being higher'.[3] This statement may seem less surprising when it is considered that the gender imbalance favouring girls in both take-up and performance has been constituted as a 'crisis' in Modern Languages (Hawkins, 1981). Why is girls' achievement in French not celebrated? Why is no one saying 'learning a language is hard, look how well girls are doing.' Why is girls' success either undermined or alleged to have sinister implications for boys' achievement? (Thom, 1987).

In his monograph on sexism and language teaching, *Boys, Girls and Languages in School* (1985), Bob Powell argued that whereas girls' under-performance in maths and sciences had received a lot of attention,[4] none had been directed at boys' under-performance in languages. Powell aimed to redress the balance. Yet, despite his own evidence that in language learning there are 'more variations within the sexes than between the sexes' (Powell, 1985, p. 42), he advocated solutions predicated on the existence of categories 'boy' and 'girl' with specific and fixed gendered attributes, arguing for example that 'micros provide a useful *intrinsic* incentive to boys', and that girls should be *'encouraged'* to use them. He also hoped that girls would get 'fair access' to the machines. Other solutions included making language learning more 'mathematical' by introducing more computer-based teaching and problem-solving exercises (Powell, 1985, p. 62).[5]

Powell's solutions are important not because I want to discuss his essentialist notion of sex-difference but because they highlight what the problem is. The interventions promoting girls' take-up and achievement in maths and sciences, which Powell aimed to emulate, were organized as compensations for a *deficit*: girls' 'nature' as well as their 'conditioning' had to be altered, their subjectivity changed. There is no question of boys' deficit in language learning, nor is their conditioning an issue. Motivating boys to take-up and do well in French is a matter of changing not the boys, but the *methods*.

My argument is that the very terms of the discourse on education are organized so that practices have the performance of boys as their main concern — even while girls' attainment appears now to be the focus of attention. The discourse presupposes that boys' failure and girls' success is due to an external cause — a pedagogical practice, a method. The possibility that girls' success and boys' failure might be due to something in them is not envisaged because the discourse rules out the possibility that boys might be deficient — at least in comparison to girls. One consequence is that boys tend to be perceived as potentially, if not actually, able but not so girls (Walkerdine, 1989). It is neither a conspiracy, nor a deliberate attempt to discriminate against girls; this is how the discourse is structured. I want to argue not only that these gendered positionings have a long history, but that the presumption of boys' potential has been integral to the construction of males since at least the eighteenth century, when the notion of a gentleman was, as John Barrell has put it, 'one in a condition of empty potential, one who is imagined as being able to comprehend everything, and yet who need not give any evidence of having comprehended anything' (Barrell, 1983, p. 203).

To be effective, interventions for girls' pedagogy must first take into account the historical baggage attached to discourses on difference and the way it has informed the construction of gendered achievement. In other words, the terms of the debate must be challenged and re-thought. The problematization of girls' achievement is neither a recent phenomenon, nor the result of changes in the status of women or in their jobs prospects. This problematization is not a *result*, it is historically constructed and woven into the fabric of gender difference. I want to trace the conditions for its emergence and persistence in the educational discourse, for, as Jeff Weeks once said, if gendered discourses are understood to be historically constructed, then 'they are open to transformation' (Weeks, 1982, p. 116).

Learning French in the Eighteenth Century

In the late seventeenth century, when my story begins, both males and females of rank learned French and were expected to speak it. While girls outnumber boys by perhaps a third in today's French classrooms, the situation was quite different then. 'French', remarked the author of *An Essay in Defense of the Female Sex*, 'has become a very fashionable language. There are now almost as many Ladies as Gentlemen speaking it' (Astell/Drake, 1696, p. 37). Throughout most of the eighteenth century, French was indispensable to the education of ladies and even more so to the fashioning of gentlemen. It was one aspect of what I call the 'cultivation of the tongue' necessary for men of rank to achieve politeness and gentlemanliness (Cohen, 1992a). Correctness, fluency and a good accent were deemed the most desirable of accomplishments for both sexes. Young men of rank travelling in France on the Grand Tour often spent a year in Blois to perfect their accent as the

French spoken there was held to be very pure. Back in England, their sisters — who did not travel abroad — had to make do with governesses and tutors (Cohen, 1992b). Thus, in Lainé's *The Princely Way to the French Tongue* (1677), a girl writing in French to her brother who is travelling in France apologizes for her mistakes, implying that *he* would not make such errors. But, she adds, he is more fortunate than her, 'vous êtes à la source', in France, while she has to remain in England (de Lainé, 1677, p. 345).

Boys also had the advantage of knowing Latin and therefore grammar while their sisters did not.[6] Not only was this not perceived to present particular problems for girls, but they might, like Fauchon's pupil Isabella Carr, make even more progress 'without any previous knowledge of Grammatical Rules' than someone trained 'scholastically' (Fauchon, 1751, Dedication). At the end of the eighteenth century, when the Grand Tour had ceased to be an essential part of upper class boys' education, they were more likely to study French, like their sisters, at home or at school. At that time, too, more girls than ever were studying French, a trend facilitated by the influx of aristocratic French exiles.[7] Boys' and girls' instruction in French had become more similar, and can thus be compared more easily, as a dialogue in Porny's *Practical French Grammar* reveals (Porny, 1796). Porny was the French master at Eton at the time.

The dialogue involves a girl and her brother. She has been learning French for six months and 'understands it better . . . construes it, writes it, and even speaks it better' than her brother, who has been learning it for six years at school (Porny, 1796, p. 316). Two features of the dialogue deserve attention. The first concerns the boy. His reluctance to learn is obvious — he finds French 'too hard' and does not see 'what use it is'. But his failure is located not in some weakness of his body or mental faculties but in an aspect of the educational process, the method. 'Tis none my fault,' says the boy, and his interlocutor agrees; the blame rests with the master. The second feature concerns the girl. Though her superior performance seems meant to discipline the boy, we should not lose sight of the fact of that achievement nor of how it is represented. The girl says that she has taken 'much pains' to learn, and believes that 'Science and Languages are only acquired by diligence and labour' (Porny, 1796, p. 319). She succeeds not because she is able, nor because she is said to have a special talent for languages, but because she is diligent and has a good teacher. Positioned as hard working rather than clever, she does not undermine or threaten the boy's potential. Indeed, once he is convinced of the 'benefits' of learning French, he endeavours to 'take so much pains' that he is sure to speak it in a short time.

Even though girls might be said to owe their success in French to a good method or to their hard work, even this modest claim was viewed with ambivalence. Bright girls, ladies of 'no contemptible natural parts', as Hannah More delicately put it (More, 1811, p. 61) had to steer a clear course between 'display' on the one hand, and 'pedantry' on the other. That course was often 'modesty'. Not surprisingly, virtuous young ladies who knew French well did not show it, something for which they were highly praised (Fordyce, 1748; Day, 1789). The others were suspect of having become 'Frenchified'.

French and the Sexed Mind

Towards the end of the eighteenth century, a new discourse on sex-difference emerged which both forged and hardened gender boundaries (Laqueur, 1990). For my purposes, the most important feature of the discourse was the claim that there was sex in mind. The 'mind of each sex', asserted Hannah More, 'has some kind of natural bias.' This difference in *mind* 'marked' the sexes and determined their 'respective, appropriate qualifications'. 'Women', she explained, 'have generally quicker perceptions; men have juster sentiments. — Women consider how things may be prettily laid — Men how they may be properly laid. — ... Women speak to shine or to please, men to convince or confute. — Women admire what is brilliant, men, what is solid. Women are fond of incident, men of argument ...' (More, 1785, pp. 4, 9–10, 13).

To examine the way the discourse on the sexed mind was constituted, I have chosen to discuss three texts concerned with female education published between the end of the eighteenth and the beginning of the nineteenth centuries: Hannah More's *Essays on Various Subjects*; John Bennett's *Strictures on Female Education*; and J.L. Chirol's *Enquiry into the Best System of Female Education* (More, 1785; Bennett, 1787; Chirol, 1809).

The discourse on the sexed mind was premised on the problematization of the female mind and achievement. Thus, More, Bennett and Chirol were unanimous about the quickness, vivacity and versatility of woman's mind, and unanimous as well that these constituted the visible manifestation of her mental inferiority. Vivacity, wrote Bennett, is unfavourable to profound thinking and accurate investigation, while More counterposed women's 'quicker perceptions' to men's 'juster sentiments'. Chirol was more blunt: woman has scarcely a thought she can call her own, except what is fugitive and transient as lightning (Bennett, 1787, p. 107; Chirol, 1809, p. 8). 'The very structure of woman's mind renders her incapable of the profound thought and careful reasoning that carry knowledge to its zenith of perfection,' Bennett concluded.[8]

What is striking about these comments is that the very presence of certain mental qualities in the female constructs her as lacking, whereas their absence in the male was held to construct *his* mental powers: the more invisible, the greater their strength. Nowhere is this more evident than in Bennett's discussion of the differences between little girls and boys, which he used to mark the 'precise bounties' of nature to each sex to demonstrate the natural truth of difference. Though he reckoned that little girls were quicker and generally more advanced than boys the same age, this was not a proof of their general superiority. Quite the opposite. It was the boy's thoughtfulness that prevented more brilliant and showy exertions. The deep and true worth of the boy's mental apparatus and the shallow and worthless brilliance of the girl's were summarized in one sentence: 'gold sparkles less than tinsel' (Bennett, 1787, pp. 105–6). By a rhetorical *tour de force*, the sexed mind was constructed so that the female's generated the mental space which allowed the superior intellectual powers of the male to be produced.

The discourse on the sexed mind did not imply that males had minds and females not, but that the faculties of each sex must be cultivated to follow 'nature'. Both sexes must be educated for their 'destination in society': the upper-class male eventually to rule his country, and the female, 'to constitute the happiness of the other half' (Chirol, 1809, p. 15). This did not mean that women had to remain ignorant; rather, it became more imperative than ever that what they learned be related to their femininity, and not transgress 'natural' boundaries. Education was meant to emphasize difference. As Frances Power Cobbe was to remark in 1862, Latin kept a man masculine by exercizing and strengthening his mental faculties. Thus, for women to learn it — and gain access to university education — became heavy with the menace of an 'assimilation' of the training of the sexes, a step which was 'fatal' in that it obliterated the 'natural differences between them'. Learning French, on the other hand, kept women 'feminine in mind' (Cobbe, 1862, pp. 8, 10).

Learning French in the Nineteenth Century

A convenient vantage point for considering the way education in general, and the learning of French in particular, developed in the nineteenth century is provided by the evidence of the two major Royal Commissions on education of the 1860s: the Clarendon Commission of 1864 and the Taunton Commission of 1868. The Clarendon Commission investigated the public schools; and the Taunton Commission middle-class secondary schools for girls as well as boys. Taken together, they provide a detailed picture of the educational discourse in the nineteenth century. The main pedagogical concern of the assistant commissioners was to investigate whether a particular subject trained and disciplined the mind.

Given how important speaking French had been for upper-class males in the eighteenth century, one might have thought that in the nineteenth century, Eton would sustain something of that tradition — it was the public school which trained the men who occupied most of the highest government and diplomatic posts (Bamford, 1967, p. 230). But no. Of the nine public schools which the Clarendon Commission investigated, Eton was the only one in which French was not part of the curriculum. After having been central to the fashioning of the men of rank for centuries, French was now the object of their scorn. The same attitude prevailed in the boys' grammar schools investigated by the Taunton Commission. 'Cultivating the faculties was the single most important educational learning theory of the nineteenth century' (Rothblatt, 1976, p. 129). Public and grammar school teachers were unanimous in their belief that Latin was the best means of achieving this aim. Because it lacked declensions and its grammar was considered simple, French could not discipline the mind. Even when French was taught, it was for no more than two hours a week. To allow it more time might 'damage . . . the intellectual tone of the place,' declared H.M. Butler, Headmaster at Harrow (Clarendon Commission, vol. 3, p. 382). At the same time, French was, as one assistant commissioner put it, the 'intellectual *spécialité*' of girls' schools (Taunton Commission, vol. 9, p. 297).

It is not possible to address here the complex issues explaining why attitudes towards French changed so dramatically (see Cohen, 1992a). My argument, in brief, is that this change was one element, one symptom of a much broader discursive shift which took place at the turn of the nineteenth century, related to the concern for the production of an English masculine national identity. Crucially, this involved a shift in the techniques for the production of the gentleman from the cultivation of his tongue to the training and disciplining of his mental faculties. Languages which were learned by or for conversation, were no longer deemed appropriate for males. Grammar alone could train the mind.

French was taught in many of the schools investigated by the Taunton Commission. Though some schools earned the Commission's highest praise, as did Newcastle Grammar School because boys were taught French 'precisely in the same way as the ancient languages',[9] French instruction was mostly severely criticized: the results of translation tests[10] — considered at the time the best gauge of 'linguistic cultivation' — were poor for both sexes. Discussing boys' schools, assistant commissioner Fearon suggested that one reason for this state of affairs was the textbooks. Most of the grammars used were not only 'exceedingly bad', they were 'defective in the scientific treatment of the language'. He particularly denounced the editions of French authors for English pupils, where the notes lacked any 'scholarship' and where there was

> no attempt to grapple with the real syntactical or idiomatic difficulties in a true spirit of philology . . . [no] attempt . . . to illustrate French usages or constructions by the light of parallel or analogous expressions in Latin, German or English authors; not one in which the origin and derivation of words and phrases was discussed, or they were traced through their various changes of signification. (Taunton Commission, vol. 7, pp. 299–301)

Similar deficiencies were noted in girls' schools. Even in the best private schools, girls could not

> discuss the origin and derivation of words and phrases; trace them through their various phases of signification; reconcile their employment, or point out their disagreement, with the general laws of grammar, illustrate the growth of such usages by other examples from the French or other languages. (Taunton Commission, vol. 7, pp. 403–5)

Ostensibly the criticisms are similar, except for one crucial detail. In the case of boys' failure, the problem was the textbooks; in the case of girls, it was the girls themselves. It should have come as no surprise that girls who were having 'conversational lessons in literature with Parisian teachers' were unable to construe, translate or 'answer such questions upon their French authors as boys in the upper sixth form of our public schools were expected to answer upon their Latin authors'. But it did. This confirmed the assistant commissioners' view that girls' education showed 'want of early and systematic mental discipline' and 'want of cultivation of the logical and reasoning faculties' (Taunton Commission, vols 7 and 8, pp. 401, 401).

The most severe criticism was of the use of the spoken language in girls' French classes. The assistant commissioners complained that the French lesson was too often conducted entirely in French; that the practice, common in the best schools, of enforcing constant use of French for a fixed number of hours outside class was 'mischievous' and even 'injurious to morals'; that girls' French language classes had wrong priorities: 'A pure Parisian accent is regarded as of more consequence than grammatical knowledge'; gaining fluency 'more important than the evil of incorrectness' (Taunton Commission, vol. 9, p. 297). The assistant commissioners' conclusion that the girls 'knew French better than the boys' (Taunton Commission, vol. 8, p. 49) might therefore seem startling, except that this was taken as evidence of their failure. Because no girls were found whose mind had been 'trained' or 'strengthened' by learning French — i.e., who could do translation accurately — their superior performance had no significance. Being able to speak French had no educational value or status (Taunton Commission, vols 8 and 9, pp. 250, 809) and girls' achievement was no achievement.

When the Direct Method, inspired by the German Reform School, was hailed as a revolution in language teaching methodology thirty years later, at the turn of the century, one of its foremost proponents could write: 'In pre-reform days . . . the learner never handled the language himself for the purpose of expressing his own experiences and ideas' (Repman, 1907, Introduction). This was precisely what the assistant commissioners had condemned in girls' language classrooms. In fact, the main 'innovative' tenets of the Direct Method comprised precisely those features of girls' French instruction criticized by the Taunton Commission: it advocated the use of the foreign language at all times in the classroom and opposed parsing, analysis and translation.[11] Because of the way educational achievement had been defined in the Taunton Commission, what girls had learned did not count and how they had learned did not constitute a method. Their classroom practices did not impact on the history of language learning. Citing the Taunton Commission in his historical survey of the teaching of French in England, Eric Hawkins quoted the comment that 'girls knew French better than the boys' and a few pages later the remark that girls failed at French — i.e., at translation (Hawkins, 1981). Hawkins, in 1981, saw no contradiction either. What history has recorded is the unsystematic 'slipshod chatter' of French conversation lessons in nineteenth-century girls' schools.

My focus on French may have been misleading: perusing the testimonies contained in the many volumes of the Taunton Commission, I read again and again the evidence of girls' superior performance and 'eagerness to learn'. One assistant commissioner found that they were better than boys in reading, spelling, geography and history; another, that they were better at arithmetic. Yet girls were believed to have done well only *because* of some extrinsic factor. Either they had 'a correct ear', 'quicker perception', 'greater aptitude'; or they were more mature than the boys; or had spent more time learning the subject, and more time at school.[12]

The Taunton Commission is a powerful illustration of the way girls' performance is construed. It was not located, like boys', in their intellect, it was not based, as Eynard and Walkerdine put it, 'on the same intellectual foundations as the performance of boys' (Eynard and Walkerdine, 1984, p. 4). As I argued earlier, this was not a conspiracy: the commissioners cannot be charged with having failed to 'recognize' the 'truth' deriving from the 'evidence': they saw, and reported, girls' performance. But the attribution of achievement requires a method for producing it. Education was defined as mental discipline produced by grammar-translation-parsing. Because girls' instruction was not based on these techniques, their achievement was simultaneously noticed and rendered insignificant, harmless, immaterial.

It is not surprising that the discovery of girls' superior performance did not have the force of a revelation for the assistant commissioners. What is surprising, however, is the tenacity of the mechanism by which girls' superior performance is repeatedly construed as insignificant at its point of insertion into the discourse on achievement. Deborah Thom, for example, quotes how Philip Vernon, 'the most prominent writer on intelligence testing' in the 1950s, explained why girls did better than boys at the intelligence and arithmetic groups tests as well as in English in the period 1940–50. 'Boys', he argued, 'were likely to have been more seriously affected by war-time relaxations of home discipline and upsets to schooling.' Girls' superior performance was not discussed. Caused by 'social factors', it was assumed to be only temporary. 'By the later 1950s,' the quote continues, 'boys had generally caught up in intelligence tests and regained their superiority in arithmetic' (Thom, 1987, pp. 138–9).

Following the Taunton Commission's findings that girls were able to learn the various subjects of education, girls finally (if briefly) had access to the same curriculum as boys. Only five years later, in 1873, Henry Maudsley's polemical article 'Sex in Mind' appeared in the *Fortnightly Review*.[13] Maudsley claimed that the energy required for intellectual exertion was subtracted from that required for menstruation.[14] Education was therefore debilitating girls' reproductive system and would make them sterile. Girls now became the object of a medical discourse about overwork and overstrain. Since girls could not regulate themselves — a female trait — they were bound to work 'too hard,' with dire consequences for motherhood and the nation. Maudsley's voice carried the authority of his position as physician. The anxieties he raised could not be ignored by the educational establishment. They are expressed most candidly in the section on sex-differences in texts promoting co-education published in the early twentieth century. One text thus contrasted each sex's response to schoolwork: 'the boy's breezy attitude to life . . . successfully secures him from morbid concentration on the acquisition of knowledge'; the girl is said to 'brood over her tasks and reproach herself her imperfections' (Grant and Hodgson, 1913, pp. 128–9). In 1923, the Board of Education institutionalized the difference: 'Boys have, as a rule, a habit of healthy idleness', while 'girls are much more conscientious' (Consultative Committee to the Board of Education, 1923, p. 61). Girls' high performance as pathology became an integral part of the educational discourse and was a determining factor in the differentiation of the curriculum according to sex.[15]

This anxiety was possibly, in part, a way of accounting for girls' superior attainment while protecting boys' potential, now that their overall performance could be compared. Thus, Bob Powell can be said to have been endorsing a long tradition when he attributed girls' success in French to their gender conditioning so that girls, both conditioned and compliant, accepted to do the repetitive and meaningless tasks required by the current language teaching methods. Boys, neither 'conditioned' nor docile, did not. Their lack of success was construed as a healthy rebellion against bad methods, leaving their potential for success intact (Powell, 1985, pp. 48, 62).

The initial question I raised in this paper was: Is there a space for the achieving girl? Perhaps the question ought to have been: Why does the fiction of the boy's potential continue to be sustained? The answer seems clear: While there is no space for the achieving girl, girls' achievement itself continues to create the space for the fiction of the boys' potential to be sustained.

Notes

1 This paper was written with the support of a Jean Monnet Fellowship at the European University Institute in Florence, Italy. I also thank the Gender Group at the EUI, Diemut Bubeck, Stella Tillyard and Phil Bevis for their criticisms and suggestions on various versions on the paper.

2 For example, in histories of language teaching: HAWKINS, E. (1981) *Modern Languages*, Cambridge, Cambridge University Press; KELLY, L.G. (1976) *25 Centuries of Language Teaching: 500 BC–1969*, Rowley, Mass., Newbury House; WATSON, J.F. (1971) *The Beginnings of the Teaching of Modern Languages in England*, [1909], Wakefield, S.R. Publishers. In general histories of education (where girls' education is discussed): BARNARD, H.C. (1969) *A History of English Education from 1760*, London, University of London Press; HANS, N. (1966) *New Trends in Education in the Eighteenth Century*, London, Routledge and Kegan Paul. In social histories of girls' education: AVERY, G. (1991) *The Best Type of Girl: A History of Girls' Independent Schools*, London, Deutsch; O'DAY, R. (1982) *Education and Society 1500–1800*, London, Longman; DYHOUSE, C. (1981) *Girls Growing Up in Late Victorian and Edwardian England*, London, Routledge and Kegan Paul; KAMM, J. (1965) *Hope Deferred: Girls' Education in English History*, London, Methuen. In literary histories: ARMSTRONG, N. (1987) *Desire and Domestic Fiction: A Political History of the Novel*, Oxford, Oxford University Press.

3 Symposium on Language Teaching, St Pauls' Girls' School, London, June 1987. Michael Buckby is a member of Eric Hawkins' language department at the University of York, and author of several popular French courses, for example *Action*. See my comments in COHEN, M. (1995) *French's 'Adulterous Charms': The Sexualisation and Gendering of French in England*, Modern Foreign Languages Academic Group, Occasional Paper No. 4, London, Institute of Education, 1995.

4 He is referring to the intervention of agencies such as the Equal Opportunities Commission or the Girls into Science Group (GIST).

5 My emphasis. Though maths is associated with abstraction, in the paper he presented at the Symposium, Michael Buckby pointed out that boys have been said to respond better to a 'more realistic, less theoretical approach' in language teaching.

6 French syntax followed the framework of Latin — which girls did not usually learn. This implied for example noun declension, such as 'le roi, du roi, au roi'.

7 As portrayed in 'The Governess', a moral tale written by Maria Edgeworth in *The Good Governess and Other Stories*, London, n.d. N. Hans also noted that 'almost every

exiled aristocrat . . . resorted to giving private lessons as a living', *New Trends*, p. 188. See also CLAPTON, G.T. and STEWART, W. (1929) *Les Etudes Françaises dans l'Enseignement en Grande-Bretagne*, Paris, Les Belles Lettres.

8   Bennett, *Strictures*, p. 107. More used almost the same words: the female mind, she wrote, is not 'capable of attaining so high a degree of perfection in science as the male', *Essays*, p. 6.

9   Taunton Commission, vol. 8, p. 401. See also the testimony of Charles Cassal, Professor of French Language and Literature at University College, vol. 5, p. 190, Question 10,760.

10 This consisted of translation from English into French, and from French into English, with grammatical questions. Taunton Commission.

11 By 1907, the Board of Education asserted that 'accurate knowledge [of a language] implies accuracy of pronunciation', *Memorandum on the Study of Languages*, London, p. 6.

12 Assistant Commissioner Bompas referred for example to girls' 'natural aptitude' for languages and to the fact that fluency was more important than accuracy, Taunton Commission, vol. 8, pp. 49, 53, 54; vol. 9, pp. 291, 292, 807, 811.

13 His views were similar to those of Edward Clarke of Harvard University, whose book, *A Fair Chance for Girls*, published in the USA in 1873, was very widely read.

14 The view that different parts of the body competed for energy resources was based on a finite energy model of the body current at the end of the nineteenth century. See SPENCER, H. (1966) 'Education: Intellectual, moral and physical', *The Works of Herbert Spencer*, vol. XVI, Otto Zeller, Osnabruck, p. 180.

15 See F. Hunt for a summary of the views held by Janet Campbell, medical officer at the Board of Education at the turn of the century, on the subject of overstrain.

References

(1696) *An Essay in Defense of the Female Sex*, London. (This essay has been variously attributed to Judith Drake or Mary Astell.)

BAMFORD T.W. (1967) *The Rise of the Public Schools: A Study of Boys' Public Boarding Schools in England and Wales from 1837 to the Present Day*, London, Nelson.

BARRELL, J. (1983) *English Literature in History 1730–1780: An Equal, Wide Survey*, London, Hutchinson.

BENNETT, J., (1787) *Strictures on Female Education*, London.

CHIROL, J.L. (1809) *An Enquiry into the Best System of Female Education or Boarding School and Home Education Attentively Considered*, London.

COBBE, F.P. (1862), 'Female education, and, how it would be affected by university examinations,' Paper read at the Social Science Congress, London.

COHEN. M. (1992a) 'A genealogy of conversation: Gender subjectivation and learning French in England,' PhD thesis, University of London.

COHEN, M. (1992b) 'The grand tour: Constructing the English gentleman in eighteenth century France', *History of Education*, 21(3), pp. 241–57.

CONSULTATIVE COMMITTEE TO THE BOARD OF EDUCATION (1923) *Report on the Differentiation of the Curriculum for Boys and Girls Respectively in Secondary Schools*, London.

DAY, T. (1789) *The History of Sandford and Merton*, London.

EYNARD, R. and WALKERDINE, V. (1984) *The Practice of Reason: Investigation into the*

Teaching and Learning of Mathematics, Vol. 2: Girls and Mathematics, London, University of London.

FAUCHON, J. (1751) *The French Tongue*, Cambridge.

FORDYCE, D. (1748) *Dialogues Concerning Education*, London.

HAWKINS, E. (1981) *Modern Languages in the Curriculum*, Cambridge, Cambridge University Press.

KELLY, A., WHYTE, A. and SMAIL, B. (1984) *Final Report of the Girls into Science and Technology Project*, Manchester, Manchester University Press.

LAINÉ, P. DE (1677) *The Princely Way to the French Tongue*, London.

LAQUEUR, T. (1990) *Making Sex: Body and Gender from the Greeks to Freud*, London, Harvard University Press.

LOCKE, J. (1989) *Some Thoughts Concerning Education*, in YOLTON, J.S. and YOLTON, J.W. (eds) Oxford, Clarendon Press.

MAUDSLEY, H. (1874) 'Sex in mind', *Fortnightly Review*, **15**, pp. 466–83.

MORE, H. (1811) *Strictures on the Modern System of Female Education*: Vols. 1 and 2, London.

MORE, H. (1785) *Essays on Various Subjects Principally Designed for Young Ladies*, London.

PORNY, M.A. (1796) *Practical French Grammar*, Dublin.

POWELL, B. (1985) *Boys, Girls and Languages in School*, London, CILT.

REPORT OF HER MAJESTY'S COMMISSIONERS APPOINTED TO INQUIRE INTO REVENUES AND MANAGEMENT OF CERTAIN COLLEGES AND SCHOOLS (1864) *Clarendon Commission*, 4 volumes, London.

REPORT FROM THE COMMISSIONERS, SCHOOLS INQUIRY COMMISSION (1868) *Taunton Commission*, 23 volumes, London.

ROTHBLATT, S. (1976) *Tradition and Change in English Liberal Education: An Essay in History and Culture*, London, Faber.

THOM, D. (1987) 'Better a teacher than a hairdresser?'; 'A mad passion for equality' or, 'Keeping Molly and Betty down', in HUNT, F. (ed.) *Lessons for Life: The Schooling of Girls and Women 1850–1950*, Oxford, Blackwell.

WALKERDINE, V. (1989) *Counting Girls Out*, London, Virago.

WEEKS, J. (1982) 'Foucault for Historians', *History Workshop Journal*, **14**, August, pp. 106–19.

11   A Socially Just Pedagogy for the Teaching of Mathematics

Leone Burton

The Story Begins — *What* Is Going On?

It was not until the 1970s in the USA that attention was given to differentiation in mathematics achievement by sex, led by the work of Elizabeth Fennema. (See, in particular, Fennema and Sherman, 1977; 1978; Maccoby and Jacklin, 1975.) The focus of this early work, which has been the first stage of activity in many different countries, was data gathering. Observations of apparent gender bias in rates of participation in mathematics course taking, as well as performance results on tests which were publicly administered or reported, led to attempts to answer the question: *What* is going on? Nel Noddings has called this the first of three generations of feminist research where women are seeking equality with men (see Hart, 1992).

Explanations for Gender Differences — *Where* and *When* Are They Observed?

Differences in participation depend upon circumstances, educational, but more generally social. In the USA, secondary school mathematics courses are optional so who opts and what are their outcomes are questions which have been addressed. Where mathematics is a compulsory subject, as for example in the UK, participation differences might be interpreted in terms of levels of achievement and, if it exists, subsequent 'streaming' or 'tracking' of students such that top and bottom streams are likely to be dominated by males (see Burton, 1986; 1990; 1994). In some countries, single-sex classes or schools have provided evidence on differences in achievement and experiences in classrooms, although it is not clear that these are simply related. Jan Harding (1983), amongst many other researchers, has suggested that the single-sex status of a school might not be as important to female achievement in science as other factors such as its teaching and organizational style. What is clear is that we cannot look at one without the others.

Work done on the impact of different assessment strategies demonstrates that gender is an indicative factor. Differences in performance have been recorded on multiple choice tests (see Anderson, 1989; Harding, 1983; Murphy, 1982) and unseen written paper and pencil examinations compared with classroom-based, pupil-driven project work called 'coursework' in the UK (see Bolger and Kellaghan,

1990; Goulding, 1992; Stobart, Elwood and Quinlan, 1992) and a range of innovative assessment strategies in the Netherlands (see de Lange, 1987) and Australia (see Forgasz, 1994, Chapter 3). Increasingly, evidence suggests that achievement data from so-called 'objective' tests, whether national, or international and comparative, provides only a very meagre picture of *who* achieves at *what* mathematics under *which* assessment regime. As Caroline Gipps and Patricia Murphy point out:

> Differences in achievement, the APU, NAEP and international surveys show, are related to differences in opportunity to learn to a large extent. Attitudes, APU studies have shown, also have an important effect on achievement ... the psycho-social variables affect how boys and girls come to view themselves, how they become viewed by others, how the subject is 'constructed' and how achievement within it is defined. (1994, p. 264)

How class, 'race', age and experience act together with sex to produce the recorded differences is often left unquestioned (although Reyes and Stanic, 1986, offer one rare analysis).

The social stereotyping of classrooms has been the focus for many studies. Eileen Byrne sums up her conclusions on science classroom domination by males:

1 No study shows females to have had generally more interactions with or help from teachers than male peers; a substantial body of research shows males to be favoured in interactions and receipt of positive help; but a significant number of studies show no sex differences. We cannot conclude that all co-educational settings are lethal to girls.
2 There is consistently strong evidence that males are cued, prompted or questioned more than females in co-educational classrooms.
3 Twenty-nine studies show no sex differences in positive teacher–student interactions, twenty-six demonstrate that males receive more positive interactions, and seven show that females are favoured.
4 More studies show that males receive both more praise and more criticism than females, but many studies show no sex differences. But the more soundly constructed and reported research shows that it is frequently a small minority of boys in a classroom who dominate, are disruptive and receive more attention — not all, or most, boys. (1993, p. 183)

The links between these classroom experiences and the mathematical diet which the learners have been offered, and between this diet and societal and academic views on the nature of mathematics, remain largely unexplored.

Why?

The observation of these differences has not provided an explanation for why they exist. Researchers have tended to offer explanatory models. For example, Laurie

Reyes and George Stanic (1986) draw attention to five factors: societal influences; school mathematics curricula; teacher attitudes; student attitudes and achievement-related behaviours; and classroom processes. Gilah Leder's (1990) model differentiates environmental variables, emerging through society (the law, media, peers, cultural expectations), the home (parents, siblings and socio-economic status) and the school (teachers, organization, curriculum, textbooks, assessment, peers) from learner-related variables, including cognitive development (particularly in relation to spatial and verbal abilities) and beliefs (confidence, utility of mathematics, sex-role congruency and motivation — particularly fear of success, attributional style, learned helplessness, mastery orientation and performance following failure) (Leder, 1990, p. 15). Elizabeth Fennema and Penny Peterson's model of Autonomous Learning Behaviors (1985) identifies behaviours necessary to independent pursuit of high-cognitive-level activities in mathematics. Females are perceived as exhibiting fewer such behaviours. A fourth model, Academic Choice, has been developed by Eccles, Adler, Futterman, Goff, Kaczala, Meece and Midgley (1985) and associates the taking of particular academic decisions with their perceived value and expectations of success, themselves a function of environmental and learning-related factors.

Rosie Walden and Valerie Walkerdine draw attention to the 'important circularity or circulation between evaluation, practice and performance: no simple analysis of cause and effect will sufficiently explain this complexity' (1985, p. 81). They point to the devaluation of girls' performance in spite of success and to the manner in which classroom practices interact with power and knowledge relations to produce gendered effects on learning. In particular they argue that 'the practices of mathematics teaching relate to procedural rules' (1985, p. 84):

> If there are considerable pressures specifically on girls to behave well and responsibly, and to work hard, it may well prove more than they can bear to break rules. Firstly, they would risk exclusion by others for naughtiness and secondly they would require the confidence to challenge the teacher. Such contradictions place them in a difficult, if not impossible position. (Walden and Walkerdine, 1985, p. 84)

I argue below that pedagogical practices of this kind are not only implicated in gendered pupil behaviour but also in distorting mathematics as a discipline. Too often, the mathematics syllabus, with its related classroom practices, remains unquestioned in studies which investigate gender differences in learning the subject.

More recently, the striving for 'equity' has become a feature of many approaches to social justice (see Rogers and Kaiser, 1995). Elizabeth Fennema defines three different kinds of equity in learning mathematics: equity as equal educational opportunity; equity as equal educational treatment; and equity as equal educational outcome (1990, p. 2). As she points out:

> ... gender differences in mathematics have been studied intensively for about 20 years. In many countries, the incentive for such study has been

the recognition that lack of mathematical learning and negative beliefs about themselves and mathematics hampers females from achieving equity with males. (1990, p. 1)

Bennison, Wilkinson, Fennema, Masemann and Peterson (1984) identify this approach, consistent with Nel Noddings' first generation thinking, as a deficit approach to equity since it appears to assume that pupils react similarly to education and that deficits on entry should be compensated so that outputs are comparable. They describe three other approaches in the literature: the assimilationist, in which learning characteristics are similar despite sex; the pluralistic, which acknowledges diversity in learner characteristics; and the social justice, which evokes fair treatment across similarities and differences. Some of these fit comfortably into Nel Noddings' second generation in which female qualities are identified as particular and impetus to be accepted as the same as males is rejected. Some research into classroom experiences falls into this category.

Nel Noddings' third generation of feminism involves a critique of the first two so that new approaches can be expected to take advantage of what has been done as well as address what still needs to be done. In this spirit, Eileen Byrne is critical of the power distribution in society, in particular with respect to the ways in which myths are created about women and science to excuse those in power from accepting responsibility and taking action.

It has been predominantly the men in schooling, science and industry who have created masculine images and attached them territorially to disciplines and occupations. It is primarily male students who define the presence of women students in a discipline as normal or abnormal, who assert exclusive territoriality, and who dominate hands-on experimentation with equipment and computers to exclude girls and women. It is the men in the leadership of higher education who (albeit often unconsciously) act as mentors to male but not to female students, to the great advantage of the former. In essence, *the problem with girls and women is boys and men,* and these issues are factors which critically affect the learning environment of girls and women. (Byrne, 1993, p. 6, original emphasis)

Eileen Byrne draws our attention to the manner in which stereotyping structures behaviour, expectations and consequently outcomes of schooling. Like everything else, including mathematics the discipline, stereotyping is a social construct which leads to the question: what could mathematics be like if it were not sexually stereotyped and, consequently, in what ways would the pupils' experiences of mathematics be changed? Walden and Walkerdine (1985) emphasize the complexity and shifting nature of living in an educational world where your positionings can be neither 'unambiguous nor gender-neutral' (p. 102).

I have recently queried the status and derivation of knowledge and knowing in mathematics from a gender perspective (see Burton, 1995). This would seem to fall into the category of third generation thinking. Such epistemological inquiries are distinct from the former focus on learning and teaching although clearly contribute to an understanding of mathematics classrooms.

Moving Towards a Socially Just Mathematics

I recognize that seeking answers to the questions What? Where? When? is a necessary part of information gathering. However, the central question is Why? to which we have, and might only ever have, a partial answer. Nonetheless, in recognizing both the personal and the social loss that failure to engage with mathematics ensures, I have no option but to pursue the implications of a non-socially just mathematics education. Two issues seem to me to be central. One is the way in which mathematical knowledge is understood and the impact that this has on how it is taught, learned and assessed. The other is related to this — and is the pervasiveness of homogeneity within mathematics and its pedagogy.

For me, and many others, mathematics is not an 'objective' discipline, the contents of which are 'discovered'. Nor is it 'invented' by outstanding individuals who write history. Mathematics is socially constructed, and consequently socially responsive.

> All sciences and technologies . . . arise out of people's historical experiences and as such carry values and cultures of the people concerned. Science is not neutral. It carries the values of the society where it evolved. Nor is technology just products or hardware. Technology is a combination of objects, techniques and skills, contributing to a process which is only meaningful in a social and cultural context. (Byanyima, 1994, p. 59)

Despite this, the myth of mathematical 'objectivity' continues to pervade and, in the process, to distort perspectives on the discipline as well as on how it is taught and learned.

> A recent study at the University of Sydney (Crawford *et al.*, in press) demonstrated that about three-quarters of first year university mathematics students have a fragmented view of the mathematics they studied at school, regarding it primarily as a collection of numbers, rules, and formulae. Over 90% of the students with this view had adopted a surface approach to learning mathematics at school, concentrating on rote memorisation and practising lots of examples. By the end of the first year of university studies, these students were tending to achieve at a lower level than those who had a more cohesive view of mathematics and had adopted a deeper approach to studying it. (Coupland, 1994, p. 3)

Kathryn Crawford and her colleagues draw attention, in particular, to the ways in which conceptions of the discipline *and* approaches to studying it are 'constituted dynamically in relation to each other. That is, students' conceptions of mathematics are formed by their approaches to learning it and also form their approaches' (1994, p. 343). As a consequence, they conclude that 'university teachers need to consider not only the content of their course, but also how the students conceive of what that content is about and how they go about learning it' (1994, p. 344).

Mathematicians are highly respected as contributors to social progress. As such, it is not surprising to find that they themselves reflect the power structures within a society. Almost always male, middle class and often white, what they contribute to whose definition of 'progress' is rarely unpicked, although sociologists of science are more and more frequently offering insights. 'The mathematician explicitly creates a mathematical reality very much the way a Tolkien or a Frank Herbert creates a fantasy world. And the mathematician, like the science fiction or fantasy writer, carries over into his or her new world certain preferences, taken for granted notions, etc.' (Restivo, 1992, p. 167). This mathematical reality supports the pervading directions of the times. In doing so, it privileges mathematicians which, in part, explains how they can, simultaneously, act as 'the brains (and to some extent the hands too) of political, military, and economic interests ... and ... members of a professional community whose autonomy guarantees them certain perquisites, especially a certain degree of apparent independence in the pursuit of their teaching and research goals' (Restivo, 1992, pp. 171–2). It is not a big step from this to a definition of a school syllabus which reflects particular social imperatives, a classroom which permits a pedagogical reality which is unbalanced in the experiences offered to girls and boys, and an assessment system which protects the interests of one group over the rest of the society.

To generate a mathematical experience which is more likely to be socially just, I believe that we have to relocate authority from the discipline to the learner. Instead of trying to ensure that learners acquire powerful and effective knowledge and techniques in mathematics, it would be more appropriate, in my view, to validate the knowledge and skills that learners bring with them into the classroom as we exercise our professional insights in challenging, stretching, informing and questioning learners. Instead of allowing pupils to be 'grossly underestimated' (van den Heuvel-Panhuizen, 1990, p. 76), we need to accord them respect for what they know and can do and place them in a context where they generate, compare and negotiate meanings amongst themselves. In this way not only would we be working on the educative function of the classroom, but we would also be nearer to the potential multiple meanings present in the mathematics.

Heterogeneous is an apt description of any mathematics classroom. It is heterogeneous in terms of potential mathematics and its interpretations, but also in terms of the learners. With Eileen Byrne, I recognize the need for serious work to be done in schools with the boys whose socialization most surely supports the very aspects of epistemology and pedagogy in mathematics that ensures the perpetuation of exclusion. But I also see the need to celebrate the diversity to be found in classrooms rather than attempting to turn all pupils into carbon copies. The clash of meanings, interpretations, styles of learning, methods, representations, knowledges, uses for mathematics — all of these, and others I have failed to mention — underpin a rich culture in every classroom. This culture is most frequently denied as attempts are made to match every pupil against a desired 'norm'. There is content which must only be taught at a particular time, no matter what the pupils know and can do. There are methods which must be acquired with no more reason than that they are the methods which the teacher or text find comfortable. The literature abounds with examples of pupils whose mathematical discomfort can be traced to attempts to 'learn' competing methods with no comprehension for why they should work. The many different ways in which pupils understand and can make sense of some mathematics provides a teacher with a rich source of investigation for that mathematics which underlies these differences. Far from denying heterogeneity, in a socially just classroom it becomes a cause for celebration.

It seems to me that we have constructed educational systems which fail to serve many, if not most, of the communities within our world-wide society. What we are learning to identify, by focusing on the pedagogical experiences of girls, are the fallacies which support a system which is unsatisfactory for all but a very small number of privileged people.

> We are now beginning to understand some of our past curriculum practices in mathematics which have disadvantaged groups of students. For example, many of the contexts in which mathematical concepts were developed, applied and assessed were more likely to be central in the lives of boys than in the lives of girls. In some subtle and other not-so-subtle ways, the message was communicated to girls and boys that mathematics was of more relevance in the lives of adult men than adult women. In a similar way, the mathematics curriculum has tended to emphasise values and concerns which are more middle class than working class, and to draw on experiences which are more relevant to children of Anglo-Celtic descent. (Australian Education Council, 1991, p. 9)

By shifting our understandings about the nature of mathematics, together with the conditions which support its learning, we might move towards developing a pedagogy which is flexible, responsive and effective. Either we continue to operate with the myth of mathematics consisting of 'objective' knowledge, independent of the communities who have derived and work with it, or we begin to engage with the difficulties of mathematics as a human construct. 'What is clearly lost in the process of objectivation, even more if it is accompanied by reductionism, is what I want to call the human factor, the relationship between people and mathematics' (Fischer, 1992, p. 10).

What is gained, in shifting from an 'objective' to a 'relative' view of the derivation and use of mathematical knowledge, is access to a growing body of work which emphasizes 'relationships rather than properties' (Turkle and Papert, 1993, p. 50) and consequently enables the mathematics and its pedagogical practices to come together into a coherent, and mutually supporting, whole. The important shift is one from knowledge control by authorities external to the student, to the development of a community of voices with whom authority, and indeed authorship,[1] rest. In a primary, or secondary, classroom this would consist of those children whose work was responsible for the derivation of some new understanding. Part of their responsibility is to address the parameters within which their understanding is valid and to build bridges from their own to 'public' understanding. This kind of coherence has been achieved in other disciplinary areas, such as English. Mathematics, and to some extent the sciences, stand out as still clinging to an epistemology of 'truths' which validates a transmissive educational mode. This is despite a world- and discipline-wide shift in learning theories to embrace some form of constructivism. However,

> ... we should not be so concerned with motivating everyone to do well in mathematics but, rather, with giving everyone a chance to find out whether he or she is interested in doing mathematics. To reject the study of mathematics as a free and well-informed decision is the choice of a responsible citizen; to plod through it docilely is a slavelike response, and to drop out without reflective consideration is to lose an opportunity both to learn mathematics and to learn about oneself. (Noddings, 1993, p. 156)

When provided with such an opportunity to exercise discretion and choice, pupils offer teachers evidence of how responsibly they can do so, how positively their learning is affected and the substantial difference made to their understanding and achievement. Under such conditions, not only can we begin to see an outline of a socially just pedagogy, but the possibility of that pedagogy supporting learning appropriate, in their own eyes, to the many different communities which make up nation states and, ultimately, a world society.

Note

1 I am indebted to Hilary Povey for this description of the meaning of mathematical empowerment.

References

ANDERSON, J. (1989) 'Sex-related differences on objective tests among undergraduates', *Educational Studies in Mathematics*, **20**, pp. 165–77.
AUSTRALIAN EDUCATION COUNCIL (1991) *A National Statement on Mathematics for Australian Schools*, Carlton, Vic., Curriculum Corporation.
BENNISON, A., WILKINSON, L.C., FENNEMA, E., MASEMANN, V. and PETERSON, P. (1984) 'Equity or equality: What shall it be?', in FENNEMA, E. and AYER, M.J. (eds) *Women and Education: Equity or Equality?* Berkeley, Calif., McCutchan Publishing Corporation.
BOLGER, N. and KELLAGHAN, T. (1990) 'Method of measurement and gender differences in scholastic achievement', *Journal of Educational Measurement*, **27**(2), pp. 165–74.
BURTON, L. (ed.) (1986) *Girls Into Maths Can Go*, Eastbourne, E. Sussex, Holt, Rinehart & Winston.

BURTON, L. (ed.) (1990) *Gender and Mathematics: An International Perspective*, London, Cassell.

BURTON, L. (ed.) (1994) *Who Counts? Mathematics Achievement in Europe*, Stoke-on-Trent, Trentham.

BURTON, L. (1995) 'Moving towards a feminist epistemology of mathematics', *Educational Studies in Mathematics*, **28**(3), pp. 1–17.

BYANYIMA, W. (1994) 'The role of women engineers in developing countries', *RSA Journal*, **142**(5454), pp. 57–66.

BYRNE, E. (1993) *Women and Science: The Snark Syndrome*, London, Falmer Press.

COUPLAND, M. (1994) 'When you ask different questions, be prepared for different answers', Paper presented to the Australian Bridging Mathematics Network Conference, Sydney, July.

CRAWFORD, K., GORDON, S., NICHOLAS, J. and PROSSER, M. (1994) 'Conceptions of mathematics and how it is learned: The perspectives of students entering university', *Learning and Instruction*, **5**(4), pp. 331–45.

DE LANGE, J. (1987) *Mathematics: Insight and Meaning*, Utrecht, OW & OC.

ECCLES, J., ADLER, T.F., FUTTERMAN, R., GOFF, S.B., KACZALA, C.M., MEECE, J.L. and MIDGLEY, C. (1985) 'Self-perceptions, task perceptions, socializing influences, and the decision to enrol in mathematics', in CHIPMAN, S.F., BRUSH, L.R. and WILSON, D.M. (eds) *Women and Mathematics: Balancing the Equation*, Hillsdale, N.J., Lawrence Erlbaum.

FENNEMA, E. (1990) 'Justice, equity, and mathematics education', in LEDER, G. and FENNEMA, E. (eds) *Mathematics and Gender*, New York, Teachers College Press.

FENNEMA, E. and PETERSON, P. (1985) 'Autonomous learning behavior: A possible explanation of gender-related differences in mathematics', in WILKINSON, L.C. and MARRETT, C.B. (eds) *Gender Related Differences in Classroom Interaction*, London, Academic Press.

FENNEMA, E. and SHERMAN, J.A. (1977) 'Sex-related differences in mathematics achievement, spatial visualization and affective factors', *American Educational Research Journal*, **14**, pp. 51–71.

FENNEMA, E. and SHERMAN, J.A. (1978) 'Sex-related differences in mathematics achievement, spatial visualization and affective factors: A further study', *Journal for Research in Mathematics Education*, **9**, pp. 189–203.

FISCHER, R. (1992) 'The "human factor" in pure and in applied mathematics', *For the learning of mathematics*, **12**(3), pp. 9–18.

FORGASZ, H. (1994) *Society and Gender Equity in Mathematics Education*, Geelong, Vic., Australia, Deakin University Press.

GIPPS, C. and MURPHY, P. (1994) *A Fair Test? Assessment, Achievement and Equity*, Milton Keynes, Open University Press.

GOULDING, M. (1992) 'Let's hear it for the girls', *Times Educational Supplement*, February 21, pp. 38–9.

HARDING, J. (1983) *Switched Off: The Science Education of Girls*, York, Longman for Schools Council.

HART, L.R. (1992) 'Two generations of feminist thinking', *Journal for Research in Mathematics Education*, **23**(1), pp. 79–83.

LEDER, G. (1990) 'Gender differences in mathematics', in LEDER, G. and FENNEMA, E. (eds) *Mathematics and Gender*, New York, Teachers College Press.

LYNCH, K., CLOSE, S. and OLDHAM, E. (1994) 'The Republic of Ireland', in BURTON, L. (ed.) *Who Counts? Assessing Mathematics in Europe*, Stoke-on-Trent, Trentham Books.

MACCOBY, E.E. and JACKLIN, C.N. (1975) *The Psychology of Sex Differences*, Oxford, Oxford University Press.

MURPHY, R.J.L. (1982) 'Sex differences in objective test performance', *British Journal of Educational Psychology*, **52**, pp. 213–19.

NODDINGS, N. (1993) 'Politicizing the mathematics classroom', in RESTIVO, S., VAN BENDEGEM, J.P. and FISCHER, R. (eds) *Math Worlds*, Albany, State University of New York Press.

RESTIVO, S. (1992) *Mathematics in Society and History*, Dordrecht, Kluwer Academic Publishers.

REYES, L. and STANIC, G. (1986) 'Race, sex, socioeconomic status and mathematics', *Journal for Research in Mathematics Education*, **19**(1), pp. 26–43.

ROGERS, P. and KAISER, G. (1995) *Equity in Mathematics Education: Influences of Feminism and Culture*, London, Falmer Press.

STOBART, G., ELWOOD, J. and QUINLAN, M. (1992) 'Gender bias in examinations: How equal are the opportunities?', *British Educational Research Journal*, **18**(3), pp. 261–76.

TURKLE, S. and PAPERT, S. (1993) 'Styles and voices', *For the learning of mathematics*, **13**(1), pp. 49–52.

VAN DEN HEUVEL-PANHUIZEN, M. (1990) 'Realistic arithmetic/mathematics instruction and tests', in GRAVEMEIJER, K., VAN DEN HEUVEL, M. and STREEFLAND, L. (eds) *Contexts Free Productions, Tests and Geometry in Realistic Mathematics Education*, State University of Utrecht, The Netherlands, OW & OC.

WALDEN, R. and WALKERDINE, V. (1985) *Girls and Mathematics: From Primary to Secondary Schooling*, Bedford Way Paper No. 24, London, Institute of Education.

III

Interventions

12   Redefining Achievement

Gaell M. Hildebrand

Assessment is frequently the engine that drives pedagogy and the curriculum. Hence, assessment has the power to endorse or to challenge the ways in which fields of knowledge, school subjects and understandings about learning and about gender are constructed through the delivered curriculum. This chapter shows how gender, science and assessment are all built on a fundamental set of dualistic concepts associated with power and privilege.

I argue that the gendered achievement profiles which exist in many subject areas of the school curriculum have been partly built up by assessment techniques which have privileged some masculine constructions of knowledge and ways of knowing (Belenky, Clinchy, Goldberger and Tarule, 1986). By this, I mean that those bodies of knowledge, skills and experiences that have been more highly regarded within many subject areas, indeed more richly rewarded within our culture, have been traditionally defined as those associated with hegemonic masculinity (Connell, 1987).

> To invoke the importance of pedagogy is to raise questions not simply about
> how students learn but also how educators . . . construct the ideological
> and political positions from which they speak. (Henry Giroux, 1992, p. 81)

To uncritically perpetuate practices implicitly underpinned by an ideology that privileges the masculine is to jeopardize work towards effective pedagogies for all students. This chapter goes on to tell the story of a challenge, and a consequent re-definition of achievement in physics, undertaken in the state of Victoria, Australia. By transforming assessment practices it became possible to change both what was taught and how it was taught and this has altered the historical achievement profile so that girls have suddenly become very good at physics.

As this chapter draws on changes to physics it seems appropriate to use two visual metaphors to illuminate interactions between constructions of gender, science and assessment. The metaphor used for the process of looking, is that of sets of spectacles or 'frames of reference', whilst the scene being observed, pedagogy, is like a 'multi-faceted diamond'.

Three Feminist Frames of Reference

If we look at the lens itself — through which we view the world — we can see that the very specifications of that lens (the paradigm) shapes how we are able to interpret what we see. If we are a conservative male physicist from a high status university then the lens through which we view changes which impact on gendered achievement profiles will be quite different from the lens used by a liberal feminist physics teacher and different again from that of a Turkish-Australian girl from a working-class area who chooses to study physics. The lens of the frame of reference, or standpoint, from which we construct our perspective will colour, focus and shape the version of reality we interpret.

Three useful frames of reference, which can be looked through to revision issues and possibilities, and which are loosely parallel to the three tiers of feminism described by Julia Kristeva (1981), are linked with the differing perspectives of liberal, radical and post-structural feminisms. There are times when operating from an 'access and equity', or liberal feminist, frame of reference will generate an appropriate response to a particular issue. At other times, or for other people, the radical feminist approach of valuing women's experiences and approaches to learning can be more appropriate. A post-structural feminist perspective, where dualisms and discourses are used as sources of critique and challenge (Weedon, 1987) and multiple subjectivities are acknowledged, is a third frame of reference to employ. In deliberately using a different frame of reference we can observe dimensions to which we were previously blind.

A Multi-faceted Diamond — The Scene Under Observation

Like a brilliant-cut diamond, there are many facets to pedagogy. A schema of facets which indicates the multiple factors that interact to construct gender in schools includes: the life experiences that students and teachers bring to school; the organizational structure of the curriculum; the constructions of knowledge inferred by the way the curriculum is devised and taught; the degree of social context and theory–practice links in the content of the curriculum and the integration or separateness of its components; resource availability and utilization; the power differential associated with communication and decision-making patterns; the degree of integration of work education into the curriculum; the physical environment; the frames of reference used by teachers and their ideologies about pedagogy; the ways sex-based harassment is dealt with; and assessment practices (see Allard, Cooper, Hildebrand and Wealands, 1995, pp. 81–2).

Also, the setting (or school context) within which the diamond (pedagogy) sits enhances or dulls it; the light (outcomes of intervention ideas) reflected out of the facets will depend on the circumstances (students and curriculum); particular facets will produce a rainbow of coloured light (be a focus of energy and attention) at different times; and the more brilliant light (better outcomes of intervention) will come from a multi-faceted diamond (multiple sites of action). This chapter only highlights the facet of pedagogy related to assessment-linked profiles of achievement and recognizes that no single dimension, alone, can transform the outcomes of schooling for all girls.

Linking Constructions of Gender, Science and Assessment

It is now widely acknowledged that gender is a social construction and that understandings about 'appropriate' versions of femininity and masculinity 'vary across different cultures; are informed by social class; and change over time both individually and collectively. They can be endorsed, negotiated, challenged, reconstructed and resisted on an individual and collective basis' (Allard et al., 1995, p. 21). Whilst we have some agency to choose or resist gendered practices and codes, particular constructions of masculinity and femininity are accorded higher status.

Hegemonic masculinity is the 'culturally exalted' version (Connell, 1995, p. 77) that is publicly admired, rewarded and aligned with hierarchical power, objectivity and competition. 'Emphasized femininity', an unequal opposite (Connell, 1987, p. 183) is the traditional form where there is a compliance with the subordination of women to men, a focus on physical appearance and a narrow range of life options centred on the private realm. Emphasized femininity is aligned with emotions, subjectivity and cooperation and its asymmetry with hegemonic masculinity is played out in both institutional and interpersonal spheres.

There have been many critiques of science that have revealed its social construction (e.g., Sandra Harding, 1986; 1991; Bleier, 1986; Tuana, 1989; Rosser, 1990; Lemke, 1990; Thomas, 1990; Code, 1991; Kirkup and Keller, 1992; Shepherd, 1993). These analyses have revealed the masculine bias in the practice of science, in the image of science and in the way dimensions have been selected for inclusion in school studies. Many factors in the dominant paradigm of 'good' or 'real' science, aligned with those defining hegemonic masculinity, are so deeply embedded in our understanding of what science is that they have become invisible. The branch of science called physics, has been socially constructed this century to link directly with power and control through militarism, and thus more closely to hegemonic masculinity than most other fields.

The status accorded science has influenced knowledge production and authentication in many other fields and the positivist paradigm, which science has created and cultivated, has, in turn, strongly influenced research methodologies across many fields, including educational evaluation (e.g., Lincoln and Guba, 1985; Lather, 1991; Reinharz, 1992; Cambourne and Turbill, 1994). Through its grounding in psychometrics, with its heavy reliance on positivism, assessment of achievement in education is also a construction linked directly to hegemonic masculinity.

All three of those constructions — gender, science and assessment — are based on a common set of asymmetrical dualisms where the concepts in the left column are valorized, taken as the norm and used as the measuring stick of worth.

abstract	holistic
quantitative	qualitative
outcomes	process
competition	cooperation
objective	subjective
knower/mind	knowable/nature

| hierarchical | multiplicity |
| value-free | value-laden |

The concepts in the right column are associated with the 'other' (not the norm), are of lower status and represent a supposed inherent inferiority. These asymmetrical dualisms thus create implicit assumptions about (hegemonic) masculinity and (emphasized) femininity; about science and non-science; and about so-called 'good' and 'bad' assessment practices. Looking through the first frame of reference, that of liberal feminism, the task would be seen as fixing the girls, science and assessment practices so that they fit the conceptual model built by the left column, taking the malestream as the standard. Looking through the second frame of reference there would be a focus on the strengths of the feminine (right) column and an attempt to bring that into a symmetrical balance with the left column — equally valuing both concepts in each dualism. Using the third frame of reference, that of post-structural feminism, a contestation of these dualisms would ask provocative questions such as: Are they dualisms or continua? Whose purpose is being served by the valuing of one set over the other? Would the multiple truths generated by using 'both/and', rather than 'either/or', produce a more acceptable reality?

I will now explore how these dualistic concepts distort science and assessment. The dysfunctional processes and outcomes arising from the dualisms that produce hegemonic masculinity and emphasized femininity permeate this chapter and this book and will not be further discussed here.

Gendered Dualisms and Science

The image of science is strongly gendered and aligned with hegemonic masculinity (e.g., S. Harding, 1986; Tuana, 1989; Thomas, 1990; Kirkup and Keller, 1992) but this mystique is a distortion of the concealed reality which frequently accommodates concepts from the right column of dualisms. Linda Shepherd (1993) reveals the existing, but heavily veiled, feminine face of science that includes:

- knower/known interactivity: Heisenberg's uncertainty principle in physics (you cannot measure both the momentum and the position of an electron because in measuring one you interfere with the other) along with Chaos theory reveal the interdependence of the observer and the observed;
- subjectivity: feelings are significant when research is motivated by love and desire and where hunches come before hypotheses;
- multiplicity: a web of interactivity exists between and among phenomena;
- cooperation: the importance of care and empathy in sustaining an harmoniously working research team;
- intuition: another way of knowing which is valued in highly esteemed, speculative scientists; and
- holistic: seeing the relatedness of ideas through interdisciplinary studies

which show larger patterns, challenges underlying values like simplicity, abstraction and reductionism in science.

She argues that only when science integrates the feminine with the masculine, and replaces either/or conceptualizations with both/and thinking, will there be an acceptance of the complexities of reality.

Yet, as Jay Lemke (1990) shows, school science further distorts the field of science by:

- generating a catalogue of 'facts' for students to recall, and presenting science as if it is possible to produce absolutely objective truths;
- pretending that a scientific method exists — even when we know that real scientists, funded through politically driven sources, seek evidence through using the research techniques that will most likely provide what they desire;
- teaching with the expectation that only a 'super-intelligent elite' can ever understand science's concepts, and thus teaching most students to trust powerful technocrats and politicians who make decisions based on scientific, and hence unchallengeable, evidence.

Gendered Dualisms and Assessment

For each pair of gendered dualisms, looking through the third, post-structural feminist, frame of reference, and challenging the implicit assumptions underpinning the dominant paradigm, can lead to a more equitable definition of assessment.

Reward Holistic Learning
(both abstract and holistic)

Assessment has largely valued abstraction and analysis over holism, relatedness and synthesis, particularly in science where the real world is often seen as too 'messy' and complex to illustrate with neat mathematical models. If our assessment procedures only examine students' ability to suspend what they know about their world, while they blindly manipulate formulae or regurgitate information, then we ought not be disappointed when students fail to apply concepts to the real world.

> Ensuring science and technology are considered in their social context with assessment of their benefits for the environment and human beings may be the most important change that can be made in science teaching for all people, both male and female. (Rosser, 1990, p. 72)

Anecdotal evidence suggests that many girls do prefer to learn concepts situated in their social context rather than abstract, fragment and compartmentalize their understandings. To value holistic learning, assessment tasks ought to be set within a social context and reward synthesis of ideas where theory and practice are clearly interconnected.

Encourage Qualitative Understanding
(both quantitative and qualitative)

Testing the authenticity of a proposed assessment task by checking whether it seeks evidence of qualitative understanding, rather than simplistic manipulation of quantitative data, is one way to recognize that many girls strive for this. For example:

> My curiosity simply did not extend to the quantitative solution. I just didn't care to figure out how much. I was more concerned with the 'why' and the 'how'. I wanted verbal explanations with formulae and computations only as a secondary aid. Becoming capable at problem solving was not a major goal of mine. But it was a major goal of the course. (Michelle in Tobias, 1990, p. 40)

There is considerable anecdotal evidence from teachers which suggests that girls are more troubled by a feeling that they 'don't really understand', an important factor in their withdrawal from subjects/courses. Boys appear to be less concerned by this and will continue a subject when their grades indicate that they 'know enough'. If we value deep understanding then we should build it into our assessment processes. Also, many students, frequently girls, want feedback on their work that goes beyond a quantitative grade. As assessors of student achievement we need to provide extended oral and written feedback that helpfully indicates areas of success whilst specifying ways in which the quality of work can be improved.

The Means Effects the Ends
(both outcomes and process)

A narrow focus on outcomes, products and endpoints leads to a tendency to rely on summative assessment modes that are too late for student action. Judgments should be based on a rich record of student progress that is built up over time and which gives due recognition to an ongoing commitment to attend to their work, as many girls do. Paul Black concluded from his comprehensive review of formative and summative assessment that 'good formative assessment can be a powerful tool for raising standards of learning' (Black, 1993, p. 84) and that it ought to be 'embedded' into, and support, learning programs.

Integrated formative assessment has the potential to monitor a range of competencies meeting all the course goals. Many courses aim to cover multiple aspects of learning, such as: knowledge; skills (including communication, thinking, problem solving and social); values (including attitudes, ethics and morality); and metacognition (learning how to learn). Those things that are easiest to summatively assess should not take precedence over those tasks which encourage the full spectrum of intended learning outcomes. Unless all curriculum goals are built into the assessment processes they will be read as unimportant; for example, many girls do well in research and cooperation which are not valued as they are not assessed.

Intrinsic Motivation Through Explicit Guidelines
(both competition and cooperation)

The extent to which we have indoctrinated our students into competitive assessment can be gauged by the number of times we hear the question: 'What did you get?' Assuming that all students are extrinsically motivated by competition pitches the students in a battle against the assessor and against each other. Norm-referencing builds in competition through its winners and losers system, but assessment 'should be essentially criterion-based rather than norm-based' (Australian Curriculum Studies Association, 1992, p. 37) to create the possibility of all students being winners.

Many teachers argue that girls are more focused than boys in trying to 'guess what's in the teacher's head' and in their desire to meet expectations. Also, those students whose learning is undermined by blatant competition, with its frequently shifting or unclear benchmarks, can be highly motivated by the intrinsic pleasure in understanding and in completing assigned tasks. To remove some of the guesswork and competition, teachers and assessors could cooperate with students by providing clear guidelines and criteria for evaluating student work. Also, many girls like to work jointly on projects and assessment processes should provide ways to reward such cooperation which, after all, is highly valued in the workplace.

Explicit guidelines specifying achievable, yet challenging, work requirements and assessment tasks should include:

- topic or theme of the learning area;
- process tasks or work requirements;
- product types and formats to be completed;
- product extent or length;
- time-lines (including interim and final dates);
- the criteria which will be used to judge the quality of work; and
- the weighting of each task in the overall assessment package.

Recognizing the Pervasiveness of Subjectivity
(both objective and subjective)

Traditional assessment practices, drawn from and located within the positivist, psychometric paradigm, have assumed that it is possible to build in total objectivity, as well as validity and reliability, and that these are simply technical problems for assessment designers. Lorraine Code (1991) asks 'Out of whose subjectivity has this ideal [of objectivity] grown? . . . whose values does it represent?' (p. 70). She contends that we can be neither value-free nor value-neutral because of the subjectivities interwoven in the knower/assessor such as: their location in history and in specific social and linguistic contexts; their racial, ethnic, political, class, age and other identifications; their enthusiasms, desires, commitments and interests; and hence their value system (Code, 1991, p. 46).

Thus, '... all assessment is a human and subjective process' (Withers and Cornish, 1984, p. 3). Even so-called objective tests (usually multiple choice items) involve subjective judgments about: the choice of language used; the contexts deemed appropriate; the distinctions used to define the distracters; and in the selection process used to determine which items to include on a particular test.

The questions that must be raised concerning objectivity and lack of precision have been masked by an over-reliance on numbers as represented by 'marks'. This association of numbers with truth, a feature of the positivist paradigm, has been critiqued by many researchers (e.g., Lather, 1991; Code, 1991; Shepard, 1993; Gipps, 1994; Cambourne and Turbill, 1994; Gipps and Murphy, 1994) and assessment must be recognized as an 'inexact process which involves varying degrees of errors both in measurement and in judgement' (Australian Curriculum Studies Association, 1992, p. 38).

Responsive evaluation, which recognizes the complexities of constructivism and assessment of performance, would rather ask questions about trustworthiness and confirmability than objectivity; about credibility and applicability than validity; about dependability and authenticity than reliability (Guba and Lincoln, 1989; Cambourne and Turbill, 1994; Gipps, 1994). In this model of assessment, the teacher, as a human being, is seen as a responsive instrument, able to detect many nuances of performance from multiple sources, which no external, objective test can ever perceive. Compare this with the dominant paradigm that values external assessors over the teacher, testing over work requirements, written over oral, quantitative over qualitative, print over other text forms, and so on.

The Knower Is Not Distanced from the Known
(both knower/mind and knowable/nature)

Within both science and assessment, the dominant view is that the knower is distanced from the known, the relationship between the two 'is that between a subject and an object, radically divided, which is to say, no worldly relation' (Keller, 1985, p. 79). Hence, a corollary of the objectivity/subjectivity dualism is the desired separateness of the learner from the material they learn, and from the observer judging their learning. Yet we know that learners are not distanced from, but are formed by, their learnings, and that observers/assessors make decisions based on their understandings of what learners ought to be able to know and do.

Yet, students arrive in our classrooms with prior understandings and conceptions that have been constructed over time through their unique interactions with their world. This is the basis of constructivism (Fensham, Gunstone and White, 1994) which is currently producing a revolutionary paradigm shift (Kuhn, 1970) in the teaching and learning of science. Girls and boys, as groups, generally have had very different out-of-school experiences which result in their school learning beginning at different starting points. Sometimes these prior experiences are assumed for all students and assessed accordingly, even though one group such as girls, may have had little opportunity to learn the skills, or about the phenomena, outside the classroom.

Because of prior experiences and constructions, assessment practices have commonly given an unfair advantage to particular groups of boys. For example it has been shown (e.g., R. Murphy, 1982; J. Harding, 1981, 1991; Blum and Azencot, 1986; P. Murphy, 1989; Gipps and Murphy, 1994) that many girls tend to do better in assessment tasks composed of structured and extended response questions, whereas boys, as a group, will do better if questions are posed in a multiple choice format. Thus, designing a test exclusively using a single question format would advantage one sex over the other, simply by the question format.

Additionally, students bring gendered interpretations of their own success or failure. For example, causal attribution studies (e.g., Ames, 1984) show that when girls do well they often attribute their success to external factors such as luck, a good teacher or easy assessment tasks, whereas many boys attribute their success to internal factors such as innate ability. Constructions of gender also interact with self-perceptions of performance when boys tend to over-estimate strongly in mathematics, less so in English, while girls tend to be closer in estimation of their actual performance, but to under-estimate more in mathematics than in English (Bornbolt, Goodnow and Cooney, 1994). Reliance upon any one particular assessment device, such as testing or self-assessment, will thus be open to the possibility of systematic discrimination.

Teachers also come to the classroom with prior experiences, assumptions and values with which they are constructing understandings about what they see as 'acceptable' feminine or masculine behaviours, for themselves and their students. They also bring gendered perspectives on the way knowledge itself is organized. For example, when Spear investigated teacher blind-marking of student work — the same pieces of work were arbitrarily labelled as being done by either sex — she found that '. . . work attributed to a boy received higher mean ratings than the same work attributed to a girl' (Spear, 1984, p. 373).

Valerie Walkerdine goes further when she finds that 'girls are still considered lacking when they perform well, and boys are still taken to possess something when they perform poorly' (Walkerdine, 1989, p. 4). Walkerdine found that the girls often performed at least as well as the boys, but the teacher's interpretation of their work was very different and unintentionally influenced by the student's sex. Teachers' gendered assumptions can be displayed in many ways such as when capacity judgments are based on future promise for boys/men and past performance for girls/women.

Thus three ways that assessment processes could privilege the masculine are: assuming equivalent out-of-school experiences for both sexes; assuming assessment techniques are gender-neutral forms of knowledge demonstration; being blind to gendered expectations that teachers bring to school. Recognizing these interactions between the knower and the known would suggest that more equitable assessment would use: negotiation of starting points for learning; multiple data collection techniques; and a variety of assessors.

Multiplicity Provides Higher Quality Information
(both hierarchical and multiplicity)

Introducing multiplicity and variety into assessment practices can break down some past hierarchical patterns where particular assessors and types of data are considered more important than others. For example, a variety of assessors, including the student, a peer, the teacher, an external authority, can provide moderated authenticity where there is an in-built checking mechanism against the gendered constructions of each assessor and the reports from each are all valued and moderated against each other. Students have a high level of personal engagement with their learning when it involves a degree of self-management (Hildebrand, 1991), although teachers need to remember that many girls under-rate themselves whilst many boys over-rate themselves (see Bornbolt, Goodnow and Cooney, 1994). Responsibility for learning can be shared and assessment is not done to students but done with students.

A second way that assessment can value multiplicity is to draw on a number of data-collection devices which provide students with a range of opportunities to show what they know and can do. In establishing a fair and equitable assessment process that removes systematic disadvantage, a variety of assessment techniques are utilized and seen to be of equivalent importance and validity. Data-collection devices may include: annotated timelines, concept maps, scientific posters, briefing papers, working models, investigative projects, simulation games, case-study reports, photographic sets, audio/video tapes, observation checklists, journals, interview records, portfolios of class work, critiques of models/metaphors, anthropomorphic stories, etc. Similarly the products that are the outcomes of student assessment tasks should also vary in extent or length and in their forms: oral, written, visual, etc. This ensures that no particular mode is privileged over another.

Ideally, the students would negotiate the particular assessment formats that are used to assess their work. Negotiation means a 'letting-go' for the teacher of some of their power and control of the learning/teaching/assessment system.

Valuing Values
(always value-driven)

There can be no such thing as value-free gender constructions, value-free science or value-free assessment. Our values are implicit in the choices we take. The simple act of choosing to prioritize abstraction, objectivity, quantitative approaches, hierarchies, competition, outcomes, and to desire freedom from values, is making a value judgment. Constructing assessment practices upon such a biased set of concepts generates gendered achievement profiles and cannot be valid, that is 'equally fair and sound for all groups' (Gipps and Murphy, 1994, p. 2).

'It is through our assessment that we communicate to our pupils those things which we most value' (Clarke, 1988, preface). If we value: qualitative understanding; formative assessment to improve learning; synthesis and holistic learning in a social context; explicit criterion referenced assessment; cooperation; variety in sources of evidence upon which to make judgments; and variety in assessors; then we must avoid either/or conceptualizations and give value to **both** dimensions when considering the gendered dualisms which underpin our assumptions.

A Change Opportunity: The Victorian Certificate of Education

The Victorian Certificate of Education (VCE) had a long gestation, and painful birth, but has been in place now for over three years. It is used as a schooling completion credential and as a means for competitive selection into limited tertiary and workforce places. It is thus a critical and publicly accountable stage of schooling and the potential for a paradigm shift at this transition phase appeared more possible than at any other phase of schooling. The story of redefining achievement in the VCE is interwoven with the action of the McClintock Collective, a network of educators in (McClintockers) Victoria, who have been working together on gender and science education since 1983.

The McClintock Collective took up the development of the new VCE courses as a site of political action and a vehicle of challenge to the conventional paradigms of science, gender, curriculum, teaching and assessment. There was a deliberate, yet subtle and effective, campaign of the Collective to be represented on all committees having an influence on the new courses. Thus people with a strong background in gender and science became instrumental as course writers, advisers, textbook authors and monitoring committee members. These women struggled as outsiders who were often seen as (and were) infiltrators attacking the hegemonic paradigm of the 'real' science curriculum and assessment: a paradigm that had served the interests and needs of males well across generations.

The changes to the VCE began with a widely held conceptualization that centred on a notion of 'gender-inclusive' curriculum (see Sue Lewis's chapter in this volume). Like pedagogy, the multi-faceted diamond, a gender-inclusive curriculum includes all those dimensions that contribute to the construction of gender in schools — providing ways for teachers and students to actively engage in negotiating, resisting and interrupting processes that assume gendered boundaries. Whilst the new VCE could not alter all possible facets, the feminist advocates on the committees did focus on the curriculum, pedagogical and assessment practices that were under the locus of control of the central accrediting body.

I do not want to give the impression that all McClintock Collective members work from a single frame of reference. Any changes which will facilitate access into science, and equity within its current construction, are considered worth pursuing. The majority of McClintock members are actively working towards creating a new construction of science, at least in schools, in which

> ... the values traditionally ascribed to women are given a positive and central place ... and there is a ... belief that the quality of life has priority over economics or efficiency or 'rational' planning ... [where] scientific activities ... reflect a balance with and not an exploitation of nature ... [and there is] an alteration of world view ... from the analytical fragmentation of modern science to a holistic view in which social, ethical and moral considerations are unquestionably involved ... [where the] scientific community [is] based on co-operation, social accountability and accessibility and ... a respect for and equal valuations of different forms of knowledge, including the 'irrational' and the 'subjective'. (Manthorpe, 1982, p. 75)

The development of 'McClintock' approaches can be seen as radical feminist: celebrating the feminine and women's ways of relating to the world — the second frame of reference. The concept of a 'pedagogy for girls in science' has become a major focus of the work of the McClintock Collective. Whilst it is still unclear what feminist pedagogies might be, speculation on them is becoming more focused as a central concern of feminist educators (e.g., Shrewsbury, 1987; Roy and Schen, 1987; Gore, 1992; Luke and Gore, 1992) and influencing the work of the Collective, which has largely grown out of the 'personally relevant pedagogy' (Hollingsworth, 1992, p. 384) of its active members. Many strategies and practices (e.g., Gianello, 1988; Lewis and Davies, 1988; Hildebrand, 1989) have been advocated in extensive professional development programs as a means of making a new version of science accessible to girls. McClintock members using this frame of reference value highly: multiplicity, synthesis, holistic learning, qualitative understandings, cooperation, intuition and subjectivity and try to build these into assessment practices.

McClintockers work on multiple fronts to deconstruct the restrictive and dysfunctional dualities of gender and of science. In that sense, a glimpse through the third frame of reference, that of post-structural feminism, is available within the Collective's work. Most McClintock Collective work has centred on the 'development and "dissemination" of alternative forms of non-discriminatory and empowering pedagogy, which may challenge schooling's complicity in reproducing gendered inequality' (Kenway and Modra, 1992, p. 141). The manifest ways of doing this, and the frames of reference of the viewers/actors, are in a constant state of flux and are characterized by their very fluidity and flexibility. While very little direct analysis on the impact of this work has been undertaken, the publicly available outcomes of the new VCE are, at least to some degree, a measure of the success of the Collective's work.

Lessons from Physics

While the pattern of assessment practices outlined here are common to all the VCE subjects, physics is chosen as a barometer because of its extreme position as the most 'masculine' of the science subjects, at least in terms of participation and achievement.

The opportunity that the introduction of the VCE created, provided two catalysts to speed up the implementation of the McClintock pedagogies. Firstly, there was much professional development time for VCE teachers that the Collective organized. Secondly, the study designs incorporated assessment approaches, advocated by McClintockers, which necessitated changed classroom practice. Thus we were able to build in integrated, formative work requirements and assessment tasks, with explicit guidelines and criteria, which valued qualitative understanding, assessed all course goals, were set in a real world context, required a variety of types of data sources, and used different assessors. As an example of new data sources illustrates: teachers who had never considered the 'visual' as a legitimate way of summarizing learning were required to ask students to submit a poster on their research (in physics) or produce a concept map of ideas (in chemistry).

A distinguishing feature of the new assessment processes is the embedding of continuous formative assessment into the learning program through a two-tier system of 'work requirements' and 'common assessment tasks'.

Work Requirements

The work requirements are designed so that by doing these tasks at specified points during their studies, students would, almost necessarily, learn the intended curriculum. In physics, each of the four semester units studied consecutively across the last two years of secondary school, require the satisfactory completion of six or seven work requirements. Students are given specific guidelines on how to complete the work requirements which '. . . place emphasis on the interaction between physics, technology and society' (VCAB, 1991a, p. 3), with some flexibility to negotiate real world contexts to match students' interests. The new course values different learning approaches, and thus the work requirements provide a range of ways for students to show evidence of their learning. For physics these include: posters; case studies; student-designed practical investigations; research projects; and files of changing ideas.

Common Assessment Tasks (CATs)

Common Assessment Tasks (CATs) are the basis for judging the quality of the work done in the last two semester units, usually undertaken in the final year of school. All students across the state doing a subject do the same three or four CATs and it is these grades that are used for tertiary selection. In every subject, at least one CAT is assessed internally by the teacher and at least one is assessed under test conditions by external examiners. For physics, CAT 1 and CAT 3 are teacher assessed and CAT 2 and CAT 4 have been completed under test conditions. Also the CATs are spread across the year, so that student achievement is monitored at different points and on qualitatively different types of tasks. For physics, the two teacher-assessed CATs are an extended practical investigation due in May and a research project due in September. The two external test CATs are a comprehension and application test at the end of first semester (June) and an explanation and modelling test at the end of second semester (November).

Social Context

The tenet that theory and practice should be explicitly linked and therefore learning of curriculum skills and content must be set within a social context became one of the strongest guiding principles for all VCE courses in all fields. The physics curriculum 'is based on the view that learning takes place in the same way physics itself is practised: in a social setting, trying to make sense of problems which matter to people' (VCAB, 1991b, p. 8). As assessment issues are central to the whole curriculum design process, they also incorporate physics in its social context. This is a distinguishing feature of the new physics course. One of several specified contexts must be selected as the vehicle for learning the central physics ideas. For example, the contexts for the topic Movement are 'Aristotle to Newton and beyond', 'On your own two feet' or 'Wheels'. For Nuclear Energy they are 'Development of the bomb' or 'Nuclear power'. Students, individually or in small groups, choose a context for each topic that is of personal interest.

The new assessment tasks are situated within a context which provides 'a point of connection with students' intuitive perceptions of the world' and which uses 'students' ideas as starting points for learning experiences' (VCAB, 1991b, p. 11). For example, the research project, or CAT 3, must be presented in the form of a scientific poster, and the specifications say that it must examine one of the following:

- everyday situations (e.g., sailing, bicycles, ballet)
- physics related to other forms of knowledge (e.g., biophysics, geophysics)
- issues of social or personal importance (e.g., safe road design ...)
- development of ideas in physics ... making reference to social and/or technological implications
- technological applications (e.g., lasers, jogging shoes, electrocardiograms)
- the work of physics related laboratories, industries or professions (e.g., ... designing and manufacturing sound systems, physiotherapy) ... (VCAB, 1991a, p. 35).

That is the research project must be physics set in a social context.

Even in the externally assessed test CATs, social context is important. For example, students can choose to study Sound through one of three contexts: 'speaking and hearing', 'music making' or 'recording and reproduction'. The test questions are arranged so that students select the set for their chosen context. The following items appeared in equivalent sets, accompanied by relevant diagrams and related questions, in the second CAT, the comprehension and application test, for 1993:

11. If the dinosaur had vocal cords in its throat which generated sound over a wide range of frequencies, explain the effect of the **length** of the nasal cavity on the sound emitted by the dinosaur. (Board of Studies, 1994, p. 9)

11. A wide range of frequencies is emitted by the sound-tube toy, but only a few frequencies are audible in the emitted sound. Explain the effect of the **length** of the tube on the sound emitted by the sound-toy. (Board of Studies, 1994, p. 11)

11. The background noise in the museum is made up of a wide range of frequencies, but only a few frequencies are audible in the sound emitted by the set of tubes. Explain the effect of the **lengths** of the tubes on the sound emitted by the sound exhibit. (Board of Studies, 1994, p. 13)

These items also show how qualitative understanding is now also expected, alongside the quantitative questions (now shown here), for each set.

Criteria

Each Common Assessment Task has clearly stated criteria that are used to distinguish between achievement levels, and hence determine the grades on a scale. Three of the nine criteria for CAT 3, the research project, have been: 'The extent to which the report ... explains and discusses concepts through: synthesis and integration of relevant ideas; communication of the understanding gained; identification of related technological and social issues' (VCAB, 1991a, p. 38). Not only are the desired skills specified but they include ones which have not previously been valued in physics marking schemes in Victoria.

New Teaching Approaches

An example of one new teaching strategy used in the Nuclear Energy topic is 'a role play of people at a public meeting held to decide if a nuclear power plant should be built in the area' (VCAB, 1991b, p. 15). Teachers now also used brainstorming, creative writing, jigsaw techniques for cooperative learning and other McClintock Collective teaching strategies (see Gianello, 1988; Lewis and Davis, 1988; Hildebrand, 1989). In the Year 11 topic, Nuclear Energy, those students who have chosen the context, 'Development of the bomb', can complete one work requirement with a briefing paper that responds to a focus statement such as: 'A group of students from your school is visiting Japan on a study tour, and one of the places they will go to is Hiroshima. They ask your physics class to prepare some information for them on the physics of the atomic bomb and its effect on people' (VCAB, 1991b, p. 24). Many other focus statements for this briefing could also be negotiated with students. The quite radical shift in the conceptualization of learning, built by the work requirement system, means it is no longer possible to teach physics in the old ways.

Assessment Matching the Course Aims

Three of the ten aims in the new physics course are:

- become aware of physics as a particular way of knowing about the world which interacts with the setting, both social and personal, within which it is pursued;
- understand some of the practical applications of physics in present and past technologies, examining the social usefulness of such technologies as well as problems associated with them;
- develop the capacity and confidence to communicate their knowledge of physics effectively (VCAB, 1991a, pp. 1–2).

A genuine attempt has been made to ensure that these are built into the assessment program: the first is highlighted in the work requirement where students have to build a file of changing ideas about light and matter; the second in the research project (CAT 3); and the third in both the extended investigation, (CAT 1) and in CAT 3.

How Has the Assessment Transformed the Curriculum?

The actual physics curriculum statement is not markedly different from that in other similar level courses. It includes: light, heat, sound, electricity, electronics, motion, forces, structures, radioactivity and nuclear energy, etc. The difference here is that the integrated assessment processes created by the formative work requirement system necessitated new approaches to curriculum implementation. For example, in order to enable students to satisfactorily complete the prescribed work requirements, teachers were required to base all the central ideas in real world contexts. Also, as the work requirements demand a range of learning tasks, a broader repertoire of teaching strategies must be employed. The guidelines and criteria are explicit for each assessment task which now value qualitative understanding as well as quantitative ability, and, together, the assessment tasks cover all the course goals. These changes have meant that girls experience a physics curriculum which is very different from that of the old course.

Has this Redefinition Altered Outcomes for Girls?

Looking through the first frame of reference — access and equity or liberal feminist — an analysis of girls' participation and achievement in physics can now be undertaken.

Participation of Girls in Physics

In 1970, 16 per cent of all girls and 49 per cent of all boys studied physics in Year 12. (See Note 1). By 1985 this had declined to 8.9 per cent of girls and 34.8 per cent of boys. This pattern continued for the final years of the old course. But for 1992, the first year of the full new course, the proportion of girls increased with 9.4 per cent of all girls choosing the new physics course while the corresponding figure for boys continued to decline to 28 per cent of all boys. By 1994, physics educators were concerned about the overall drop in physics participation, down to only 7.8 per cent of all girls and 26.9 per cent of all boys; but this occurred at a time when the overall retention rate had increased, suggesting that the extra students who now stayed on to complete their VCE were not taking up physics. Many more boys than girls are studying physics, but the new course has made a small shift in the participation of girls given that 53 per cent of the cohort are now girls.

Achievement

Satisfactory completion or passing grades

All items on the external exam of the old physics course (which dominated the grading system through being used as a tool to moderate teacher assessments) were dichotomous response: either multiple choice or numerical answers. Between 1970 and 1985, the percentage pass rate for boys in Year 12 physics was consistently greater than 3 points above that for girls. When the research clearly suggested that this examination format might discriminate against girls, some extended response and social context questions were included in the papers at the end of the 1980s. This did have an impact on the overall success rate of girls so that by 1991 (the last year of the old course) 87 per cent of girls and 84 per cent of boys passed.

With the new VCE physics in 1992, 97 per cent of girls satisfactorily completed, whilst 94 per cent of boys did so. This 10 per cent increase in one year suggests that the work requirement system is more accessible and equitable for all students. These completion rates have remained stable for both girls and boys.

Mean scores

Because of the way data was retained for the years before the introduction of the VCE it is not possible to calculate mean scores for girls and boys on the old course. However, it is reasonable to assume, because of the outstanding degree of difference in passing rates and A-grades awarded, that mean scores for boys were greater than those for girls. Cox and Nash (1994) have analysed the first two years of VCE physics data and show that the mean scores of girls have been better than those for boys at statistically significant levels ($p = 0.01$). They further analysed the data for each Common Assessment Task (CAT) and found that girls' mean scores were greater than those for boys at statistically significant levels across all CATs (p = 0.001 for all but the first test, CAT 2, in 1993 where p = 0.01).

Excellence

Another dramatic impact of the changes in physics is in the sudden capacity of girls to demonstrate 'excellence' as is evidenced in the awarding of A-grades.

Under the old system, from 1970 to 1985, the percentage of boys awarded A-grades was consistently more than 8 points higher than the corresponding figure for girls. For example in 1985, 11.5 per cent of girls were awarded A-grades whilst 20.7 per cent of boys were so rewarded. This gave fuel to the argument that girls just could not do physics very well. With the advent of the new extended response and social context questions in the exam, the margin narrowed so that by 1991, the last year of the old course, there was only a difference of 4 points, still in favour of boys (14.3 per cent of girls and 18.1 per cent of boys received A-grades).

The remarkable change in the A-grades awarded for the Common Assessment Tasks in the VCE (see Table 12.1) indicates that suddenly girls have become excellent at physics!

As can be seen in Table 12.1, girls achieved excellent results in all the physics CATs and were only outperformed, in the awarding of A-grades, by the boys in CAT 2 (1993 and 1994) and CAT 4 (only in 1993), although girls' mean scores overall, and on each CAT, were still better than those for boys (Cox and Nash, 1994). In particular, for the two internally (teacher) assessed physics CATs (CAT 1 and CAT 3), the girls' results were considerably better than those for the boys with almost half the girls being awarded A-grades for their research projects (CAT 3). Whilst both sexes improved on these two internally assessed CATs in 1993, the gap between them widened from 1992 to 1993 and remained fairly steady for 1994. This confirms the work done in western Australia by Rennie and Parker (1991), which showed that girls achieved better results on internal assessments than did boys.

The changes in assessment practices have led to an educationally important transformation in girls' experience of, and success in, the physics curriculum. The data suggests that the assessment processes are now more equitable: girls are a very select group and it ought to be expected that they would outperform boys. Girls' mean scores were greater than those for boys in all but two Common Assessment Tasks — the two test CATs in chemistry — across all five science subjects (Cox and Nash, 1994); and, over the full range of forty-four studies within the VCE, girls consistently outperformed boys. Looking through the first frame of reference, liberal feminist, it would seem that the changes to the VCE have been good for girls.

Why Do Girls Achieve Better Grades with the VCE?

I recorded the following reactions, which were given by unidentified science teachers at the workshop on 'CATs and Sex' run by Peter Cox and Mary Nash (Cox and

Table 12.1   Excellence defined by A-grades in VCE physics

Common Assessment Task (CAT)	Girls awarded A-grades (%)	Boys awarded A-grades (%)	Diff (G–B) (%)	Mode of assessment
CAT 1				
1992	27	19	8	internal
1993	40	26	14	experimental
1994	44	29	15	investigation
CAT 2				
1992	17	17	0	external exam
1993	15	17	–2	comprehension
1994	15	17	–2	and application
CAT 3				
1992	36	28	8	internal
1993	44	30	14	research project
1994	43	29	14	
CAT 4				
1992	18	16	2	external exam
1993	15	16	–1	explanation and
1994	16	15	1	modelling

Nash, 1994), in response to: 'Why do girls do better, especially on the teacher-assessed CATs?'

> Girls choose physics, but boys get told to do it.
>
> Girls are a more select group, ability-wise.
>
> Girls are more careful and they read the assessment criteria.
>
> Girls ask the teacher what the criteria mean.
>
> Girls put in a draft and get feedback.
>
> Boys tend to be 'slap-dash' in their submissions.

Some of these answers reflect a view through the second frame of reference, that of radical feminism, extolling the qualities which young women bring to their study of physics. One of the physics curriculum specialists (Firkin, 1993) places much of the credit for the shift in achievement profiles to the style of assessment which 'does seem to allow girls to show what they know and what they can do much better than the old system'. She also suggests that the first physics CAT, the internally assessed, extended investigation, has a confidence boosting effect for girls which continues into the test CATs. Firkin stresses that the course itself is no less rigorous or difficult.

Girls apparently do '. . . respond better to science if more co-operative and interactive modes of learning . . . [are] part of the pedagogy' (Tobias, 1990, p. 70). While there are grounds for celebration, a number of concerns remain.

Good for All Girls?

Using the first (access and equity or liberal feminist) and the second (valuing female qualities or radical feminist) frames of reference these changed assessment practices could be said to have been good for girls. But looking through the third, post-structural feminist, frame of reference we see the need to recognize the many differences within the broad category 'girls' and see that the interactions based on socio-economic factors and ethnicity, at least, challenge claims that all is well.

Some research, (e.g., Jones, 1989; Wyn, 1990) suggests that girls from lower socio-economic backgrounds actively resist pedagogical and assessment practices based on 'interpretation, exposition and independent work' (Jones, 1989, p. 29), precisely those practices which are now being given greater status. Teese, Charlton and Polesel (1994) clearly show that not all girls are doing well in the new VCE. Their data shows that both in enrolment patterns and achievement levels, girls from low socio-economic areas are well behind girls from areas with higher proportions of the population having tertiary qualifications and higher status occupations. For example: the 1992 participation rate of girls in physics for the working-class north-west region of Melbourne was less than 7 per cent compared to 12 per cent of VCE girls in the more affluent inner-eastern region. The differences are even more dramatic when achievement is considered: in 1992, less than 14 per cent of girls from the north-west region gained high grades (defined as in the top 20 per cent) whereas 39 per cent of girls who lived in the inner-eastern region did so (Teese *et al.*, 1994).

Other evidence also suggests that some girls suffer pressure and trauma caused by teachers who expect girls to live up to the prejudices that their teachers have of them as belonging to particular ethnic categories. For example, Chinese-Australian girls who do not like, and are not highly competent at, mathematics and science are treated negatively by many teachers who believe they should fit an unrealistic stereotypical pattern (Fan, 1994).

The current curriculum and assessment changes are obviously not broad enough in scope to ensure effective pedagogies for all girls and all boys. A way forward might be to build in more negotiation of curriculum content and assessment processes, within broad parameters, which maintain 'public credibility' (Gipps, 1994, p. 173) in the entire credentialling process, whilst allowing for differences in interest, learning styles and preferred assessment modes to cater for distinct groups of students.

Two Steps Forward, One Step Back

During 1994, a General Achievement Test (GAT), basically a conventional 'aptitude' test, was introduced and all teacher-assessed CATs are now moderated by it. The GAT creates several educational concerns: the presumption that external ('content-free') tests are more valid than teacher assessments; the validity of assuming that performance on qualitatively different types of tasks can be compared; the degree of inclusivity of the GAT for ethnicity, race and socio-economic factors as well as for gender; the performance differences on the GAT which are driven by the format chosen (predominantly multiple choice); and the removal of the powerful professional development experiences which occurred while teachers shared ideas during their previous Verification Days which had been used to moderate teacher assessments.

Girls have done very well on the internal, teacher-assessed tasks. However, changes to the physics study design from 1995 mean the deletion of CAT 3 (in an effort to reduce student workload only three CATs remain for each subject), the very CAT which allowed girls to shine! (Remember almost half of girls were awarded A-grades in the research project.) This means that from 1995, two thirds of the physics result will come from test CATs, whereas previously the new course had half the final assessment derived from teacher-assessed CATs. Another change, from 1995, which is expected to be detrimental to girls, is the removal of the obligation for teachers to present all learning within a social context and the subsequent optional place of context in the test CATs. That is, physics could now go back to 'a point mass moved at 3m/s across a frictionless surface . . .' A cynic might comment that the men, back in power on the physics committee, have taken the opportunity to re-assert their dominant paradigm of assessment which privileges boys.

Conclusions

Consistent with the arguments at the beginning of this chapter, McClintockers have been able to make considerable shifts in the balance within each pair of gendered dualisms which underpin assessment. Unlike tertiary physics courses, VCE physics now presents scientific knowledge not as an objective or universal truth, but as a social construction grounded in our complex world. There is now a firm commitment to multiplicity as a way of resolving some subjectivity issues and a recognition that assessment is a value-laden activity. The struggle to do this was never easy. Despite these shifts, the following dualisms are still evident in the new physics course:

abstract	holistic
quantitative	qualitative
outcomes	process
competition	cooperation
knower/mind	knowable/nature

Whilst both columns are now recognized as having something to offer the study of physics, the term on the left is still given a higher status over its partner. There is much to be done before these dualisms are fully challenged as the ideological foundation of assessment (or for that matter, gender and science), but even the small shifts that were possible have interrupted previous performance patterns.

As Connell *et al.* (1992) state, 'assessment practices are not technical devices which are socially neutral, but social techniques that have social consequences'

(p. 23). By selecting particular assessment tasks and techniques we are giving clear messages to students about what is valued as knowledge and which ways of learning are rewarded. To premise our choices on an ideology which privileges the masculine is to build a fundamentally flawed system which will produce gendered achievement profiles. In working towards effective pedagogies for all students we must look through the post-structural feminist frame of reference to deconstruct and redefine the implicit gendered dualisms which act as powerful stabilizers of current paradigms.

Notes

Statistics in this paper came from: VCAB, 1992, 1993; VBOS, 1994; Hildebrand, 1987; Firkin, 1993, unless attributed to other sources.
VBOS is the Victorian Board of Studies (established 1993).
VCAB was the Victorian Curriculum and Assessment Board.
VCE is the Victorian Certificate of Education.
CAT is a Common Assessment Task.
GAT is the General Achievement Test.

References

ALLARD, A., COOPER, M., HILDEBRAND, G. and WEALANDS, E. (1995) *STAGES — Steps Towards Addressing Gender in Educational Settings*, Carlton, Vic., Curriculum Corporation.
AMES, C. (1984) 'Achievement attributions and self-instructions under competitive and individualistic goal structures', *Journal of Educational Psychology*, **76**(3), pp. 478–87.
AUSTRALIAN CURRICULUM STUDIES ASSOCIATION (1992), 'Principles of assessment', *Curriculum Perspectives*, June.
BELENKY, M.F., CLINCHY, B.M., GOLDBERGER, N.R. and TARULE, J.M. (1986) *Women's Ways of Knowing: The Development of Self, Voice and Mind*, New York, Basic Books.
BLACK, P. (1993) 'Formative and summative assessment by teachers', *Studies in Science Education*, **21**, pp. 49–97.
BLEIER, R. (1986) *Feminist Approaches to Science*, New York, Pergamon Press.
BLUM, A. and AZENCOT, M. (1986) 'Multiple-choice versus equivalent essay questions in a national examination', *European Journal of Science Education*, **8**(2), pp. 225–8.
BOARD OF STUDIES (1994) *VCE Official Sample CATs — Physics*, North Blackburn, Vic., Collins Dove.
BORNBOLT, L., GOODNOW, J. and COONEY, G. (1994) 'Influences of gender stereotypes on adolescents' perceptions of their own achievement', *American Educational Research Journal*, **31**(3), pp. 675–92.
CAMBOURNE, B. and TURBILL, J. (1994) *Responsive Evaluation*, Armadale, Vic., Eleanor Curtain.
CLARKE, D. (1988) *Assessment Alternatives in Mathematics*, Canberra, Curriculum Corporation.
CODE, L. (1991) *What Can She Know? Feminist Theory and the Construction of Knowledge*, Ithaca, Cornell University Press.
CONNELL, R.W. (1987) *Gender and Power*, Sydney, Allen and Unwin.

CONNELL, R.W. (1995) *Masculinities*, St Leonards, NSW, Allen and Unwin.

CONNELL, R.W., JOHNSTON, K. and WHITE V. (1992) *Measuring Up*, Canberra, Australian Curriculum Studies Association monograph.

COX, P. and NASH, M. (1994) 'CATs and sex: Gender differences in the VCE science subjects', Paper presented at the annual conference of the Science Teachers' Association of Victoria (STAVCON), Melbourne, November.

FAN, C. (1994) 'Academic adjustment of Chinese immigrant girls in Australia,' Paper presented at the International Congress on School Effectiveness and Improvement (ICSEI), Melbourne, January.

FENSHAM, P., GUNSTONE, R. and WHITE, R. (1994) *The Content of Science — A Constructivist Approach to Teaching and Learning*, London, Falmer Press.

FIRKIN, J. (1993) Curriculum Officer, VCAB, Personal communication via fax and telephone, January.

GIANELLO, L. (ed.) (1988) *Getting into Gear: Gender-Inclusive Teaching Strategies in Science*, Canberra, Curriculum Development Centre.

GIPPS, C. (1994) *Beyond Testing — Towards a Theory of Educational Assessment*, London, Falmer Press.

GIPPS, C. and MURPHY, P. (1994) *A Fair Test? Assessment, Achievement and Equity*, Buckingham, Open University Press.

GIROUX, H. (1992) *Border Crossings — Cultural Workers and the Politics of Education*, New York, Routledge.

GORE, J. (1992) *The Struggle for Pedagogies*, New York, Routledge.

GUBA, E. and LINCOLN, Y. (1989) *Fourth Generation Evaluation*, London, Sage.

HARDING, J. (1981) 'Sex differences in science examinations', in KELLY, A. (ed.) *The Missing Half*, Manchester, Manchester University Press.

HARDING, J. (1991) 'Can assessment be gender fair?', Paper presented to Schools Programs Division, Melbourne, August.

HARDING, S. (1986) *The Science Question in Feminism*, Buckingham, Open University Press.

HARDING, S. (1991) *Whose Science? Whose Knowledge? Thinking from Women's Lives*, Buckingham, Open University Press.

HILDEBRAND, G.M. (1987) 'Girls and the career relevance of science', Unpublished MEd thesis, Monash University.

HILDEBRAND, G.M. (1989) 'Creating a gender-inclusive science education', *Australian Science Teachers Journal*, **35**(3), pp. 7–16.

HILDEBRAND, G.M. (1991) 'Student managed assessment', *Australian Science Teachers' Journal*, **37**(4), pp. 19–24.

HOLLINGSWORTH, S. (1992) 'Learning to teach through collaborative conversation: A feminist approach', *American Educational Research Journal*, **29**(2), pp. 373–404.

JONES, A. (1989) 'The cultural production of classroom practice', *British Journal of Sociology of Education*, **10**(1), pp. 19–31.

KELLER, E.F. (1985) *Reflections on Gender and Science*, New Haven, Yale University Press.

KENWAY, J. and MODRA, H. (1992) 'Feminist pedagogy and emancipatory possibilities', in LUKE, C. and GORE, J. (eds) *Feminisms and Critical Pedagogy*, New York, Routledge.

KIRKUP, G. and KELLER, L.S. (1992) *Inventing Women — Science, Technology and Gender*, Cambridge, Polity Press.

KRISTEVA, J. (1981) 'Women's time', *Signs*, **7**(1), pp. 13–35.

KUHN, T. (1970) *The Structure of Scientific Revolutions*, Chicago, University of Chicago Press.

LATHER, P. (1991) *Getting Smart — Feminist Research and Pedagogy within the Postmodern*, New York, Routledge.

LEMKE, J. (1990) *Talking Science — Language, Learning and Values*, Norwood, Ablex.

LEWIS, S. and DAVIES, A. (1988) *Gender Equity in Mathematics and Science*, Canberra, Curriculum Development Centre.

LINCOLN, Y. and GUBA, E. (1985) *Naturalistic Inquiry*, Newbury Park, Sage Publications.

LUKE, C. and GORE, J. (1992) *Feminisms and Critical Pedagogy*, New York, Routledge.

MANTHORPE, C. (1982) 'Men's science, women's science or science? Some issues related to the study of girls' science education', *Studies in Science Education*, **9**, pp. 65–80.

MURPHY, P. (1989) 'Gender and assessment in science', in MURPHY, P. and MOON, B. (eds) *Developments in Learning and Assessment*, London, Hodder and Stoughton.

MURPHY, R.J.L. (1982) 'Sex differences in objective test performance', *British Journal of Educational Psychology*, **52**, pp. 213–19.

REINHARZ, S. (1992) *Feminist Methods in Social Research*, Oxford, Oxford University Press.

RENNIE, L. and PARKER, L. (1991) 'Assessment of learning in science: The need to look closely at item characteristics', *Australian Science Teachers' Journal*, **37**(4), pp. 56–9.

ROSSER, S. (1990) *Female Friendly Science: Applying Women's Studies Theories and Methods to Attract Students*, New York, Pergamon.

ROY, P. and SCHEN, M. (1987) 'Feminist pedagogy: Transforming the high school classroom', *Women's Studies Quarterly*, **15**(3 and 4), pp. 110–15.

SHEPARD, L. (1993) 'Why we need better assessments', in BURKE, K. (ed.) *Authentic Assessment*, Cheltenham, Vic., Hawker Brownlow.

SHEPHERD, L. (1993) *Lifting the Veil — The Feminine Face of Science*, Boston, Shambhala.

SHREWSBURY, C. (1987) 'What is feminist pedagogy?', *Women's Studies Quarterly*, **15**(3 and 4), pp. 6–13.

SPEAR, M.G. (1984) 'Sex bias in science teachers' ratings of work and pupil characteristics', *European Journal of Science Education*, **6**(4), pp. 369–77.

TEESE, R., CHARLTON, M. and POLESEL, J. (1994) 'Curriculum outcomes in Victoria: A geographical and gender analysis of the VCE in 1992, educational outcomes for disadvantaged groups project', University of Melbourne, paper.

THOMAS, K. (1990) *Gender and Subject in Higher Education*, Buckingham, Open University Press.

TOBIAS, S. (1990) *They're Not Dumb, They're Different*, Tucson, Research Corporation.

TUANA, N. (ed.) (1989) *Feminism and Science*, Bloomington, Indiana University Press.

VBOS (1994) *Statistical Information on the VCE 1993 Assessment Program*, Melbourne, VBOS.

VCAB (1991a) *Physics Study Design*, Melbourne, VCAB.

VCAB (1991b) *Physics Curriculum Development Support Material*, Melbourne, VCAB.

VCAB (1992) *Statistical Information on the VCE 1991 Assessment Program*, Melbourne, VCAB.

VCAB (1993) *Statistical Information on the VCE 1992 Assessment Program*, Melbourne, VCAB.

WALKERDINE, V. (1989) *Counting Girls Out*, London, Virago.

WEEDON, C. (1987) *Feminist Practice and Poststructuralist Theory*, Oxford, Blackwell.

WITHERS, G. and CORNISH, G. (1984) *Assessment in Practice: Competitive or Non-competitive?* Melbourne, Victorian Institute of Secondary Education, Occasional Paper No. 11.

WYN, J. (1990) 'Working class girls and educational outcomes', in KENWAY, J. and WILLIS, S. (eds) *Hearts and Minds: Self-esteem and the Schooling of Girls*, London, Falmer Press.

13   Single-sex Settings: Pedagogies for Girls and Boys in Danish Schools

Anne-Mette Kruse

Abstract

Teachers in the Danish co-educational elementary school system (the 'folkeskole' with pupils from the age of 6 to 16) who are involved in innovative pedagogical projects have used segregation as an organizational method in introducing and developing equal opportunities and anti-sexist pedagogical initiatives. The idea of arranging single-sex settings started out as a means to provide space for girls and to enhance their competence professionally as well as to empower them personally. In setting up 'Project Girls' Class–Boys' Class' — a developmental project about gender equity — the teachers, a woman and a man, have mixed their two classes and segregated the girls and the boys for longer or shorter periods or for a whole term in certain subjects, thus giving them space and tutoring on their own terms. The involved girls developed self-confidence and prefer to be in their girls-only setting whereas it is the teachers (more than the involved boys themselves) that find that the boys' class can provide important learning experiences for boys in raising their awareness of values and attitudes — both among the boys themselves and in relation to the girls. From the point of view of educational theory and of how learning can become true learning affecting the cognitive, emotional as well as moral and behavioural attitudes, the chapter reflects on why the segregation projects have given such clear results, whereas much other excellent tutoring by committed teachers seems not to have had the same impact. The preliminary conclusion is that, in the hands of devoted teachers (people committed to the issues of gender equity and anti-sexism and who are close and caring to their pupils), the technique of polarizing can be very effective.

Introduction

Research on the Method of Single-sex Settings and the Development of a Pedagogical Theory

Since the beginning of the 1980s I have taken part in action research and innovation programmes on how to improve conditions in the elementary school with the intention of improving the opportunities for girls especially. During the last seven

173

years I have been in touch with many projects and committed teachers engaged in gender equity projects and equal opportunity initiatives for both sexes. Together with teachers — on the basis of their practice and my observations and interviews — I have reflected and explored how to effect changes that will strengthen and empower those pupils who normally lose out. In doing this I have had intensive contact with six projects and know of forty-nine other projects that have used single-sex as an organizational and pedagogical means.

Proposing a girls-only environment as a strategy was an obvious result of my own experience with women's consciousness raising groups and Women's Studies. But in the mid-1980s, when the projects started to appear, we were met with resistance and opposition to this strategy. Mostly, reactions have been that the idea is reactionary and old-fashioned: 'Are you mad?' 'Why are you digging trenches?' 'Do you really think that we want to go back to the old times with girls' schools, schools that restricted them, gave them a holy fear of sex, and put the poor girls in fetters so they didn't know how to cope with the opposite sex and have a realistic approach to society?' or 'What about the boys — I wouldn't let my son attend a boys' class; like boys' schools they are repressive, rough and sexist. Should he be kept away from associating with and learning from girls?' These are statements that illustrate some of the responses I have experienced. In the 1990s the opposition is this: 'Gender identity is something you choose, why then segregate?' Or 'Middle class girls and boys are becoming more alike in terms of the values they hold and the identities they share so what is the problem?' On the whole, power theories are not 'in' any more in the Scandinavian discourse.

My research into the possibilities of single-sex settings within the Danish co-educational school system is unique, it has only become possible because of the committed teachers, who have had the courage to counter prejudice to try out their ideas in practice. Today, we are very encouraged by the results of the first projects. We find that the idea of developing a feminist pedagogy for girls in single-sex settings as a strategy to empower them personally and professionally is a most effective method and one that has been consolidated.

Setting up girls' classes within co-educational schools has meant that boys' classes invariably emerge. The question that then arose was whether boys can benefit from these and whether they are adequate tools for developing gender equity — or will they have the opposite effect and make boys' attitudes more stereotypically sexist? Or, if we succeed in making boys softer and more open, less competitive — non-violent and non-abusive — will this just result in men who in subtle ways will be able to be more manipulative in their domination as they still hold power over women and maintain more power than women?

We have to be aware of this possibility, but having taught and observed lessons in boys-only settings, having interviewed many boys about their experience in single-sex settings and also having done assertiveness training with boys and talked to teachers who are devoted to anti-sexist work, I have now changed my view and motivation in relation to pedagogical work with boys. Today, I find this work to be both important and necessary. I think that boys, directly as well as indirectly, can benefit from exploring what it means and can mean to be a man and what masculinity may be. Boys need the opportunity to explore and change their ambivalent views of women, to be confronted with the effects of the misuse of power and men's role and responsibility in this. In Denmark, the pedagogical work with boys-only groups has been relatively undeveloped and anti-sexist work with boys is mainly done by women. Very few men have engaged in this because they do not find it important and do not themselves engage in developing their norms of masculinity and sexuality or take part in political movements to challenge male hegemony. But having now followed and analysed the results of the anti-sexist projects that have been developed so far, I have come to the conclusion that a pedagogical method based on alternating between single-sex and co-educational settings will polarize and thus help improve the pupils' feelings of self-esteem, develop their gender identity and potential for acting out changes (Kruse, 1989, 1996). In this chapter, I therefore argue for the development of a pedagogical method and theory of polarization.

Politics and Strategies

Equal Rights, Equal Opportunities or Equal Worth — Which Strategy?

Danish and Scandinavian women have achieved a high degree of formal rights, approaching the same rights that men hold. But in reality there is still a long way to go. The struggle for both equality and equal opportunities is one that must continue. It is true that women who have fought for the rights and equal opportunities for women have done a necessary job. But through the new women's movement some of us have come to the conclusion that the ideology inherent in much of the early work for equal rights and equal opportunity reflects an adaptation to male institutions and a society based on patriarchal values. We as women have to go further.

Today there are a number of materialist-radical feminists who put emphasis on a term in Denmark called 'equal worth' (equal status). Within the concept of 'equal worth' there are different goals to that of obtaining equal opportunities within a male-dominated society. As the goals are different so are our politics and strategies. At the same time as working towards equity for all groups that are being disadvantaged, we as women are also working for a qualitative transformation of society, its hierarchies of power and the division of labour. It is a feminism that focuses on abolishing the unequal power between women and men, between social classes and ethnic groups. It acknowledges differences but not inequality within the group of women. Working from the point of 'equal worth', we call for political action on the basis of the values and commitment that we as women (ironically) have developed in the struggle against our oppression. We have learnt that formal rights, equal access or equal opportunities alone do not lead to equality. Put another way: 'Nothing is more unjust, than to give equal rights to people who have been socialized to inequality' (Hansen and Ørum, 1975). If this statement was applied to the gender debate, we can see that equity can only truly be realized if we acknowledge the power differences between women and men, permit affirmative action and develop different strategies for change for the two groups. When we as policy-makers, researchers or teachers, work on making changes in society and in schools, we need to be aware of the fact that obtaining formal equality is a prerequisite for obtaining real equality but never a direct consequence of this. We must continue to work for both equal opportunities and equal worth and we need to understand how they, though different in their politics, are connected and which strategy is most appropriate according to specific situations.

The Issue of Empowering Girls

Our minds are full of contradictory messages that we are unaware of, and we tend to unconsciously accept and grow insensitive to everyday phenomena around us. We do not question why is it like this — we tend to accept things as they are. A statement often heard is, 'Boys will be boys'. (The underlying assumption is that boys cannot change so either girls have to — or adapt). Another statement often made by girls: 'I'll never be outspoken in class.' (Assumption: this is a characteristic and organic part of being female.) Many girls feel that 'Boys are better than us girls.' (Assumption: the message we get from the surrounding society as well as in the classroom that boys are more valuable than girls, is true.)

Put in psychological terms: Danish women have to face what Eva Ethelberg (1983) calls the contradiction of femininity. It means that every day we have to face a contradictory situation; we have to face reality while maintaining our self-esteem. As reality is male dominance and women's subordination, we have to struggle for our self-respect. This is not easily done. Based on her work as a therapist, Eva Ethelberg has recognized three different survival strategies that women use.

The first and 'heaviest' strategy involves repressing the contradiction completely. Women who have developed this way of coping have difficulties developing a realistic approach to life because of deep structures of fear and anxiety that act as blocks. The second strategy involves adapting to the definition of women's subordinate position. Many women have 'chosen' this strategy but either find their own ways to move on to the third strategy or are open to help from others in this respect. The third strategy means facing the contradiction of existing in a reality with male dominance on the one hand and maintaining one's self-esteem as a woman on the other. Only by facing reality — not accepting it — can we develop the potential and the strategies that, on an individual level, can help us change imbalances of power. The third strategy is likely to give women voice and inner power to cope, and, when appropriate, to challenge male dominance. Women can learn to cope with the contradiction if they are not too blocked psychologically or too oppressed in their environment.

Girls who use the first two strategies may learn to see and to deal with imposed power structures in a caring and supportive setting. Girls who use the third strategy can be encouraged to hold on to it. This recognition of the difference in the girls' individual coping strategies can be a valuable help to feminist teachers in dealing with individuals and groups of girls.

In all classrooms there will be girls who have learnt to survive by unconsciously employing one of these strategies. In addition, schoolgirls are situated in an institutionalized educational setting with little influence. It is a setting in which the 'hidden agenda' expects them to balance the contradiction of being good pupils (adaptive, patient, obedient, cooperative) with becoming competitive, individualistic and assertive. As members of a co-educational pupil culture they tend to develop strategies that are protective against this massive and overwhelming domination and repression. They withdraw and develop their own spaces and their own intimate culture within cliques and one-to-one relations with other girls.

Girls tend wisely to defend this space from intrusion of either boys or teachers and in doing so they often lose out in influence and qualifications. Our research project, 'School Life — Girlhood' (Jensen, Krogh-Jespersen, Reinsholm, Kruse and Reisby, 1984), shows that many develop a double strategy of coping in which they convince teachers that they are listening and are present as good pupils while they are actually fooling the teachers. This is their immediate way of maintaining their self-respect, but in the long run they both 'cheat' the teachers and lose out. Girls thus act and react in a variety of ways according to the socio-cultural background and personality of the individual. Some girls are openly deviant, others are very subtle and indirect and others again are unaware of their coping strategies for an oppression they have not even recognized. The latter are the most vulnerable and powerless.

The first step in this struggle against repression is to face this situation. The next step is to let the girls explore and express in their own terms how they feel and how they cope. Then it is important to find out whether they are confident enough to help each other change some of their strategies of coping in order to gain more power and influence and in order to constitute themselves as subjects of their own decisions instead of always reacting to the contradictions and domination of others.

Consequently there are good political as well as psychological reasons for establishing girls-only classes and settings and developing a pedagogical practice in solidarity and together with girls. Some of the main issues that may then become obvious are those of power and the oppression–submission pattern. With the support of sympathetic teachers, girls can learn to identify and face the contradiction of their reality (male dominance) and, at the same time, develop strategies to maintain their self-esteem and challenge and puncture the power structures. This will help them explore similarities and differences within their own gender group and train themselves in developing supportive coping strategies to counter the different types of hegemony they are exposed to.

My research supports the theory that when girls gain the opportunity to be in girls' groups their approach is often somewhat insecure, quiet and restrained. But this does not last. Safety and acceptance seem to be an important prerequisite, more important than they seem to be to boys. Gradually, girls grow more and more comfortable, free, open, talkative and better at holding on to their own opinions than when they were in mixed settings. The relationships between girls most often improve when boys are not present. One explanation is that they stop being 'ruled and divided'; another, that they do not have to compete for the attention of the boys.

When back in mixed settings the new insights and skills are tested. Mostly, the empowering effect does not becomes obvious before the girls have had longer as well as frequent periods in their own settings on their own terms.

Teaching Girls is Different from Teaching Boys

Although teachers often have problems controlling boys' behaviour, they usually have a positive view of boys. But teachers — female as well as male — are often ambivalent in their opinions of girls. There are different reasons for this, e.g., some teachers do not find girls as exciting or as interesting as boys; they do not approve of and do not understand the intimate friendship relations of girls, their ways of communicating, or their conflicts. Somehow, they do not approve of either girls who are too conventional, nice and adaptable or the opposite, too noisy, too demanding, too rebellious, too challenging. In this way, we are all carriers of society's double conceptualization of women ('Damned if you do — and damned if you don't'). Furthermore, teaching girls is not easy for teachers who, for more than a generation, have been used to the fact that 'pupils' are synonymous with 'boys'. Another type of pedagogy is required when pupils are extrovert and dominating than when they are withdrawn or resistant. The latter calls for creative empathy rather than disciplinary measures.

An interesting illustrative example is Haarup School where 14–15-year-old girls and boys from one class were segregated during four lessons a week in their 8th and 9th year at school. They were separated in German, English, mathematics and physics. This was initiated by Grethe Biil (1988) a feminist teacher, who, as their 'form-teacher', was responsible for the social welfare of the pupils. She also taught them Danish and German. I observed both in the class and the single-sex settings and interviewed all involved. Grethe Biil enjoyed being alone with the girls. But she also discovered that it can be enjoyable to work with boys on their own. This experience has been confirmed by other women teachers, including myself. It reduces the reproach heaped on boys for being too dominating. Teachers feel that at least now the boys are not suppressing the girls, and this can bring relaxation and greater openness towards them. But teaching an all-boys class is a different matter from teaching an all-girls class. Even lessons that have the same text or content or result in the same homework go through processes that are very different. In the two 8th to 9th grade settings Grethe Biil experienced the following differences:

The girls-only setting:
1 The girls work in a concentrated way. The subject matter is worked through in half the time used by boys.
2 The girls are well prepared.
3 The girls keep strictly to the subject.
4 The girls see the lesson as a shared venture.
5 The girls listen and show respect when others speak. They laugh in a caring way: 'Aren't we having a nice time together?'
6 The girls are helpful to each other.

The boys-only setting:

1   The boys are active in an anarchistic way.
2   The boys have a low degree of preparation.
3   The boys broaden the subject and include new angles and points of view.
4   They see the lesson as an individual matter.
5   The boys constantly interrupt each other with funny or ironical remarks. They are tough with each other, use swear words and garbage language.
6   The boys compete with each other and in getting the teacher's attention.

In the girls-only setting Grethe Biil rarely scolded. Each girl became visible, and appeared as an individual with certain characteristics. In the boys-only setting she often told the boys off and lessons were often interrupted, especially when changing from one discipline to another. Also, the quiet boys became more visible, and the power structures within the boys' group became more obvious.

When the girls had concentrated on the subject matter and on finishing their schoolwork, they wanted to talk: talk about vital things in their lives and share reflections about their futures about which they felt insecure. Thus many a German lesson became the place where the girls bettered their German qualifications and additionally gained the attention and support of a committed feminist teacher on other vital matters.

The very different ways in which the pupils interacted forced Grethe Biil to change her teaching style completely when in the girls' or in the boys' setting. At first she herself reacted spontaneously, but gradually she became aware of the need to develop different teaching strategies and to set different goals for each of the two groups.

Empowering Boys — and Developing Awareness of and Commitment to Counter Sexism

In my introduction I argue for the importance of anti-sexist work with boys. Now I go one step further and talk about empowering them. This may sound both contradictory and deeply problematic. How can I, who claim to be rooted in a materialist-radical feminism, seriously talk about empowering boys? Have I not argued that men have more power than women, that men exert power over women, and that the effect of this calls for a pedagogy for girls which empowers them so that they can become autonomous, take control and define their own strategies? How, then, dare I argue for empowering boys, who as it is, hold far the most resources, attention and influence? My research, has shown me the necessity of teachers concerned with sexism dealing directly with boys, with their gender identity, with their concepts of masculinity and with their attitudes and behaviour. Focusing only on girls will result in imposing upon them the whole responsibility for change, and it will underpin the assumption that 'boys are boys' and therefore cannot change. The sexist behaviour of boys is a result of a socially constructed relationship in which men will denigrate women. Boys are not personally responsible for this but they will be the unconscious propagators of a sexist ideology if they are not confronted with this and supported and challenged in their attempt to find ways to change their culturally given roles. Research in education shows that schools generally are important agents in the reinforcement of social inequality. We have to develop new politics and new models of practice.

When I refer to empowering boys, I use a concept of power that I have acquired in my training as an assertiveness trainer. This defines power as a psychological position from within rather than needing to oppress or submit to others (Dickson, 1982; Jeffers, 1987). It is an important aspect of personal development, and even if it is only one step in creating an anti-sexist attitude and behaviour, it is an extremely productive place from which to begin when working with boys as well as girls. In this I have been greatly inspired by the work of Sue Askew and Carol Ross (1988). They offer much information, examples and ideas of how feminists may organize anti-sexist work with boys. And since there are more women teachers than men teachers, we ought to take steps to change our ways of working with boys. In her book *Education For Peace*, Birgit Brock-Utne (1985) also discusses and provides examples of what feminist mothers and teachers can do in order to bring up boys to be non-violent and caring.

In several English-speaking countries (USA, Britain, and Australia), men active in the men's movement or men supportive of the feminist ideology have taken steps to work towards a revaluation of masculinity. Some are also developing programs, training sessions and courses for men who work with boys, and for boys themselves. Some of these initiatives have served as personal development for the boys involved, and some have proceeded to integrate personal development and political perspectives.

Encouraging boys to talk about their personal experience is not easy. But, in London, Trevor Lloyd and fellow youth workers use the methods from the women's movement: changing attitudes through the exploration of personal experience. Lloyd makes several stipulations before discussions begin: There is to be no ridicule, and when someone is speaking, the rest must listen. From here the next step is to establish an overall view of boys'/young men's experience and a collective view of relationships with other men and with women, of men's sexuality, etc. These findings are then related to boys' experiences, stressing the oppression of young people and the contradictory nature of manhood. Similarities and differences between the youth workers and the boys of today are explored. And new strategies for work with the boys are developed.

A more radical policy has been developed by Colin Hocking in Australia. He began as a member of the Men against Patriarchy group. Then he went through a period of radicalization and, together with other men, organized Men Against Sexual Assault. Since the early 1980s he and others have set up and developed counter-sexist programs for boys. Debates have been critical of the programmes that have attempted to build on personal development. The programmes were criticized for not being efficient enough in their dealings with pressing social problems such as sexual assault and other forms of violence. Thus, attempts were made to '. . . rebuild our experience in providing education programmes for boys, so that they more effectively integrate the personal development and social/political perspectives . . .' (Hocking, 1991).

In Denmark only a few men work with boys in either way. Erik Wittrup's work centers on personal development but also raises anti-sexist issues. I welcome this work and hope that more male teachers and researchers will engage in this issue and form networks with people with more experience in other countries. This could stimulate political and pedagogical discussions and radicalize ideas and practice.

Segregation and Pedagogical Practice

Single-sex Settings as Means to Heighten Self-esteem and Awareness of Sexism in Girls as well as Boys

It seems to me that the main pedagogical purpose for setting up single-sex settings is threefold: to promote self-esteem and gender identity by acknowledging and attending to the individual pupil, to challenge by broadening the spectrum of qualifications — personally as well as professionally — and to raise the political awareness of anti-sexist issues in the light of trying to alter socially constructed gender patterns. At the personal level, this means giving support to individual gender-identity (you are ok) and challenge to the general sex-role as formed by society (your attitudes and behaviour may not be ok). At group level, for either girls or boys, it means providing space and possibilities for experiencing alternative coping techniques and ways to consciously try, step by step, to act differently and thus create change.

Girls and boys have met different expectations and treatment during their childhood and this means that they need to be supported and challenged in different ways, necessitating periods of segregated pedagogy alternating with mixed settings. I suggest starting off by offering pupils the possibilities of experiencing single-sex settings and learning situations as early as possible in the educational process, involving the pupils in the theoretical and political issues in accordance to their history, their age and psychological development.

Project Girls' Class and Boys' Class — a practical example

The following is a short description of one of the innovation projects that I have evaluated. I have 'hung around' in classrooms; undertaken both long- and short-term mostly 'passive-participation' observations; written 'day-books', i.e., diaries consisting of a mixture of objective (tape-recorded) as well as subjective observations; carried out semi-structured qualitative interviews with pupils, teachers and parents.

The reason for focusing on this particular project is that it may be seen as exemplary in its ideas and in the efforts of the two committed teachers. Seeing the ways in which the pupils' consciousness of gender and their sexist behaviour have

Anne-Mette Kruse

been challenged and have started to change has also inspired me to further develop the theory of a polarizing pedagogy to undermine the hidden curriculum of sexism. First the practical example:

The Girls' Class: The project started out when the pupils were in their 5th form and lasted until the end of their 9th grade in the school year of 1991–92. Two teachers, Lotte Rasmussen and Erik Wittrup, proposed to segregate girls and boys from two 5th grades for two months in all subjects. The pupils were then 10–11 years-old. The parents had given their hesitating consent, but especially the girls were very reluctant. However, during this first period of the single-sex classes the boys — who from the beginning had welcomed the idea — competed and fought and thus painfully became aware of their own lack of social skills. While the girls who had been the staunchest opponents to the experiment to their surprise found an environment of new possibilities:

> *Line*:   I think attending a girls' class is wonderful. There are so many things we can do. The boys haven't laughed at us the way they used to do. We've had more freedom and have been much more outspoken — and best of all, we can walk around without being kicked and things like that.

This statement expresses the experience of a new learning situation: space to be safe from being ridiculed, freedom to act on one's own wishes, encouragement to speak up, development of personal skills, and safety from harassment and violence. Of nineteen girls from different social backgrounds, eighteen gave expression to similar statements and feelings. One girl claimed that she did not experience any difference between a girls' class and mixed class. Some of the girls admitted to having missed the boys, their cheek and out-spokenness, and still — out of the classroom — sought for the attention of the boys. But the girls now recognized how their classes used to be dominated by boys and realized their own part in letting them. They also experienced that it was both fun and vital to be at the centre of their own learning situation. When asked if girls speak less in co-educational settings, Line replied:

> Yes, there are some that speak less . . . 'cause if you say something wrong or incorrect, the boys will laugh at you. And then you feel small. So you don't really dare say anything. You then keep your mouth shut and hold back.

The girls became closer knit and achieved an awareness about those factors that often keep them back in class; the 'put-downs' and ridicule suffered particularly from the more attractive boys. And together they developed and learned (in role-play) how to overcome male dominance in the classroom:

> *Line*:   And when we have sat in the circle, we have talked about us — girls. We have talked about ourselves, and Lotte has presented us with topics

that concern girls. Usually we sit there listening to teachers talking with boys about boys. We aren't really interested in that, and in the girls' class we haven't been forced to spend our time on them . . . Apart from that we have learned not just to sit back, twiddle our thumbs and let them [the boys] take over.

The work in the girls' class at first centered around getting to share opinions and feelings about different topics. Nobody was allowed to withdraw, every single girl was expected by the teacher and the group, in a supportive way, to express herself. The group did different kinds of body-work exploring the body's potential and also worked on increasing sensitivity and confidence. It studied and explored matters of sex education and devised role-plays, as training to be more assertive. In addition, they analysed a typical short story from a woman's magazine. In pairs, the girls made a survey of the working conditions and pay for women in the local community. They learnt interviewing techniques, how to handle tape recorders, overcome fear of making contacts, and they ended up providing descriptions as well as statistics and giving talks in front of the whole group about their findings. Of their own choosing they explored attitudes to fashion and did group work where both content, process and performed results were totally within their own control. The teacher did not intervene unless asked to and this group work, in particular, struck home. The girls were encouraged to develop a new conception of self and individual as well as the group gender identity, which was strengthened and extended. All of which was confirmed through my observations and the girls' own statements.

Lotte Rasmussen was compelled to take two aspects into consideration: on the one hand, the level of socio-psychological development and the needs of these pre-pubescent girls, and on the other hand, her own wish to compensate for what she considered to be their lack of experience. She accepted the role as the supportive feminist teacher who recognized the need for care and security, but who, in addition, wanted the girls to experience an extension of their own limited knowledge and understandings.

The girls' learning became both supportive and challenging with an emphasis on the latter. It was not an incubatory pedagogy, as voices critical of learning processes involving only girls, have argued. And the girls' learning did not become adaptive, though it began from the position of respect for the girls' own concepts of femininity and choice of coping strategies. The fundamental point was that it did not accept the status quo but in a supportive way set out to challenge this at many levels.

A common experience for both girls and boys was sitting in a circle and having everybody express their opinion about a subject matter, a method inspired by the American civil rights movement and the women's movement as it aims to strengthen symmetry and equality in communication. It also aims to counter hegemony and dominance. It is democratic: everybody has a right to express her/his opinion, and everybody can expect to get a response. By using this device, Lotte Rasmussen helped the girls to achieve insight into the mechanisms (e.g., strategies of dominance) that oppress them. As they gradually gained these insights she encouraged them to express themselves — at first verbally, later via role-plays — thus allowing these new experiences to be integrated. The final goal was to encourage the girls to act in a more supporting way towards each other in situations where they shared interests, objectively as well as subjectively.

The Boys' Class: The boys differed in their opinions about being in a boys-only class and could be divided into three groups. One group of boys — the leading boys — stuck together and took control of the class. They took every opportunity to decide who, what, and when — for example, that all must play football during breaks. They felt good about the changes and enjoyed being able to recruit a whole football team. They felt that they gained the undivided attention of the male teacher Erik Wittrup, and that he was much more fair and open to them now than in the usual co-educational class, where they felt that he was protecting and defending the girls. They claimed that they would not mind continuing three more years at least in a boys-only class.

> David: ... I think that he (Erik) has become more kind.
> Martin: I totally agree. Before we were always quarreling with Erik.
> David: We don't quarrel so much any more, now we sort of talk about things. ... He listens more to what we have to say. Yes, and I also think that he being a man makes it easier for him to understand the feelings of boys ...

A group of boys that did not take on leadership, but were friendly with the leaders, liked being with boys only but also missed the girls. They wanted to continue in the boys' setting for certain periods only, alternating with a mixed setting.

> I: Would you like the boys' class to continue?
> Per: Yes. And then we could stop for a while, and then start again.
> I: What do you see as advantages?
> Per: Well, we boys we would rather read about motors and football and things like that. The girls are maybe more interested in fashion and things like that. But Erik, he arranges things in such a way that it is on our premises — on our terms.

A third group of boys (who had low status in the boys' class) did not like being in the single-sex setting. First, because they found it noisier, but also because the level of conflicts and teasing was higher in the boys-only class, and because the boys missed the attention and services of the girls.

> Peter: We are a lot noisier than when the girls are here.
> I: What's that like?
> Simon: One can easily hear that we are only boys in the class, if the girls

had been here we wouldn't have shouted as much — cause then they would have asked us to be quieter.

Peter: But when there aren't any girls, we shout so much, and as no one hushes at us, we get scolded more [by the teachers].

Simon: If I ask one of the boys if he will help me or lend me something, he can't be bothered. If the girls were here, they would have helped. Now I have to sit and wait for the teacher to come, no-one else will help me.

Having experienced working with a boys-only class and having started to develop a pedagogy for boys, Erik Wittrup states that he finds it important for male teachers wanting to work with boys — as a departure — to reflect on the following:

- That the values of boys differ from those of the girls.
- That boys simply have to react against an educational institution that focuses on theoretical knowledge, adaptive policy, predictability, repetition and boredom.
- That if teachers tried to 'follow' some of the wishes of the boys maybe schools could change in ways that could benefit all pupils.
- That pursuing and making changes in cooperation with the pupils can help develop democracy in schools.

Summing up work with boys he advocates:

- Understand them.
- Accept them.
- Go along with them.
- Control the situation together with them.
- Recognize your own male identity in your being together with them.

Erik Wittrup claimed that in the boys' class the room became a lively and a creative area for work. He also experienced that, as a teacher, he was forced to respond to the needs and wants of the boys, and sometimes found it difficult to set boundaries — sometimes in negative ways — as the school framework in itself is restrictive. But he also saw the possibilities of development if one cared and dared to 'go along' with the boys. Having set this scene of acceptance, and having created a space of solidarity, the work could begin: exploring relationships within the group such as the constant conflicts that the boys suffered. Erik Wittrup wanted the boys to see and experience the possibilities of being and working together in non-competitive and cooperative ways, and, as the content of the tutoring and the group work began to reflect the wishes of the boys, they gradually began to open up, thus feeling important and influential. From here, Erik Wittrup gradually began to introduce demands and to intervene in social processes. Conflicts were approached in new ways, feelings were shared and assertive skills were developed. Also 'rounds' were set up when decisions were to be made or in dealing with examples of violence and abuse within the group.

The boys' curriculum was different from that of the girls'. Like the girls, the boys were allowed to exert considerable influence on themes and work methods. The day they were responsible for was devoted to fish and fishing. The day the girls were responsible for dealt with fashion and personal appearance. Under these circumstances one feels tempted to ask: have these pupils had their sex-roles challenged? On one level the answer may be no. But in the interviews, the girls and boys revealed that on such days they felt their identity and self-confidence strengthened because they were free to follow a common interest and to organize according to their own wishes. The pupils felt an exhilarating sense of control so that the actual adaptive and conventional sex-role nature of the activities seemed to become less important.

On the occasions when the girls were challenged to work in unconventional fields, e.g., with statistics, work pattern analyses and interviewing, the boys were challenged to do practical work with a theme, which was unconventional for them: unpaid domestic labour. Both the girls and boys explored emotions and behaviour patterns through assertiveness training, and within their respective groups they worked on conflict solving and anti-sexist issues.

The girls' and the boys' classes planned and worked separately and with different topics. As a point of departure the two teachers took on the leadership role and focused on the subjective interests of the respective groups. Then they decided what the two groups of pupils needed in terms of challenges and improved competency but also gave space for self-management and autonomy.

Back in the co-educational setting: When, after 8 weeks, the pupils went back into their usual co-educational classes, the girls openly struggled for more space and mounted fierce reactions to boys' dominant behaviour. The boys were irritated but showed more respect for the girls than they had done earlier. Only a few of them openly expressed this in interviews, but both the teachers and I observed this. As an example, boys who wished to associate or chose to work with girls no longer got teased by other boys. However a few months later it was noticed that some of the quieter girls had relapsed into their old well-known patterns; they were again withdrawn and did not speak up in class. The teachers thus decided that the single-sex settings were to be utilized again mainly to help maintain the confident and assertive behaviour that the girls had shown so strongly during and immediately after the first segregation period. So, when it was possible, the girls and boys were taught separately. In the 6th form, this was the case in home economics; and in the 7th form, in physics and some of the German lessons. In the 8th form they were segregated for a term in sociology.

The two teachers and the two classes have continued their efforts to create positive gender identities and to deal with anti-sexism. Gender equity concerns pervade all levels of the teaching process from planning through the actual teaching practice to the assessment of the results. At age 16 the pupils had actively been involved in developing a learning practice where girls and boys were encouraged to try out different democratic models of cooperation, and in trying out a variety of forms of self-expression.

Gender Segregation and Pedagogical Theory

Personal Development, Awareness of Discrimination and Political Understanding

Alternating between periods of mixed settings and periods of single-sex settings polarizes and makes more obvious the stereotyped gendered behaviour patterns and contradictions of inequality. The method used here is a means to raise the consciousness of girls and boys about their own gendered behaviour.

The pupils can enjoy a new form of attention from their teachers. This attention is focused on their different learning styles, ways of responding and the way in which they express themselves as members of that particular group. The gender identity and self-confidence of individual pupils and their gender group are supported; the sex-roles, attitudes and behaviour are challenged. Being segregated gives the groups the experience of focusing on and learning about similarities and differences between the values and behaviours of girls and boys, makes them sensitive and more open to variations within each gender group, and they meet and learn about power structures, equity issues and other forms and models of femininity and masculinity than the stereotyped ones when dealing with topics of sexism.

The Pedagogical Method of Polarization

The theoretical assumptions contained in this study of how knowledge about the hidden curriculum is obtained and how understanding about socially constructed behaviour can become empowering have been based on and adapted from the concepts of *The Pedagogical Method of Polarization* (Nordström, 1979). Originally, this theory was developed to describe how students could learn to understand the impact of class society in artistic and creative production. Briefly, the pedagogical method of polarization originally has four consecutive levels: 1) It seeks to understand knowledge by bringing to light the contradictions in the subject matter; 2) It is a dialectic and dynamic model of pedagogy and emphasizes critical thinking and consciousness raising; 3) Theory is deduced from the actual practice of interaction, and; 4) It demands a production of meaning through expression and communication.

My empirical based research indicated that utilizing a polarization pedagogy is a possible way of capturing how pupils can come to understand and start to counteract the realities and mechanisms of power inequality between the sexes. I have adapted and developed this theory into five levels, adding some aspects and interpreting them in accordance with the gender equity issue of the hidden curriculum:

Level 1

Seeking to understand knowledge by bringing to light the contradictions in the subject matter and making them obvious. When girls and boys periodically get the chance to be taught apart from each other, and the usual pattern of mixed interaction is broken, it has an immense effect on the insight of especially the most subordinate and suppressed pupils. Both girls and boys see themselves and their own gender group in a new way: power structures and power strategies suddenly become apparent. What before was part of the hidden curriculum now becomes obvious and is actively experienced by the participants themselves. In this phase it is vital that the 'message' is not taught, but that the new setting, in addition to the support of a pro-feminist or feminist teacher as a kind of 'midwife', helps the pupils to explore, feel, analyse and express their own understanding and learning.

Level 2

The dialectic and dynamic model of pedagogy emphasizes critical thinking and consciousness-raising. The actual shift between being in a single and a mixed setting frees the pupils' own experiences from the differences/similarities between themselves. In the project mentioned above, both gender groups gained a new grasp of individual as well as general contradictions and of the differences of being in a mixed setting as opposed to a single-sex setting. At this level the teachers can confront, ask provocative questions and, together with the pupils, explore aspects in their lives where gendered power imbalances occur. The teacher may challenge stereotyping, attitudes and behaviour. They may study books, material and videos that raise important issues, e.g., sexual harassment, unequal pay etc., by using different means of pupil-centered cooperative and interactive learning methods.

Level 3

Studies of the indisputable evidence (the objective reality) of inequality between women and men — and the oppression of women — locally as well as globally. This phase is an extension of level 2 for pupils in the older age groups. Here the pupils in pairs or groups can study historical or current evidence on issues they would like to know more about. Teachers and pupils can prepare talks on matters they and/or the pupils find important.

Level 4

Deducing theory from the actual interaction practice. After having conceptualized their own experiences (level 1) and together having gained new insights and a new awareness about the issues in their own lives (level 2) and in general (level 3), the pupils (still in their respective single-sex settings) with the support of the teachers analyse, organize and categorize what they have learnt and operationalize the evidence in specific and concrete ways, e.g., What in our daily environment do we no longer accept? What is within our reach to change? How do we work on changing a) our attitudes b) our behaviour?

Level 5

The production of meaning through expression, communication and action. Having first identified the perceived results of inequality in a socially unjust and sexist society, then analysed in a theoretical and practical way the nature of the social interaction between the involved girls and boys themselves, and when each single-sex group with their teachers have decided what they find the most urgent issues to address, the pupils enter a phase of communicating the results and acting out the changes. Communicating what one has learnt is of vital importance. Here, all means of creative expressions are welcome including drama, information boards, tape-recordings, video or slide displays, dance, talks, creative writing in the form of songs, poems, essays, etc. The presentation of work that groups, pairs or individuals have prepared has two purposes. It is a way of clarifying one's new learning for oneself at the same time as the meaning is communicated to others. Not until then does it become true learning.

Going back into the mixed setting, preparing to share one's new insights and dealing specifically with counteracting the oppression/submission pattern is the next step. Here the goal is for all pupils to get an equal share of attention, influence and time to express ideas and feelings and support to manage this in assertive and clear ways. And this is not obtained at one go. There will be both progression as well as regression.

Reflections

Single-sex education is not a goal in itself. Single-sex pedagogy in these projects is a means to help girls as well as boys understand sex-roles and attitudes as social constructions that can be changed by those involved. By this I do not mean to say that single-sex classes or schools are always likely to be positive. We have also seen how in previous generations the effect of women being regarded as second rate created a special limitation in the opportunities and possibilities available to girls in or out of schools.

Sex-segregated education can be used for emancipation or oppression. As a method it does not guarantee an outcome. The intentions, the understanding of people and their gender, the pedagogical attitudes and practices, are crucial, as in all pedagogical work. The aim here is equal rights and equal worth for girls and boys, so that they can meet and experience equal and mutual appreciation and respect. Experience shows that respect for other people is greatest where people openly and honestly understand their own strengths and limitations. This requires a realistic idea of oneself and a stable and well-founded gender image, self-identity and feelings of inner power. Sex-segregated processes that are organized around the specific conditions and interests of a particular sex can support the development of a positive gender identity based on authentic values, rather than merely becoming reflections of the stereotypical ideas of the opposite sex. A person is better qualified to participate on an equal footing with the opposite sex, if that person has had a chance to develop according to her/his own terms. The advantage may, at first view, appear to be greatest for girls, but, in the long run, both sexes can profit if boys are able to see girls contesting boys' immediate sovereignty instead of having their false assumptions reinforced. Back in the mixed class, girls show less inclination to accept patriarchal values and patterns of work.

In a racist class society which is also based on sex inequality, alternating between sex-segregated and mixed learning processes can contribute to the creation of conditions for change, while at the same time serving to enhance people's sense of the conditions that can bring about consciousness-raising — a prerequisite for change. The aim is to create an awareness of our similarities and differences as human beings, and an awareness of how social divisions based on race, class and sex structure our experiences and opportunities in life.

Note

The chapter is a revised edition of 'We have learnt not just to sit back and twiddle our thumbs and let them take over', in *Gender and Education*, 4(1–2), 1992.

References

ASKEW, S. and ROSS, C. (1988) *Boys Don't Cry: Boys and Sexism in Education*, Buckingham, Open University Press.

BIIL, G. (1988) *Ligeværdsundervisning: Kønsadskilt undervisning i folkeskolen*, Aarhus, Forlaget LIS.

BROCK-UTNE, B. (1985) *Education for Peace*, New York, Pergamon Press.

DICKSON, A. (1982) *A Woman in Your Own Right*, London, Quartet Books.

ETHELBERG, E. (1983) *Kvindelighedens modsigelse*, Copenhagen, Antropos.

JEFFERS, S. (1987) *Feel The Fear And Do It Anyway*, London, Arrow Books.

JENSEN, P.-E., KROGH-JESPERSEN, K., REINSHOLM, N., KRUSE, A.-M. and REISBY, K. (1984) *Skoleliv — Pigheliv*, Copenhagen, Unge Pædagoger.

HANSEN, E.J. and ØRUM, B. (1975) *Illusioner om uddannelse*, Copenhagen, Socialforskningsinstituttet.

HOCKING, C. (1991) 'Counter-sexism programmes for boys — Developments and dilemmas', Paper presented to the Local Domestic Violence Committee's Conference, Medlow Bath, New South Wales, Australia.

KRUSE, A.-M. (1989) 'Hvorfor pigeklasser?', in HILDEN, A. and KRUSE, A.-M. (eds) *Pigernes skole*, Aarhus, Klim.

KRUSE, A.-M. (1990) 'Kønsadskilt undervisning som kønsbevidst pædagogik', in JACOBSEN, H. and HØJGÅRD, L. (eds) *Skolen er køn*, Copenhagen, Ligestillingsrådet.

KRUSE, A.-M. (1991a) 'Metoder til fremme af ligeværd', in PEDERSEN, G. and REISBY, K. (eds) *Ligeværd — Mangfoldighed*, Copenhagen, Danmarks Lærerhøjskole.

KRUSE, A.-M. (1991b) 'Was kann die schule für die mädchen tun?', in MARKER, B., SJØRUP, L. and WOLF, K. (eds) *Island, Grönland, Dänemark und die Färöer der Frauen: Reise and Kultur*, München, Frauenoffensive.

KRUSE, A.-M. (1992a) '¿ Cómo pueden ayudar a las chicas las experiencias escolares? ¿Pueden ser las instituciones para un solo sexo y las agrupaciones dentro de escuelas mixtas parte de una solución', in BALLARIN D.P. (ed.) *¿Desde las Mujeres Modelos Educations: Coeducar/Segregar?* FEMINAE, Seminaro do Estidios de la Mujer, Universidad de Granada.

KRUSE, A.-M. (1992b) 'We have learnt not just to sit back, twiddle our thumbs and let them take over. Single-sex settings and the development of a pedagogy for girls and a pedagogy for boys in Danish schools', *Gender and Education*, 4(1–2), pp. 81–103.

KRUSE, A.-M. (1993) 'Non-koedukativer unterricht als geschlechtsbewußter unterricht', in GLUMPLER, E. (ed.) *Erträge der Frauenforschung für die LehrerInnenbildung*, Flensburg, Klinkhardt.

KRUSE, A.-M. (1994a) 'Hvorfor kønsopdelt pædagogik? Om polariserende pædagogik som metode til at modvirke ulighed mellem kønnene belyst via Projekt Pigeklasse-Drengeklasse', *Arbejdsnotat*, no. 20, CEKVINA.

KRUSE, A.-M. (1994b) 'Er drenge bare drenge?', *Tidsskrift for børne — og ungdomskultur-forskning*, no. 34, pp. 51–65.

KRUSE, A.-M. (1995) 'Pigepædagogik og drengepædagogik — debat, praksis og perspektiver', *Utbildning och genusperspektivet, Tidsskrift för didaktik och utbildningspolitik*.

KRUSE, A.-M. (1996) 'Approaches to teaching boys and girls.' Article for forthcoming issue of Women's Studies International Forum.

NORDSTRÖM, G.Z. (1979) *Kreativitet og Bevidsthed: Den Polariserende Pædagogiks Grundlag*, Copenhagen, Borgen.

14 Intervention Programs in Science and Engineering Education: From Secondary Schools to Universities

Sue Lewis

Introduction

Recruitment, retention and educational development programs for teaching staff all come under the broad label of intervention programs and the foci and theoretical underpinnings of these programs are constantly being reappraised and challenged within Australia. Intervention programs in science and engineering sit at a controversial intersection between feminism and these masculine identified fields. They are the site of one of the main feminist challenges to the masculine professions and as such they have been contested, debated and developed. Over the past ten years I have collaboratively developed and implemented a number of educational programs, working with teaching staff to provide more gender-inclusive practices in science and engineering education. I have implemented these programs at both the secondary and tertiary levels of education, as well as in Australia and the United States. Over that time, many layers of complexity have been explored through developments in feminist theory, feminist theories of education, feminist critiques of traditional science and engineering and major developments in our understanding of gender construction. Unfortunately, particularly in Australia, there has often been a separation of the theory from the practice of intervention programs and programs have suffered from excessive pressures for 'action' and 'change' at the expense of research, reflection and theorizing.

The National Centre for Women (NCW), based at Swinburne University of Technology is a unique university centre in Australia whose current brief is to research and enhance women's recruitment and equal participation in 'non-traditional' employment, education and training. In the late 1980s, however, the NCW, like many other Australian programs, had explicit aims to increase the participation and retention of female students in the areas of engineering and science and it performed most of the recognized advocacy tasks: it targeted recruitment through attractive promotional materials, participation in seminars, 'hands-on' taster days; and support for women enrolled in engineering and science through support groups, mentors, use of role models, intervention classes in areas from engines to assertiveness. With recruitment or outreach programs, the focus is women in schools and in the community. With retention and support programs the focus is the women within 'non-traditional' courses and training. Whilst many feminists are retrospect-ively critical of these 'women focused' approaches during the 1980s, they were, and continue to be vital — without them we would not have the practical or theoretical base to reflect or the increased numbers of women within these fields of work and study. Participation in these programs has provided a base to identify their strengths as well as their theoretical and practical limitations.

Just as the 6th (1989) and 7th (1991) international Gender and Science and Technology (GASAT) conferences started to shift the theoretical underpinning of intervention programs from 'changing women and girls' to 'changing science and engineering', so did the NCW. In 1993, we reassessed our theoretical position and shifted our emphases from changing women's career aspirations and support once they had enrolled, to working toward change at organizational and cultural levels. Consequently, within the tertiary sector, a third layer has been added to recruitment and retention initiatives — educational development programs where the focus is curriculum and teaching. Here the focus is not women and girls but faculty lecturers, the majority of whom are male (96 per cent of engineering faculty academics are male in Australia).

Most of our work intersects with science and engineering areas of study and employment, although this is shifting as we examine and redefine the discourse of non-traditional work and study. Hence our major focus currently is on challenging the educational and workplace assumptions within non-traditional environments through a mixture of activism, research, theorizing and change processes. Interven-tion programs in the 1980s unwittingly sprang from the position that women needed to change in order to recognize and enjoy the wonders that science and engineer-ing careers have to offer. Again, the male norm is the universalized reference point. In these recruitment approaches, it is women who are problematized and targeted whilst the masculine epistemological processes that determine both the educational assumptions and the workplace practices are left unquestioned. Curriculum and teaching review and reform shift the spotlight to the assumptions and practices within faculties.

This chapter will revisit the reasons for the differential participation of women and men in the sciences before exploring the historical directions of intervention programs within the secondary sector. Finally I will discuss the current position and directions of intervention programs within the Australian tertiary sector.

What is 'Gender-Inclusive'?

'Gender-inclusive' has become a shorthand term in Australia for including a com-prehensive gender analysis in all educational practices. 'Inclusive of whom?' has often been asked. Whilst the term has been criticized for excluding an analysis of the power relations between women and men, the power relations between classes and cultures in our society, and power relations between different groups of women, it has been a useful shorthand for the transformed curriculum that would arise from females and males becoming equally valued in education. It is also a term that has evolved in meaning through the many theorists and practitioners that have enriched its usage (see one collection of papers in the Australian journal *Curriculum Perspectives*, **7**(1), 1987).

Definitions of gender-inclusive convey many of the same themes:

> Curriculum materials are gender-inclusive in content when the content is equally representative of the experiences and interests of women and men, when women's experience is recognised and valued equally with men's and is represented as an integral part of each area of study, subject, topic and theme. (A Fair Go For All — Guidelines for a gender-inclusive curriculum, Office of Schools Administration, Ministry of Education, Victoria, 1990, p. 16)

Equity practitioners in Australia have used gender-inclusive to refer to gender understandings in relation to staff approaches to lectures, tutorials, teaching strategies, types and frequency of assessment, decisions about content, staff selection and promotion, the physical environment, laboratory design and usage, as well as timetabling, course structure and options.

Different Gender, Different Interests, Different Cognitive Styles

In order to consider the directions for current intervention programs in Australia, it is important to first revisit the eternal question: 'Why do more women than men choose to reject science and engineering education?'

Much of the theoretical underpinning for intervention programs in gender and maths and science education draws on the literature that describes females and males as having different interests and learning styles. Social conventional wisdom describes women as interested in people and the environment and men as interested in machines and things. These patterns have been characterized by the feminist movement as the private versus the public domains. Other dualisms follow: the emotional versus the rational, subjective versus the objective, soft versus hard. These popular manifestations of the differential treatment of girls and boys during childhood are exhibited in science classrooms through girls' and boys' preferences for human-centred versus machine-centred science topics respectively (Smail, 1984; Johnson and Murphy, 1986).

Nancy Chodorow's (1978) work *The Reproduction of Mothering* is often the starting point in the literature for the psychoanalytic interpretation of these patterns. Her work has drawn attention to the different formative experiences for girls and boys in relation to parental care patterns that are dominant in our society. She explores the gender difference arising from the mother being the primary care giver for both young girls and boys in our society. Through the differential parenting patterns common in most families, she describes the development of the gendered human and has provided 'a subject object schema that permits us to analyse, criticise, and, it is hoped, transform the subject/object relations that organise curriculum and the disciplines' (Grumet, 1994).

When the mother is the primary caretaker of her infant, the attachment to her precedes the infant's attachment to the father and influences it profoundly: particularly during the first six months. Within this way of looking at childhood, the mother is the child's first object. The mother identifies with the daughter, but perceives her son as sexually other. Hence from very early on, because they are parented by a person of the same gender, 'girls come to experience themselves as less differentiated than boys, as more continuous with and related to the external object world and as differently oriented to their inner object world as well' (Chodorow, 1978). As Grumet (1994) summarizes in *Conception, Contradiction, and Curriculum*:

> The achievement of masculine gender requires the male child to repress those elements of his own subjectivity that are identified with his mother. What is male is that which is not feminine and/or connected with women. This is another way in which boys repress relation and connection in the process of growing up. Girls, on the other hand, need not repress the identification with their mothers. (p. 156)

Separation from the mother is part of the masculine development of independence in our society. As Head (1985) describes:

> The consequences of such childhood experiences are that the girl reaches adolescence with a developed sense of interpersonal responsibilities but possibly with a weak sense of personal identity and autonomy. The boy possesses the latter but has paid a price, an inability to handle explicit expression of emotions and some insensitivity to other people's needs. (p. 61)

These differences in gender construction interact with the stereotypical patterns of child rearing. The adult world conveys different messages to girls and boys about what are acceptable and unacceptable ways to behave. Hence we encourage girls to be more social and boys to be more physically active. We encourage boys to play out-of-doors more often than girls, we encourage boys to play competitive games more often than girls (Clark, 1989; Lever, 1976; Lever, 1978). We give different toys to girls and boys (Rheingold and Cook, 1975; and any children's toy shop).

The work of Carol Gilligan (1982) and Belenky *et al.* (1986) indicate that these patterns often persist into adult life and lead to differences in cognitive style between women and men. Attribute style is one of the fields of cognitive style where gender differences have been identified (see Head's earlier Chapter in this volume) and is the pattern of causes attributed by a person to the events in their life. When these events are educational, such as success or failure on tests or examinations, females attribute a 'failure' to lack of ability (unchangeable) and success to easy test problems or simply luck (arbitrary factors outside their control) (Beyer and Reich, 1987; Beyer, 1991). This attribute style also means that she does not expect to achieve success in the future — even if she has already experienced some success. In comparison, males often attribute 'failure' to arbitrary or temporary causes such as lack of preparation or misfortune. Success is perceived as a result of ability. This attribute style enables the male to maintain his self-confidence despite failures, and to expect success in the future.

Nona Lyons (1994) follows the transition in the 'nature of knowledge' research from William Perry who derived his theories largely from male college students through to Mary Belenky, Blythe Clinchy, Nancy Goldberger and Jill Tarule's (1986) now famous study of *Women's Ways of Knowing*. Lyons reviews these together to reveal some gender dimensions to ways of knowing. Perry describes nine positions for students during their undergraduate years, where they move from a 'dualistic understanding of knowledge as either right or wrong to a position of relativism; that is, an understanding that all knowledge is constructed' (Lyons, 1994). He saw that a capacity for detachment and an ability to stand back from oneself in objectivity and the relativism of one system of thought to another are necessary to achieve this transition. Belenky *et al.* (1986) showed that women were able to act in detached objectivity, to see and respond to demands of external authorities. However, they also showed that women were especially concerned with understanding the background, perspectives and beliefs of others. Women seemed to connect with others in their own particular situations and contexts rather than to challenge them.

Belenky *et al.* (1986) interviewed 135 women, including women in urban and rural environments, and elaborated a theory to include five different epistemological categories from these interviews — ways of knowing. These categories range from

> ... silence, a position in which women experience themselves as mind-less and voiceless and subject to the whims of external authority; received knowledge, a perspective from which women conceive of themselves as capable of receiving, even reproducing, knowledge from all knowing external authorities but not capable of creating knowledge on their own; subjective knowledge, a perspective from which truth and knowledge are conceived of as personal, private, and subjectively known or intuited; procedural knowledge, a position in which women are invested in learning and applying objective procedures for obtaining and communicating knowledge; and constructed knowledge, a position in which women view all knowledge as contextual, experience themselves as creators of knowledge, and value both subjective and objective strategies for knowing. (p. 15)

This final category is similar to Perry's view (1970) that all knowledge is contextual and constructed, and that women are capable of making theory. This work of Belenky *et al.* (1986) also suggests another way to interpret the classroom. As a teacher or student we hold various stances toward knowledge and ways of knowing. They describe two different approaches for procedural knowers. One approach is more like the traditionally known, objective, rule-seeking ways of evaluating, proving or disproving truth — separate procedural knowers. A second approach seeks understanding a meaning from the individual's perspective — connected procedural knowers — for people who look for connections between ideas, events and personal factors such as circumstances and background experiences.

The former description characterizes the traditional view of the physical sciences and the teaching of physics-related subjects in particular. Belenky *et al.* (1986) identify the need to look more fully at the gender patterns for connected and procedural knowers, but this connection is another way of interpreting the differential participation of women and men in physics and engineering. As a society we continue to construct women and men differently. In turn, men unwittingly influence the practices and processes within the physical sciences and engineering so that they embody the very characteristics of their gender — separation of the knower from the knowledge. One position orients toward that to be known (traditional view of physics and the physics curriculum) and the other toward the knower (more the gender-inclusive perspective). Lynda Stone (1994) calls this the epistemic orientation. Not all women and not all men approach learning and teaching the sciences and engineering in these ways — it is the complex processes leading to the gendering of these professions that are important.

How these differences express themselves in the relationship that girls and boys forge with science is the parallel framework that we know more about. A number of authors have used the psychoanalytic perspectives of Chodorow (1978) and object relations theory to explain the different subject choices of female and male students (Harding and Sutoris, 1987; Head, 1985). It is at the crucial adolescent age when females seek interrelatedness and males seek independence that we ask students to make their subject choices. Girls who choose the physical sciences or engineering not only have to show a strong sense of independence by choosing a non-traditional subject, they are also asked to choose a set of maths and science subjects which are characterized as abstract laws disconnected from their social and physical worlds. Boys, on the other hand, can make a decision in tune with their peer group, and overlapping their need for emotional separation through disconnected abstract laws. Hence, do many men choose the certainty of physics and the allied engineering discipline? Do many women also choose these areas for the same reasons and our society constructs fewer women this way than men? Or do women make adjustments and incorporate the accepted ways of knowing in physics in order to succeed?

The implications for the gender reform of the physical sciences and engineering that follow from these analyses are interesting. If we are seeking a transformation of the ways of knowing within the discipline, we are really asking for individuals to move from certainty to uncertainty at many levels and here begin many of the issues that relate to the educational and staff development challenges in universities.

The Evolution of Intervention Programs in Secondary Schools: A Case Study

I will briefly outline the major directions for Australian intervention programs in the secondary education sector before focusing on current tertiary developments. This link is important as programs in secondary schools have been the most frequently funded and prolific. McIntosh (1984) and Schuster and Van Dyne (1984) developed two similar models of curriculum change out of analyses of arts curriculum changes when challenged by gender reform. They depict the incorporation of women into the curriculum as a process with identifiable phases. Both start from the historical situation, where the absence of women in the curriculum was not noted, through to the transformed gender-balanced curriculum where women's and men's experience can be understood together. Schuster and Van Dyne (1984) also include the changed relationship between teacher and student that each stage requires. I have re-labelled the Schuster and Van Dyne stages to apply to science education:

1 Absence of women in science not noticed.
2 The search for the missing women in science.
3 Why are there so few women in science?
4 Studying women's experience in science.
5 Challenging the paradigm of what science is.
6 The transformed, reconstructed gender-balanced curriculum.

Using this framework I have analysed the intervention strategies and programs associated with the McClintock Collective from 1983 to 1993 (Lewis, 1993). The first four stages focus on women and their attributes and experiences whereas stages 5 and 6 shift the microscope to science (or technology, engineering) itself. The McClintock Collective have represented many of Schuster and Van Dyne's stages in the evolution of their research and intervention programs. As a result of equal opportunity and non-sexist programs of the 1970s and early 1980s, as well as an increasing number of Australian women scientists, the first stage of 'not missing the women' (Stage 1) had passed in science education by 1983. The search for the missing women scientists to profile in science classrooms (Stage 2 above) was a phase that started in the early 1980s in Victoria with the publication of the resource packages and posters depicting women as scientists and mathematicians in the past as well as the present. As Schuster and Van Dyne (1984) point out, this approach adds to the existing data within the conventional paradigms. Essentially it was a compensatory exercise and asked the same question as conventional science — who are and were the great women scientists? It also transferred the same criteria that defined men as famous scientists, forgetting other female contributions to science; for example, the women who did all the technical work in research laboratories who were rarely given credit.

Questions such as 'Why are there so few women in science?' (Stage 3) framed much of the early work of the McClintock Collective in the mid-1980s and exemplified the first state-wide professional development program for teachers in Victoria. The low numbers of women in science employment, and of girls in physics and chemistry classes, were profiled. These numerical differences were attributed to social and educational influences, particularly the classroom dynamics experienced by girls in the science laboratory classroom. Strategies developed by the McClintock Collective focused on challenging these classroom practices. At this time however, the curriculum itself, teaching practice, and the views of science they reflected were only beginning to be challenged. Women were 'disadvantaged' because individual females missed out on being part of male achievement. It was a protest rather than a direct challenge to the conventional paradigm of science and science education.

In late 1984, there was a shift in focus to challenging the traditional curriculum and teaching of science. The McClintock Collective received some government funding to develop a gender-inclusive curriculum for science. We subsequently spent considerable time asking 'What is a gender-inclusive science curriculum anyway?' Other questions followed. What is women's experience of science and what are the informal science experiences of girls (Stage 4)? What are the differences amongst girls? How does an inclusive curriculum differ from the traditional curriculum? Do girls learn differently from boys and what are the implications for science education? What are curriculum materials for girls? How do you start from female experience in science but extend girls from there? What is the influence of different teaching approaches? What areas of the science curriculum are most urgently in need of better materials? What about the boys ... ? These and other questions challenged us and were discussed more over the next three years (McClintock Collective, 1987). They still represent the questions that many teachers and theorists ask today.

Out of this questioning, our focus became 'how science is taught' and versions of the 'McClintock Teaching Strategies' were developed with a comprehensive array of student-centred teaching approaches for science. Essentially these teaching approaches fitted one of three types. They provided active learning contexts for students (e.g., constructing with lego), they described alternative ways of organizing the classroom (e.g., cooperative groups) and they reorganized the curriculum (e.g., starting from and valuing students' experiences) whilst at the same time recognizing that stereotyped female and male experiences of the world are different. Underneath these approaches was the assumption that if teachers could teach and present science experiences in innovative and active ways there would be an increased participation in the physical sciences by girls in their post-Year 10 choices.

The Collective focused on: cooperative group work, creative drawing and writing, role-playing, media, social implications of science, discussion, tinkering, negotiation, construction of models, using materials and tools, and values clarification exercises. These ideas culminated in the McClintock Collective resource book *Getting into Gear — Gender-Inclusive Teaching Strategies in Science* (Gianello, 1988). Many of these strategies were present in other projects, but often without a gender perspective.

Perhaps the most direct challenge to 'the paradigm of science' (Stage 5) is the development of more gender-inclusive curriculum models that challenge conventional '*content-driven*' approaches. Content-driven curriculum is the curriculum model that dominates the tertiary teaching of science and engineering (and hence the secondary school science) and continues to reinforce the masculine characterization of science as abstract and disconnected from social and environmental concerns. The content-driven curriculum is one of the most strongly defended notions in the physical and engineering sciences. Here the curriculum developers start with the list of mandatory theory when approaching course development. Allied to this curriculum approach in Australia is the common view within science and engineering education of teaching as telling or transmission that is so prevalent in the tertiary sector. The underlying assumption of gender-inclusive challenges is that if the curriculum is presented in a more connected style, where the social and environmental contexts are integrated, then we will attract a wider diversity of female and male students to scientific endeavour, and ultimately diversify the culture of science.

In a *context-driven* curriculum, instead of starting from the abstract laws and theories of chemistry or physics, the starting points are the contexts of the social, environmental, and physical worlds and the investigative processes lead to the theories, models and perspectives that make up the culture of science. Contexts are often open-ended, holistic rather than closed and compartmentalized. Harding (1986) worked with students in teacher training to develop a curriculum that begins with students raising questions about the science issues in their lives. This issues-based curriculum starts from, for example, lead in petrol, household appliances, X-rays, acid rain, supermarkets, roller skates. The Girls and Maths and Science Teaching project in Australia (GAMAST) also started topics with student-led enquiries about sunblock creams, heat resistant materials, playground equipment and bicycles (Lewis and Davies, 1988).

A context-developed curriculum has other implications for teaching and learning. The relationship between the teacher and student becomes more central. The teacher fosters connections with students, begins with knowledge of the student's background and prior learning, recognizes the value of subjective ways of knowing, has a democratic and non-authoritarian style. She also has diverse models of classroom organization where students may learn collaboratively through role-plays, model building, discussion, investigations or through individual research. She has diverse assessment practices where the students are continuously assessed, sometimes anonymously, often through extended answers (Spear, 1987; Gipps and Murphy, 1994; Murphy, 1993; Hildebrand and Allard, 1993; Parker and Rennie, 1993; Rennie and Parker, 1993). The teacher also collaborates with other staff to review, read and reflect on her teaching and assessment and how her teaching affects different groups of students and different individuals.

Constructing curriculum in this way can challenge the traditional views of science and approaches to science teaching through the inclusion of key issues and questions that surround students' lives. Context-driven curriculum also challenges the definition and boundaries of what has been traditionally accepted as the science curriculum. It provides the basis for diversifying the approaches to curriculum and assessment to include multiple ways of knowing as well as questioning the established view that there is only one way of knowing — a scientific way.

The political context for this historical sequence of programs must be further explained for other education communities. In 1982 a new state government (Labor) was elected in Victoria after twenty-eight years of conservative (Liberal) government. New ideas and possibilities were sweeping the education community at the same time as there was national and international attention on gender issues in education. In addition, a national Labor government was elected in 1983 which set up the Commonwealth Schools Commission and initiated a funding base for special 'Projects of National Significance'. GAMAST was one of the projects funded under this Commission from 1986 to 1988. Whilst funding was, and is, always hard to secure for gender reform, these events are important to document as they provided the political as well as infrastructure support for the establishment of the McClintock Collective's early intervention programs. Since 1992 there has been a return to a Conservative state government in Victoria which has subsequently cut funding to all equity programs and shown no commitment to gender justice in schools.

The Process of Change

To quote Fullan (1982), 'change is a process not an event'. The ideas and programs described above have to be incorporated into effective teacher professional development programs — changing the practices of real people. In the 1980s intervention programs in Australia carried the label of 'gender' and consequently had to deal with the multiple positions of female and male teachers in their views of gender. Gender justice workers felt, and continue to feel, this acutely (Kenway and Evans, 1991). The McClintock Collective and the GAMAST project aimed to engage teachers in a collaborative process to develop new classroom practices that would lead to changes in their attitudes and values as outcomes of changes in student learning. The inservice model of curriculum consultants supporting small, ongoing, school-based teams, or key groups of teachers who owned their starting points and action research pathways, was already widespread in the Victorian education system. The GAMAST project principles illustrate these characteristics:

- commitment to formal and informal workshops extending over time;
- participating teachers applied for, and were selected for the project on the basis of, their interest and commitment to the issues of a gender-based review of their curriculum and teaching;
- ongoing support and follow-up from consultants throughout the year;
- teachers worked together in small teams;
- external consultants participated in a formative evaluation of the program;
- programs started from the individual needs and understandings of the participating teachers;
- mandatory support of the school principal;
- both school- and project-based at different times.

Action research has been the common thread determining the investigative process within most of the programs. Essentially, action research is a form of self-reflective enquiry which aims to improve practice through understanding and to involve others in all phases of an open process. Practitioners research their own practice. Action research leads to formulating recommendations and putting these into practice. It also represents a cyclical process of ongoing change without a predetermined end point (Carr and Kemmis, 1983; Zuber-Skerritt, 1992).

In the GAMAST project we attempted to meet all three of Fullan's (1982) criteria for successful change: the overlap of the individual participant's needs with those of the central funding body; the support of the Ministry, region and school principal; and the opportunity for staff to interact with each other, share ideas and have access to external support and assistance. The McClintock Collective also evolved toward this model with the benefit of hindsight. Following some harrowing experiences when we were included in a compulsory program we decided to only work with staff who were self-selecting.

Having explored the directions of secondary intervention programs using the McClintock Collective programs as a case study, I want to focus on the tertiary sector. How have gender reform issues been taken up by tertiary science and engineering faculties within Australia these past ten years? The comparison with secondary is revealing.

Gendered Faculties in Tertiary Education

Background

Tertiary education in science and engineering continued in the 1970s and 1980s without the gender reforms that took place in the primary and secondary sectors during this time. In primary and secondary education in Australia, women have been the majority of the advocates for change. Until recently, tertiary intervention programs focused entirely on recruitment and retention initiatives where the focus was changing women's career choices and experiences. More importantly, the focus remained safely outside the faculty. Intervention program managers in higher education have been predominantly female also, but with one significant difference: the intervention program workers have not been faculty teaching staff but women employed to work in programs outside the departments or in centres for women's access to education. Hence the teaching staff themselves, and the curriculum and teaching practices within these science and engineering faculties, have been largely unaffected and unchallenged by these programs. Instead, intervention programs have focused on recruitment and retention strategies. Consequently, most male staff in these faculties have not personally worked through the complexity of the issue from the perspective of implementing gender-inclusive strategies or reforming their curriculum and teaching. There is much learning and experience from the secondary sector that has not been transferred to the tertiary sector.

In every primary and secondary school, it is mandatory that all teachers have teacher training. There is a very different history in the tertiary sector, however, where the theoretical knowledge of a discipline has often been the central criterion for appointment, without consideration of teaching and educational knowledge. Unlike the secondary sector, the pressures on the tertiary sector to be educationally accountable are very recent. Now there are expectations of performance appraisal and consideration of teaching as a criterion for appointment and promotion, as well as national funds for educational development in departments and faculties. The knowledge of gender and education research and theory has consequently been confined to education faculties and has rarely been applied within a science or engineering faculty for examining curriculum, teaching and assessment practices faculty-wide. Hence, much of the learning in the primary and secondary sectors about educational change and the importance of gender in educational improvement have not been applied in tertiary education.

Since 1991 I have worked within universities in an educational development role, usually with gender as a lens and more recently with student diversity as a lens. Here, the issues for intervention programs are different. Perhaps the central obstacles for intervention programs in higher education are the pervasiveness of the culture of autonomy, individuality, competition, and hierarchical models of management prevalent in engineering and science faculties, compared with a more democratic culture of teamwork and decision-making in the secondary sector. Added to this, research in universities is being maintained as a higher priority than teaching and educational development, despite the ambitious rhetoric during the transition of Australian universities to a unified system after 1988. By contrast, teaching and educational development are the central priorities in the secondary school sector (although the professional development of teachers is devalued within the current political system in Victoria). Female science teachers have been a 'critical mass' of 30–40 per cent, sometimes 50 per cent, in many schools and have led the gender reform movement there. There is no such critical mass in science and engineering faculties, where faculties of engineering can still have few or no women (national data is 4 per cent).

Science and engineering faculties are more directly linked to the culture of scientific research and its technical applications. Universities continue the education of scientists and engineers arising out of the physical science curriculum at the secondary school level. The personality characteristics of scientists and engineers show that males tend to be 'emotionally reticent, disliking overt emotional expression in others and themselves . . . they also tend to be authoritarian, conservative and controlled in their thinking' (Head, 1987). The research questions, methods, criteria of success, and styles of teaching are male-defined and, consequently, the knowledge itself reflects a bias towards a male cognitive style in its practices, theories, ways of teaching, and ways of managing and organizing faculties. The science and engineering makers have created professions where the separation of theory from social context, and the top-down, expert authority is the dominant paradigm.

Higher education science and engineering faculties have a double layer of masculinity: the rules and accepted practices for the generation of knowledge and the transmission of this knowledge have two layers of power relations that make women (as well as some men) and their ways of knowing invisible. The distance between science and society is large, as is the distance between lecturer and student.

The Chilly Learning Environment — Factors for Change

One of the central issues facing engineering faculties in Australia, and some of the physical science majors, is the male student learning environment. Many women students experience these environments as uncomfortable, 'chilly' and consequently many intervention strategies in universities have focused on retention strategies. A range of inside and outside classroom behaviours can create a chilly learning environment. They relate to how women are treated in the classroom or the laboratory, the undergraduate and graduate relationship with teaching staff, and the less formal student exchange. All these contexts may affect how women students view themselves and hence their full development and career aspirations. Not all male dominated engineering and science learning environments exhibit characteristics that make them uncomfortable for women, but many do. In 1994, women comprised 13.1 per cent of engineering undergraduate numbers in Australia. There are physical science majors within science and applied science degrees where the women are often in the minority from 10 to 30 per cent. Like all statistics they hide as much as they reveal — by the time you get to the final years of an engineering degree, there may be very few women remaining depending on the field of engineering. For example there may be final year classes in some fields of engineering, such as mechanical or electrical, with few or no women studying (Lewis, 1995).

Marginalization

Putdowns and sexist harassment of female students (and many male ethnic students) appears to be worse in the 1990s compared with the 1970s and 1980s. Prior to the 1970s the small minority of female students were treated as a separate species but with almost Victorian era politeness, compared with the blatantly sexist behaviour that some male students now exhibit towards them. Data on how many female students 'drop out' of male dominated courses, when and why they do so has been largely ignored as a research question and source of valuable information in the tertiary sector.

Subtle forms of discrimination such as putdowns can often inflict the most damage because they occur without recognition and they occur repeatedly over time — where individuals or groups are singled out or ignored because of their sex, race or age or disability. These putdowns often occur in the course of everyday interchanges but the cumulative effect of these interchanges throughout the undergraduate experience can create a chilly learning environment. Putdowns can place women students at an educational disadvantage through discouraging their classroom participation, preventing them from seeking help outside class, causing them to drop or avoid certain classes and even to leave an institution. All of these can have the effect of undermining confidence and dampening career aspirations.

Prior Experience

One of the most striking aspects of women student interviews is the common reporting that undergraduate lecturers start their lectures at a level that assumes prior knowledge outside their secondary studies curricula (Lewis, 1995). This prior knowledge overlaps with the typical informal experience of the male students. A typical male student in the 1970s or 1980s did have a tinkering and model building background and often came from a technical background. Now, many women, as well as an increasing number of men students, do not fit this stereotype. Males often have significant informal experience outside their schooling that gives them language and mechanical concepts as well as provides them with both knowledge and motivation to choose engineering. One interview study of forty students found that 85 per cent of men students had previous informal tinkering experience; had built houses with their families; had pulled cars and tractors apart; had lived in Dick Smith kits and stores during their adolescence; or had been tinkerers and builders with their father (Lewis, 1995). This pattern has also been reported from the UK (Carter and Kirkup, 1990) and from the US (McIlwee and Robinson, 1992).

Attribute Style and Retention

Attribute style is one of the other central issues within the climate of male-dominated courses. The importance of gender related attribute differences, interest levels and curriculum context all play a part in an environment where women students are feeling singled out or ignored. They are part of a set of factors that contribute to some women students feeling less confident about their abilities and their place in a chilly course. Consequently, women's educational experiences may differ considerably from those of men even when they attend the same lectures and practicals or work with the same supervisors. Faculty behaviours which lead women to feel their academic and career ambitions are not as important as those of men students may play a major role in limiting women students' development.

All these faculty-based factors have led to the proliferation of a range of retention strategies within, and adjacent to, faculties: 'drop-in' centres, special events, mentor schemes and support networks for women undergraduates. One of the current issues for concern is the identification of these programs with feminism in the minds of many of the students. Feminism is the target of many of the putdowns and trivializations by the male students and it is understandable that women students are ambivalent about adopting overt expressions of feminism — such as participation in feminist identified programs conducted by a women's centre. These recent backlash issues are causing many programs to rethink their retention strategies.

Some Tertiary Case Studies of Intervention Programs

The following three boxes illustrate some of the current issues within science and engineering faculties in Australia. They form the third category of intervention programs that I identified in the introduction — curriculum and teaching programs where the focus is faculty teaching staff. The names of the universities and grant agencies have been changed or omitted.

Intervention programs have not had significant federal funding within Australian universities to develop the lighthouse programs that have occurred in the secondary and primary sectors. Consequently, universities assemble small amounts of funding to conduct small projects that are short term. Universities are also experiencing severe economic constraints in the 1990s and the finances for educational development and the implementation of more student-centred practices are very limited.

Focus on First Year

The project's focus was to review and develop the common first year of the undergraduate engineering program. In Australia, a common first year sees all first year undergraduate engineers studying the same course before choosing their fields of specialization in second year. The major focus of the project was the many challenges facing post secondary/tertiary engineering education due to the increasing diversity of students and the rapid changes to the engineering workplace over the past fifteen years. Women students, and students from language backgrounds other than English, were the central diversity concerns.

Initial planning for the project adopted an action research methodology as the appropriate way of initiating and developing the project. The project team had part-time release from teaching and developed their own understandings of action research principles. The team also had to articulate their own understanding of the educational reasons for the project. There was much recognition that most proposals for reform focused on quick solutions rather than a deeper understanding of educational problems. The team developed through planning, acting, observing, and reflecting during the many stages of the project. This was often a confusing process: directions became blurred and then more focused, members sometimes reverted to their previously held opinions, and the overall development was certainly not linear.

The team's first task was to collate and document a picture of the first year and this was a revealing process for all the teaching staff. The critical issues identified were:

- the curriculum, content sequencing and assessment of most first year subjects were decided independently of other subjects and with little collaboration between first and second years;
- staff knew little of what was happening educationally outside their own subject;
- the practical component of the subjects had diminished over the past ten years due to diminishing resources and this was having a detrimental educational effect;
- there was very little continuity or uniformity in the description of the subject goals and objectives given to the students;
- some content areas overlapped between subjects and resulted in confusion for students due to different terminology and symbols.

Here was critical learning for gender reform: there were considerable and basic educational issues that needed addressing before or in parallel with any gender reform of the curriculum and teaching.

One of the central research strategies involved the staff in interviewing and surveying students. Listening to students was unusual in this context and there were many gender patterns and revelations about different prior experience and the very different student environments they experienced. These findings became the bases for further curriculum and faculty development. The team accumulated relevant information on research and practice in engineering education and used this as the basis for informed discussion and further development. Out of this process the team developed an overall set of aims for a common first year, and consulted with the wider faculty through structured staff meetings. The project team explored educational and structural changes to the first year to achieve these educational aims and implemented these through extensive committee processes. A first year curriculum panel came into existence as a body to monitor and coordinate educational development of the first year. With time this committee was the most significant outcome of the project long after the funding had expired — there was the potential for ongoing change.

Making Connections

'Making Connections' has federal higher education funds and has developed, trialed and evaluated a project-based component of design engineering in two universities. One of the central rationales for this program was that further improvement in the participation of women in undergraduate engineering will only be achieved through changing the traditional practices within engineering education and employment. Professional and industry reports have also emphasized the need for undergraduate courses in engineering to adjust to changes in the profession more rapidly and equip graduates with broader skills, particularly in the areas of communication, interdisciplinary skills, creative problem-solving and management.

Students are undertaking design projects in teams, as well as presenting and evaluating their projects in a simulated workplace situation. This program has implemented the shift from content- to context-driven curriculum and assists student learning by starting with a familiar curriculum context and building the technical and professional skills components through connecting with the engineering concepts.

The gender-inclusive model for this project was characterized by:

- open-ended, problem-based learning;
- social and environmental curriculum contexts;

- collaborative team approaches;
- diversity of teaching and assessment approaches.

These principles have been the focus for the staff development component of the project.

Students were allowed to choose the subject of their projects and many semester classes were structured to guide students through the design process, and integrating the social and environmental contexts into their design. Interdisciplinary and group work featured rather than the traditional educational models characterized by lectures, separate disciplines and individual work. Staff impressions and experience were recorded through individual interviews as well as group discussion. Student feedback was documented from evaluation sessions.

Student feedback was very positive with students expressing their enjoyment of the design project as a chance to work as real engineers and develop their understanding of engineering. They also viewed the vicissitudes of teamwork within a real world context: this was the reality of the workplace and it was important to develop teamworking skills. Women students pointed out the informality of the subject and the importance of socially getting to know and work with other male students who subsequently treated them with more respect. They saw many subjects as learning 'which numbers to plug into which formulae' and appreciated that a different teaching approach also improved their social and learning environment.

Staff reactions were very positive with the exception of one staff member who remained convinced that such a subject was 'content free' and as such was a waste of student time compared with technically centred subjects. Positive comments related to creating a real workplace task and teamwork context through to enabling students to connect previous learning into meaningful engineering tasks. Staff also commented on their difficulties in effectively teaching team skills and conflict resolution and this was the focus for further staff development as a consequence. Due to the external funding, staff had funded time to attend weekly planning and curriculum development meetings and these were highly appreciated by all staff. Here again was important learning for gender reform: there are very few collaborative processes within engineering faculties and these processes are central to gender reform. Most faculties have very few opportunities for staff collaboration.

Maximizing Diversity

A cluster of projects at another university has arisen out of a sequence of staff development sessions conducted over six months. These sessions focused on factors that create a warm classroom environment for both female students and students from other cultures, as well as inclusive curriculum and teaching issues. Again the focus for this program was a faculty concern over the plateau and possible decline in the number of women within the undergraduate engineering programs and recognition that the assumptions and practices within engineering faculties have to be challenged in order to examine how engineering can become more inclusive of 'non-traditional' students. The faculty wanted to improve their educational strategies to teach in gender and culturally inclusive ways.

The culmination of these sessions was the development of a cluster of educational development projects within the engineering faculty. Staff were offered central funds to collaboratively conduct projects that supported student diversity in learning. The focus was both women and students from language backgrounds other than English. Staff were asked to make a brief submission for the funds and were provided with consultancy time for this project development phase. These projects will be linked together with a common faculty reporting and publication timeline.

Funded projects are very diverse and cover:

- training of laboratory tutors to be more gender and culturally sensitive;
- analysing the assessment data within the faculty in order to reveal any patterns of achievement in different assessment tasks;
- interviewing female and male students about curriculum and assessment issues;
- videoing mechanical practical exercises in order to understand and intervene in any gender and culture dynamics within the class;
- the development of a multimedia library resource to cater for students from less technical backgrounds.

The most meaningful model for change in science and engineering faculties has the same characteristics as secondary models: staff collaboratively designing and developing their change programs over time with the support of senior staff and an external consultant. These programs cannot be prescriptive, but must follow the emergent ideas and viewpoints. They must also be legitimated by teaching staff being given both time and material resources to develop changes to their curriculum and teaching. The importance of monitoring and documenting the programs is also one of the lessons learnt from the 1980s.

The Loneliness of the Long Distance — Resistance to Change

There are emerging concerns about the likelihood of success of intervention programs in science and engineering faculties in higher education. As outlined earlier, the culture is male defined and most academics in these disciplines are male. There are very few advocates for a more gender-inclusive curriculum within the male academies of science and engineering. Experience of advertised programs for gender-inclusive development within these faculties has shown that very few staff apply. Some reform programs have an enlightened Dean pushing their staff to attend a session on gender and education, and the various stages of awareness of the participants inevitably span all six stages of Schuster and Van Dyne's curriculum change model. There are many forms of resistance exhibited by such staff groupings.

Intervention programs in science and engineering faculties are particularly vulnerable to resistance since they threaten the comfort zone of many staff members and students. There are a number of resistance discourses operating in faculties and they can be described politely as politics and educational priorities but they can be avoidance, sabotage and attack. Not all staff approach gender dilemmas and challenges in these ways. Avoidance statements are the most commonly encountered and centre on assigning all educational problems to the student deficit model — the poor quality of student intake (always decreasing from earlier times) or the poor motivation or preparedness of students. Other avoidance mechanisms involve defending current practices based on the longevity of their degree-conferring ceremonies, drawing on one particularly successful woman to justify current teaching practices, or problem recognition equals problem resolution. Sabotage can extend to appointing an unqualified person to a change position, or appointing the right person in a far too junior position with low salary. It can also take the form of cynicism where everything has been done before or is an assumed part of current educational practice. Attack is often saved for any written material by questioning its grammar, meaning or research validity or the attack targets the workshop opportunity where the facilitator is assumed the enemy and asked the most aggressive question. The forms of resistance can be many and varied.

The success of a particular change project is subject to a number of local variables including institutional culture, role and status of the program and manager in the faculty, and the nature and strength of the relationships formed. It must pay attention to the process of change. The following list of change strategies have emerged with time:

- Change is slow, so patience is very important.
- Work with the support of a group where possible. If that group contains highly regarded, competent staff all the better, since this broadens your credibility.
- Be sensitive to the needs/values and history of the particular culture with which you are dealing.
- Target and work with people receptive to your ideas. Accept that some people will *never* change. Attempting the impossible wastes time and proves discouraging.
- Encourage ownership of change at both an individual and organizational level.
- Avoid imposing your changes/ideas. Seek involvement from those who will be affected by the change.
- Have a strong case! Be prepared with research/data/'one liners' to support your actions/demands.

- Be flexible. Don't forget the importance of one-to-one informal strategies.
- Acknowledge and recognize the odds stacked against you. Know your opposition!
- Operate within a strong policy framework — this gives you support and validates the change process.
- The big stick! While legislation will not in itself change ideas and attitudes, it will change actions and behaviour which can, eventually, lead to changed beliefs.

Towards a Transformed, Gender-balanced Curriculum

Needless to say, we have not yet achieved a transformed, gender-balanced curriculum (Stage 6). In the future, writers such as Evelyn Fox Keller envisage a world where gender is not an organizing category; 'a transformation of the very categories of male and female, and correspondingly, of mind and nature' (Keller, 1985, p. 178). Many of our questions about 'what is our vision of science' need new initiatives and theoretical frameworks. We need to develop new ways of transforming critiques of science into innovative curriculum and develop ways of incorporating these perspectives in the classroom.

Here is the opportunity for the post-structuralist feminist frameworks to influence the science curricula of the future: critically examining the assumptions behind the culture and practice of science. Processes such as deconstruction need to be explored for their potential for classroom teaching. How will we provide programs in the future that enable students to understand the construction of scientific knowledge in our society, and, in particular, the historical relationships of the past that have led to the male construction of science? We need curricula which include the history and philosophy of science and engineering, which include gender critiques, which connect the knower with the subject/object, which include the intended and unintended outcomes of scientific discoveries and their technologies, and which expose the undemocratic ways that science and engineering often operate (the process of scientific research funding, for example).

There are a range of issues raised through feminist critiques of science that represent many of the visions of what a socially critical science could be, but these are filtering into gender and science education communities very slowly. There seems to be some perpetuation of the academic divisions between the theoretical feminists critiquing science and engineering and the practitioners translating these ideas into classroom practice. The development of the inclusive curriculum and teaching ideas must learn from and incorporate these theoretical ideas more rapidly. To do this there has to be more joint work to consider effective ways of translating these ideas into the classroom. Theorists also need to be engaged in the practical meanings of their ideas as well as practitioners engaged with theory.

The assumptions that underpin gender-inclusive curriculum and teaching developments always need to be questioned. To treat all girls and women as a single category is to deny the diversity of class and ethnic backgrounds of women and girls.

To assume that all females learn in a common way is as problematic as the assumption that female and male students must learn in the same way. The interaction of gender, class, and culture in relation to science and engineering education has yet to be researched in any depth in Australia, let alone be put into practice. It is already the challenge for the last half of the 1990s and beyond.

References

BELENKY, M.F., CLINCHY, B.M., GOLDBERGER, N.R. and TARULE, J.M (1986) *Women's Ways of Knowing: The Development of Self, Voice and Mind*, New York, Basic Books, Inc., Publishers.

BEYER, K. and REICH, J. (1987) 'Why Are Many Girls Inhibited From Learning Scientific Concepts in Physics?', Contributions to the Fourth Girls and Science and Technology (GASAT) Conference, Michigan, USA, University of Michigan.

BEYER, K. (1991) 'Gender, Science Anxiety and Learning Style', Contributions to the Sixth International Gender and Science and Technology (GASAT) Conference, Melbourne, Australia, The University of Melbourne.

CARTER, R. and KIRKUP, G. (1990) *Women in Engineering: A Good Place to Be?* London, Macmillan Education.

CARR, W. and KEMMIS, S. (1983) *Becoming Critical: Knowing Through Action Research*, Geelong, Australia, Deakin University Press.

CHODOROW, N. (1978) *The Reproduction of Mothering: Psychoanalysis and the Sociology of Gender*, Berkeley, University of California Press.

CLARK, M. (1989) *The Great Divide: The Construction of Gender in the Primary School*, Woden, ACT, Australia, Curriculum Development Centre.

FULLAN, M. (1982) *The Meaning of Educational Change*, New York, Teachers College Press.

GILLIGAN, C. (1982) *In A Different Voice*, Cambridge, England, Harvard University Press.

GIANELLO, L. (1988) *Getting into Gear: Gender-Inclusive Teaching Strategies in Science: McClintock Collective*, Canberra, Curriculum Corporation.

GIPPS, C. and MURPHY, P. (1994) *A Fair Test? Assessment, Achievement and Equity*, Buckingham, Open University.

GRUMET, M. (1994) 'Conception, contradiction and curriculum', in STONE, L. (ed.) *The Education Feminism Reader*, New York, Routledge, pp. 149–70.

HARDING, J. (1986) 'Foundation Chemistry Course from Issues', *McClintock Memos*, **5**, pp. 1–9.

HARDING, J. and SUTORIS, M. (1987) 'An object-relations account of the differential involvement of boys and girls in science and technology', in KELLY, A. (ed.) *Science for girls?*, Milton Keynes, Open University, pp. 24–36.

HEAD, J. (1985) *The Personal Response to Science, Cambridge*, Cambridge.

HEAD, J. (1987) 'A Model to Link Personality Characteristics to a Preference for Science', in KELLY, A. (ed.) *Science for Girls?*, Milton Keynes, Open University, pp. 18–23.

HILDEBRAND, G. and ALLARD, A. (1993) 'Transforming the Curriculum Through Changing Assessment Practices', Contributions to the Seventh International Gender and Science and Technology (GASAT) Conference, Waterloo, Ontario, Canada, The University of Waterloo.

JOHNSON, S. and MURPHY, P. (1986) 'Girls and Physics. Reflections on APU Findings', *Assessment of Performance Unit*, Occasional Paper No. 4, p. 40.

KELLER, E.F. (1985) *Reflections on Gender and Science*, New Haven, Yale University.

KENWAY, J. and EVANS, M. (1991) *Working for Gender Justice in Schools*, Melbourne, Australia, Ministry of Education and Training.

LEVER, J. (1976) 'Sex differences in the games children play', *Social Problems*, **23**, pp. 478–87.

LEVER, J. (1978) 'Sex differences in the complexity of children's play and games', *American Sociological Review*, **43**, pp. 471–83.

LEWIS, S. (1993) 'Lessons to learn: Gender and science education', in KELLY, F. (ed.) On the edge of discovery, Melbourne, Australia, Text, pp. 255–80.

LEWIS, S. (1995) *Chilly Courses for Women? Some Engineering and Science Experiences: Women, Culture and Universities: A Chilly Climate?*, University of Technology, Sydney, UTS.

LEWIS, S. and DAVIES, A. (1988) *Gender Equity in Mathematics and Science: The Girls and Maths and Science Teaching Project*, Canberra, Curriculum Corporation.

LYONS, N. (1994) 'Dilemmas of knowing: Ethical and epistemological dimensions of teachers' work and development', in STONE, L. (ed.) *The Education Feminism Reader*, New York, Routledge, pp. 195–217.

McCLINTOCK COLLECTIVE (1987) *The Fascinating Sky: Introducing the McClintock Collective and Some of its Work*, Melbourne, Australia, Victorian Government Printer.

McINTOSH, P. (1984) 'The study of women: Processes of personal and curricular revision', *The Forum for Liberal Education*, **6**(5), pp. 2–4.

McILWEE, J.S. and ROBINSON, J.G. (1992) *Women in Engineering: Gender, Power and Workplace Culture*, Albany, NY, State University of New York.

MURPHY, P. (1993) 'Equity and Assessment', Contributions to the Seventh International Gender and Science and Technology (GASAT) Conference, Waterloo, Ontario, Canada, The University of Waterloo.

PARKER, L.H. and RENNIE, L.J. (1993) 'Towards Gender Fair Assessment in Science 1: The Process of Research', Contributions to the Seventh International Gender and Science and Technology (GASAT) Conference, Waterloo, Ontario, Canada, The University of Waterloo.

PERRY, W.G. (1970) *Forms of Ethical and Intellectual Development in the College Years*, New York, Holt, Rinehart and Winston.

RENNIE, L.J. and PARKER, L.H. (1993) 'Towards Gender Fair Assessment in Science 11: The Initial Outcomes of the Research', Contributions to the Seventh International Gender and Science and Technology (GASAT) Conference, Waterloo, Ontario, Canada, The University of Waterloo.

RHEINGOLD, H.L. and COOK, K.V. (1975) 'The contents of boys' and girls' rooms as an index of parents' behavior', *Child Development*, **46**, pp. 459–63.

SCHUSTER, M. and VAN DYNE, S. (1984) 'Placing women in the Liberal arts: Stages of curriculum transformation', *Harvard Educational Review*, **54**(4), pp. 413–28.

SMAIL, B. (1984) *Girl Friendly Science: Avoiding Sex Bias in the Curriculum*, York, UK, Longman.

SPEAR, M. (1987) 'The Biasing Influence of Pupil Sex in a Science Marking Exercise', in KELLY, A. (ed.) *Science for Girls?*, Milton Keynes, Open University, pp. 46–51.

STONE, L. (1994) 'Towards a Transformational Theory of Teaching', *The Education Feminism Reader*, New York, Routledge, p. 380.

ZUBER-SKERRITT, O. (1992) *Professional Development in Higher Education: A Theoretical Framework for Action Research*, Kogan Page, ASTAM.

15 How Do We Get Educators to Teach Gender Equity?

Jo Sanders

How Do We Get Educators to Teach Gender Equity?

There have been many grant-funded projects in the United States — probably hundreds, possibly thousands — that have dealt with advancing gender equity in education. Nevertheless the low level of awareness of gender equity among classroom teachers is astonishing. Why hasn't there been more progress?

One reason is that, for the most part, the education establishment has not been lining up to buy what we are selling. Professional education associations rarely feature major speeches on gender equity, and when a workshop on gender equity is given most of those in attendance are people who are already convinced of the importance of the issue and are doing something about it. The mainstream educational media occasionally run articles on gender equity but it is hardly a top priority. As a result, we preach to a relatively small choir and have few ways of enlarging the pool of choir members.

Another reason for the lack of awareness of gender equity among so many teachers has been in the types of activities we have carried out over the past twenty years. It seems to me that we have put most of our efforts into two activities which are undoubtedly necessary but apparently not sufficient.

First, we have produced vast numbers of print and audio-visual materials for educators on gender equity. A member of my staff and I recently produced a bibliography, for example, that contains a full fifty-two pages on gender equity materials only in mathematics, science and technology and only developed since 1980 (Sanders and Rocco, 1994). While many of the materials are excellent and of great value to educators who use them, I think it is fair to say they are not, by and large, widely used. Most developers, scattered at universities, non-profit organizations, education agencies and schools nation-wide, have no organized distribution channel. The only two systematic distributors with catalogue and professional order processing are the Women's Educational Equity Act Publishing Centre in Newton, Massachusetts which distributes some of the materials produced by Women's Educational Equity Act grantees, and the National Women's History Project in Windsor, California, but together they carry only a fraction of the materials that exist. And even if developers were knowledgeable about the commercial publishing process (though most are not), commercial publishers tend to be uninterested in publishing gender equity materials for classroom teachers because the market is too thin. It is therefore unlikely that a typical educator is aware of the available resources. Another reason for the low level of use of the materials that have been produced may have to do with the imbalance between supply and demand. We have been concentrating on increasing the supply of materials, but the demand for them has not grown correspondingly.

The second major gender equity activity in the last twenty years has been to increase the awareness of classroom teachers about gender equity, and the primary vehicle has been the in-service workshop. Over the past twenty years there have surely been thousands of them: held at local, state and national professional meetings, at universities, and in schools, and taught by gender equity specialists who are professors, gender equity grantees (such as myself), the occasional classroom teacher or administrator, and local, state or national education agency employees. Again, I see several reasons why this vast effort has not had as much effect as we might have hoped. For one, most of the workshops are the 'quick-fix' type of an hour or two. While activities designed to create an awareness of gender inequities are certainly essential, teachers have developed sexist attitudes and beliefs over a lifetime. An hour or two is not enough to create substantial 'cognitive dissonance.' Second, most of the workshops stop with awareness of the problem and pass lightly over solutions to the problem, and without solutions there can be no progress. Third, classroom teachers have many professional agendas competing for their attention. A one-shot workshop on gender equity, even a powerful one, tends, before too long, to recede into the background with new issues taking its place in the foreground.

Nevertheless, gender equity specialists must have the active and widespread cooperation of classroom teachers. We do not personally teach girls in classrooms, and most of us do not teach prospective teachers either. Without enlisting classroom teachers and professors of education in substantial numbers to address gender equity in their work, our work can be of no benefit to girls in schools.

Other chapters in this book address the specifics of what works or why it works to increase girls' participation, performance, and/or persistence. Here, I will talk about what I increasingly see as a critical link, the involvement of educators in gender equity, and specifically the ways I have found to be successful in moving them from a lack of interest to active commitment, keeping them interested, and making them effective.

I would like to describe my experiences with two large nation-wide American projects, the Computer Equity Expert Project and the Teacher Education Expert Project. The first served educators in grades 6–12 (ages 12 to 18), while the latter serves professors of education.

The Computer Equity Expert Project, 1990–93

This project served 200 classroom teachers and administrators in grades 6–12 in mathematics, science or computers in a trainer-of-trainers model. The project was funded primarily by the National Science Foundation, with additional funding from IBM, Hewlett Packard, Chevron, Intel, American Express, Xerox, and Westinghouse over two and a half years. We had a full-time staff of three.

Participants (whom we called trainers) attended a six-day seminar taught by internationally renowned gender equity specialists in the United States, a three-day follow-up meeting a year later, a stipend of $100 per participant, a grant of $150 to each trainer's school, and considerable publicity about their participation.

The major seminar sessions were:

- *Gender Equity in Education*: a review of gender equity issues in over a dozen education areas such as guidance, vocational education, testing, and athletics. Instructor: Jo Sanders.
- *Girls in Mathematics and Science*: an overview of what we know about achievement, persistence, motivation, etc. Instructor: Patricia B. Campbell.
- *A Feminist Analysis of Mathematics and Science*: current thinking on feminist pedagogy. Instructor: Judith Jacobs.
- *Educational Technology*: how to create gender-fair lessons using computers. Instructor: Carol Edwards.
- *Building Presentation and Training Skills*: on the techniques of delivering equity training to faculty groups. Instructor: Dolores Grayson.
- *Workshops*: two workshops developed in an earlier pilot project were taught to the trainers to prepare them to teach these workshops to faculty groups in their schools (Sanders and McGinnis, 1991a, b).

Evaluation results indicated a high degree of satisfaction with the seminar, as 91 per cent of the trainers agreed with the statement, 'Overall, I found this seminar to be of high quality.' Back home, trainers taught the two workshops to their faculties and convened 'equity teams' of faculty, often administrators, and sometimes students as well, to carry out strategies of their choosing designed to close the gender gaps in mathematics, science or technology identified in their applications. Follow-up contact over 18 months consisted of frequent mailings, two lengthy telephone interviews, a bi-monthly newsletter, an electronic network, and site visits to a small number of trainers.

Results cannot be simply summarized, since the 'presenting' problems and the strategies were so varied. However, by trainers' estimates they reached a combined total of over 77,000 girls with their strategies, and taught or otherwise involved 9,400 of their colleagues. Many of the trainers reported to us pre/post results such as the following:

- The ratio of boys to girls in the after-school computer lab of a New York middle school was 25:2 before the project, 1:1 after.
- In a Wyoming high school, girls' enrollment in Physics rose from 46 per cent to 62 per cent, and in Introduction to Calculus, from 45 per cent to 71 per cent.
- An Oklahoma high school had no girls in the elective computer science class before the project, but 31 per cent girls afterward.

- The mathematics team in a Massachusetts middle school increased from less than 20 per cent to 50 per cent female.
- The Advanced Placement Pascal course went from 0 per cent to 50 per cent girls in one year in a Virginia high school.
- In an Oregon high school, girls' enrollment in Advanced Mathematics rose from 37 per cent to 64 per cent; in Advanced Chemistry it was 20 per cent to 63 per cent.
- In a Maine high school, girls signed up for Physics for the first time in 12 years.

Ninety-eight per cent of the trainers carried out the activities required by the project. Seventy-one per cent of the trainers gave equity presentations not required by the project. A book of the trainers' strategies has been widely distributed (Sanders, 1994).

Teacher Education Equity Project, 1993–96

Thinking about the two hundred trainers in the Computer Equity Expert Project who most likely failed to encourage girls' educational interests before they learned about gender equity in the project, I designed a new project to reach teachers with gender equity instruction *before* they entered the classroom: at the pre-service teacher education stage of their careers. The Teacher Education Equity Project serves sixty professors of education in mathematics, science and technology at thirty-eight colleges and universities in twenty-six states from Alaska to Florida, It is funded primarily by the National Science Foundation, with additional support from IBM, Hewlett Packard, and AT&T over three years. We have a full-time staff of three.

Participants attended a five-day seminar, a three-day follow-up meeting, received a small grant of $750 each ($750 per individual, $1,500 for teams of two from an institution, or $2,250 for teams of three), and extensive publicity about their participation. In exchange, they carry out three activities: teach gender equity to their students in education methods classes using three books of activities (for math, science and technology) developed earlier in the project; share what they learned at the seminar with their colleagues; and carry out an approved mini-grant project relating to gender equity in pre-service teacher education.

Seminar sessions were again given by international gender experts from the USA and included:

- *An Overview of the Issues in Gender Equity in Education*: a review of twenty areas of gender equity (language, legislation, testing, sexual harassment, and others) to convey a sense of the systemic nature of sexism in education. Instructor: Jo Sanders
- *Research Overview of Girls and Women in Mathematics, Science and Technology Education and Careers*: an analysis of the effect of societal norms,

educational experiences, and student dispositions on girls' and women's attitudes, grades, test scores, motivation, and persistence. Instructor: Marcia Linn
- *Classroom Interaction and Peer Harassment*: an examination of biased classroom interactions via a role-play and strategies for making the classroom a more equitable place. Instructor: Bernice Sandler
- *Feminist Approaches to Teaching Mathematics, Science and Technology*: a session that presented three approaches to syllabus design based on models of feminist pedagogy. Instructor: Kate Scantlebury
- *Gender Equity in Pre-service Mathematics/Technology/Science Education*: three concurrent sessions at which a book of activities for professors of education to use in methods courses with education students was presented to participants. Instructors, respectively: Josephine Urso, Laura Jeffers, Janice Koch

Participants were highly positive in their evaluation of these sessions, rating them 1.8 on a five-point scale where 1 was 'Very Useful' and 5 was 'Not at All Useful'.

Participants are teaching the gender equity activities to their students, holding sessions on gender equity for their colleagues, and carrying out their mini-grant projects. There last are quite varied, as the following examples show:

- To team female elementary mathematics and science education students with upper-class female mathematics and science majors. They construct hands-on mathematics and science exhibits and present them to middle-school children.
- To have education students design and carry out a research project to determine gender equity understanding among mathematics, science and technology teachers at five to ten area high schools. The professor will compare the classroom equity behaviour of participating students to those who receive gender equity instruction but do not take part in the research project.
- To integrate a component on children's literature with female protagonists into an elementary mathematics methods course.
- To develop, test and disseminate a hypercard stack on gender equity to be used by education students as an alternative instructional vehicle.
- To involve education students in the planning and teaching of an existing week-long summer camp program on mathematics, science and computers for 150 7th and 8th grade girls.
- To create a Technology Scholars program by enlisting female education students with computer skills to assist education faculty to plan and implement gender-equitable instruction involving computers.
- To have mathematics and science education students design and carry out gender equity action research projects in their field experience schools for course credit, and to have them create a multi-media presentation on their findings for teachers, administrators and others.

Professors who have completed their mini-grants have expressed great satisfaction with them, primarily because they are good ways to have education students learn about gender equity issues for themselves. Active learning is almost always more effective than lecturing. Many professors have said that their students chose to do extended reports or term papers on gender equity topics after being introduced to the issue through the mini-grants. These students, it seems to me, can be counted on to do the right thing in their classrooms when they graduate.

Follow-up continues through 1995 in the form of periodic mailings, telephone interviews, an electronic network, a three-day follow-up meeting, and site visits ultimately to about a third of the participants. As of this writing, *after only one year* of active participation in the project, the education professors have taught gender equity to a collective total of 5,000 student teachers and another 5,000 others (colleagues, classroom teachers, and parents). They have made a collective total of over 150 presentations to local, state and national educators at all levels and have published over a dozen articles, things they are doing because they have become deeply committed to the 'cause' of gender equity, not because the project required them to do this.

What Works?

It is clear to me that most of the participants in these two projects have become committed and effective activists. As one current participant from Oregon wrote,

> It is difficult to pinpoint exactly what it was that changed my lens for viewing the world, but that's exactly what happened. I can't go into a classroom without thinking about these issues . . . My teaching looks and feels different. It is very exciting.

This outcome is all the more remarkable, in my opinion, in that most of the participants did not start out with background knowledge in women's studies or gender equity. Many were not even aware of the widely publicized findings, a few years ago of two studies on biased classroom interaction patterns — teachers calling on boys more than girls, etc. (AAUW, 1991, 1992). The Computer Equity Expert Project trainers, who achieved the wonderful before-and-after results listed earlier, for example, had not known anything about gender equity before beginning the project.

What, then, accounts for the transformation of classroom teachers, administrators, and professors of education into genuine feminist activists (even though some of them might not consider themselves to be that)?

Seminar Content

A participant from South Dakota wrote that 'the intense training we received during our training session in Minneapolis made a lasting impression.' It *was* intense and deliberately so, with people working hard from 8:45 am to 5:00 pm, because I thought that the strength of years of unexamined sexist assumptions would require considerable force to pierce.

Aside from the fact that I am not sufficiently knowledgeable about all the areas that were important to cover in seminar sessions, I chose to hire additional instructors to reinforce the message. As a Computer Equity Expert Project trainer put it last year, 'I began to believe it when I heard the same thing coming in different ways from all of you,' and as a Teacher Education Equity Project participant recently wrote, 'Your guest speakers were great people who raised the credibility of the entire program.' The instructors were chosen not only for their expertise but their teaching ability: clarity, liveliness, warmth, and ideological moderation, the last because I was concerned that speakers perceived as 'radical' would alienate novices.

The first session at each seminar was important in setting the tone. Dinner was first on the program, after a very brief welcome from me. After dinner I asked people to introduce themselves and say where they were from, partly to establish the geographic diversity of the group. I then introduced the discussion by saying that since I had read all their proposals I knew about the various gender gaps they had written about, but they didn't know about each other's. I invited them to describe what they had discovered in their schools, colleges or universities. For the next hour and a half that's what they did. This had several purposes: each saw that her or his gender imbalance wasn't unusual; they learned that most of them had been surprised at what they had discovered; and they began to get a sense of each other as people.

Many participants have mentioned the materials they received at the seminar as particularly helpful. At the Teacher Education Equity Project seminar, professors of education received a packet of eighteen brochures and books plus five loose-leaf binders: one a 540-page compendium of materials for my overview session on gender equity, one of handouts for the other sessions, and three of activities to be used to teach pre-service education students about gender equity in mathematics, science and technology (Sanders, Koch and Urso, in press). For people new to gender equity, the vastness and the range of materials was a revelation and helped to convince them that there was indeed a problem with education for girls and that researchers and teachers had developed extensive solutions. My intention was to give participants so much material that they would be obliged to pick and choose from it to work with at home, thus making it theirs. An Oregon participant said,

> The notebooks presented things in a global way and broke the issue apart
> in a more systematic way. The research base was really helpful in con-
> vincing our faculty there is validity in what we are trying to do here.

Her second sentence is very important. I felt it was essential that participants take home a good selection of research on gender equity, because they needed to have tools readily available to use for dealing with resistance from colleagues charging 'feminist extremism.' As a participant from Idaho said,

> I love the resource materials we came away with. They are a much needed
> crutch and springboard, particularly because they are 'middle of the road'
> and not 'radical.'

There was also much diversity of books on the book table. I shipped virtually my
entire professional library to the seminars, and I recall one participant at the seminar this summer telling me she became convinced that gender equity in education
was important when she saw the dozens and dozens of research and practical
volumes out on the table.

Seminar Atmosphere

I think a critical element of the atmosphere I tried to create was based on advance
planning. I knew that people would be coming to these seminars worrying that they
might have gotten involved in educational quackery, in some off-the-wall weirdo
feminist nonsense that some of their colleagues back home had already begun to
ridicule. To counter this image, I tried to make the seminar a model of a well-run
conference. Registration procedures were welcoming and streamlined. Materials
were distributed on time and efficiently. Two staff members were assigned full-
time to trouble-shooting. Everything was where it should have been, when it should
have been there. This was accomplished by my thinking through every session in
advance, writing down everything that would be required and when, and then giving my 'Seminar Book' to my staff so that they could figure out exactly when and
how their specific responsibilities would need to be done. As a result, the seminar
schedule was gently but strictly adhered to and there were virtually no last minute
foul-ups.

> Your professionalism, your staff's professionalism and the professional-
> ism displayed by your speakers added true style to the entire project.

A second element of the atmosphere was that I tried to make it relaxed, warm and
friendly. In my experience, the tension created by questioning sex roles for the first
time can be quite powerful, and the hours of hard work can make the atmosphere
even more tense. I and the other instructors were as informal as possible. I also
tried to present material factually and calmly, as opposed to emotionally or ideologically. The goal was to create an environment in which sexism could be thought
about intellectually and in which participants could feel comfortable and safe. The
emotional processing, an inevitable and necessary part of discovering for the first
time how systemically sexist our world is, needed to be done and was done pri-
vately both during and after the seminar.

From the first evening, I told participants at each seminar that the gender
imbalances they reported in their schools, colleges and universities were not their
fault. I told them they did not create the problem, although they inadvertently contributed to it like everyone else in a sexist society (including myself), but it was in

their power to fix it. This point is essential, I think, because many newcomers to gender equity are afraid we are going to accuse them of oppressing poor defenseless little girls. They are angry with us before we say a word, which obviously does not produce a good learning environment. The no-blame message removes this pitfall.

Similarly, I permitted no male-bashing right from the first evening's discussion, a fairly strenuous effort on my part because most novices assume simplistically that sexism is exclusively men's fault. ('There are no girls in physics because all the science teachers in my school are men,' for example, could not go unchallenged.) First, it is simply not true that male teachers are the problem and female teachers are the solution: there are plenty of helpful men and sexist women. Second, male-bashing effectively releases men from any responsibility for gender equity solutions — if maleness causes sexism then they cannot help being sexist, which I do not accept. Last, male-bashing would have insulted and alienated the fifth of the Computer Equity Expert Project participants who were men and the third of the Teacher Education Equity Project participants who were men, thus defeating the very purpose of the projects in their case.

Another aspect of the seminar atmosphere is the issue of ownership. A feeling of ownership cannot be ordered up, of course, but I did stress the great variability there is in educational institutions, in student populations, in community standards, in resources, and especially among the participants. I emphasized fairly often that the materials and instruction they were receiving were theirs to adapt, change, and use as they saw fit, that there is no 'recipe' for gender equity success, that their gender equity activities would need to be personalized, in effect, for their own situations. A Montana participant said,

> The program has provided us with a plethora of ideas which can be used by a variety of personalities. Some of us like the subtle approach and there are activities which are more subtle. Some of us like the more direct approach and we can find those activities too. There is a bit of something for all of us.

The last aspect of the atmosphere I'd like to discuss here is the creation of a group ethos. Newcomers to gender equity can feel quite alone when their new commitment is not shared, or is even disparaged, by colleagues. Eventually enough colleagues become interested that the isolation tends not to last, but initially it is very important to reassure the novice that she or he is not alone. Contributing to the creation of a sense of community were a private dining room for all our meals, a warm, welcoming and outgoing staff, and a genuine concern for people's physical and emotional comfort. A group feeling was apparently created: you will have noticed that most of the participants who were kind enough to provide suggestions for this paper did so with the pronoun 'we' rather than 'I.' A participant from Alaska expressed it this way:

> Something that is very beneficial in the project is the diversity of the group in terms of the types of institutions represented. Each of us can find other

people in similar situations to share and relate to . . . I feel as though I'm part of a team.

Another person referred to 'the family spirit that was developed [at the seminar] in making us all feel like a part of a big family.'

Follow-up

The essence of the follow-up I have tried to create is one described well by a participant from Pennsylvania:

> This project works because you've made us accountable for portions of it. So many workshop/seminars are simply presentations of information without any responsibility for participant involvement afterward. You've maintained contact and pushed us to be active. By making us accountable, you've brought us into the project fully.

Stated another way by an Idaho participant:

> I love the subtle, friendly pushing (not too much, but just enough) your staff employs. You seem to provide just enough challenges for us to meet, at a variety of levels, so that we can all function in very diverse environments, so we can all feel we are contributing to an important project which will make a significant difference in the long run.

The electronic network we began for the Computer Equity Expert Project trainers was not effective because of its limited use. Perhaps thirty of the 200 trainers in 1990–93 had access to telecommunication either at school or at home, and it was used regularly by fewer than that. As a result, the medium could only be used for chatting purposes: pleasant but basically irrelevant. The important communications went into a newsletter produced every two months which grew from four pages in length to forty pages over the six issues. Newsletters contained news of trainers' activities, strategies they were carrying out in their schools to increase girls' participation in mathematics, science or computers, trainer-created tips for gender equity workshops, and miscellany, most of which was harvested from indepth phone interviews.

The electronic network we established for the Teacher Education Equity Project, however, has been extremely successful. All but five participants are members. The network contains information about participants' activities, entered either by me or my staff and gleaned primarily from telephone interviews, summaries of newly approved mini-grant projects, news of resources (print, electronic media, conferences), requests for panelists for conference sessions on the project, discussions of various project-related topics — a recent one is 'How do you deal with resistance?' — quotes of interest to us all, requests for information, and so forth. Participants strongly preferred that the network remain private among ourselves rather than be opened up to the world at large, to keep the volume of messages under control. This enables the network, which is moderated by a project staff member, to function as group 'glue.'

The network has become our main vehicle for follow-up. The Montana participant wrote:

> All too often teachers are subjected to the wonderful weekend of ideas and then come back to the workplace. As the daily routine takes over, the memories of the 'wonderful weekend' begin to fade and before long the enthusiasm and excitement are nonexistent. Even though I rarely respond on the e-mail, I faithfully read it every day. I pick up ideas for classroom activities and (somewhat silently) commiserate with the problems and frustrations I see expressed.

An Idaho participant:

> I love the feeling that resources are only an electronic minute away.

An Alaska participant:

> The listserv has been very beneficial. Even though I haven't sent a lot of messages to the group, I feel that reading the messages posted on a weekly basis keeps me informed and committed to the project. I believe without the bulletin board it would be easy to get distracted with other projects and let things slide. When I see what others are doing, I feel a real obligation to follow through.

We also produce a newsletter every two months with material that has appeared on the network, partly to give everyone a hardcopy organized by topic that they can share with others if they choose, partly to send to the five non-network participants, and partly to have an ongoing report to send to funders, seminar instructors, advisory committee members, and others. The newsletter and the network have essentially the same group communication function, but the network, because of its immediacy and interactivity, is much the superior medium. I would not do a group project now without it.

I maintain an electronic network and write and send a newsletter for very specific purposes. First, I sincerely believe in the power of peer pressure, or, if you prefer, recognition and honor. When a participant reads that other participants are teaching their students about gender equity in innovative ways, teaching their colleagues about gender equity, or presenting sessions on gender equity at professional meetings, she or he feels a motivation or an obligation to do likewise. Put another way, the participant would like to see her or his name there for the group to read and admire, too. (To promote recognition and honor, I wrote a generic press release shortly after the seminar and sent it to participants for their use. Several have told me about television and radio interviews that resulted, and about articles written about them in local newspapers. This cannot hurt!) Second, the exchange of information enhances the group feeling, also maximizing their commitment and activity level. Third, describing participants' activities sparks new ideas in others. Last but certainly not least, frequent communication enables me to offer praise and congratulations often and publicly, which I do because I think it is encouraging and strengthening. Besides, achievement *deserves* praise.

Another form of follow-up activity is the participants' mini-grant projects. In one project I visited recently in Utah, a professor chose to use her $750 to pay modest stipends to students who helped her teach a five-hour workshop for area teachers on gender equity, and to pay for lunch and materials for the teachers. The seven undergraduates, who had met with the professor a number of times to pre-pare, taught about two-thirds of the workshop, and they did it very well. They were confident and comfortable teaching gender equity to people twice their age, and the teachers in turn were receptive. Soon these students will be reading short essays by the teachers on how they would use a check for $50 for gender equity materials, and choosing the best one to receive the award. The entire experience was extremely impressive.

A couple of project participants mentioned the mini-grants when I asked for advice about what I should mention in this paper. From two North Carolina participants:

> What makes it worthwhile for me is having a chance to decide how we want to use and disseminate the information at our own institutions. In other words, I liked being able to propose a project that I wanted to do.

> I think that for me the most significant feature of the project is that the participants are funded to conduct research and develop projects that we think are important. This has kept me involved despite my time commit-ment to other activities.

There was a three-day meeting in Seattle in August of 1995 for participants in the Teacher Education Equity Project, which corresponds to a similar meeting for the Computer Equity Expert Project trainers in New Orleans. The follow-up meeting was taught primarily by the participants, as they reported on what they have learned in their mini-grant projects and share what they have accomplished in their class-rooms and institutions. There was also time reserved at the follow-up meeting for small-group discussions; to let them process the new experiences they have had, and for social purposes. It was extremely successful, with participants rating their peers' concurrent sessions, the major part of the meeting, at 1.4 on a scale of 1 to 5, where 1 was 'Very Useful.'

What Happens When Educators Teach Gender Equity?

In 1993, Computer Equity Expert Project trainers were asked to complete short reports to obtain their $100 stipends at the end of the project, and they were asked to describe the impact of the project upon them. Here are some of the trainers' com-ments, with the states they are from:

This experience has changed my life. (Texas)

I have always been interested in the issue, but now I have the tools to teach non-believers and to spread the word. (Arkansas)

I can honestly say that I had no idea, before beginning the project, that I was not meeting the needs of my female students ... I do feel I am making a difference now. (Colorado)

I have made a concerted effort not to assume that a male science or mathematics teacher is more knowledgeable merely because he is a he. (New York)

Because of my association with this program, I now have practical, successful strategies for working with females, and I can assist my colleagues in their efforts to interest more females in their areas of computers, mathematics and science. (Pennsylvania)

In all, for me this has been a wonderful learning experience that I plan to continue passing on to others. (South Carolina)

I see no end to the learning for me and my colleagues, and this project sparked it all. Thank you. (Washington State)

I will never be the same since I was exposed to this project. (New Jersey)

Similarly, professors of education in the Teacher Education Equity Project made the following comments as they evaluated the project:

This project has changed my way of viewing the world. There couldn't be a greater impact.

I see things I never saw before. The project has provided me with a launch pad for a dimension of my work that will span a career.

My students told me that this has really opened their eyes.

I've had a definite paradigm shift.

This was an opportunity of tremendous growth for me.

There has been an exceptional impact on what I teach: an integrated thread of equity.

Being a member of this project has enhanced my self-worth as an educator. This has been the most award-winning experience for me. I have learned how to be a much more effective teacher.

I am a better teacher of young women and men because of the project.

All I teach goes through a new gender lens. This project has made a significant impact on my life, personally and professionally.

Conclusion

For all the success these two projects have achieved, I have not described the nirvana of educational interventions. I am frustrated that it has taken so much work and time, not to mention money, to create only 200 classroom teachers who are feminist advocates, and the situation is the same for sixty teacher educators. In the United States there are 2.8 million teachers in 110,000 elementary and secondary schools, and there are 35,000 education faculty in 10,000 colleges and universities (National Center for Education Statistics, 1993). Obviously, I am working at a snail's pace. On the other hand, both projects were intended to train new trainers, and clearly the 260 participants are doing this. But while I applaud all the workshops they are giving and the articles they are writing, and while I recognize that their activities reach far more people than I ever could personally, I have the same concern I expressed at the beginning of this chapter — that the intensity level of a short workshop or an article is too low to make more than a transitory difference.

Then on my more optimistic days I think to myself that a snail's pace may be the only possible pace at which one can achieve *real* change in gender equity, and trying to reach a lot of people quickly means that we reach them more superficially and less profoundly. I try to content myself with a response a Computer Equity Expert Project trainer from Arizona gave in assessing the impact of the project on her:

How can you put into words a total transformation?

References

AAUW (1991) *A Call to Action: Shortchanging Girls, Shortchanging America*, Washington DC, American Association of University Women.

AAUW (1992) *The AAUW Report: How Schools Shortchange Girls*; Washington DC, American Association of University Women. This study was carried out by the Wellesley College Centre for Research on Women.

NATIONAL CENTER FOR EDUCATION STATISTICS (1993) *Digest of Education Statistics, 1993*, Washington DC, NCES, Tables 4, 1, 221 and 5 respectively.

SANDERS, J. and McGINNIS, M. (1991) *What is Computer Equity in Math and Science Metuchen*, New Jersey, Scarecrow Press.

SANDERS, J. and ROCCO, S. (1994) *Bibliography on Gender Equity in Mathematics, Science and Technology: Resources for Classroom Teachers*, New York, Center for Advanced Study in Education, City University of New York Graduate Center.

SANDERS, J. (1994) *Lifting the Barriers: 600 Strategies that Really Work to Increase Girls' Participation in Science, Mathematics and Computers*, Port Washington, New York, Jo Sanders Publications.

SANDERS, J., KOCH, J. and URSO, J. (in press) *Gender Equity in Teacher Education*, New Jersey, Lawrence Erlbaum Associates.

227

16   Gender, Teachers and Changing Practices: Voices from Schools

Liz Wyatt, Jo Whitehead and Christina Hart

'Gender' Packaged as Another Change Product to Buy
Liz Wyatt

When a new consumable product is introduced into a supermarket, much time, effort and energy (not to mention money) goes into its creation and promotion. The success of the product depends on many factors such as the marketing strategies which are necessary to make the consumers aware of this new product, why it is better than other similar products and why it is worth the change. The viability of this new product will be continually assessed to see if it satisfies consumers' changing needs and to see if it is effective/profitable.

Reform of curriculum and teaching practices based on gender equity in schools is like a new product in the supermarket. It too has to be promoted to teachers who can be seen as the consumers of this change product. Marketing of this agenda has occurred through professional development programs, through the publication of resource materials and through campaigns to promote the principles and processes associated with the gender equity reforms. The expectation of effectiveness/success was that teachers would take up some/many of these initiatives and this would directly impact on changed outcomes for girls and boys.

But change is never easy to instigate. In the supermarket there are many new products vying for the consumers' attention. Likewise, in schools, there are many demands for schools and teachers to change multiple dimensions of their practices, and each of these sites becomes a point of tension. Gender equity is just one such call for change and teachers, with their demanding workloads, can only 'take on board' and actively commit themselves to a few changes in any one schoolyear.

In the school where I have recently been working, a conservative school in a middle-class area, about half the student population is female and close to 90 per cent of the staff are female. I decided to ask individual staff members to, metaphorically, place themselves somewhere along a continuum with one end representing gender as an important issue in their lives and at school, and the opposite end of the continuum representing gender as not being an issue at all. I followed up this paper exercise with interviews, or conversations, with each teacher.

I found that the staff formed three distinct groups. The first group, to which I belonged, I shall call the 'highly motivated' group. They felt that gender equity and reform of the curriculum was a highly motivating issue which energized them to alter their own pract⎯⎯⎯⎯⎯⎯⎯⎯⎯⎯⎯⎯⎯⎯⎯⎯⎯⎯⎯⎯⎯ number, but active, energet⎯⎯⎯⎯⎯⎯⎯⎯⎯⎯⎯⎯⎯⎯⎯⎯⎯⎯⎯⎯⎯⎯⎯ ol and teaching practices and t⎯⎯⎯⎯⎯⎯⎯⎯⎯⎯⎯⎯⎯⎯⎯⎯⎯⎯⎯⎯⎯⎯⎯ wealth Schools Commission, 1987) as a stimulus for the establishment of a local committee including parents, which built a school-level policy on gender equity. This group then committed themselves to strong ongoing action to change teaching, classroom and school practices to make our school more gender equitable.

The second group of teachers, about half the staff, positioned themselves around the middle of the continuum and I shall refer to them as the 'partly-committed' group. In discussions it became clear that these teachers were aware of gender issues in schools but they no longer actively cultivated innovations premised on gender equity, either in their own beliefs or in their teaching and classroom practices. This group was not opposed to gender-driven reforms in their teaching. They believed they had undertaken some changes in the past, but felt there were more important issues which took their energy at the moment.

The final group I shall call the 'oppositional' group. Whilst being very small in number, they were vehemently, and loudly, opposed to any change requested by other staff members which used the word 'gender' anywhere in the argument. Most of these teachers felt they had 'successfully' taught for considerable periods of time (mostly more than twenty years) and were entrenched in their practice. Working to change practices with this group seemed to be an overwhelmingly energy-draining task.

I decided to focus on understanding the perspective of the large middle group, the 'partly-committed' staff. I began by seeking out what this group 'knew' about gender equity and curriculum and teaching reform. Each teacher in this group was able to articulate examples of changes which had occurred in their own teaching and classrooms because of gender concerns. They were aware of past inequities and recognized the desirability of re-dressing these injustices. They could trace their own changed beliefs over time, and realized that when their own expectations changed so did those of their students. Each teacher in this group identified the issues of 'classroom dynamics' as a starting point for their past changes: they recognized that boys had been demanding more of their time and effort during class and so they had taken steps to rectify these imbalances by organizing their teaching in new ways.

In particular, this group of apparently only 'partly-committed' teachers had individually experimented with new ways to achieve a balance in the gender dynamics within their classrooms. In this step they were very similar to the 'highly motivated' group. Some had moved the classroom furniture and altered seating arrangements; others had set up rosters for jobs and timetables for access to computer equipment and other hands-on resources in their rooms; yet others had changed their teaching practices to cater for a range of learning styles which they felt girls preferred, such as using more cooperative learning activities, role-playing and consensus-discussion groups.

They frequently identified the Australian expression of a 'fair go' for girls which appears to be in line with that of liberal feminism — change teaching and

school _____ s in, everything boys and
men d _____ ....ging ... power dimensions built into the current structures of schools or of society. They were moved to try new practices by arguments
(marketing) which centred on highlighting disadvantages that girls had experienced
compared with boys. They expressed their motivation in terms of a focus on social
injustice and linked this to their moral concern that the girls and boys in their classes
should be provided with an education that was equally valuable for both sexes, seen
as fitting into society as it is currently organized. This was a point of difference to
the group of 'highly motivated' teachers who saw their task as one which ultimately ·would lead to shifts in the power structures in schools and in society.

The 'partly committed' group frequently expressed notions of being gender-
inclusive in their teaching practices as a goal for changed practices. They had each
tried to support girls in the learning areas of mathematics and science — domains
that they accepted had previously been thought of as belonging to males and which
ought to be opened up to girls and women. Many of the teachers in this group
spoke of trying to be gender-inclusive with the use of language in their classrooms:
both in everyday speech and in the texts that their students were reading and producing. They discussed examples of literature which they had once deemed suitable
but now discarded because of the negative images of femininity and masculinity
that they portrayed. They expressed regret that financial limitations required them
to continue to use some resources that they now saw as inappropriate from a gender
point of view.

Many of the teachers in this group at my school related gender inequities to
other forms of injustice that were clear to them — such as those linked to students
with disabilities, students from language backgrounds other than English and students
from certain cultural groups whose values system exacerbated gender disparities.

Some teachers from this group expressed a perceived feeling of inadequacy
in the gender equity area — believing that they were a bit 'shaky' on their terminology and theoretical understandings and articulated a desire for more professional
development that would enable them to more confidently discuss gender issues within
our school community. An example of this was one teacher who had a support person working in her classroom to help a student with a disability. When the integration aide started playing a game of 'hangman' with the student concerned, the
teacher called her aside and tried to explain that this game was not consistent with
the school's policy on gender equity. When she next looked, she was amazed to see
that the game was now 'hangwoman'. She tried to explain that changing the sex
did not alter the masculine connotations of violence and images of aggression that
were associated with the game. She felt frustrated because she couldn't articulate
a clear understanding of her concerns about this task from a gender point of view.

Similar stories arose from other teachers within this group: they expressed a
desire to have open discussion about notions of gender-inclusivity and other specialist terminology that the 'highly motivated' group used freely because they felt
inadequate and uncomfortable when gender issues arose in the staffroom due to
their unfamiliarity with key terms. In other words, they felt excluded and intimid-
ated by the specialist language of gender equity and curriculum reform.

Whilst this group placed themselves about the middle of the continuum on the importance of gender issues, most felt that their position was not set in concrete and that they had moved forward and retreated a number of times since gender equity had become a focus of discussion in our school. While most of these teachers expressed a desire to act on gender reform in their practices, they felt there were too many other attractive, and easy-to-use, products available to them in the change supermarket. They tried to keep up with a constantly changing government policy initiatives and felt that their energies were constantly being channelled into the latest memorandum.

Lack of time and energy to focus on all demands for change was the major reason these teachers saw themselves as unable to do more for gender equity in our school. They were willing to undertake a critical reflection and self-analysis of their practices but desired more support from the 'highly motivated' group to do so. There was a sense of embarrassment and of concern at being seen by their peers as not coping well with change in this area.

I believe that what we have to do now is change the culture of our school so that we are all seen as competent professionals working towards addressing gender issues. Because gender reform begins with teaching practice we need to work through the emotional baggage we all bring to the staffroom and classroom, and openly discuss our attitudes and values without resorting to jargonistic terminology. This large group of 'partly committed' staff, who have in the past undertaken considerable effort to alter their practice and who are willing to act further, need the active support of those in the 'highly motivated' group. We have tended to exclude them from our enthusiastic attempts by the very energy and discourse levels we thought were so productive.

For the 'partly committed' group of teachers in our school, gender reform of our practices has had many parallels with the new supermarket product: there have been times when it stayed on the shelf, untried; at other times it was selected, tried and adapted; on yet other occasions it was seen as too costly, in terms of effort and a threat to competence levels, to take down from the shelf. What this points to, using the supermarket analogy, is to more continuous marketing of this product. We need more time and space for issues of gender equity to be discussed and addressed through ongoing professional development experiences within our school community. We also need more sensitively to recognize our colleagues' willingness to change and provide the appropriate amount of support so that we can reach shared understandings about the issues and potential actions in our school.

Towards Gender Awareness Through Discipline and Welfare Issues — A Model for How Teachers Change
Jo Whitehead

This is the story of increasing awareness of gender issues in my own life and the life of the small country school in which I work. It is a story of growing understandings of both the need for change and the facets which contribute to effective change when gender is the focus.

The construction of gender was not a major concern of mine, nor of my fifteen colleagues, until a series of policy documents beginning with the National Policy for the Education of Girls in Australian Schools (Commonwealth Schools Commission, 1987) and other state-level initiatives began to filter into our staffroom. This began a period of personal reading which I found quite amazing. I had not realized that gender was such a critical factor in issues affecting me as a child and as an adult: I had accepted my life as it unfolded, learning to not disagree with males (my father, my teacher, my husband, my principal) and to not question the available choices and rights which I now recognized were frequently influenced by my sex. I acknowledged that, as a teacher, I too was perpetuating the established system, where males were advantaged, through ways I operated in my school, the language I used, the expectations I had for myself, my daughters and the girls in my classes.

I could see that I, and others in my school, could choose change. We could work towards a gender-inclusive curriculum that actively supports the needs of girls on many fronts, although I knew that the majority of staff in my school did not accept that girls were disadvantaged. It would be an enormous task, which began with the questions: 'What can I do?' and 'How can I encourage other teachers to recognize the gender issues here?' My role in the school had given me responsibility for professional development and curriculum coordination and I had staff confidence in my ability to do this job well, as I was locally selected for the position.

I wanted to improve outcomes for girls now that I was looking at situations through a different lens and was challenged by writers who were promoting the view that teachers could make major changes to gendered outcomes. I could now see that gendered dualisms in our school were being reinforced through the hidden curriculum, school and curriculum organization, resourcing, staffing practices and assessment, as well as the more obvious content and teaching approaches. But gender issues were not widely accepted in our school and my early attempts to bring them into curriculum and teaching discussions resulted in comments such as, 'Everyone is happy with things as they are', and I was advised by the principal not to get 'too carried away with all this'.

The school community, with School Council approval, had identified discipline and welfare, self-esteem, assertiveness and conflict resolution skills as the key areas for action in the forthcoming year. I could see the possibilities of linking these as we worked on a whole school approach to change, and incorporating gender as a factor. Although I could find very little research linking gender issues with discipline and welfare, I had seen enough evidence in our school grounds and classrooms that monitoring and collecting our own data from students would produce hard facts that could not be ignored, negated with denial or demeaned by humour.

I realized that it was important to establish a non-threatening, supportive environment in which to address these issues and we would need a slow and gentle approach so that staff opinion did not quickly become antagonistic.

I began to explore the literature on teacher change processes and could see that

8">

Table 16.1 *Working model for gender and change*

Source and purpose of change
- Identify locally recognized needs.
- Collect and share local data.
- Use creditable practitioners as promoters and facilitators.
- Emphasize practical strategies and activities for teachers that lead directly to improved learning outcomes for all students.

Degree of change required
- Endeavour to bring about a real change — in pedagogy and teaching repertoire — approaches, methods, processes, content, language, evaluation techniques. (Adoption not just adaptation of changes.)
- Change to teachers' and students' personal viewpoint, values, responses, behaviours is required.

Teachers as learners
- Active in-school support strategies — discuss, model, try, feedback.
- Collegial atmosphere, climate of trust, tolerance and patience.
- Whole school approach; provide affiliation, achievement and ability to influence.
- Value existing knowledge and skills, share positive outcomes and strategies.
- Work with a change agent in the school.
- Work toward readiness to identify bias in current practice.
- Document and communicate observable changes in students.

The school organization and its response to change
- Very well-prepared ground, awareness raised, change oriented, energized environment.
- Strong leadership support, recognizing the real issues (e.g., principal or other active change agent who has staff respect).
- Model gender-inclusive practice in all staff development programs.
- Creditable non-school-based personnel may be helpful.
- Monitor change and provide ongoing support.
- Use action research or action planning strategies — small areas of change at a time, accumulate in cycles.
- Celebrate small successes.

Time
- Create time for professional development and trialing of ideas.
- Extended period for action, reflection, consideration and assimilation.

---

additional factors were important when gender is an issue in the teacher change process. It became obvious that there was a gap in the teacher change literature, which tended to focus on adoption of new curriculum or organizational practices which were seen as unproblematic. But my mapping of the gender and education literature indicated that in this field any change is considered controversial, is often strongly resisted, finds it harder to gain widespread support, takes longer, slips back more quickly, and requires different sensitivities than less personal and political changes.

I then developed a Working Model for Gender and Change (see Table 16.1) which incorporates the key factors that I could find when gender is a focus of the change. Next, I began to implement as many facets of the model as possible across a full year of ongoing school-based professional development activities centring on building a new discipline and welfare policy consistent with our agreed whole school Action Plan. I took on the roles of researcher (finding and providing background information and resources), motivator (modelling actions, identifying positive outcomes, enabling discussions on gender) and change agent (collecting feedback by recording and collating responses, chairing discussions, planning and running staff workshops).

This is not the place to detail the extensive activities we undertook across the whole year. But I will outline one example of a particularly important activity which illustrates the quality of the local data that was so powerful in convincing staff that gender was an issue in our school.

During second term, when we did a series of workshops on building self-esteem, the teachers of grades 2, 3 and 5 cooperated to provide some time when their students were able to meet in single-sex groupings to discuss such questions as:

- Have you any concerns or worries in the playground?
- How does this make you feel? What can you do about it?
- Is there anything that happens in the classroom that worries you?

The students, still working in girls-only and boys-only groups, also completed the following sentence stems. For girls:

- It's great being a girl because . . .
- It's bad being a girl because . . .

and parallel stems for boys.

The teachers collated the data together, and noticed some amazing trends. Girls saw that *all* of the negative aspects of being a girl, quite a long list, related to the behaviour of boys towards them. They expressed this in a matter of fact way, as if that is just how it is in the world. Samples were:

It's bad being a girl because . . . boys kick you on the bars.
boys are not letting the girls play with the basketball.
boys laugh at you.
boys don't let us join in their games.
boys have more fun than girls.
and so on.

Conversely most of the positive aspects identified by boys, another long list, related to having higher skill levels than girls. Samples were:

It's great being a boy because . . . boys are stronger.
boys are better at playing basketball.
boys can do more dangerous things.
boys can ride roller blades, girls always trip over.
boys have more adventures.

> boys are braver than girls.
> boys can run a lot faster than girls.
> boys aren't afraid of spiders.
> girls aren't too keen on computers.

When the girls gave the positive aspects of being a girl, they, in sharp contrast to the parallel stem for boys, listed only a few aspects summed up by:

> It's great being a girl because ... girls can do anything.
> we can play any sport we like.

Only three boys could complete the stem:

> It's bad being a boy because ... my little sister never gets into trouble.
> girls can type faster than boys.
> it is also good being a girl as well.

No other comments were given by the boys — a stark contrast to the equivalent stem for girls.

When the male teacher in this trio presented the data from this exercise to the whole staff we had some shocked teachers! The reaction was, 'No wonder girls need their self-esteem built up!' and boys 'really think they are better!' This sharing of student opinions carried considerable weight and increased staff awareness in a way that no data imported from another school could have achieved. This was a key turning point in recognizing that gender-linked factors were fundamental to our school's commitment to addressing discipline and welfare practices.

There were, of course, many other key change moments across the year: incidents initially reported to us by parents added strength to a gender focus when staff were forced to admit that sex-based harassment did happen in our school; the principal's readiness to speak out in support of changes carried much influence and promoted greater confidence and consistency across the school; some teachers who monitored each other's classrooms, and shared their data with the whole staff, surprised many, and literally convinced others, that boys do demand more time and attention, even in our school; and when students in the upper-end of the school began to show changes to previously gendered attitudes and behaviours staff were encouraged to intensify their efforts.

I believe that the single most effective impetus for change was the continuous collection and sharing of local data — on many levels and from various sources. This proved to be very powerful in raising awareness, generating a climate of collegiality and motivating further changes in teaching practices. Change is harder when gender is a focus and all aspects of the model appear to be important when designing professional development that makes a difference to practice.

Our new discipline and welfare policy reflects a much greater awareness of gender issues and the way they impinge on discipline and welfare matters in our school. The policy identifies ways in which our girls are disadvantaged; records strategies we have found which work to reduce this; and it addresses sex-based harassment as a major problem which will be named as such, will not be tolerated and is now dealt with as a major misdemeanour. This represents a major shift in understanding and readiness to act both as individual teachers and as a whole school. The climate is more supportive and collaborative for staff and there is an expectation that teachers reflect individually and collectively on their understandings, values and current practices. The change process based on the model has built a culture of success and trust in our school.

Students now show more awareness of each others' rights and they speak up and express their views and feelings more readily. They assertively resolve conflict among themselves but they also have greater confidence in talking to teachers who now make an effort to actively listen to their concerns. Students know we have a strong emphasis on an equitable and harassment-free environment.

I set out on a journey and I travelled a long way, moving myself and my colleagues towards a new horizon, opening up new vistas, new opportunities for action, new understandings of practices. Our action plan mapped the way; discipline and welfare was the path we trod; gender awareness was the meeting place; and in moving barriers we learned to negotiate with each other. This journey has had its mountains and valleys, with gentler paths in between, but it is a journey that has no end, only new beginnings. Travelling on is the choice our staff has made, continuing to make changes and improving our practices as we consider gender as a significant issue in our school.

Change that lasts, takes time. Time in the busy weekly schedule to discuss gender issues; time at staff meetings to run workshops; time across the entire year to cumulatively build, and share, a picture of current practice, to try new ideas and to be rewarded by observable improvements in student behaviours and attitudes. Professional development that works for gender equity requires considerable planning so that the key elements listed in the model are incorporated into the change processes. It has been a demanding process, but extremely worthwhile: gender is now firmly on our agenda.

Changing Physics to Suit the Girls?
Christina Hart

I find myself changing hairdressers quite often. As I get to know each one — and she gets to know my hair — she leaves to follow a boyfriend or have a baby, and the conversation has to start all over again with the young woman who takes her place. 'Do you work?' 'Yes, I'm a teacher.' 'What do you teach?' 'Physics!' The scissors clatter to the floor as my attendant retreats, then offers her apology: 'I was never very good at physics.' The interchange illustrates two elements of the relationship between women and physics. There is the young woman's fear of the incomprehensible and the implied question about what kind of woman I can be if I survived my encounter with the subject.

I was a relative late-comer to teaching. When my youngest child began school I went back on a promise, made to myself in high school, that I would never become a teacher. From the perspective of a mother it was clear that the scientific profession I had entered as a young graduate could not match the pragmatic advantages offered by school hours and holidays. A shortage of physics teachers ensured that I easily gained a position in a girls' school, and I embarked on a new career believing I already had a good understanding of the issues that contribute to girls' low participation in physics.

My initial experiences in the classroom were, however, profoundly discouraging. In my second year at the school I had a very able group of twenty-two girls in Year 11 and, to my satisfaction, they consistently gained high marks in the tests I regularly set. But, at the end of the year, only five of them elected to continue physics in Year 12. In response to my dumbfounded query they told me that they simply could not understand physics. It took me several years to understand the truth behind this apparent untruth.

At this stage I was fortunate to become involved in two groups of teachers, the Monash Children's Science Group and the McClintock Collective. The members of the Children's Science Group were concerned with the implications for teaching of constructivist views of learning; and the McClintock Collective was concerned with increasing girls' participation, competence and confidence in science (see the chapters by Sue Lewis and Gaell Hildebrand in this volume). It was the overlap between these two areas of concern that enabled me to resolve the conundrum that my students had posed.

I began to listen attentively to the questions and puzzles that the girls had about the physical world: 'What attracts the earth to us — is it a magnetic field surrounding us?' 'If friction is a force, what is it, exactly, and what does it do?' 'Why does our weight change when we are submerged in water?' 'What is the sun's gravity balanced by?' I started to think of ways of using these questions as the basis for building students' understandings of concepts. I realized that previously I had disregarded their intuitive understandings of the physical world and dismissed as trivial the questions that, to them, were vital in making sense of their experiences.

At first I saw myself as just trying to teach physics better. It took a while before I began to understand that, while what I was doing would probably be better for boys as well as for girls, it had specific advantages for girls. Influenced by the writing of Jan Harding (Harding, 1985; Harding and Sutoris, 1987) and Evelyn Fox Keller (1985) I began to revise the view I had formed during the early years of my feminism: that there were no significant differences between males and females, except in their reproductive anatomy. I reconsidered the importance of 'relatedness' in a young woman's search for identity and recognized the importance for my students of being able to relate to me and to one another in the course of their search, rather than seeing me as a dispenser of impartial knowledge.

More importantly, I began to realize that the impression that most students have of physics — that it is boring, hard, abstract and unrelated to other aspects of their lives — has particular significance for girls. Boys, of course, are more likely to have had experiences that relate easily to the concepts, but perhaps they are also more ready to accept what they are told without questioning how it applies to other areas of their life. By contrast, a girl may acknowledge that she is unable to see connections between the abstract concepts and her everyday experiences, but mistakenly assumes this means that she does not have the ability to understand the subject.

She may even be relieved to discover that abstract thought is beyond her. The concern with 'relatedness', which is so central to her search for identity, is mirrored in the intellectual realm as a concern to relate new knowledge and ideas to experiences in other areas of life. A young male, on the other hand, is more likely to construct his identity in terms of independence, and he may find personal relationships threatening. For him the 'unrelatedness' of abstract thought may be very reassuring. Furthermore, abstraction is often represented as the highest and most difficult form of disciplined thought and, as such, it provides an avenue for the heroic expression of male identity.

In most traditional physics courses the abstract nature of principles is emphasized and the complexity of applying the principles to familiar experiences is deprecated. This approach may be quite reassuring for some boys, while others may find it merely boring. But it can be profoundly alienating for most girls. It is not surprising that the girls I teach consistently tell me that physics is still seen as a boys' subject and that a girl needs to have an exceptional level of confidence in herself to take it on.

Of course, many other factors also influence girls' enrolments in physics. In the past, females as well as males have persisted with physics if the subject is a prerequisite for their preferred tertiary course. Girls, being less likely than boys to have career plans of any kind, have generally had less incentive to tolerate boredom and irrelevance. The girls in my classes still vouch for the importance of sound careers advice in drawing their attention to the importance of physics as preparation for many tertiary courses.

However, as girls are becoming more conscious of their career decisions, physics is actually declining in importance as a prerequisite: it has not been required for entry to medicine for many years, and is no longer absolutely necessary even for some engineering courses. These changes have helped produce an interesting divergence in the participation rates of girls in the two physical sciences, chemistry and physics. Until the end of the 1970s these two subjects enrolled similar percentages of girls. But chemistry remained a prerequisite for medicine and, as girls' aspirations rose during the following decade, the enrolments in chemistry rose also, reaching almost half by the end of the 1980s. (Coincidentally, changes to the chemistry course during this period placed a greater emphasis on the relevance of chemical concepts to everyday life, and this probably also contributed to girls' increased enrolments.)

The narrowness of the standard science program — consisting of physics, chemistry, two mathematics subjects and English — seems to be particularly unappealing to girls. They will often sacrifice career options in order to take a humanities subject, particularly a language other than English, and physics appears to be the most dispensable of the science subjects. I suspect that broadening the Year 12 program would have a substantial impact on girls' participation in physics. At the university level in Australia, the introduction of broad combined degrees such as Arts/Engineering has certainly helped encourage more young women into engineering, previously regarded as an exclusively male domain.

However, changes within physics itself are also required. As I began to appreciate the validity of my students' questions and understand their underlying meaning, I felt increasingly frustrated by the constraints within which I had to work. The syllabus was weighed down by concepts (such as 'gravitational potential' or 'kinetic energy of the centre of mass') which were intractably abstract, while the questions that characterized the physics examination at the time began to look trivial beside those with which my students wanted to grapple. After all, who, in their right mind, was concerned with what happened to a 'block of mass 1.0 kg . . . connected to a light spring of natural length 0.50 m, and placed on a frictionless surface'? (1985 Physics examination, question 22). I believed that it ought to be possible to devise a course, with appropriate assessment, which, rather than viewing abstract principles as ends in themselves, would focus on the links between physics concepts and the real life experiences of both girls and boys.

In 1987, I became involved in writing a new physics course which was to be implemented as part of a major reform of the structures, curriculum and assessment for post-compulsory schooling. The policy for all subjects in the new Victorian Certificate of Education (VCE) placed considerable emphasis on the 'encouragement of participation'. It urged the development of 'courses that are appropriate and reflect the lives of both females and males' and that 'include a balance of theory and practice . . . [and] relate knowledge to its social context and uses' across all fields of study (Victorian Curriculum and Assessment Board, 1987, pp. 75–8). This appeared to provide clear support for my hopes of a physics course that would encourage girls' participation and make physics more appealing and genuinely challenging for all students. I embarked on the task with considerable optimism.

In addition, the committee charged with overseeing the development of the new course included broad community representation and enlightened members of the science teaching profession. Academics, who had considerably influenced the course in the past, were represented, but only as one of several groups with a legitimate interest in school physics. Increasing the participation of girls in school physics was high on the agenda of the committee, and approaches based on constructivist views of learning and emphasizing the social and technological implications of physics were also embraced as being valid in their own right and valuable for a wide range of students.

It turned out that, even in such favourable circumstances, changing the guise in which physics is presented in school courses was no easy task (Hart, 1995). A syllabus document describes its content in very sparse terms and is able to effectively communicate its intentions only by implicit reference to a background of commonly accepted practices in teaching and assessment. Communicating the intention to depart from established practice, I discovered, cannot be achieved within similarly sparse terms. Teachers and students want to know exactly what they will be required to teach and learn. In the case of VCE physics, demands that the syllabus should unambiguously prescribe the content effectively enforced a traditional presentation of the subject.

Of course academic physicists also vigorously defended the traditional abstract version. Their arguments were lost in the forum of the overseeing committee but, by an indirect route, their views nonetheless became very influential. Bureaucratic personnel charged with administrative responsibility for the development and implementation of the new certificate intervened. Overriding the decisions of the committee, they ensured that the new physics course expressed a more traditional view of the nature and purposes of school physics. However, while the bureaucrats acknowledged that they had received representations from the academic community, they justified their action by reference to what they themselves saw as the essential nature of physics. Although they were not scientists, they were personally convinced that physics could not be anything other than what it always had been.

In its final form the new VCE physics course does represent a significant departure from tradition. However, the achievement is minor compared with what had seemed possible at the outset. The constraints that operated during the process of developing the course were compounded by problems with assessment during implementation. For the first three years of the new course, students' assessments were based on the completion of two externally set tests, one at the end of each semester, and two school assessed tasks, an extended experimental investigation and a poster based on library research. However, in response to concerns about unreasonable workloads for both students and teachers, the number of assessment tasks was reduced to three in all subjects, with two school assessed tasks and one externally set test becoming the norm for most subjects. But in the case of physics, concern with assessing content prevailed: the research project, which had encountered opposition from physics teachers, was dropped, meaning that two tests were retained.

Nonetheless, small but significant gains have been made. According to data compiled by Dan O'Keefe (1994), there was a gradual increase in girls' enrolments in physics between 1989 and 1991 as teachers began to implement some of the intentions of the new course. This was followed by a substantial increase in 1992, the first year of the new full VCE physics course at Year 12. The participation of boys also increased, however, so that girls still represented only 27 per cent of physics candidates, compared with 26 per cent in the early 1980s. There have also been significant changes in the patterns of girls' performance on the new course (see Gaell Hildebrand's chapter in this volume).

A particular problem has been the difficulty of devising questions for the externally set tests which genuinely reflect the intentions of the new course. Widespread anecdotal evidence suggests that students have generally found the tests to be onerous and discouraging. A lot of work remains to be done to develop a style of question that matches the intentions of the course, and which appropriately values the diversity of students' relevant capacities.

Teaching the VCE physics course has led me to make further changes in my approach, but those changes are a consequence of my experience in devising the course, rather than a result of its prescriptions. I have realized that, whilst at first sight the task of presenting physics in a way that builds on students' experiences and concerns seems relatively straightforward, it in fact represents a huge challenge. This challenge exists at the purely pragmatic level of 'How do we teach?' and, more importantly, 'How do we assess?'

But I have also learnt that the view which people have about the nature of physics touches on existential questions about how we, in the late twentieth century, express our individual and collective search for identity and meaning. I discovered that attempts to change the traditional version of physics threaten our notions of how we determine right and wrong, and our mechanisms for allocating power and privilege. I now see girls' exclusion from physics as a symptom of the essentially exclusive social purposes that physics fulfils. We can include girls by demanding of them what was demanded of me: that they sacrifice their 'femininity' on the grounds that it serves only to make them inferior persons. Or, we can include so-called 'feminine' values into physics and embrace the challenge which girls offer, that of replacing power and privilege as the basis of social order with a new concern for relatedness.

References

COMMONWEALTH SCHOOLS COMMISSION (1987) *The National Policy for the Education of Girls in Australian Schools*, Carlton, Vic., Curriculum Corporation.

HARDING, J. (1985) 'Values, cognitive style and the curriculum', Contributions to the third international conference on Gender and Science and Technology (GASAT 3), London, UK, pp. 159–66.

HARDING, J. and SUTORIS, M. (1987) 'An object relations account of the differential involvement of boys and girls in science and technology', in KELLY, A. (ed.) *Science for Girls?* Milton Keynes, Open University Press.

HART, C. (1995) 'Access and the quality of learning — The story of a curriculum document for school physics', Unpublished doctoral thesis, Monash University.

KELLER, E.F. (1985) *Reflections on Gender and Science*, New Haven, Yale University Press.

O'KEEFE, D. (1994) 'Analysis of year 12 physics numbers', Unpublished paper presented to the Science Key Learning Area Committee of the Victorian Board of Studies.

VICTORIAN CURRICULUM AND ASSESSMENT BOARD (1987) *Developing the Victorian Certificate of Education: Options Paper*, Melbourne, Victorian Curriculum and Assessment Board.

17 The Emotional Dimensions of Feminist Pedagogy in Schools

Jane Kenway, Jill Blackmore, Sue Willis and Léonie Rennie

Introduction

This chapter rests on the premise that if it is to move towards its desired ends, the movement for gender justice in and through schools must reach a much better understanding of what actually happens in schools as gender reform policies and principles are translated into educational practices. It draws data from case studies of gender reform practices in schools in several Australian states (see further, Kenway, Willis, Blackmore, Rennie, in press). Our argument is that feminist teachers must pay more attention to the reception and re-articulation of feminist practices in schools and that, in particular, this is the case with regard to its emotional dimensions. Drawing from our data, we will point to the complex interpersonal, educational and emotional dynamics that feminist work for change evokes. In so doing, it will become clear that some feminist approaches to the curriculum need to be revised.

There was a range of ways in which the teachers in our research schools sought to effect gender reform. These can be roughly categorized as seeking to *change girls' choices* (i.e., their subject choices and post-school ambitions); to *change girls themselves* (i.e., to enhance their self-esteem, to encourage them to value femaleness and to value their differences); to *change the curriculum* (i.e., the development of gender-inclusive and/or socially critical curriculum), and to *change the learning environment* (i.e., the development of school and classroom policies and the appointment of committees and personnel to change the gendered culture of the school). Certainly there was some overlap between these categories and within each broad approach a range of perspectives and activities existed. For elaborations see Kenway and Willis with the Education of Girls Unit, South Australia, (1993). Many attempts at feminist reform were read and reworked in ways which had unintended and often paradoxical and ironical results.

Overall on the matter of feminism in and beyond schools, emotions almost invariably ran high. These emotional responses were most extreme amongst feminism's proponents and opponents where, it seemed, matters of gender identity and/ or feminist identity and investment were most keen. However it was almost always the case that people in our schools experienced feminism as some sort of challenge.

For some, the challenge was negative and it provoked emotional resistance of various sorts and degrees; defensiveness and hostility, for example. For others, the reverse was the case and feminism brought forth feelings of relief and hope because it represented a challenge to injustices of various sorts. For yet others, it evoked mixed feelings depending on its particular manifestation. Certain feminist ideas were easily tolerated, others quickly produced a knee-jerk negativity. Feminism was indeed a heady emotional cocktail, the effects of which were not easy to predict.

The Mixed Emotions of Teachers

For many of the teachers involved in gender reform, feminism was a core part of their identity. It provided a different, and in their view, preferable way of being and shaped decisively their educational and world views and the way they acted in and on their schools. Feminism held out to them the promise of a better education system; a better world. Through the rectification of injustices based on gender, it offered a different future to women and girls; one rich with hope and possibilities. It offered new ways to understand current problems and to reinterpret old wounds. Their feminist work for change was usually fuelled by a deep sense of commitment, determination and often outrage and frustration.

To these teachers, small victories, such as timetable or uniform changes, felt significant because of the difficulty of achieving them. Grander victories such as school equal opportunities policies or major curriculum changes tended to be the result of lengthy processes of contestation and compromise. Almost every success was fragile, open to dispute and often temporary, dependent as it was on the energies of a committed few. The gap between the promise, the practice and the price of feminism was almost always considerable. For some this resulted in feelings of anxiety, distress and alienation from their colleagues and even their students. Burnout was not unusual for feminists flying solo in their schools. Most teachers had a strong sense that the results of their work were complex, diffuse and difficult to assess: not easily pinned down. Given the fragile and marginal position of feminism in most schools, small wonder these teachers yearned for predictability and certainty.

Let us consider an example of the gender politics of feminist pedagogies. The following story points to the sensitivities that the feminist reform agenda invoked amongst male colleagues.

In this inner-city suburban school with a wide social mix of Indo-Chinese, Greek, Italian and Anglo-Celtic students, most staff agreed that the hegemonic masculinity of the 'macho Greek boys' was a major problem for the school generally and for the girls particularly. Sex-based harassment, bullying, sexist arrogance and lack of concern for others were rife. Most female teachers felt that addressing this problem was the responsibility of male staff members and did not want to divert their over-taxed feminist energies to it. Nonetheless, two female Affirmative Action (AA) team members had gained some state funding for an inservice day to allow male staff to seek to change the attitudes of the boys and (they hoped) themselves. From their viewpoint, this reform initiative sought to provide space for men to work up their own agenda and to try and shift the focus away from changing girls to changing boys. Despite such good intentions, this caused considerable resentment amongst all the males, even those who were pro-feminist. In their view it implied that the male staff were unable to 'get their act together'. It was regarded as high-handed, heavy-handed and non-consultative. According to a pro-feminist male AA team member, it was also rather threatening to the men's sense of who was in control. He observed that when the inservice occurred, the male participants spent much of the time 'feminist bashing', and even the most liberal men enjoyed joining in. Collective resistance to any programs for boys and men which were initiated by feminists resulted, and the upshot of the day was that the males explored the question 'What can we do to help the girls?' They thus reclaimed control at the same time as appearing to nurture the feminist agenda. As the pro-feminist male member of the Affirmative Action (AA) group who attended this workshop commented, 'A necessary therapeutic phase of the change process may well be one which allows male anger to surface and be given vent.' Whether this is so or not is a moot point. Certainly though, in this instance, it was counter-productive and allowed men to again shift responsibility for action back on to the feminists and onto changing girls, not changing boys. At a later stage, when the antagonism had died down, there were moves, initiated by males, to organize a specific day addressing the problem of boys and violence. Ironically, these men were largely uninterested in and even antagonistic to equal opportunity. They saw it only as a career path for ambitious women who had rejected their proper nurturing role in the home and the school.

This example suggests that feminism generates certain fears in male teachers about their loss of responsibility, control and initiative. But it also raises questions about collegial courtesy and tact and shows how a lack of both on the part of the feminist teachers, in a sense gave the men permission to claim the moral high ground and to appear to nurture the feminist cause while at the same time withholding their support for it. Reconstructing masculinity could then be done without reference to any feminist agenda. This is a predictable result when the male/ female dualism is mobilized as a way of allocating blame and responsibility. Potential male allies were alienated and lost, at least temporarily. Our studies revealed many examples of the gender politics of feminist pedagogy which we will not elaborate here but see, further, Kenway (1995).

Feminist Pedagogies: Pleasure and Pain

It is possible to group feminist pedagogies into two broad camps, one which demonstrated elements of therapy; the other, elements of authoritarianism. Neither was a particularly successful form of pedagogy either with other teachers or with students. In the last instance the tendency was to ignore altogether the world of feelings and to resort to highly rationalistic and even authoritarian policies and pedagogies. Hyper-rationalistic solutions were offered to deeply emotive issues. In many cases these subverted their intentions and alienated many students and staff. Alternatively, when they did attend to such matters, it was often the case that the approach was more therapeutic than educational. Ensuring that students and colleagues enjoyed themselves and/or felt good about feminism became more important than helping them to become critical, informed and skilled advocates for a better world. Usually for the people on the receiving end, either too much or too little was demanded and at stake. Of course, to suggest that such approaches were purely authoritarian or purely therapeutic would be a misnomer. Usually they were rather complex amalgamations of the two — and more! And no approach evoked the same reaction from all those it pertained to. For some, the voice of feminist authority was a comforting reassurance. Yet for others it was experienced as oppressive. The same point pertained to therapeutic approaches.

Therapy and Nurturance

The more therapeutic and nurturant feminist discourses in the schools were most associated with attempts to 'change girls' and to 'change the learning environment'. The idea here was to value the girls and what they did in order that they would value themselves; to provide them with the space and the support to explore topics near and dear to their hearts and to encourage them to take risks with their bodies and their identities. Nonetheless, even this discourse was, on occasions, also underpinned by a deficit model of girlhood. In broad terms, their 'lack' was seen to be largely psychological — they didn't have a strong and enabling sense of self. They were thus often positioned by feminism as the victims of society's systematic devaluing of femaleness; victims who had learnt to be limited. The therapeutic feminist curriculum was designed to give them lots of positive strokes, to make them believe they could 'do anything'; that 'the sky's the limit' (two popular slogans). Alternatively they were positioned as unsung heroines who must value and celebrate femaleness. Our evidence indicates that some programmes articulated their feminist positions more clearly than did others but most tried to offer them almost subliminally. A rare few attached them to an overt feminist agenda.

The girls in our research schools were often surprised and rather uncomfortable at intimations that they were all essentially the same. Further, they were usually confused by and resented an attributed victim status, or any suggestion of their inevitably low self-worth. They seemed to see themselves as clusters of strengths and weaknesses. Predictably, they were attracted to the position of unsung heroines, especially when it involved celebrations, fun and games; many of which amused and delighted them. Learning to ride horses and surf boards, to survive as country girls in the city, dining out together, using drama and pop music to explore ideas were some of the many celebratory aspects of the feminist reform agenda that turned girls on rather than turned them off. Let us explore some of the issues raised in the above discussion a little further through some specific examples.

Since 1986, the Year 7 and 8 girls at Foster have annually attended the Lakeside Riding Camp. This programme is seen to promote 'self-esteem, confidence, awareness of self-importance, personal relationships and phys-ical fitness'. It consciously chooses a single-sex approach so as to indicate to the girls that they are being taken seriously and with a view to encour-aging the free sharing of ideas and the consensual reaching of conclusions. The camp includes horse-riding and a number of workshops. Over the years the program has varied and has included issues to do with contraception and sexuality. The year that we visited, the theme was *Self Esteem*.

On Day One the girls joined in two workshops, one on Health and Personal Relationships run by school staff and the other called Being Assertive, run by the local Equal Opportunity Officer. When I arrived on Day Two the remains of one of these activities was taped around the room. Each girl had a paper bag with her name on and all others are asked to write out 'Warm Fuzzies' to include in the bag. During Day Two they unfortunately had to be reminded to put more in, as some bags were rather empty. Scattered in the corner were sheets from the Assertiveness Work-shop. The girls filled in the sheets under the two headings below. Their answers indicated that many were confused by the concept 'assertive'. The following response was typical:

Times when I was not assertive: When I stole a dollar, I blamed it on my sister. (How I could have improved the situation?) I could of said it was me.

On Day Two the mood was rather subdued when the Equal Opportunity Officer started her program. She had three activities planned. The first was a simple exercise involving mingling and getting to identify each others' characteristics — colour of hair, birth sign, etc. The delivery was rather lack-lustre and so was the response. A Community Relations Officer then had them doing a similar activity but despite a vibrant delivery the re-sponse remained at best half-hearted. A further exercise which required that they get into groups and go through a work sheet on future options was equally lacking in inspiration for them. The sheet was relatively com-plex. It was clear from the outset that they have not attended sufficiently well to the explanation offered by the increasingly disheartened Equal Opportunity Officer to be able to adequately go through the required activities in the way anticipated. Some groups knew what to do, others did not but still went through some semblance of the activity. In part this involved discussing their strengths. This they did relatively easily and compliments were handed around generously. But the activity still ground to an early halt, three quarters of an hour before anticipated. The girls then wandered off to do their own thing. My later discussion with the two visitors indicated that they were rather disgruntled by their inability to energize the girls. They tended to blame lack of forward planning. Having identified at least one major reason for the failure of the exercise the Equal Opportunity Officer also concluded that another contributing factor was the girls' low self-esteem — which she claimed was clearly in evidence.

It is difficult to see how, under the circumstances, such activities could significantly enhance girls' self-esteem. In our view, most of the activities were so simplistic that they trivialized and indeed denigrated the girls. The compulsory 'Warm Fuzzies' implied firstly that the girls would be convinced by superficial compliments and secondly that they needed help in giving and receiving praise and more generally at the interpersonal level. And, as they demonstrated by their resistant participation, the girls did not feel the need to do this and neither did they feel affirmed by what they were asked to do. Expectations of the girls were low, they were offered no challenges that sparked their interest or tapped into what they perceived as their needs, and so the girls performed accordingly. Had the assertiveness class been more effective, the girls may have been able to articulate this grievance but, as it was, the overall exercise was, again, very much one of the politics of niceness and this is a familiar politics for girls.

> Fortunately for the Foster girls, other Lakeview workshops had tapped into the girls' perceived needs. Older girls' reflections on earlier camps revealed a strong sense of pleasure, female connectedness, security and support. The camps were seen as a sign that although they were small in number in the school, they were an important part of it. 'It was us girls, all together, it was really good. It made us feel wanted by the school.' The girls also said that the programs encouraged them to be positive about themselves and to think about all aspects of their futures. 'It was just like self-discovery. It made you look on the inside, not on the outside.' What they particularly liked was the way it dealt with the personal side of life — sex, contraception, family relationships and friendships. One of the noticeable things about the camp was its focus on the private, the personal, the emotional and relational aspects of girls' lives.

This was relatively typical of 'changing girls'' approaches. While this may be considered inclusive, and it may well have helped girls to deal much better with these aspects of their lives, it could hardly be described as expansive. It positioned girls in the same old identities and offered them few, if any, new positions to occupy. Certainly the personal was not often made political. Clearly, though, the girls felt gratified that they were able to talk about the personal side of their lives and that discussions focused on matters of importance to them. Currently, the private is often constructed as a girls' place and so these aspects of their lives should not be dismissed. Nonetheless, the public/private dichotomy is a problem for girls and requires deconstruction. 'Changing girls'' strategies are well placed to do this deconstructive work but in our study they did not do it.

And, as the following story demonstrates, taking girl students seriously, to paraphrase Adrienne Rich, means more than caring them into a state of dependency.

> In this inner suburban school with a large proportion of Greek, Italian and Indo-Chinese students, there was a wide range of equal opportunity policies and activities for girls ranging from special girls-only classes in maths, science, computers, self-defence, and gym to girls' camps, career days, community based activities and women speakers. The equal opportunity activities at this school, of which there was a wide range, were well received by most girls, who saw them as fun and as a clear indication that the teachers cared for girls because they provided information about careers and 'boy free' space for girls in a school environment dominated by macho males. The AA team and the principal in the school were seeking to implement a whole school approach to equal opportunity by integrating it throughout the curriculum. There was a strong health and human relations program which focused upon raising girls' self-esteem.
>
> Whilst these girls felt gratified and strengthened because the school attended to them particularly, there was also a feeling that the teachers were 'a bit slack' in terms of their expectations. The additional programs for girls were seen to compete with the 'important' subjects for time and resources and, because of their social rather than knowledge orientation, to be less important and 'easier' because they did not have the same academic demands but were about making pretty things (Technology Studies) or just talking about themselves and people's behaviour (Health and Human Relations). In that sense, the knowledge hierarchy of secondary schools only legitimated certain types of gender reform programs, e.g., encouraging more girls to do maths and non-traditional subjects. Furthermore, whilst there was a wide range of programs addressing equal opportunity, there was little attempt to actively involve the girls in the politics of the school, e.g., student council or in running the girls' programs. Nurturance here meant dependence. The girls often felt rather ambivalent about the school's feminist programs. They were fun but soft options; it appeared to them that they both valued and undervalued them simultaneously. Certainly, at one level, they did not take them as seriously as they would have wished.

One of the difficulties of the therapeutic model of feminism in schools was its limited intellectual agenda. It did not help girls to understand the politics of gender and how they pertain to the politics of knowledge. While it sought to elevate and celebrate the female side of the gender divide, it did not explain how and why it was constituted as other than and less than the male side or why such elevatory practices were 'necessary'. It also demonstrated a certain innocence or ignorance about material culture.

> The setting was a school in a lower middle-class, newish suburb in a large country town. The key player was a charismatic gender equity coordinator

called Carole who could jolly most kids and many staff into doing things associated with gender reform. She had taken under her wing the school's 'naughty girls'. The dissident voice of feminism became aligned to the dissident voices of these girls' close knit anti-school culture. They 'rocked along' to all the feminist activities organized by the Equal Opportunity Coordinator. They made streamers and badges on International Women's Day, they talked about feminist issues at assemblies and attentively attended career sessions for girls. Feminism promised them that they could do anything and they took it at its word. Indeed, they became ambitious as a result; they wanted to become engineers and mechanics, journalists and lawyers. The problem here wasn't simply that in some cases their grades didn't match their ambitions — their lives outside of school didn't either. The future mechanic had to leave the school and her friends, to follow her sole parent mother to a nearby city. The mother had to leave town due to ongoing harassment by her father. She didn't know what the future held for her anymore. The future journalist became pregnant and her fantasies revolved around motherhood and going to the North of Queensland to live with her boyfriend and the Aborigines. Her best friend, the baby's aunt, took time off school to be with her while she was suffering from morning sickness and shingles. She had missed lots of classes anyway, in order to look after her invalid, sole parent father.

The feminism that this school offered wasn't much use to these girls. Indeed, it both betrayed and abandoned them. The popular feminist slogan 'Girls can do anything' is premised on the principles of choice, free will and the work ethic. The principle that it is possible to do anything if you want to badly enough and work hard enough did not have much purchase in this situation. This liberal fantasy had very little to do with the grim reality of many girls' lives, as the previous story about a school's 'naughty girls' fantasizing through feminism demonstrates. Coming to grips with the material realities of these girls' lives and assessing what sort of help really helps would have been infinitely more appropriate than feeding their fantasies.

Generally students' responses to the therapeutic and the authoritarian feminist agendas in schools were strongly coded by class and ethnicity. It was often the case that attempts at reform were informed by white middle-class values even when their intended audience was neither. As a result there was not only a total mismatch between production and consumption but a great deal of pain on the part of those students who felt their identities were negated. Alternatively, some approaches adopted a deficit or romanticized view of their audience, again missing their mark.

Clearly the cultural background of the students and the teachers was a crucial variable. We believe that the concept of 'positionality' is particularly useful for helping gender reformers to read both the culture of the school and its patterns of power relationships and their own work for change. Implicit in much school education and, we might add, gender reform is the notion of 'normal' girls, usually seen to be middle-class and Anglo. Such girls are positioned positively; their culture is made central. They therefore receive an education couched in their own values. Girls who are not positioned as 'normal' are positioned as other than and as less than 'normal' girls. They are seen as different from what is normal and preferable; as special or 'at risk'; not because this is how they have been positioned by schools, but because of some sort of dysfunction in their backgrounds. This sleight of hand allows two things to happen. It allows schools to shift responsibility for any of the problems such girls may have at school to their home or their culture. Blame can be transferred elsewhere and girls and their parents can then be asked to accept the onus to change. Alternatively, schools develop some sort of compensatory measures couched in terms of 'normal' girls to make up for these other girls' 'deficits'. That is, schools try to reposition them as someone else. As a result, such girls are positioned by education structures and practices in such a way as to marginalize and dispossess them (see Kenway and Willis, 1990).

The benefit, then, of using the concept 'positionality' is that it requires schools to look at themselves rather than elsewhere, to ask both how is it that they position some girls at the margins of school life and value systems, and how can they reposition them at the centre. It requires them to reconsider the use of such terms as 'girls with special needs', 'girls at risk' and 'girls from non-English-speaking backgrounds'. Another benefit of the concept 'positionality' is that it allows for the recognition that, rather than being from one social grouping or another — say working class or cultural minority — girls occupy a range of social and cultural positions simultaneously. Society positions them in many ways, all of which are part of their identity and all of which influence the ways schools treat them and the ways they treat schools. Had Carole considered more carefully the positions she was offering her 'naughty girls' and the positions they were coming from she may well have offered them programs which attended to the issues they were facing in real life rather than those they fancied in their dreams.

A process of regulating feminism and mobilizing femininity, which we have noted elswhere (Kenway, 1995) in our discussions of male teachers, had its parallels in the behaviour of many boys. And this had its effects on a number of girls' responses to feminism. Unwilling to have their feminine identity brought into question and to have the pleasure of their relationships with boys placed at risk through appearing to blame or neglect them, many girls took on board and replayed the anti-feminist discourse.

> In this school a variety of girl-centred strategies had been developed. These included single-sex maths classes, computer sessions, and camps, self-defence classes, a Girls' Council and a sexual harassment policy. Within the girls' single-sex maths class at Year 9, there was a divergence of opinion amongst the girls, regarding the usefulness, fairness and effectiveness of these policies. For a small group of girls, girl-centred policies, those which seemed to give girls special treatment, were seen to be unfair as they treated girls differently from boys. The girls adopting this position were largely those most closely associated with the boys in friendship groups. They saw boys as being their 'good mates' because they were

'more loyal' and 'less bitchy' than the girls. These 'strong' girls gained their pleasure from 'being one of the boys', from being able to compete with them equally (better in one instance) in sport, but also in 'knowing' the boys' personal weaknesses and insecurities and thus being in the position to 'mother' them. They were on the surface, strong, independent and sure both of their capacity to look after themselves and to cope with the boys' ongoing name calling and denigration. Although these girls were in the single-sex class and on the Girls' Council, they nonetheless perceived feminism as being anti-male and did not see the necessity for sexual harassment policies or for girls-only activities. Indeed, one argued that she went on to the Girls' Council to represent the boys' perspective because all boys were labelled as 'bad' by the equal opportunity discourse. These girls argued that whilst it was 'quieter' in the all-girls class, they worked just as well in a mixed class. Their teachers, whilst pleased that these girls were participants in the class, were simultaneously irritated and puzzled by their resistance to equal opportunity policies. It brought into question the teachers' status as 'strong role models' and undermined their claims to be representing 'the best interests' of girls. Given that the predominantly male staff either saw gender as irrelevant or as adequately dealt with by the strategies noted above, these teachers felt they needed all the support they could get. Indeed, they felt rather betrayed by these girls.

But the 'strong' girls in this class, rather than seeing their teachers as 'good role models', considered them 'over the top feminists'. Indeed, women teachers in this school, whether they saw themselves as feminist or not, were immediately labelled as feminist by other staff and students as soon as they indicated any concern for girls or women teachers. Feminism was a term of derision, and feminists were characterized as anti-male, humourless and without a sense of fun. This was most evident when the male teacher of the rather noisy all-boys maths class over the corridor visited the girls' class. He joked to the girls that the boys were doing more difficult maths than them. The female teacher publicly chastised him in front of the girls for putting the classes into a competitive relationship. One of the strong girls commented, 'There she goes again . . . over the top. Feminists can't take a joke.'

The view that 'feminist' teachers were 'over the top' was also expressed by other 'strong' girls with reference to other equal opportunities strategies such as sexual harassment policies. These policies were seen to protect the girls who the 'strong' girls tended to hold in contempt and so their feelings of contempt flowed over to the policies themselves. They were also seen to provide teachers, particularly those concerned with equal opportunity, with the opportunity for excessive surveillance and generalized condemnation of boys by teachers. Boys were seen to be the victims of such policies. One teacher went so far as to interpret the girls' antagonism to equal opportunity as their response to being separated from the boys. She implied that they were 'boy mad' and assumed that their relationships with the boys were sexual rather than as preferred friends. So, whilst she listened to their view that equal opportunity was 'unfair' for boys, she made little attempt to rectify the blanket portrayal of 'boys as bad'. These girls eventually came to feel that being with boys meant being a 'bad girl', whereas being with girls made you a 'good girl' — at least in the eyes of the feminist teachers. In this way, these girls who found pleasure in being with their male peer groups felt both ashamed and defensive about their association with boys, who in turn were blamed for the girls' disadvantage.

In our schools the discourse of equal opportunities was readily and constantly subverted both by its own logic and by the fear of rejection and will to nurturance which the girls often demonstrated in relation to the resistant males. The boys often felt 'discriminated against' when policies related particularly to girls and did not like to be 'blamed and made to feel accountable' for inequalities which they were not convinced existed or which they did not feel responsible for producing. They envied and resented the attention given to the girls and could not comprehend that under 'normal circumstances' they had held the lion's share, which was now simply being more evenly distributed. Generally, boys read feminist reforms of any sort as an affront to a natural and preferred educational and social order, they demonstrated varying degrees of negativity and engaged in rituals of refusal which ranged from banter to vigorous debate to extreme hostility. Another regular response was to play victim and to punish the girls for being on the side of the oppressor. When this happened the girls tended to feel guilty, rejected and anxious about the loss of connectedness. They would thus tend to support the boys' case in order to maintain and mend the social fabric of their relationships with their male peers. This in turn tended to undermine the power of the original discourse as both girls and boys appeared opposed to it.

Authoritarian Feminisms

What often put girls off feminism was its association with negative authority; with what seemed like relentless criticism of girls' pleasures and fantasies, and a portrayal of women's lives, past, present and future as a struggle without relief. Deconstruction too frequently took the form of destruction and, as we will show shortly, feminists came to be seen as anti pleasure.

It was not at all unusual for a number of feminist curriculum practices to offer girls the implicit message that somehow or other they were in the wrong: that their 'choices' of subject and future and their preferences with regard to reading, television and sport were less than they could or should be, that their homes, and indeed their mothers, were somehow deficient and that overall girls were 'their own worst enemy'. The things that many girls took pleasure in were often the object of particular criticism: romance novels, soap operas and fashion magazines came in for a particular drumming. It was largely only in our research schools where reform was sought through changing girls' views of themselves, i.e., by enhancing their self-esteem and encouraging them to value femaleness and difference that girls' pleasures were attended to positively and drawn on for teaching purposes. When other discourses did so, it was largely in a negative way. However, as we have argued elsewhere, neither had a sufficiently nuanced view of pleasure (Kenway, Willis, Blackmore and Rennie, 1994).

The implicit message of these feminist discourses was 'girls are not good enough as they are, they therefore must change, and become more like boys. They must stop doing the things they like and do the things that we think are good for them.' Along-side this was another implicit message which offered girls an image of themselves as passive victims and/or dupes overwhelmed by negative gender stereotypes or by the unequal relationships between the sexes. Generally it was believed that a good dose of information about alternatives or of critique or deconstruction would set them right. It was the 'changing choices' and the 'changing curriculum' discourses which were most at fault here.

Needless to say, classes that employed these logics did not often meet with a very positive reception. The girls did not tend to appreciate teachers who made them feel ashamed about themselves, their choices, homes and lifestyles — all in the name of helping them. Indeed a number found this insulting and hurtful. Ironically though, as the following story shows, this did not necessarily prevent them from doing as they were told — to a certain extent — or from benefiting from the extra attention.

This single-sex maths class was initiated as a strategy for feminist reform in a school which was previously a boys' technical school and which sought to assume the image of a high school with a comprehensive curriculum. Girls were in the minority in a largely masculinist culture. The proclaimed purpose of this strategy was to change the girls' choices of subjects and therefore to increase their post-school options. In reality, however, changing their choices often meant simply doing more maths.

The girls who were good at maths in Year 9 were encouraged and bribed by three female teachers (the Year Level Coordinator, Equal Opportunity Coordinator and a maths teacher) to choose a single-sex extended maths class in Year 10. In their view, the girls in this single-sex maths class had made the 'right' choices by selecting to do more maths. And, it appeared on the surface that the girls felt the same way. When asked why they had decided to take on this class, most of them responded that maths would 'multiply their choices' — a slogan drawn from a major publicity campaign intended to encourage more girls to do 'non-traditional' subjects (see Kenway, 1993). They spoke of how they believed it was 'good' to do maths, and how they received additional attention from their teachers who they saw as caring and having their interests at heart.

However, in talking to them about what they enjoyed at school and about their post-school study, training or work aspirations, it was clear that few of these girls had real need for further maths. While they enjoyed the 'boy free space', and the social aspects of the 'girl-friendly' pedagogies of group and assignment work, many of the girls did not enjoy maths and only continued with the subject because their teachers had actively encouraged them and would have been disappointed. Having been subject to the media campaigns designed to expand girls' choices, their parents also valued the study of maths for girls. While, on the one hand, these parents informed their daughters that they were free to choose a career which would make them happy and, where possible, pay well, on the other hand, they strongly encouraged them to do what the teachers suggested and to take the maths class. For many girls, doing this extra maths option meant not taking up art, design or the humanities subjects. Ironically many had an aptitude and a preference for these subjects. 'I love to play with colours,' said one. 'I'm really enjoy drawing and would like to do something with design,' said another. A third found pleasure in writing short stories at weekends. Most of these girls aspired to careers in interior design, fashion design or journalism. But they were advised that the humanities and art subjects 'could be picked up at any point'. Two years later, of the fifteen girls in this class, only one had continued mathematics into Year 12.

As this story indicates, doing as they were told was not without its rewards. Many of the girls involved in our research enjoyed the companionship and relaxed comfort of girls-only classes, no matter what the subject or location. They also felt valued by the fact that the teachers had gone to so much trouble for them. Indeed, in certain cases they felt duty bound to the teacher for this, and had great difficulty in expressing the view that while they appreciated the effort they still had other preferences or some criticisms or concerns. Caught in a bind between self-interest and obligation, between guilt and resentment, many did what girls often do; they gave into the pressure to nurture the feelings of others and put their self-interest and perspectives second. There were many complex ironies here; not the least being the fact that often a feminist discourse reinscribed the girls within the politics of nurturance, an aspect of female subordination. This occurred at the same time as the discourse sought to move them beyond the constraints that their gender was seen to impose. Usually, though, girls made the most of their second choices and the teachers were relieved that their cause had not been subverted by the girls' inability to 'see what was good for them'. Nonetheless, adolescent girls struggling to become young women (i.e., adults) do not respond very positively to being told what to do or to proclamations and intimations that they are 'wrong'.

In the girls-only maths class at Year 9 there was a specific intervention on girls and careers. This involved the Equal Opportunity Coordinator talking about careers and maths, but also, more generally, about the changing position of women in work. The teachers saw these programs as broadening the perspectives of the ethnic minority girls who they saw as coming from cultural backgrounds which positioned women as 'unequal' and in more traditional familial roles. They tended to believe that these girls needed special 'protection' and greater encouragement. This special session, held every two weeks, was enjoyed by most of the girls in the class, largely because it was not maths. As Yotta, a Greek girl who wished to go to university and be a lawyer said: 'It opens up new opportunities for us. Being in an all-girl maths class which other girls who also want to get a good job and not just get married and have babies was good.' The regular discussion on maths and careers allowed them an opportunity to talk about themselves and their futures without being denigrated by the boys as being dumb or stupid. However, not all adhered to the notion of getting a career, and one girl, Oksan, from a Muslim background, saw her future as being looked after by her husband whilst she had the babies.

For Tan, a Cambodian girl, one of six in the all-girl maths class, this regular equal opportunity session was seen as an unwelcome intrusion, taking up valuable time in the subject she felt was the most important for her to get into university. For her what the school did for girls generally in terms of the many equal opportunity programs and activities for girls was clouded by the interruption to her maths class. Her response shifted from passive resistance to anger. Whenever the Equal Opportunity Coordinator spoke, and even when asked to be more actively involved by her male maths teacher, she continued to do her maths problems. He did not push her to stop doing maths, but spoke quietly to her afterwards, enquiring as to why she was so uncooperative. She said she wanted to finish her maths homework for the test. Her anger was more overt when, two weeks later, the class was asked to shift rooms in order to watch a video on careers arranged by Ms Roberts. Tan threw a chair as she left the room, muttering 'all this girls' stuff is a waste of time' under her breath.

This highly unusual occurrence raised particular concern with the maths teacher and Ms Robers, about how they were possibly alienating Tan and, apparently, the other Indo-Chinese girls. Tan later indicated that she would be happy for such discussions to occur in Health and Human Relations or History, but not English, Science, Maths or Computing. Her view was: 'We come to school to study and not learn about blood and sex.' She believed that these special sessions in maths were supposed to be 'good for girls' but was not certain how. She expressed the view that women can do anything men can and more — have babies — and that women should continue work. She felt the sessions had little relevance to her. When asked about how she saw her future, she said that her parents wanted her to go to university. She felt she had to do maths so she could fulfil her parents' ambitions for her. However, what she really wanted to be was an actress and singer. At this point, her manner changed. She visibly brightened and spoke animatedly. She really wanted to travel, to be by herself, to be free. She loved pop music and drama. She smiled and laughed when talking about her drama teacher. He said Tan took on a new life in his classes, became the centre of attention and was unrecognizable from her quiet unassuming behaviour in other classes. Tan was anxious about her future options which she felt were restricted by her limp (as a result of polio), her parents' lack of money to support her in university and by the fact that she was 'not that good at maths'. She felt she was destined to become a hairdresser. Her pleasure in music, acting and drama was sublimated to others' perceptions about what was important for her.

This story points to the importance of moving beyond authoritarian feminisms which impose themselves on reluctant students, towards a feminist politics of difference in schools. As we indicated earlier, girls are positioned very differently by the discourses of the school and elsewhere. They are positioned by the primary discursive fields of race, class, ethnicity, 'disability' and sexuality, and by more subordinate discourses to do with, for example, age, intellectuality, competence, appearance, popularity and personality. Our research indicated that most — but, we stress, not all — feminist work for change did not address the matter of difference in any adequate way at all. The tendency was to essentialize all girls in the terms of the 'normal girl' and to assume that all girls have similar needs, interests, pleasures and anxieties, that what oppresses one oppresses all, and that what 'empowers' one 'empowers' all.

The girls in our schools, who were different from 'the normal girls' by virtue of their cultural background, often found themselves on the margins of the feminist discourse; welcomed because of their femaleness but misunderstood because of their otherness. This caused them pain, confusion and a great deal of anxiety. Ironically, most of our feminist teachers had a sense of this. Their difficulty was, what to do about it. Those teachers who tried to address this issue, inevitably got caught on the horns of all sorts of dilemmas associated with either cultural relativism or with the cultural prejudices, ignorances and negativities arising from their own locations around these discursive regimes. As we have pointed out, students and teachers read attempts at feminist reform intertextually and, in the case of teachers, it was often the common sense associated with the practice of teaching which undermined feminist work for change. The ideas associated with individual differences and, strangely, with a refusal of difference and differential treatment were frequently mobilized as part of a counter-discourse and prevented them from attending to issues associated with different cultural groupings of students.

To their credit, some of those teachers who sought to change the curriculum did attempt to inform students about the social construction of knowledge and value, and the relationships of power involved. However, they largely failed to contend with the emotional fall-out of such explanations. Many students, female and male, were strongly resistant to de-naturing anything at all — but particularly matters of gender. We found that, in broad terms, this resistance was associated with matters of identity, investment, pain and pleasure.

Some girls from our studies saw feminism as risky, if not downright dangerous. It expected too much of them, confused and even, in the view of some, misled and betrayed them by being inconsistent or by making promises it could not keep. Also, sometimes, it just simply bored them by being repetitive and predictable, by preaching rather than teaching and by failing to connect with their interests.

While feminist programs can avoid being boring, they cannot always avoid perplexing and in some cases frightening students. Getting to know the unknown, within and without, is difficult and sometimes painful, and future research on pedagogy must explore ways of addressing girls' fears of feminism and its ideas for them and their futures. In our research schools, such fears were too often read by teachers as examples of misguided thinking rather than as matters to be sensitively worked through. This suggests that although feminist pedagogy must attend to power and pleasure, it must also have a nurturant or therapeutic dimension. However, we don't mean the sort of nurturance noted above that 'cares' girls into a state of dependency, but that which is attentive to the difficulties they experience with aspects of feminism. In helping girls both to understand 'why they want what they want' (Walkerdine, 1990, p. 89) and to extend the range of their lives, teachers must work *with* and, just as importantly, *through* their pleasures and fears; helping them to understand how female pleasures and fears are constructed, and how to address them in their own and other females' interests.

Of course, gaining an understanding of the politics of gender does not necessarily prepare girls to re-envisage themselves as current and future actors in the processes they have come to recognize as political. Too often, critique and deconstruction seemed only to offer girls negative politics. It wasn't at all clear what positive alternatives it made available to them. In our view, negative critique is not the best we have to offer girls in schools. Also important are feminist visions of a better world and matters of political mobilization. If girls are to become advocates for a better future for themselves and for others then they need to have some sense of political organization and strategy. Certainly, some schools did position them as agential. Feminist assertiveness training, negotiation of the curriculum, active participation in the formal politics of the school, the development and over-seeing of action plans by girls, Girls' Councils and the use of sexual harassment grievance procedures were concrete and powerful examples which assisted girls to become active citizens within the politics of gender in their schools. It was these sorts of approaches that actually strengthened girls' sense of self and which gave them the courage to act on their worlds in ways they thought were important.

Now, it has to be said that there was no necessary agreement between what they thought important and what their feminist teachers thought. As we indicated earlier, sometimes girls 'in power' ran rather anti-feminist agendas. They had the skills but not the knowledge necessary to act on behalf of girls and women. Clearly both are necessary. However, the tendency in our schools was not to explore with girls the ways in which it all came together for them — how girls put together the scripts of the gendered and feminist discourses which made up their lives. Aspects of feminism were taught to them separately: negotiating the confusing tensions, contradictions and ambiguities of the big picture was left to the girls. Teachers taught the bits and whether and how girls made sense of the collections of bits generally was not considered. There was no doubt that this left girls variously confused, amused and cynical.

Having said all this it is important to note that, overall, girls were remarkably polite and tolerant of what was done to/for them in the name of feminism.

They usually managed to rescue something positive from even the most bother-some practices, providing their investments in femininity, romance, pleasure and particularly friendship were not portrayed negatively or put at risk. They tended appropriately to select what was of use to them and reject anything regarded as too extreme or disruptive. In our view, they were too tolerant too often. We believe that authoritarian pedagogies which imply a deficit view of girls or of femaleness and which position them as passive or light-weight should not be part of the feminist agenda in schools. Equally, while those therapeutic approaches which simply and uncritically value girls should be treated less harshly, they should not necessarily be seen as the alternative choice. The pedagogical project should certainly include girls' starting positions and celebrate femaleness to some extent, but this is not sufficient if the idea is to get beyond the constraints that gender imposes. The task is to move beyond the limitations of both approaches and, as we have suggested, one way to learn how to do this is to attend to the ways in which feminist reform is experienced subjectively by students and other staff.

Conclusions

In this chapter we have shown that although the various texts of feminist reform were encountered somewhat promiscuously by individuals and groups in schools, it was also possible to see certain regularities in their responses and that the emo-tional dimension was a regularity of significance. To be more specific, we have also illustrated some of the diverse ways in which feminist curriculum reform positions and is received by diverse people in schools, the investments and fantasies that it mobilizes or places at risk, and the positive and negative emotions it generates. We have suggested that attending to and understanding these matters enables us to explore the limits and the possibilities of the feminisms which are actually used in schools. Working with and through the emotional effects of our work can only make it work better.

References

KENWAY, J. (1993) 'Non-traditional pathways: Are they the way to the future?', in BLACKMORE, J. and KENWAY, J. (eds) *Gender Matters in Educational Administration and Policy: A Feminist Introduction*, London, Falmer Press, pp. 81–101.

KENWAY, J. (1995) 'Masculinity: Under siege, on the defensive and under reconstruction', *Discourse*, first international edition, **16**(1), pp. 59–81.

KENWAY, J. and WILLIS, S. (eds) (1990) *Hearts and Minds: Self Esteem and the Schooling of Girls*, London, Falmer Press.

KENWAY, J. and WILLIS, S. WITH EDUCATION OF GIRLS UNIT, SA (1993) *Telling Tales: Girls and Schools Changing Their Ways*, Canberra, Department of Employment Education and Training, Curriculum Division, Australian Government Publishing Service.

KENWAY, J., WILLIS, S., BLACKMORE, J. and RENNIE, L. (1994) 'Making hope practical rather than despair convincing: Feminism, post-structuralism and educational change', *British Journal of the Sociology of Education*, **15**(2).

KENWAY, J., WILLIS, S., BLACKMORE, J. and RENNIE, L. (in press) *Answering Back: Students Teachers and Feminism in Schools*, Sydney, Allen and Unwin.

WALKERDINE, V. (1990) *School-girl Fictions*, London, Verso.

18 Review and Conclusions: A Pedagogy or a Range of Pedagogic Strategies?

Caroline Gipps

In this final chapter we look across the research to highlight the messages that are emerging about girls' and boys' learning. We then examine how this has influenced the interventions, and the outcomes of these. Finally, we summarize and put forward directions we feel need to be taken in future.

Science and Technology

Science and technology in western cultures are seen as masculine subjects and they emerge as some of the most strongly sex-stereotyped areas of the curriculum. As Jan Harding points out, we must recognize that there does exist in these subjects a pedagogy for boys: through the overwhelming number of scientists who are males; through illustrations and examples used in teaching; through the world views, experiences and ways of working that are assumed; and the way in which students and teachers in the lab context reconstitute gender in their interactions.

In other cultures the situation may be different: in Thailand, for example, where boys and girls are equally represented in the 15–18-year-old school population choosing science, and where girls do better than boys in chemistry and as well as boys in physics, science has a high status in the education system (even humanities students must study some science). No choice is allowed with the science course, which is practically based, and both boys and girls associate the operations used in chemistry (but not in physics) with women's work in the kitchen. Although presentation in science is not linked to social issues, most science teachers are women and the expectation is that girls' participation and success in science will be as great as that of the boys. Despite their good performance at school in the physical sciences, and the cultural expectations which support this, women in Thailand are, however, underrepresented in science-based employment, except teaching.

Karen Littleton's chapter showed that classroom studies in England, the USA and Australia indicate that in the area of computing:

- boys are more confident than girls in approaching working with computers;
- the participation level in computer-use by girls (and female teachers) is lower than that of boys;

- boys are also more likely to use computers out of school which contributes to their greater ease with them at school.

The difference in boys' and girls' confidence in the use of computers is also found in maths and science: in both science and computer lessons boys are found to dominate the equipment and its use. In these three subjects there is international evidence that boys continue to have more positive attitudes than girls, although there are national exceptions. These differences can be linked to boys' greater experience with computers outside of school and with science-related activities.

The nature of software and computer games is a key influence in this gender separation: girls are likely to see the material as typically 'masculine', even sexist, relying on activities and content that boys are more familiar with, and requiring combative role-play with which boys are more comfortable than girls. Similarly, in science and technology the content and approaches to learning have been found to influence girls' ability and willingness to engage with the subject, which in turn affects their performance. The long hours that many adolescent boys spend playing computer games which require no language skills, while their sisters are talking, reading and doing schoolwork, is considered to be one of the contributing factors to boys' relatively lower levels of performance at school. The early belief that time spent by boys with these machines would be beneficial to their later careers, particularly in computing, has proved to be misguided as the linguistic and educational content of much of this activity is very limited. Changing the focus and content of games and software is vital to counteract their macho and violent image, so that girls want to engage with computing. The level of violence with which boys engage in these games, we argue, should in any case be reduced.

Mathematics

Research on mathematics performance among girls indicates that the picture mirrors that of the sciences, technology and computing: where mathematics is seen as a preserve of males, girls choose not to participate in or engage with it; either physically when the subject is optional or emotionally when it is not. Elizabeth Fennema responds to this: 'Instead of interpreting the challenges related to gender and mathematics as involving problems associated with females and mathematics, I begin now to look at how a male view of mathematics has been destructive to both males and females. I begin to articulate a problem that lies in our current views of mathematics and its teaching. I am coming to believe that females have recognized that mathematics, as currently taught and learned, restricts their lives rather than enriches them.'

Girls' own low expectations of success in mathematics, which are again the product of cultural, family and societal pressures, are self-fulfilling. Furthermore, the type of approach required to do advanced-level mathematical problem-solving requires girls to behave outside their typically socialized ways of behaviour: being independent, active, questioning and rule-breaking. Rather than blaming girls for not breaking the rules, we point out that it is particularly difficult to break rules when one is socialized to be compliant (Walden and Walkerdine, 1985).

But, it is not only girls who may find school mathematics inaccessible '. . . the mathematics curriculum has tended to emphasise values and concerns which are more middle class than working class, and to draw on experiences which are more relevant to children of Anglo-Celtic descent' (Australian Education Council, 1991).

The 'objective' nature of mathematics consisting of facts out there to be 'discovered' (which is now the subject of post-structural critique) also disengages many girls. Leone Burton argues that we cannot continue with the myth of mathematics as consisting of 'objective' knowledge, independent of the communities who have derived and worked with it. Science, like maths, typically makes claims to be objective and teachers struggle with the notion of socially constructed and selected knowledge. The messages from the research make it clear that not only must the socially determined nature of knowledge become part of the curriculum to be learnt about, but pedagogy must also allow alternative perspectives and ways of knowing to emerge within the classroom whatever the topic to be learnt.

Language

There is a weight of research evidence to indicate that girls do extremely well in reading and writing in their language of instruction. This simple statement, however, masks a complex set of issues. First, boys' underachievement in the subject is excused by downgrading that subject. Extraordinary though it may seem, the argument in England (until very recent) has been that boys' poor performance in English language studies at school does not matter, since English is a girls' subject anyway, and boys get on well without it. The latter point is, of course, true and we must ask why this lack of success seems to be of so little hindrance. Janet White argues in her chapter that boys' competence in oral language has been thought to be one factor, although more recent evidence from public exam data in England suggests that girls are out-performing boys on the assessment of oracy. The nature of their out-of-school reading is another: the comics and fact-based books which boys prefer prepare them for engaging with textbooks and support their development of a scientific style of writing.

Michele Cohen's study of French teaching in England since the mid-seventeenth century indicates that girls' performance has largely been better than that of boys, but their superior performance has been downgraded: girls are diligent and hard working which does not count, while boys' poor performance is explained by poor motivation or poor teaching. By the late nineteenth century, French was not taught at Eton, then (and now) the most prestigious boys' school in England, and it was downgraded to being the intellectual speciality of girls' schools. Although French is taught in all secondary schools in England now, it is still very much a girls' subject: in 1994, 22,500 girls took the advanced-level public examinations in French at 18 compared with 8,500 boys. (For English the equivalent figures were 61,000 girls and 27,000 boys.) By contrast, in countries where another language *has* to be learnt in order to achieve — for example, English in The Netherlands — it is a high status subject; boys are engaged with it and at the centre of the lesson.

Teachers' understandings, beliefs and expectations, together with students' understandings, beliefs and expectations are crucial in schooling. These define and normalize what is considered appropriate, reasonable and effective for different groups and category of pupil. The role of language is a major theme in the construction of knowledge and meaning; the many pupils who do not speak the language of instruction, or indeed to not share the dialect and social and cultural mores of the dominant educator groups, are therefore at a disadvantage.

Interventions

We now outline some of the findings of intervention studies which have focused on girls' performance. Some interventions focus on separating gender groups for longer or shorter periods in order to offer 'space' to the girls, tutoring on their own terms for both groups, an opportunity to reflect on the values and attitudes of the other sex, and on working together in mixed classrooms. Separating the genders in an Icelandic nursery school in order to develop physical courage and a love of adventure in girls and reflective, caring qualities in boys has had significant effects. As Anne-Mette Kruse's chapter shows the technique of polarizing can be very effective in the hands of committed teachers. Kruse, in developing the theory of the pedagogical method of polarization, describes a process which begins with seeking to understand knowledge and how it is created: using critical thinking (shifting from single-sex to mixed settings) to raise consciousness of stereotypes, gender inequalities, attitudes and behaviour; reflecting on the experience to develop understandings and insight; communicating and acting on the new understandings. It is the alternating between single-sex and co-ed settings, and reflecting on differences, which seem to be the powerful factors. In this way boys, as well as girls, are brought into discussion about knowledge and gendered, appropriate or inappropriate behaviour. The space offered allows the girls to be outspoken, to take chances and to engage with the teachers without the boys' usual negative reaction and harassment. The girls come to recognize how the boys had dominated the classes and how the girls had let them; the girls in this intervention then learned how to overcome male dominance in the classroom. Single-sex teaching in these projects is a means to help, as well as to understand sex-roles and attitudes as social constructions that can be changed by those involved. Back in the mixed class, girls show less inclination to accept patriarchal values and patterns of work.

But we cannot separate the 'how' of learning from the 'what'. Janet White in her chapter argues that in relation to the teaching and learning of English in England, three things are needed before we can begin to develop a truly effective pedagogy for either girls *or* boys:

- a wholesale re-evaluation of the position and status of the subject English in our national consciousness, which would lead to

- a changed set of expectations for boys in English, and hence,
- a change in the language practices which make up the daily work of every classroom, it no longer being accepted that English 'doesn't matter so much for boys', or that girls are naturally 'good' at English.

These reflect the underlying principles of subject status, expectation and classroom interaction and so have a relevance beyond English language performance: we would make the same claim with regard to science or mathematics.

Jan Harding points out that in western cultures, a successful pedagogy for girls in science and technology, different from the traditional approach appropriate mainly for males, has been identified. This places teaching/learning in a social context, relating to human need and 'real' problems; allows for collaborative ways of learning, including discussion-based exploration of understanding; and provides assessment procedures that allow for the recognition of complexity and the identification of a range of problems.

Gaell Hildebrand's work shows that a network of science educators in Victoria, Australia has challenged both the definition of the physics curriculum and its teaching and assessment practices. A programme in which physics is learnt in context and assessed innovatively has enhanced the performance of both boys *and* girls, but has in particular elicited excellence from girls (although not those from lower socio-economic status (SES) families).

At tertiary level, too, Sue Lewis' work indicates that successful interventions need to focus on a range of issues together. These include addressing the knowledge content of the curriculum and the way the knowledge is contextualized and presented: a content-driven curriculum with a teaching-as-telling pedagogy is the norm in physical and engineering sciences. Presenting the curriculum in a 'gender-inclusive' way, that is in a more connected style with social and environmental contexts integrated, can attract a more diverse range of students to study science at tertiary level and will diversify the culture of science. Her experience also tells us how such curriculum change can be brought about: with staff working collaboratively with the support of senior staff and an external consultant.

Interventions in curriculum and pedagogy will not, it is clear, alter the pattern of success unless the assessment system is also changed to be consistent with the heterogeneity of the learning population. Using a range of assessment processes, together with clarity and openness about what is being assessed and how, is not only more equitable, but also supports learning (Gipps and Murphy, 1994). It is important here to ensure that teachers have a good understanding of formative assessment, and how it can help them to understand and further the pupil's learning.

The research reviews and intervention studies suggest that to enhance the performance and engagement of lower performing groups — be it girls in science and mathematics or boys in language — we need to examine the knowledge-base of the curriculum being offered, as well as how that knowledge is taught. We do know from intervention studies that in order to enhance the performance of girls, teachers need to be made aware of and encouraged to use the following variations in teaching strategies:

- using more cooperative and interactive modes of learning;
- emphasizing discussion and collaboration;
- having class discussion *and* quiet reflection;
- using 'private' as well as public questioning and probing of the pupil by the teacher;
- slowing the pace of a lesson and encouraging pupils to use the time to compose responses;
- giving feedback which challenges and gives precise guidance (in a supportive manner) as well as praise, rather than the bland praise (for dutiful hard work) which girls currently tend to receive. (*All* learners need to be given encouragement to go beyond that which is known and to undertake the exploration of new ideas.)

And, as good assessment practice, to support *all* learners:

- using assessment that supports learning and reflection rather than relying upon competition with others;
- designing assessment that is open and linked to clear criteria;
- including a range of assessment strategies so that all learners have a chance to perform well.

To sum up, the preceding chapters suggest that given what we know about:

- constructivist views of learning (in which we have to take account of what pupils bring to the learning situation);
- social constructivist theory (which takes account of the cultural basis of knowledge and knowing);
- different cognitive styles and motivations of different groups of pupils;
- the variation among groups of girls, (and variation among groups of boys)

we need to talk in terms of not a pedagogy, for girls or boys, but pedagogy being composed of a range of strategies (which include a range of materials and content, teaching styles, and classroom arrangements/rules) for different groups of pupils, and for different subject areas. The key issue is for the teacher to understand which strategy is appropriate and effective in which setting and for which groups of pupils and individuals. This is a huge task and can only develop over time as teachers reflect on their teaching. The interventions identify that evaluating one's practice is a key to change.

Shulman articulates this approach very clearly:

To reason one's way through an act of teaching is to think one's way from the subject matter as understood by the teacher into the minds and motivations of learners. Transformations, therefore, require some combination or ordering of the following processes, each of which employs a kind of repertoire: (1) preparation (of the given text materials) including the process of critical interpretation, (2) representation of the ideas in the form of new analogies, metaphors, and so forth, (3) instructional selections from among an array of teaching methods and models, and (4) adaptation of these representations to the general characteristics of the children to be taught, as well as (5) tailoring the adaptations to the specific young-sters in the classroom. These forms of transformation, these aspects of *the process wherein one moves from personal comprehension to preparing for the comprehension of others*, are the essence of the act of pedagogical reasoning, of teaching as thinking, and of planning — whether explicitly or implicitly — the performance of teaching. (Shulman, 1987, p. 16, our emphasis)

Pupils, too, need to understand that there are a range of learning strategies which are appropriate for different tasks, subjects and purposes; they must learn to choose the appropriate learning strategy to use in a particular setting/occasion. This reson-ates with what we know about meta-cognition: that pupils need to be aware of and to monitor, 'to regulate', their own process of learning. The emphasis here, just as with the teacher, is on the pupil as conscious decision-maker.

Ausubel's famous quote: 'The most important single factor influencing learn-ing is what the learner already knows. Ascertain this and teach him accordingly' (1968), instructs the teacher to focus on the learner's understanding. But we now know that this is not sufficiently encompassing: what the learner knows is itself a function of context, learning style, materials and classroom interaction, all of which are deeply affected by gender.

The diversity among girls as individuals and as learners supports the proposal for pedagogic strategies rather than a unified, or unifying, pedagogy. It is clear from some of the interventions described in Section Three that girls from lower socio-economic groups resist some of the 'girl-friendly' interventions or programmes at school. A major area for work is the reaction of such groups of girls to the feminist approach. Is it that they perceive the feminist agenda as essentially middle-class, professional interference in their lives? Are suggestions that they behave in other ways and attend overmuch to learning unacceptable because they make the girls unattractive to the boys? How different would it be if boys (and men) did not find 'clever' girls and women unattractive or threatening? Jane Kenway and colleagues' work highlights the issue that girls must want to engage with an approach: a fem-inist agenda cannot be imposed. We have, instead, to provide individuals with an awareness of their own and others' strengths and limitations, and provide the poten-tial for informed choice. This tension is a real one for young women of any back-ground, but for girls living in poverty in the developing world there is, we recognize, little choice to be made.

In African society, boys and girls have traditionally been educated separately, boys by men and girls by women. Schooling still separates the sexes and girls are less likely to enter secondary school and more likely to drop out. As Sheila Wamahiu points out, development is needed on several fronts: improving access for girls; sup-porting them so that they can stay in the school system; and developing a pedagogy of empowerment which is transformative, liberating and, while recognizing bio-logical differences between males and females, rejects biological or divine determinism of gender roles and status. Sexual harassment and violence towards girls is high and this is perpetuated by a very authoritarian education system in which neither boys nor girls are taught to question.

A consideration of what happens to competent high achieving girls beyond school must also enter the frame. In Thailand and in India cultural expectations support privileged girls and young women in performing well in science at school and in university; but cultural norms prevent those young women from entering and making successful careers in science. In Finland and in England, on the other hand, girls are out-performing boys in examinations at the end of compulsory school and, while the gendered division of labour has not broken down in either country, in Britain young women are now entering the professions in increasing numbers. However, women are currently significantly underrepresented in senior positions in management and in the professions in England; as this cohort of competent, high-achieving women move through to mid-career, will we see a significant change in the proportion of senior posts held by women? Tuula Gordon argues that in Finland girls do well in school and participate widely in employment but the status of women in the labour market has changed little. Therefore we must again draw attention to Jane Martin's caution that it is not enough to change pedagogy, we must also look at the wider system.

Could it be that girls' lower take up of science and mathematics careers is something to do with 'ownership' of the subject area as opposed to simple achievement within the subject? Ownership includes defining and legitimating the knowledge and it may be that, although girls are learning to achieve in certain subjects, they do not feel an ownership of the subject matter, which leads to a weaker identification with it and no commitment to continue beyond school in a particular domain. It may be that girls are achieving in subjects like science and/or mathematics but not really engaging with them; achievement as opposed to 'ownership' will not offer the motivation required to overcome social and cultural pressures and to break norms. There is evidence that girls are rejecting science and this must be seen as a positive choice rather than as a failure to pursue. As Sue Lewis reports, girls who gained access to engineering faculties have similarly been found to drop out; they reject the 'chilly' environment and the forms of knowledge studied. (We should point out that in England there is evidence that a growing number of girls *and* boys are rejecting advanced study and careers in both science and mathematics, Smithers and Robinson, 1994.)

Conclusions

Early work on the education of girls concentrated on 'changing girls' (to per-suade them to engage with science, etc.); the approach then switched to 'changing subjects' (challenging the traditional curriculum and views of knowledge); we are

267

now moving into a phase of changing and diversifying our pedagogic strategies to suit a range of learners, in order to cater for various ways of learning and knowing.

This third approach results from a set of shifts in thinking: from a post-modernist critique of one overarching feminist approach which denies differences among girls; from a post-structuralist challenging of the 'objective' reality of science and maths; from understandings that clever/strong girls who achieve in maths/ science make a *positive* choice not to pursue these beyond school (or university); from understandings that the curriculum subject matter, material and teaching approaches have not always engaged boys or girls who are not white and middle class; from developments in cognition and learning theory that tell us to respect and engage with the learner. Pupils do not all learn in the same way and a class of pupils will need different strategies. This is similar to the argument we make in relation to assessment: if genuine equality of access is a prime requirement for equity, then in any assessment programme we need to include a range of content, context, types of task and response mode so as to offer all groups an opportunity to perform well.

There is evidence that boys tend not to use the sort of approaches to learning which current theories of learning advocate: relating knowledge to context in order to be able to apply it more widely; engaging in dialogue with other learners and the teacher in order to question and validate understanding; and using collaborative approaches to learning. These are some of the effective learning strategies which, these chapters show, are more favoured by girls; this, as Patricia Murphy suggests in Chapter 1, may go some way to explaining recent patterns of boys' lower achievement. Therefore, boys' approaches to learning also need to be reconsidered and reconstructed.

Changing teachers' approaches so that they consider a range of pedagogic strategies appropriately for various pupils, subjects and tasks, places a tremendous demand on teachers and on how they are educated. But the task is not about gender equity or working with feminist teachers; it is a much broader agenda of engaging with the learner, while being conscious of the 'white, male, middle-class' nature of knowledge as it is defined, so as to offer appropriate and effective teaching for *all* groups of pupils. In western countries ethnic minority and disadvantaged boys *and* girls are underachieving. While there is evidence that strategies to make the curriculum and teaching more 'girl-friendly' have worked with girls from majority, middle-class backgrounds (Harding; Fennema; Kenway, this volume); they have not worked with other girls; furthermore, they have often generated a 'male backlash'. As Kenway (1995) argues, we are in an age of complex, shifting social and cultural circumstances with many males (and not just those for whom manual jobs were/ would be the normal expectation) feeling threatened. Alternative ways of expressing their masculinity/power include violence and scapegoating, hence not only a growing harassment of girls and women, but also a resistance to feminist approaches or discourse. We can see now that the early feminist educators' agenda was too narrowly conceived in that it did not address men's resistance or the issue of pupil diversity (see also Deem, 1995). Now that we understand how to affect the performance of middle-class majority girls we need to apply the theoretical analysis that took us there to enhancing the performance of disadvantaged and minority girls and boys: we prefer, however, to construe this as a fundamental shift in our approach to *learners*.

Engaging teachers in the task is clearly crucial since the active cooperation of classroom teachers is essential to improving pedagogy: we must tailor our message and our materials so that they are acceptable to all teachers, while remaining solidly based in the understandings we have accumulated over the years. Only in this way will our knowledge and experience in gender equity in education have practical application in the classroom and thus impact on girls. We know much about how *not* to use inservice education of teachers and how change in schools often fails. Thus it requires more than inservice provision for teachers or some articles in professional journals; as Jo Sanders points out, this sort of fundamental change is slow for it requires a rethinking of our approach to teaching and to teacher education. 'Change that lasts, takes time,' as Jo Whitehead put it. Moreover, it must be a mainstream approach not a marginal one, since, for *all* pupils, but particularly those who are not middle-class majority boys, we need to recognize diversity and to engage with the learner, bringing into play a range of appropriate, and therefore effective, pedagogic strategies.

The influence of out-of-school activity and culture is, increasingly, important. In the current technological age the influence of television, videos, computer games, as well as reading matter, have a very significant impact on what young people learn, as well as what it is considered to be appropriate to learn. The new technologies will increasingly determine the *way* in which pupils learn. It may be that this is the moment to move forward in relation to computer, and computer game, use.

The extent to which we can transform the subjects of the school curriculum is, however, a major problem; research indicates the extent to which many subjects, and in particular mathematics, technology and the sciences, are determined by male interests, experiences and examples, while others in which girls excel are undervalued. Whilst it is possible, and indeed much interesting work has been done, there are limits to which one can transform the school curriculum. Traditional views within mainstream school education are likely to be resistant to even small changes to established subjects, let alone to transforming them. Such views have formed the battleground for the fight between right-wing politicians and traditionalists on the one hand, and liberal politicians and many educationalists on the other, about the National Curriculum in England. The tertiary curriculum, that which is experienced and offered beyond the school, particularly at university level, is even less likely to be radically altered in order to reduce the male nature of the content, ideas and practices. Where we may have little effect on the taught curriculum (and that is not to say that we should stop trying) we must work on changing the interactions. We also need to recognize that girls' preference for collaboration has been equated with dependence and their recognition of complexity with uncertainty. These are social constructions which can, and should, be challenged.

So, the simple answer to the question 'Is there a pedagogy for girls?' is 'No'. Although we can identify approaches which tend to enhance girls' engagement and performance, girls not only differ from boys, but from each other; different school subjects carry different messages and valences, and consequently interest pupils differently. The message of this book is, ultimately, about enhancing pedagogy, that is curriculum, teaching and assessment practice for *all* learners. Effective pedagogy requires reflective practice on the part of the teacher and a focus on the *pupil* as a learner; it requires access to a range of materials and pedagogic strategies.

No discussion of education can, however, be framed outside the political context: we must look at teaching and learning in relation to the education-gender system. The micro-politics of the class and the school are very powerful in the educational experience of different groups of pupils. The harassment of girls in co-educational settings and the growing misogyny of underprivileged, unemployed young males is an issue which cannot simply be set aside from girls' experience of schooling and their ability to benefit from it; this is an area in which we must now all try to act, not simply to enhance the performance of girls, or to promote equity in the classroom, but to encourage a society in which both genders can work together in mutual respect and harmony.

Bibliography

Colloquium Papers

BURTON, L. (1995) 'A socially just pedagogy for the teaching of mathematics', London, UNESCO/Institute of Education Colloquium.

COHEN, M. (1995) 'Is there a space for the achieving girl?', London, UNESCO/Institute of Education Colloquium.

FENNEMA, E. (1995) 'Pedagogy, gender, and mathematics', London, UNESCO/Institute of Education Colloquium.

GORDON, T. (1995) 'Citizenship, difference and marginality in schools: Spatial and embodied aspects of gender construction', London, UNESCO/Institute of Education Colloquium.

HARDING, J. (1995) 'Is there a pedagogy for girls? (science and technology)', London, UNESCO/Institute of Education Colloquium.

HEAD, J. (1995) 'Gender identity and cognitive style', London, UNESCO/Institute of Education Colloquium.

HILDEBRAND, G. (1995) 'Assessment interacts with gender: The case of girls and physics in Victoria, Australia', London, UNESCO/Institute of Education Colloquium.

KENWAY, J. and BLACKMORE, J. (1995) 'Pleasure and pain: Beyond feminist authoritarianism and therapy in the curriculum', London, UNESCO/Institute of Education Colloquium.

KRUSE, A.-M. (1995) 'Single-sex settings: Pedagogies for girls and boys in Danish schools', London, UNESCO/Institute of Education Colloquium.

LEWIS, S. (1995) 'Is there a pedagogy for girls?', London, UNESCO/Institute of Education Colloquium.

LITTLETON, K. (1995) 'Girls and information technology', London, UNESCO/Institute of Education Colloquium.

MARTIN, J.R. (1995) 'A girls' pedagogy "in relationship"', London, UNESCO/Institute of Education Colloquium.

SANDERS, J. (1995) 'How do we get educators to teach gender equity?', London, UNESCO/Institute of Education Colloquium.

SØRENSEN, H. (1995) 'Interventions in science teaching in Denmark', London, UNESCO/ Institute of Education Colloquium.

WAMAHIU, S. (1995) 'The pedagogy of difference: An African perspective', London, UNESCO/Institute of Education Colloquium.

WHITE, J. (1995) 'Is there a pedagogy for girls?', London, UNESCO/Institute of Education Colloquium.

Other References

AUSTRALIAN EDUCATION COUNCIL (1991) *A National Statement on Mathematics for Australian Schools*, Carlton, Victoria, Curriculum Corporation.

AUSUBEL, D.P. (1968) *Educational Psychology: A Cognitive View*, New York, Holt, Rinehart and Winston.

DEEM, R. (1995) *Do Methodology and Epistemology Still Matter to Feminist Educational Researchers?*, University of Bath, European Conference of Educational Researchers Conference.

GIPPS, C. and MURPHY, P. (1994) *A Fair Test? Assessment, Achievement and Equity*, Milton Keynes, Open University Press.

KENWAY, J. (1995) 'Masculinities in schools: Under siege, on the defensive and under reconstruction?', *Discourse: Studies in the Cultural Politics of Education*, **16**(1), pp. 59–79.

SHULMAN, L. (1987) 'Knowledge and teaching: Foundations of the new reform', *Harvard Educational Review*, **57**(1), pp. 1–22.

SMITHERS, A. and ROBINSON, P. (1994) *The Impact of Double Science*, Manchester, Centre for Education and Employment Research Unit.

WALDEN, R. and WALKERDINE, V. (1985) *Girls and Mathematics: From Primary to Secondary Schooling*, Bedford Way Papers no. 24, London, Institute of Education.

UNESCO/Institute of Education Colloquium 10–12 January 1995 'Is There a Pedagogy for Girls?'

Speakers

Leone Burton	*School of Education, University of Birmingham, UK*
Michèle Cohen	*European University Institute, Italy*
Elizabeth Fennema	*Wisconsin Centre for Education Research, USA*
Caroline Gipps	*Institute of Education, University of London, UK (Chair)*
Tuula Gordon	*Department of Sociology, University of Helsinki*
Jan Harding	*Equal Opportunities Science and Technology, UK*
John Head	*Centre for Education Studies, King's College London, UK*
Gaell Hildebrand	*School of Education, University of Melbourne*
Jane Kenway	*Faculty of Education, Deakin University, Australia*
Sue Lewis	*National Centre for Women, University of Technology, Australia*
Karen Littleton	*Department of Psychology, University of Southampton, UK*
Anne-Mette Kruse	*Women's Research Centre, University of Aarhus, Denmark*
Patricia Murphy	*The Open University School of Education, Milton Keynes, UK*
Jane Roland Martin	*Professor Emerita, University of Massachusetts, USA*
Jo Sanders	*Teacher Education Equity Project CUNY Graduate Centre, USA*
Helene Sørensen	*Royal Danish School of Education Studies, Denmark*
Sheila Parvyn Wamahiu	*Forum for African Women Educationalists, Kenya*
Janet White	*School Curriculum and Assessment Authority (SCAA), London, UK*

Observers

Audrey Jones	The Fawcett Society, London, UK

UNESCO Secretariat

Colin Power   Assistant Director General for Education
John Smyth   Editor-in-Chief, World Education Report

Staff of the Institute of Education

Jannette Elwood
Celia Hoyles
Terezinha Nunes
Debbie Epstein
Elaine Unterhalter
Iram Siraj–Blatchford
Diana Leonard
Val Hey

Notes on Contributors

Leone Burton is a Professor of Education (Mathematics and Science) at the University of Birmingham, UK. She is the author of a number of books which present mathematics as a discipline which grows out of the critical enquiry of learners and, consequently, their teachers rather than as a body of knowledge and skills which must be transmitted. Her latest book is *Children Learning Mathematics: Patterns and Relationships*. She is committed to a social justice perspective on mathematics, its teaching and learning and most recently edited a book called *Who Counts? Assessing Mathematics in Europe*.

Michèle Cohen is Senior Lecturer in Languages and Linguistics at Richmond College, the International University in London. She trained as a psychologist and linguist, and worked at the Centre for Applied Linguistics in Washington DC, at the Centre for Information on Language Teaching (CILT) and at the Psycho-linguistics Research Unit, University College London, before going on to teach. In 1994, she was awarded a Jean Monnet Fellowship by the European University Institute in Florence to write her book on the role of the French language and French practices of sociability such as politeness and conversation in the fashioning of the English gentleman and on the construction of national and gendered identities in eighteenth- and early nineteenth-century England, due to be published in 1996 by Routledge.

Elizabeth Fennema is a Professor of Curriculum and Instruction at the University of Wisconsin-Madison and an Associate Director of the National Centre for Research in Mathematics Education. Her most important research studies are the Fennema-Sherman studies and the Fennema-Sherman Mathematics Attitude Scales. In the last ten years, her attention has been focused on Cognitively Guided Instruction, which has produced many studies related to the interaction between the teaching and learning of mathematics. She is a world-renowned expert in the area of maths and gender and has published extensively in this field.

Caroline Gipps is a Professor of Education and Dean of Research at the University of London Institute of Education. She trained as a psychologist and worked as a primary school teacher before moving into a career in research. Her research has included a study of the early national assessment programme (the Assessment of Performance Unit); evaluations of: standardized testing in schools, screening programmes for allocating pupils to special needs provision, the introduction of National Curriculum assessment in primary schools; gender and other equal opportunity issues in assessment, and teacher feedback to young children. Her book *A Fair Test? Assessment, Achievement and Equity*, written jointly with Patricia Murphy, won the SCSE prize for the best Education book published in 1994. Other publications include: Gipps, C., Brown, M., McCallum, B. and McAlister, S. (1995)

Intuition or Evidence? Teachers and National Assessment of Seven Year Olds, Open University Press; Gipps, C. (1994) *Beyond Testing: Towards a Theory of Educational Assessment*, Falmer Press.

Tuula Gordon is a researcher at the Sociology Research Unit, the University of Helsinki, Finland. She has numerous publications concerned with gender. Recent ones include: *Single Women: On the Margins?* (1994) Macmillan and New York University Press; *Feminist Mothers* (1990) Macmillan and New York University Press; *Democracy in One School?: Progressive Education and Restructuring* (1985) Falmer Press.

With a first degree in chemistry, **Jan Harding** taught physical sciences in grammar schools and within a College of Education. She identified the low involvement of women and girls in science and technology as her research area, which she pursued eventually from a position of Head of Chemistry Section at the Centre for Science and Mathematics Education at Chelsea College, University of London. She has published widely in the area of gender and science and technology. Since 1985 she has worked independently as an Equal Opportunities Consultant in Science and Technology in many parts of the world.

Christina Hart is a McClintock Collective member and a secondary teacher in a private girls' school in Melbourne, Victoria, Australia. For a period of time she was seconded as a course writer for physics in the new Victorian Certificate Education and she has since researched this curriculum change for her doctoral studies.

John Head is a Senior Lecturer in the School of Education, King's College London, UK. In the first part of his career he was a science teacher in schools in the UK and the USA and contributed to a number of school science curriculum projects. More recently he has worked in psychology, particularly with issues of adolescence, gender and identity.

Gaell Hildebrand is a Senior Lecturer of the Faculty of Education, University of Melbourne. Her research interests centre around gender and education growing out of her work as a foundation member of the McClintock Collective, a girls and science education network founded in 1983. In 1991 Gaell co-convened the sixth international conference on Gender and Science and Technology (GASAT 6) at the University of Melbourne and she was the Australasian representative on the foundation GASAT Board. She is currently working on a project exploring the implementation and impact of imaginative writing as a gender-inclusive strategy for learning science.

Jane Kenway is Associate Professor in the Faculty of Education at Deakin University in Victoria, Australia. She is also Director of the Deakin Centre for Education and Change. She has published widely on the topic of gender and education and is an active participant in the professional development of teachers on the topic. Her books include Kenway, J. and Willis, S. with Junor, A. (1995) *Critical Visions: Rewriting the Future of Gender Education and Work*, Australian Government Publishing Service; Blackmore, J. and Kenway, J. (eds) (1993) *Gender Matters in Educational Administration and Policy: A Feminist Introduction*, Falmer Press. Her new book, *Answering Back, Girls, Boys and Feminism in Schools*, will be published by Allen and Unwin in 1996.

Anne-Mette Kruse is a Senior Research Fellow at CEKVINA, Centre for Gender Studies at the University of Aarhus in Denmark. For many years she has been engaged in research, innovation and evaluation projects in the field of gender and education in primary and secondary schools. Currently she is doing research in two schools for unemployed adults where women and men primarily study and learn separately. Her latest article in English is: 'Approaches to teaching girls and boys — Current debates, practices and perspectives', *Women's Studies International Forum*, 1996.

Sue Lewis, an active member of the McClintock Collective, is the research and staff development coordinator in the National Centre for Women at Swinburne University of Technology in Melbourne, Australia. Her current research projects include 'Making Connections — an inclusive approach to engineering design during 1995', funded by the Committee for the Advancement of University Teaching, and 'Maximising Diversity', a research project with a large petroleum and mining corporation. During 1989–90, Sue was Visiting Scholar at EQUALS Lawrence Hall of Science, University of California. From 1986–88 she was National Secondary Coordinator of the Commonwealth Schools Commission's K–12 'Girls and Maths and Science Teaching Project' (GAMAST). She co-authored with Anne Davies the project's Professional Development Manual *Gender Equity in Mathematics and Science*.

Karen Littleton has held research posts in the Open University, School of Education, in the Centre for Research in Development, Instruction and Training at the University of Nottingham and the Department of Psychology, University of Southampton. She is presently a lecturer in the Department of Psychology, The Open University. She has published papers on children's computer-based learning and has contributed articles on learning and new technology, classroom groupwork and gender as a factor in children's learning. She is a senior scientist on the European Science Foundation Programme on Learning in Humans and Machines.

Jane Roland Martin is a Professor of Philosophy, Emerita, at the University of Massachusetts, Boston. Her most recent books are *The Schoolhome* (1992) Harvard University Press; and *Changing the Educational Landscape* (1994) Routledge.

Patricia Murphy is Director of the Centre for Curriculum and Teaching Studies at The Open University, England. Her research on science and gender arising from the APU assessment programme is well known. Her most recent book co-authored with Caroline Gipps was *A Fair Test? Assessment, Achievement and Equity* (1994) Open University Press.

Jo Sanders is Research Professor at the University of Washington, Seattle. She has directed nation-wide projects on gender equity in science, technology and mathematics education and careers since 1979. She is currently the Principal Investigator in the three-year Teacher Education Equity Project, which is developing materials on gender equity, working with professors of science, mathematics and technology education in colleges and universities. She recently completed the Computer Equity Expert Project in which K–12 maths, science and technology educators dramatically increased girls' participation in advanced courses in maths, science and technology. Jo has written six books and numerous chapters and articles dealing with gender equity in technology, science and mathematics. Among them are *Lifting the Barriers: 600 Tested Strategies that Really Work to Increase Girls' Participation in Science, Mathematics and Computers* (1994).

Born in Karachi, Pakistan, **Sheila Parvyn Wamahiu** moved to Kenya in 1981. Since then she has established herself as an academic, researcher and female rights advocate. She has been appointed by the Kenyan Government to be a member of the recently launched Task Force on Gender and Education. Between 1982 and 1994, she worked at Kenyatta University as a Fellow then Senior Lecturer, and Chair of the Department of Development Studies. Her publications are wide ranging and cover the fields of education, gender and development. Currently, Sheila is a freelance consultant with various international and national organizations such as FAWE, Commonwealth Secretariat, CIDA and ODA.

Janet White joined the School Curriculum and Assessment Authority (SCAA) in 1994 as one of three Professional Officers for English. The English team has a broad remit for implementing and monitoring the National Curriculum for English and its associated national tests at Key Stages 1, 2, and 3, as well as responsibility for the English criteria for public examinations at 16+. Janet worked at the National Foundation for Educational Research (NFER) from 1979–93. At the NFER she was deputy director of the Assessment of Performance Unit's Language Monitoring Project, a regional coordinator of the Language in the National Curriculum project, consultant/evaluator for the National Writing Project and joint director of a project conducted with the University of London Examinations and Assessment Council (ULEAC) to investigate gender differences in performance in English and mathematics at 16+.

Jo Whitehead is a primary teacher in a country, government school in Victoria, Australia. She is coordinator of curriculum and professional development in her school and has completed a Master of Education degree on the change processes which occurred when gender was the focus of change in her school.

Liz Wyatt is a primary teacher in a city, government school in Victoria, Australia. She has trained as a Reading Recovery tutor and is an advocate of gender-inclusive curriculum in her school.

Index

ability 47, 89, 99, 126, 195, 205, 238, 261
  cognitive style 59–62
  learning theories and 10–12
abstract 35–6, 238–40
Academic Choice 138
access
  gendered 266
  to computers 81, 83, 85, 92
accountability 38, 121, 202
achievement
  change and 262, 267–8
  English 99–109
  gender and 34, 37, 55–6, 74, 88, 90, 92
  girls and French 124–33
  maths 136, 137–8
  redefining 149–70
  science and technology 111–21
action research 201, 206
activity 41–2, 48, 55
adaptation–innovation 67–8
adolescence 73, 197, 254
advantage 149
agency concept 12
alienation 89, 92, 238, 245, 255
androcentrism 30–1
assertiveness 180, 185–6, 232, 246–7, 257
assessment
  achievement and 149–70
  gender and 232
  maths 136–7, 141
  methods 200, 264–5, 268
  national 102, 113
  norm/criterion based 155
  science and technology 118, 121
  see also multiple choice assessment; responsive evaluation
Assessment Performance Unit 98, 102–5, 108, 115–18

assimilation 129, 139
attack 210
attention, seeking 34, 85–6, 178–9, 184, 187, 189, 235
attitudes
  awareness 173, 179–80, 187–9
  change and 261, 263
  gendered 235
  to computers 81–2, 86–8, 91
  to French 129
  to maths 137–8
  to science 113–14, 117
attribution 63, 76, 125, 157, 195–6, 205, 245
authenticity 15
authoritarianism 46, 55–6, 244–5, 249, 252–8, 267
Autonomous Learning Behaviour Model 75, 138
autonomy 66, 179, 186, 195, 203
avoidance 210
awareness, gender equity 214–15

behaviourism 12
beliefs 73, 75, 78–9, 138, 229, 263
bias, gendered 55, 82, 84, 99–100, 118, 136, 151, 203
brain hemisphere dominance 65
brideprice 52, 54
bullying 243

campaigns, equity 228
career choice 73–4, 111, 113, 193, 202, 204, 238, 244, 254
categorization 24–6, 36, 125, 168, 211
child–centredness 11
childhood 65–6, 195
choice 38, 116, 136, 158, 162, 197, 207, 232, 242, 249, 252–4, 260–1, 268
Christianity 52–4

circumcision 49–53
Citizenship, Difference and Marginality in
    Schools project 34–43
'class' learning theory 10
class, socio-economic 126–7, 129, 151,
    168, 177, 182, 211–12, 249–50, 256,
    262, 264, 266, 268
classroom
    climate 23
    dynamics 229
    management 10, 73–5, 87, 138, 161,
        198–200, 229, 232
co-education 23, 64, 68, 84–5, 132, 137,
    174–5, 177, 182, 184, 186–7, 263,
    270
cognitive science perspectives 76–7, 79
cognitive style 90, 116–18, 138, 194–7,
    203, 265
    and identity 59–68
Cognitively Guided Instruction 77
collegiality 235–6, 244
colonialism and pedagogy 47–56
comics 99–100, 262
common assessment tasks 161–9, 240
communication 12, 14–15, 189, 263
competence 89, 99, 107, 154, 173, 186,
    237, 262
competition 64–6, 68, 74–5, 78, 85, 88,
    118, 151, 155, 174, 182, 185, 203,
    251, 265
compulsory education 10, 113, 136, 267
Computer Equity Expert Project 215–17,
    219–20, 222–3, 225–6
computers 114, 119–20, 229, 260–1
    gender and 81–93
concepts
    maths 140–1
    scientific 156
    social 153
conditioning 125, 132–3
confidence 76–7, 86, 89, 92, 118, 121,
    138, 167, 173, 177, 183, 186–7, 196,
    204–5, 236–7, 246, 260–1
confluent education 115
consciousness raising 188, 190
conservatism 38
constructivism 12, 143, 156–7, 237, 239,
    265
content, learning theory and 10

content/context driven curriculum
    199–200, 206–7, 264
context
    and knowledge 13–14, 196, 256
    maths 141–2
    science in social 114–15, 118–19, 121,
        153–4, 161–6, 169
    social 260, 268
cooperation 15, 74–6, 78, 85, 88–90, 92,
    112, 118, 120–1, 151–2, 155, 160,
    167, 184–5, 187, 200–1, 207, 209,
    229, 264–5, 268–9
cooperation/competition 64–5
coping behaviour 60, 68, 176–7, 181, 183
coursework/examinations 106–8, 113, 118,
    136
creativity 56, 59, 189
critical thinking 17–20, 56, 188, 263
cultral relativism 256
culture
    educational ideal 30
    expectations 267
    feminism and 249–50
    gender and 151
    knowledge and 12
    learning and 149
    masculinity and 23
    nature/ 35
    out of school activity 269
    school 231
    scientific 111–13, 120–1, 209
    social practice 25
    values and 140–1
curriculum
    balance 211
    change 228, 242–3, 252, 268, 269
    critical thinking 18
    education policy and 38
    gender–inclusive 198–200, 202
    gendered 186
    maths 138
    pedagogy and 9
    relationship of reading to 98

data collection devices 158
decentralization 38
deconstruction 211, 247, 252–3, 257
determinism, biological 55–6, 65
development and learning 11–13

didactics 16–17
difference
  achievement and 168
  awareness 18–20
  cognitive style and gender 59–62, 64–5,
    67–8
  English and gender 97, 100–8
  French and gender 124–9, 132
  girls' pedagogy and 23–6
  information technology and gender 81,
    83, 88, 91–2
  interest and cognitive style 194–7
  maths and gender 73–9, 136, 139
  science and gender 115, 117, 119
Differential Performance in English and
  Mathematics 100
differentiation
  African perspective of gender 48–9, 51
  gender 34–6, 38–40, 42–3
dilemma–language 17
Direct Method of language teaching 131
disadvantage 46–7, 53, 67, 81, 83, 86, 93,
  98–100, 142, 157–8, 175, 199, 204,
  230, 232, 252, 263, 268
discipline 39–43
  and welfare 231–6
discourse, pedagogy as 18
discrimination 47, 49, 54–5, 59, 126, 157,
  160, 165, 187, 204, 252
discussion 229, 265, 268
disempowerment 32
diversity 24–6, 31, 139, 141, 203, 206–9,
  264, 266, 268–9
division of labour 37, 48, 175, 267
domesticity 27–31, 53
dual certification 106–7, 113
dualisms, gendered 149–53, 156, 160,
  169–70, 194, 196, 232, 244

education–gender system 23, 26–7, 30–2
educational development 192–3, 203, 209
educators and gender equity 214–27
emancipation, social 35, 37, 189
embodiment 34, 39–43
emotions 151
  of feminist pedagogy 242–58
empowerment 18, 20, 46–7, 54, 56–7, 97,
  160, 173–4, 176–81, 187, 256, 267
English language 97–109, 262–4

enrolment 46, 168, 238, 240
essentialism 23–6, 36, 125
ethnicity 73, 75, 81, 168, 204, 211–12,
  249–50, 254, 262, 268
examinations 46, 82–3, 100–8, 113, 118,
  136, 262, 267
excellence 166–7, 264
expectations, gendered 40, 65, 87–8, 106,
  109, 112–13, 139, 157, 181, 183, 229,
  247–8, 261, 263–4, 267
experience
  mathematical 141
  prior 156–7, 204–6, 237–9, 241, 261,
    266
extract/embed 61–2, 68

failure 63, 126, 130–1, 195–6
feedback 63–4, 88, 154, 207, 265
femaleness
  of French 124–5, 129
  value of 242, 245, 253, 256, 258
femininity 176, 183, 187, 241, 250
  emphasized 151–2
feminism
  change and 266, 268
  cognitive styles 59, 68
  definitions of pedagogy 17–20
  difference in African perspectives 47–8,
    52
  intervention programmes 192–3
  pedagogic emotions 242–58
  pedagogy 174
  perspectives on maths 73, 76–9, 125
  as putdown 205
  research 9, 11, 24–5, 32, 37, 136, 139
  see also liberal; material-radical; post
    structural; radical
feminization
  of curriculum 28–30
  of education 37
field dependence 61–2, 65
flexibility 56, 60, 99
formative assessment 13, 264
  /summative assessment 154, 161, 164
Freirian theories 13, 17
French language 124–33, 262
function of education 26–7, 30, 35, 48
funding intervention programmes 201,
  205–7, 209

GCSE
  English 100–3, 105–7
  science 113
Gender and Science and Technology 193
gender–inclusivity 159, 192–4, 197–200,
  202, 206, 208–10, 230, 232, 242,
  264
gender–sensitive approach 24, 27, 31, 64,
  67
General Achiement Test 168–9
generalization 23
Girls into Science and Technology 111
Girls and Maths and Science Teaching
  Project 200–2
Girls and Technology Education 115, 117
groupings 19, 48, 76, 85–8, 92, 118, 207,
  234

harassment 27–9, 31, 182, 204, 235–6,
  243, 251, 257, 263, 267–8, 270
heterogeneity 141–2, 264
hidden curriculum 28–9, 182, 187–8,
  232
hierarchy
  gender 34, 41
  social 50
High School and Beyond project 75
holism 152–4, 160, 200
hostility 27–9

identity
  cognitive styles and gender 59–68
  construction 18, 237–8, 240
  English and 97, 108–9
  ethnic 48
  gendered 174–5, 179, 181, 183, 185–7,
    189–90, 242, 247, 249–50
  masculinity 195
  national 130
  personal 195
  teacher 243
ideology, gendered 46, 52, 149, 170, 175
image
  of computers 83, 92, 114
  gendered 28, 253
  of science 111, 120, 151
  self 50
impulsiveness/reflection 62–3, 65
individuality 11, 13, 34–8, 48, 203

industry and school 38
inferiority 124–5, 128, 131–2, 152, 241
information technology and girls 81–93
initiation 50–1, 53
interactiveness 10, 17, 74, 76–7, 114, 137,
  178–9, 189
  computers and 85–90
International Association for the
  Evaluation of Educational Survey
  119
interventions 263–7
intuition 152, 160, 237

justice, gendered 136–43, 189, 201, 230,
  242–3

knower/known 152, 156–8, 196–7
knowledge
  base 16–17, 264
  nature of 196
  reading and 98
  relations 138, 142
  shared 13–15
  use 18–19

labour market 37–8, 43, 53
language 12, 14, 18, 48–9, 65, 230,
  262–3
learned helplessness 63–5
learning
  environment 19, 182–3, 203–6, 208,
    242, 245, 267
  involuntary 99–100
  style 89–91, 116, 119–20, 161, 187,
    194, 199, 212, 229, 265–6, 268,
    270
  theories 10–15, 19
liberal feminism 149–50, 152, 164, 166,
  168, 229
liberalism 35–6, 38
literacy 97–100, 102, 108–9
literature, English 106
locus of control 63–5

McClintock Collective 159–61, 201–2,
  237, 298–9
male-bashing 222
marginality 35–7, 41, 53, 55, 85, 98, 204,
  250

market speech 38
marriage 50
masculinity
    citizenship and difference 35–6, 41–2
    culture and 23
    hegemonic 149, 151–2, 175, 179, 243
    identity 130, 195
    Latin and 129
    personal beliefs and 78–9
    reconstruction 244
    revaluation 180
    science and 111, 114, 160, 199, 260–1
material-radical feminism 175, 179
materials, gender equity resource 214–15,
    220–1, 228
maths
    change and 230, 261–2, 267
    computers and 89
    English/ 100–1
    gender and 73–9
    performance 125
    socially just pedagogy 136–43
maturation 116
means/ends 154–5
metacognition 12, 266
mini-grant projects 217–19, 225
misogyny 28, 30, 270
model for gender and change 233–6
modelling 13
Monash Children's Science Group 237
moral judgements 62
mothering 65–6, 194–5
motivation 34, 64, 84, 86, 91–2, 114, 119,
    125–6, 155, 205, 210, 265, 267
multiple choice assessment 62–3, 68,
    118–19, 121, 136, 156–7, 165, 167,
    169
multiplicity 152, 158, 160, 169
myth and gender 52–3, 139

narrative/factual writing 108
National Centre for Women 192–3
National Policy for the Education of Girls
    in Australian Schools 229, 232
National Women's History Project 214
negotiation 14–15, 158
networking 223–4
normalization 11, 34, 37, 142, 249–50,
    256, 263

nurturance, feminist pedagogy as 245–52,
    254, 257

object relations theory 197
objectivity 140, 142, 151, 153, 155–6,
    169, 184, 188, 196, 262, 268
occupation structures 9
opportunity
    denial 59
    equality of 34–8, 46, 81, 83, 92, 97,
        173–6, 198, 243–4, 248, 251–2, 255
    learning 137
    limit 189
oppression 47–8, 56–7, 175–7, 180, 184,
    188–9, 222, 256
oracy 49–50, 99, 102, 262
out of school activity 269
outreach 192
ownership 222, 267

packaging
    gender 228–31
    science 116, 198
participation
    educational 46, 67
    engineering 206
    information technology 81–3, 91
    maths 74–5, 136, 261
    physics 237–40
    science 112–13, 160, 165, 168, 260,
        267
    science and engineering 192–3, 197, 199
passivity 41–2, 55, 83, 107
patriarchy 46, 52, 54–5, 175, 190, 263
pedagogical study and reform 9
pedagogy
    Citizenship, Difference and Marginality
        in Schools project 34–43
    cognitive styles and identity 67–8
    constructing effective 149–50
    definition 9–20
    difference in African perspective 46–57
    emotions of feminist 242–58
    female maths 78–9
    girls' 23–32
    range of pedagogies 260–70
    science 120–1
    single-sex settings for 173–90
    social jutice and maths 136–43

peer pressure and change 224
performance
  assessment 156
  change and 262, 267
  French 125–7, 131–2
  gendered 166, 168–9
  maths 136, 138
  perceptions 157
personal development 180–1, 187, 190, 204–5
personality 60, 116, 177, 203
physical education 43
physics 160–4, 236–41, 264
Piagetian theories 11–12
pluralism 139
polarization 175, 182, 187–9, 263
politics, feminist 243, 256–7
positionality 249–50
positivism 75, 151, 155–6
post modernism 268
post structural feminism 149–50, 152, 160, 168, 170, 211
post structuralism 262, 268
potential 11, 13, 47, 124, 126–7, 132–3, 175–6
power relations 9, 12, 36–7, 42, 48, 85, 138–9, 141, 149, 151, 175–7, 179–80, 187–9, 193, 203, 230, 241, 249, 253, 256
practice
  epistemology of 16–17
  pedagogy and 9–10
  theory/ 162, 188–9, 192–3, 201, 203, 211, 231, 268
praxis 16
private/public worlds 26–7, 29–32, 48, 53, 194, 247
problem solving 76–7, 114–15, 261
professional development 161, 169, 198, 201, 203, 228, 230–6
progress 154
Project Girls' Class — Boys' Class 173, 181–7
psychoanalysis 194, 197
psychological development 23, 59–60
psychometrics 10–11, 59, 151, 155
puberty 66
public spending cuts 38–9
putdowns 204, 205

radical feminism 149–50, 152, 159–60, 167–8
reading 18, 98–100, 102–4, 106–7, 262
reasoning 73
reciprocity principle 50
recruitment 192–3, 202
referencing 13
reflection 14, 19, 118, 231, 236, 263, 265, 270
regulation, social 35, 37
relatedness 237–8, 241
relations
  gender 36, 53, 66
  social 93
relationship
  dialectical 13
  teacher/student 15, 19–20, 198, 200
relativity 36
resistance
  to change 243–4, 268
  to gender inclusivity 210
resources, gendered 85–7, 179, 229–30, 232
respect 177, 189
responsibility
  personal 63
  social 47, 54, 56
responsive evaluation 156–7, 165–7
restructuring 37–8
retention 202, 204, 205, 291–3
rights 56, 175–6, 189, 232, 236
ritual, gendered 48–51, 53
role
  of education 30
  of education as preparation for adulthood 48–52, 55
  gendered 65–6, 120, 175, 180–1, 186, 187, 189, 221, 244, 263, 267
  of language 12, 263
  play 182–4, 229, 261
  of school 35
  social 23
  of socialization 9
  of student 68
  of teacher 11, 13, 15, 183, 185–6, 232

sabotage of interventions 210
scaffolding 13, 64
scholarship, gender and maths 73–9

school
  concept of 34, 39–41
  culture 231
  environment 138
  gender and 150
  gendered maths 73, 75
science
  change and 267
  and engineering intervention
    programmes 192–212
  gender and assessment 151–3
  maths and 137, 140, 230
  performance 125
  and technology 111–21, 260–1, 264
secondary school, gender intervention
    programmes in 197–202
segregation 173–90, 246, 251, 253–5, 263,
    266
self, sense of 257
self-esteem 175–6, 181, 232, 234–5, 242,
    246–8, 253
self-valuation 63
sex education 50–1, 53–4, 183
sexed mind 128, 132
sexism 54, 74, 84, 89, 92, 204, 215,
    220–2, 243, 261
  anti- 173, 175, 179–82, 186–7, 189, 198
single sex settings and pedagogies 173–90
situated cognition 14–15
skills
  curriculum 162–3
  learning 119–20
  reflective 117
  social 66, 182, 257
  study 15
  technical 115
social democracy 35, 38
socialization 9, 12, 23, 50, 53–4, 119,
    141, 175, 261–2
socio-cultural learning theories 12
software and gender bias 84, 91–2, 261
spatiality 34, 36, 39–43
specialization, limited 48
status
  of adult African woman 48–55
  computer technology and 81
  of English 109
  gender 267
  of gendered maths 73, 75

of pedagogy 9
personal experience and 20
of science 120, 151, 260
of subject knowledge 14, 16, 18
of teacher 251
stereotyping 31, 41–2, 46, 49, 66, 68, 84,
    88, 107, 111–12, 114, 116, 120, 137,
    139, 168, 174, 187–8, 190, 195, 199,
    205, 253, 260, 263
streaming 19, 136
student centredness 199–200, 206
subject
  appropriateness 9
  knowledge 16, 18, 20
subjectivity 19, 36, 39, 125, 151–2,
    155–6, 160, 169, 184, 186, 195–6
support 192–3, 266
survival, educational 46, 56
synthesis 160

Taunton Commission (1868) 129–32
teacher
  change 268, 269
  changing practice and gender 228–41
  cultural transmission 55
  emotions 243–4
  gender expectations 157, 263
  gender of 49, 89, 113, 120, 178, 180,
    222, 260
  gendered maths 73–7
  reform 9
Teacher Education Equity Project 217–23,
    225–6
teaching
  gendered 178–9
  style 113–14, 163–4, 199, 203, 211,
    265–6
technology
  information 81–93
  maths 140
  new 269
  science and 111–21
  simple 48
tertiary intervention programmes 202–3,
    205–9, 264, 269
textbooks
  gender bias 55, 99–100
  nineteenth century French 130
theorizing 18

theory/practice 162, 188–9, 192–3, 201, 203, 211, 231, 268
therapy, feminist pedagogy as 244–52, 257–8
thinking
  critical 17–20, 56, 188, 263
  gendered 23
tiering 106
tracking 19, 24, 136
training, teacher 20, 114, 201–2, 215
traits, gendered 23, 27–31

understanding
  and learning 115–21, 142–3, 188, 196, 237–8, 263
  qualitative 160, 163
  qualitative/quantitative 154
uniformity 24–5, 35, 47

validity of knowledge 14–15, 141, 143
values 158–9, 169, 173–4, 185, 245, 250, 263
Victorian Certificate of Education 149, 159–69, 239–40, 264
violence 54, 84, 99, 182, 185, 261, 267, 268
Vygotskian theories 12, 64

Women's Educational Equity Act Publishing Centre 214
work requirements assessment 161, 164–6, 240
workshop, inservice 215
worth
  equal 175–6, 189
  self- 55, 245
writing 98–9, 102–8, 262